RECOVERY THROUGH REVOLUTION

RECOVERY THROUGH REVOLUTION

ROBERT MORSS LOVETT

H. N. BRAILSFORD

LOUIS FISCHER

ROBERT BRIFFAULT

WALTER N. POLAKOV

MAX NOMAD

LEWIS COREY

CHI-CHEN WANG

JOHN GUNTHER

MAXIMILIAN OLAY

HAROLD J. LASKI

G. D. H. COLE

GAETANO SALVEMINI

CARLETON BEALS

HERMAN SIMPSON

ARNOLD ROLLER

LUDWIG LORE

SACHIO OKA

V. F. CALVERTON

EDWIN D. SCHOONMAKER

EDITED BY SAMUEL D. SCHMALHAUSEN

COVICI · FRIEDE · PUBLISHERS

NEW YORK · 1933

MANUFACTURED IN THE UNITED STATES OF AMERICA
BY H. WOLFF, NEW YORK

CONTENTS

v

INTRODUCTION

If we would guide by the light of
reason, we must let our minds be bold.

JUSTICE BRANDEIS [1]

---

[1] Quoted from his Dissenting Opinion: *New State Ice Co. vs. Liebmann*, 285 U. S. 262. Justice Stone concurring.

"The people of the United States are now confronted with an emergency more serious than war. Misery is widespread, in a time, not of scarcity, but of over-abundance. The long continued depression has brought unprecedented unemployment, a catastrophic fall in commodity prices, and a volume of economic losses which threatens our financial institutions. Some people believe that the existing conditions threaten even the stability of the capitalistic system.

"There must be power in the States and nation to remould through experimentation our economic practices and institutions to meet changing social and economic needs. I cannot believe that the framers of the Fourteenth Amendment, or the States which ratified it, intended to deprive us of the power to correct the evils of technological unemployment and excess productive capacity which have attended progress in the useful arts.

"To stay experimentation in things social and economic is a grave responsibility. Denial of the right to experiment may be fraught with serious consequences to the nation. . . . This Court has the power to prevent an experiment. We may strike down the statute which embodies it on the ground that, in our opinion, the measure is arbitrary, capricious or unreasonable. We have the power to do this, because the due process clause has been held by the Court applicable to matters of procedure. But in the exercise of this high power, we must be ever on our guard, lest we erect our prejudices into legal principles. If we would guide by the light of reason, we must let our minds be bold."

THE IDEA OF REVOLUTION

EVERYONE who knows mountain country has had the experience of following a river up its valley to the source, and looking back from the upland where innumerable brooks flow together into a turbulent stream, of which glimpses are caught through the woods as it rushes, twists, and turns, thwarted by boulders and snags, until in desperation and relief it plunges into a sheer leap with perhaps a second and third cataract before it emerges broad and tranquil, in the sunlight of the open plain below. Human society may be thought of as a mountain river, impelled by the momentum of its course, gathering power as it becomes unified, but expending it in violence and disorder; and when the urgency becomes too great, falling over a precipice which after all may be a short cut to a harmonious and useful destiny.

There is, of course, no argument in a metaphor. A few years ago, however, Mr. Lyford Patterson Edwards published a volume entitled *The Natural History of Revolution,* in which he subjected contemporary society to a rough application of tests suggested by evolutionary geology and biology, and showed that we were in a period in which various phenomena indicated a revolutionary movement as certainly as the behavior of a stream and the contour of a mountain-side give warning of precipitous falls. Since Mr. Edwards wrote his book the symptoms have multiplied. The word revolution is no longer one to be expurgated from a sane vocabulary. The report of the President's Committee on Recent Social Trends expresses a

9

pious disclaimer "of assuming an attitude of alarmist irrespon-
sibility," but declares that "it would be highly negligent to
gloss over the stark and bitter realities of the social situation."
To deal with them it prescribes "willingness and determination
to undertake important integral changes in the reorganization
of social life, including the economic and political orders"—
that is to say, in Professor John A. Hobson's phrase, "revolution by consent," but nevertheless, revolution. "The report in
itself," says the *New Republic,* "is both a revolutionary protest
and a revolutionary act. It constitutes one of the most important
of the processes of a great social change. . . . Without this
sort of activity by leaders of intelligence no social revolution,
whether violent or non-violent, ever occurred."

The term revolution carries a variety of meanings and con-
notations, honorific or derogatory. Jane Addams tells the story
of trying to disillusion a group of ladies in Geneva, just after
the War, as to the significance of revolutionary activity in the
United States. They came back soon after in triumph with
newspaper references to the Daughters of the American Revolution, in proof of the progress and vigor of such a movement.
The essential characteristic of a revolution is a sudden and
fundamental change in orientation or attitude toward the world
and the individual's place in it. The discovery of America was
a revolution; so was the Reformation. The steam engine and
power loom initiated the industrial revolution. Newton opened
the way to an intellectual revolution through natural science;
Darwin to another; Einstein to a third. The French Revolution
was political, with a shift of power from one class to another,
a result achieved in England by the Reform Bill of 1832 (and
its successors) whose authors the Duke of Wellington rightly
deemed as subversive as the Jacobins. The revolutionary movements of the eighteenth and nineteenth centuries in Western
Europe and North and South America, however, are illustra-
tions of the fact that political revolutions which merely transfer
power from one dynasty or party to another are superficial and,
so far as the mass of mankind are concerned, inessential. The
entire liberal or democratic movement of the nineteenth century has but a doubtful title to the name, for though the
machinery of obtaining governments was altered, the same type
of interested person secured power as under feudalism or
despotism, and used it for the same ends. Although the control
of the state passed from the hereditary and landed aristocracy

to the industrial and commercial middle class, the latter took
over, with more or less success, the ideals and culture of their
former sovereigns whom they protected in functionless idleness
as objects of superstitious reverence and models for imitation.
The bourgeois ruling caste exploited the industrial revolution
for its own advantage. Thus the democratic movement is a
history of betrayal of the modern world by the middle class.
The political triumph of democracy led to no fundamental
change in social attitude or way of life. A true revolution must
be lived, not merely acted on a stage. It is the recognition of
this fact which gives to Marx his preëminence as the first of
social revolutionists, and to the work of his pupils in Russia a
similar distinction as conducting a movement toward a fundamental re-organization of society, on a classless basis.

What I have called the betrayal of the world by the middle
class was the result of the limitations of that class, its lack of
vision and its lack of courage. These defects are responsible for
two dogmas which determine middle class thought: individualism and nationalism. The one finds its expression in the profit
system as the sole sanction for productive activity; and the
other, in war. These dogmas received the religious allegiance
of the middle class, the one of its intellect, the other of its
emotion. The one was the source of the chief private virtue,
thrift, rationalized into self-denial, upon which the economic
well-being of the world was held to depend. The other became
the incarnation of public virtue, wherein all the faults of an
individualistic commercial civilization—selfishness, arrogance,
cruelty, falsehood—were sublimated into their national equiv-
alents, sanctified by the name of patriotism. War was salvation
not only for the individual but also for society, a sort of national
blood-letting whereby the baleful humors arising from both
prosperity and poverty could be eliminated from the body
politic.

It is unnecessary to dwell upon the inadequacy of the economics of individual thrift, capitalistic self-denial, and laissez
faire to provide satisfaction for the material needs of the world.
The breakdown has occurred at the time when production,
speeded by technological invention, has reached a point which
promises a sufficient supply of goods necessary to livelihood for
all mankind. As John Stuart Mill pointed out, the function of
production depends on nature and natural laws, that of distribution is entirely within the control of man's collective in-

telligence. The difficulties of the former have been, to all intents and purposes, overcome. The fear of under-production which haunted the Malthusians has been exorcised so thoroughly as to permit an induced limitation of the products of field and factory to insure the profit of private capital on the margin of mass starvation. Such limitation, enforced by the actual destruction of goods in the face of such starvation, confesses the failure of society to solve the problem of distribution. It is not a failure of intelligence in the abstract; the mind already sees the solution. It is a failure in the application of intelligence, hampered by the forces of self-interest and class domination, by the selfishness of the few and the class pride and loyalty of their followers. No one can believe that such forces will always stand in the way of intelligence, deflect the light of reason and shut the gates of mercy on mankind.

The paradox of making the means of life for the many a by-product of the swollen prosperity of the few is one that cannot endure. There is a law of diminishing returns limiting the profits of exploitation whether of persons or land. That those profits have fallen to the vanishing point in many industries through lack of purchasing power of the masses, that the capitalistic system thus weakened is obliged to carry an increasing load of unemployed, dislocated by the technological progress of industry which has made control over production possible, are factors tending to weaken the opposition of the owning class to the introduction of a planned and coördinated economic system. Of such a system the essential feature is subjection of private ownership to social control—which, whether accepted peacefully or imposed by force, is revolutionary.

Still less necessary is it to discuss at length the destructive force of the dogma of nationalism which finds expression in war. One of the most insistent political aspirations of mankind is toward unity and peace. The Greeks felt it for the world which they knew; hence the bitter arraignment of division and warfare in the tragedies of Aeschylus and Euripides who foresaw the nemesis which was to overtake their race in the struggle between Athens and Sparta. The Middle Age inherited a nostalgia for world unity and the *pax romana*, and deplored its frustration through the rivalry between the two powers which expressed it, the Pope and the Emperor. The Renaissance in its political science followed Greece rather than Rome. It saw Europe take the fatal path of division and nationalism; the middle class, rising to power through trade and industry, found the nation the unit best adapted to its immediate purpose, and fixed this concept upon the world. Every high school pupil learns from teachers and text books to scoff at the poor old Holy Roman Empire, and to applaud the rise of the monarchies of England, France and Spain; to pity Germany and Italy for their delay in fulfilling their national ambitions. In the lowest schools of all countries there is induced by a kind of hypnotism that patriotism which sets the nation above all considerations of reason and ethics and leads youth from flag exercises to the trenches. It remained for an American professor to announce for the winning of the War and the settlement of the world, the formula of national self-determination, which exacerbated existing national rivalries and called into being a half score of truculent new nations.

The feeble attempts at curbing the ambition and self-aggrandizement of nations through leagues and covenants, which statesmanship has made from Henry IV and Sully to Wilson and Kellogg, have reflected the sense of impending ruin through division which has haunted progress like a shadow. To-day the press rings with prophecies of what the next war will do in the way of wiping life from the face of the earth. War is inherent in nationalism. When Mr. Kellogg interpreted his pact in the sense that every nation is judge of its own cause with respect to military action for self-defense, he confessed the impotence of restraining ordinances. The only safety for the world is in the recognition of the truth that nationalism, whatever may have been the case in the past, has to-day no value for the individual outside of the privileged classes. His welfare is bound up with that of beings like himself, the victims of exploitation the world over.

That nationalism is a resource of capitalism, both materially and psychologically, needs no proof. That in war the profit system is in its glory appears in the records of the committees of the LXVI Congress investigating Mr. Baker's management of the War Department. The British Board of Trade has given out figures of the munitions supplied by British firms to the Japanese and Chinese for their warfare. It is the threat to capitalistic control and class domination which prevents the western nations from welcoming a communist revolution in Japan and China as the only release from a state of warfare in which national ambition is a mask for profiteering, a proof that only

a nationless as well as a classless society is the solvent for war
and the alternative to annihilation.

Not only are capitalism and nationalism severally hostile to
the general welfare of mankind: they are mutually destructive.
The fanatical devotion of the possessing class to both simultaneously is the most absolute of all signs that its supremacy is
coming to an end. For as Mr. John Strachey shows in *The
Coming Struggle for Power,* the inevitable tendency of capitalism is toward monopoly; individual possession is no longer the
ownership of independent competing enterprises, but rather of
shares in nation-wide corporations controlling various fields of
production. These gigantic interests control the state for their
own purposes, but they meet in fatal rivalry at the frontiers.
Capitalism is monopoly at home but competition abroad, and
this competition, taking advantage of nationalistic patriotism,
is the fundamental cause of war. Indeed, it is now clearly
recognized that the cause of the present crisis in capitalistic
economy is the fact that the world is still at war. Among the
significant prophecies of revolution, none is more startling
than that of the experts engaged in preparing the agenda for
the World Economic Conference. Their statement is literally
an eleventh hour appeal—and they made it in June, 1932!

> "In its essence the necessary program is one of
> economic disarmament. In the movement toward
> economic reconciliation an armistice was signed at
> Lausanne; the London conference must draw the
> treaty of peace. Failure in this critical undertaking
> threatens the world wide adoption of ideals of national
> self-sufficiency which cut unmistakably athwart the
> lines of economic development.
>
> Such a choice would shake the whole system of
> international finance to its foundations; the standard
> of living would be lowered and the social system as we
> know it could hardly survive. . . ."

It will be noted that revolution is to-day generally credited
with the worthy aim of achieving a better world—a world without exploitation, oppression, and war, and that criticism is
directed either to the impossibility of building such a world
upon the foundation of human nature, or to the means employed in such construction. As for the first, it is enough to say

that if the alternative lie, as all signs indicate, between the achievement of a better world and the annihilation of civilization, then humanity with its instinct for survival will take the revolutionary course. As for the second, it has long been the fashion to subject the concept of revolution to dispraise or eulogy according as it is regarded in terms of violence or non-violence. It is significant of the growing acceptance of the inevitability of revolution that this distinction is less and less insisted upon. Mr. Reinhold Niebuhr in his recent book *Moral Man and Immoral Society* frankly scouts "the belief that violence is a natural and inevitable expression of ill-will, and non-violence of good-will, and that violence is therefore intrinsically evil and non-violence intrinsically good." There is nothing inherently evil but bad-will. "If a season of violence can establish a just social system and can create the possibilities of its preservation, there is no purely ethical ground upon which violence and revolution can be ruled out." Here Mr. Niebuhr makes the final test of the good revolution the pragmatic one of its success in achieving the establishment and *preservation* of a just social system, not the means which may be employed to bring it about.

There are two reasons, however, why believers in revolution in the United States may reject for themselves the technique of violence. One is that it is futile against the organized and equipped defenders of the existing order. Karl Marx held that a necessary preliminary to a revolution by violence was the permeation of the army by the revolutionary spirit, and this condition is one of the last likely to be fulfilled. No revolution has ever succeeded in the face of a convinced and determined exercise of power by those in possession of it. Only when the old order is thoroughly rotten and ready to fall of its own weight does successful revolution occur, as in France in 1789, and Russia in 1917.

A second reason why believers in revolution may deprecate the resort to violence is that the possessing class is so ready to invoke it. Indeed, a significant evidence of a weakening of confidence in the present social order is the disposition of its upholders to discard the principle of free discussion which is essential to the liberal philosophy and the democratic process. It remains as true to-day as when John Stuart Mill wrote *On Liberty* that the most effective method of controlling discontent in a democratic state is to grant freedom of speech, press, and assembly. The repudiation by our government of the process to which theoretically it owes its existence amounts to a cynical denial that we are a democracy, a denial which takes place when the President orders his janizaries to attack with bayonet and bomb a gathering of citizens interested like others in legislation for their own benefit, and when the police, reënforced by gunmen as deputies, break up legal meetings, arrest the audience, and torture some of them in the station house.

Mr. Louis Adamic in *Dynamite* gives a history of class violence in the United States showing that in nearly every case the possessing and employing class through its mercenaries has been the aggressor, and the losses in bodily injury and death have fallen upon the workers in the proportion of about 99 to 1. The records of the Departments of Justice and of Labor since Palmer's Red Raids show how vigorously and illegally these official agencies have been employed in defense of the present social order. The story of Sacco and Vanzetti, of Tom Mooney, of attacks upon the I. W. W. at Bisbee, at Everett, at Tulsa, at Centralia, and elsewhere, show how far the possessors of power are ready to go in using the connivance of officers of justice to withdraw the protection of law from their victims.

Yet though reprisals may be justified by the failure of the executive to control his mercenaries or of the courts to protect citizens in their civil rights, they are not practicable except as a form of terrorism which has been discredited as a revolutionary technique. What may be called the ritual of violence, formerly much in evidence in the anarchist and syndicalist press, may have a certain emotional appeal without any more relation to action than the ritual of the prayer book or the Sermon on the Mount. Real discipline comes from endurance, the discipline which the followers of Gandhi in India are gaining from the lathis of the British, or the Communists in the United States from the clubs of the police.

As the present volume amply testifies, the world is in a revolutionary phase which is taking various forms according to the incidence of pressure as determined by political and social conditions. In its world-wide aspect the revolutionary demand is for the replacement of an acquisitive by a functional economy—production for use rather than for profit, and distribution according to need rather than ability to meet the exactions of the price system. Such a change is clearly in accord with reason; opposition to it is obviously motivated in large part by the self-interest of the few. The inadequacy of the present system of private capital to the needs of human life on this planet is a matter of cruel experience; the achievement of economic and social justice is part of an inexorable demand for the survival of the race. This achievement is the most urgent function of politics in every country. How it will be accomplished is a matter of speculation. The fact that Karl Marx, more than a half century ago, predicted the necessity of a social revolution to this end, gives his answer the prestige of priority. Again, the fact that Lenin and Trotsky found in Russia conditions (the most important being the decay of the ruling power) which lent themselves to the practice of the Marxian formula—dictatorship of the proletariat—gives to the Russian revolution something of the same authority.

The Russian experiment is the most important social phenomenon in the world to-day. It should be welcomed and studied with attention and interest beyond that which the world gives to the measurement of light or the discovery of cosmic rays, for on its results hang immediate decisions affecting the problem of human well-being for men now alive. That hatred of its objectives by selfish interests, or skepticism concerning their attainment by dogmatic intellectuals, or fear of the influence of its example upon submerged masses by governments seeking self-perpetuation through alliance with economic power, should make every other nation hostile, eager to bring the experiment to failure by the violence of armies or insidious intrigue of economic warfare, is in the literal meaning of the term, inhuman.

At the same time it need not be maintained that the revolution in all countries must be organized on the Russian model or directed from Moscow. In the United States the recognition of the need for a nationally planned economy and proposals toward that end are revolutionary, if the necessary condition be implied that rights of private ownership must be abrogated in favor of social control. Again, it is conceivable that the capital sunk in such a monstrous financial and cultural excrescence as Radio City might have been used in organizing our 15,000,000 unemployed, in placing them in vacant factories, vacant farms and vacant offices, where they could support themselves en masse by the exchange of goods and services. Obvi-

ously, such an economic unit would have to be outside the
money and credit system of the country at large. Its goods would
have to be denied general circulation, along with the products
of prison labor. We should have to protect the capitalistic system from its encroachment by a *cordon sanitaire,* and refuse
recognition as in the case of Soviet Russia. It would constitute
a domestic revolutionary experiment, an investigation of the
psychology of economic incentive and the organization of distribution. Naturally, the instinctive response of capitalistic
government and economic leadership would be to reject such
a demonstration of coöperation and self-help on the part of
the people, and to continue to carry the burden of doles which
means ultimate bankruptcy.

The unemployed constitute the most important revolutionary force in this country. By whatever process revolution may
come, since its aim is social justice, the behavior of the proletariat will be the most important factor in its initiation and
survival. We have never had a proletarian movement on a large
scale in the United States. The I. W. W. with its syndicalist
philosophy came nearest to it, but the I. W. W. ran head on
into the War, with the temptation it offered labor to profiteer
in war supplies and the opportunity it gave capital to brand
as subversive and to suppress by government aid every attempt
of the workers to assert their own philosophy. The unemployed
to-day, dispossessed of all participation in social welfare except
a precarious and humiliating dole, constitute a potential proletariat. It is of intense interest to see what use they make of
their new freedom. Together with the farmers, who can no
longer live under the price and profit system, and the ruined
fringe of the middle class, they constitute a body which, while
at present incapable of taking power or of using it for their own
benefit if they could take it, may by sheer mass pressure
paralyze it as a function of privilege and private profit. One
need cherish no illusions about the proletariat while recognizing that corrupted though it is by servitude, it is not yet corrupted by the exercise of power. Through the education of
democracy, including its failure, it may derive a conception of
government as a guardian of general welfare, and the administ-
trator of equal justice, rather than as the source of special
privilege and the protector of private acquisition.

If the United States has never had a class conscious proletariat, it has had a revolutionary tradition. Although the Amer-

ican Revolution as accomplished was not strictly entitled to
the name, it was nourished in genuine revolutionary thought
and gave an impetus to revolutionary activity throughout the
world. Indeed it is amusing at the present day to compare the
attitude of the monarchist nations toward the republic of 1776
with the attitude of capitalistic nations toward the Soviet
republic of 1917—a mixture of self-interest and fear of con-
tagion. The really revolutionary phases of the American revolution were the later movements, so soon suppressed, known as
Shay's Rebellion, Dorr's War, and the rent revolt against the
patroons in New York. Nor has this country ever lacked revolutionary ideology. Jefferson, as is well known, was a revolutionist
in principle. Lincoln as member of congress stated the right of
a people to change its government by constitutional process or
by revolution. In the House of Representatives, in 1848, he said:
"Any people anywhere being inclined and having the power
have the right to rise up and shake off the existing government,
and form a new one that suits them better. This is a most valuable, a most sacred right—a right which we hope and believe is
to liberate the world. Nor is this right confined to cases in
which the whole people of an existing government may choose
to exercise it. Any portion of such people that can may revolutionize and make their own of so much of the territory as they
inhabit. More than this, a majority of any portion of such people
may revolutionize, putting down a minority, intermingled with
or near about them, who may oppose this movement. Such
minority was precisely the case of the Tories of our own revolution. It is a quality of revolutions not to go by old lines or old
laws; but to break up both, and make new ones."

Historically, the farmers have been considered representative
of the typical American character. It was the farmers who stood
embattled at Lexington and Bunker Hill. It was the farmers
who accomplished the first great change in the spirit and personnel of our democracy through the election of Andrew Jackson. It was the farmers of the North West who initiated that
most characteristic movement of American socialism, the Non-
Partisan League. The League undertook not only to use the
state for purposes of general economic welfare in production
and marketing but to make it a cultural instrument as well.
It was therefore attacked by the business interests by the
methods of financial sabotage, suppression by bloodshed, and
propaganda which stigmatized it as a free love cult. To-day,

the farmers of the trans-Mississippi Middle West are using revolutionary action against the operation of laws which make it impossible for them to function in the way of life to which they have been called. The farmers represent the old type of individualism and small capitalism which is being ruthlessly slaughtered by big capitalism and monopoly. In spite of their inherited conservatism they constitute next to the unemployed of the cities the most important revolutionary force in the United States.

The third class which may be examined with reference to its revolutionary leanings is the bourgeoisie, including the favored body of organized and employed workers who have been subjected to the process of *embourgeoisement* and whose psychology is capitalistic. This class has generally been regarded as the most conservative of all. It may be questioned whether their conservatism is not being sapped by the simple process of deflation—of reduction to a condition where they have nothing to conserve. This class it is which has profited most by the educational system of the United States. It was thus the easiest to reach by propaganda, and was led blindly into the World War. It saw and comprehended the betrayal of the world by our allies at Versailles. Since then it has had opportunity to learn how it has been duped by the men whom it trusted, captains of industry, bankers, financial authorities. To the gigantic losses of the investing public through the failure of enterprises sponsored by these gentlemen must be added the further deflation wrought by the parasites—judges, receivers, lawyers. An investigation by the members of the law faculty of Northwestern University shows that while $1,300,000,000 is the sum involved in failures in Cook County, Illinois, the sum of $130,000,000 has been extracted from bankrupt estates by legal proceedings. Truly the maggots are at the body before it is actually a corpse. The sense of disgust, however unreasoning, with a social order which like Herod is eaten with worms must be accounted a motive for change. Again, the present social order offers less and less opportunity for the exercise of ambition and training which it is the function of education to promote, an education which has been the beacon of hope to American bourgeois youth for generations. One of the most striking symptoms in the present situation is the awakening of social thought in schools and colleges, the increase of genuine social criticism in class rooms, and especially the movement toward the left of the younger intellectuals from whom leadership in the social transformation must come.

The present volume gives abundant evidence of the revolutionary aspirations and activities at work in many countries. Whether one welcome or deplore them, it would be silly to ignore them. At present they represent the objectives and policies of many nations and parties, but they have as a common goal human welfare through economic justice. Welfare is a pursuit in which national rivalry has no place. It is a world-wide motive. Wealth is relative. Welfare is absolute.

To those who believe that this goal can be reached by the stagnant stream of the present social order, a quotation from the arch-priest of capitalism, John Stuart Mill, may convey a wholesome warning.

> "If the choice were to be made between Communism with all its chances, and the present state of society with all its sufferings and injustices; if the institution of private property necessarily carried with it as a consequence, that the produce of labor should be apportioned as we now see it, almost in an inverse ratio to the labor—the largest portions to those who have never worked at all, the next largest to those whose work is almost nominal, and so in a descending scale, the remuneration dwindles as the work grows harder and more disagreeable, until the most fatiguing and exhausting bodily labor cannot count with certainty on being able to earn even the necessaries of life; if this, or Communism, were the alternative, all the difficulties, great or small, of Communism, would be as dust in the balance."

PART ONE

G. D. H. COLE

THE DÉBÂCLE OF CAPITALISM

CLEAR thinking on political and economic matters is at all times a difficult process, and most people engage in thinking about such things at all only fitfully and under some strong immediate impulsion. This is true even of thinking in national terms, despite the fresh wave of nationalism which has swept over the world since the final victory in the war to end war which was brought to a triumphant conclusion fourteen years ago. But now in the changed world which the Great War has left behind men are being called upon imperatively in the interests of their own preservation to think not merely nationally but in terms of the world as a whole. For despite the frenzied efforts of the statesmen of each country to fend off from their own political and economic systems the worst effects of the almost universal collapse of the past three years, all reasonable people have at length been driven to realize that the situation which mankind is facing to-day is not of a character to yield to purely national treatment, but demands world action if it is to be put right. This view, barren enough in itself, would receive to-day the assent of practically everyone whose opinion needs to be taken at all seriously in any country. It is a matter of agreement between politicians and business men seeking to restore the world order of Capitalism, and Socialists aiming at its replacement by a new world order, that the problems of the present can be dealt with only by simultaneous and coördinated action on a stage as large as the world itself.

There, however, agreement ends. For while the world's busi-

ness men and the great mass of the world's politicians who are
obedient to their behests are crying out more and more desperately for concerted international action to rebuild the
capitalist system, the Socialist contention is that this system can
at most only be patched up again for a time, and cannot by
any means available to the world's capitalists, however enlightened and rational their actions may be from their own point
of view, be placed ever again securely on its feet. Between these
two opinions the great mass of humanity is hovering to-day, uncertain whether to go all out for the restoration of the old
order, accepting whatever sufferings and sacrifices the capitalists and the politicians may tell them are necessary in order
to bring this restoration about, or, abandoning the old order
as hopeless, to devote all their energies and imaginations to
working for a new order based on the Socialist principles now
imperfectly adumbrated in the achievement of Soviet Russia.
Among these halters between two opinions are to be found not
only a large and rapidly growing section of the middle classes
in every developed country, but also a substantial section of
the Socialist movement. For Socialism outside Russia had grown
up in the generation before the war as a political movement
acting on constitutional lines within the framework of capitalist
society, and seeking to substitute Socialism for Capitalism by a
gradual process of social reform leading on to the progressive
transformation of industry by way of piecemeal socialization.
The Social Democratic and Labor Parties of the various countries had never anticipated that they would be faced at short
notice with a definite choice between revolution and a policy
designed to protect past gains at the cost of committing them to
help in keeping the capitalist system on its feet. Where the
choice had to be made suddenly, as in Germany, the great mass
of the Social Democrats, faithful to their tradition of gradualist
and constitutional action, took their stand against revolution
and allied themselves with middle-class parties of the Left and
Center, against aggressive nationalism on the one hand and
revolutionary Communism on the other.

The choice so made by the Social Democrats was fatal to the
achievement of any real economic revolution in the post-war
years, either in Germany or in the Succession States of the
Austro-Hungarian Empire. Be it admitted that the difficulties
which the Socialist Parties of Europe had to face in the years
immediately after the war were very formidable, and that a

plausible case could be made out for an alliance with the more liberal elements in the *bourgeoisie* for the establishment of republican institutions based on nineteenth century conceptions of Parliamentary democracy. Let it be admitted that the risks of the opposite policy of a firm institution of Socialist systems in face of the military and economic power of the dominant Allies included the risk of sheer starvation for the defeated countries, and that on humanitarian grounds the Social Democrats were strongly tempted to pursue moderate and temporizing policies in the hope that conditions would speedily improve. But no one, I think, will seriously suggest that the attitude taken up by the main body of Social Democrats in the years immediately after the war was mainly due to these extreme tactical difficulties. Far more fundamentally it was the natural reaction to a situation calling for a sudden choice between dramatically opposed policies of bodies of men who had been brought up in the traditions of Parliamentary gradualism and were unable in a moment to change their mental attitude when they were confronted by an essentially revolutionary situation. The Social Democratic Parties of those countries in which freedom of agitation and political action had existed in some considerable measure before the war had often great strength and solidarity, but they lacked everywhere the psychology of revolution or the power quickly to adapt themselves to a situation radically different from that to which they had been used.

By Communists this decision of the main mass of European Social Democracy in favor of coalitions with the liberal *bourgeoisie* in preference to a policy of Socialist revolution is commonly termed "a betrayal of the working-class movement." That it did deflect the entire course of events in post-war Europe is not in doubt. The policy of Socialist revolution *à outrance* in Germany and the Succession States might have succeeded in 1918 and 1919, or it might have failed. But whichever had happened, it is certain that the whole subsequent course of European politics would have been different if it had been tried. For the consequences of the Social Democratic decision were on the one hand the equipment of a large number of European countries with new constitutions based on a compromise between *bourgeois* political ideas and moderate gradualist Socialism, and on the other hand a sharp division in the ranks of the working classes between the adherents of gradualism and of revolution. When, as happened in Germany, the

Social Democrats found themselves suppressing Spartacist risings by armed forces, and Socialist took to killing Socialist in the streets, a disastrous rift was made in the solidarity of the working-class movement, and this reacted speedily upon the Social Democrats by diminishing their influence in the coalitions into which they had entered. For they could no longer claim to be the effective canalizers of the whole force of working-class discontent, or to be the real representatives of the working class as a whole. Accordingly their power and influence suffered, and gradually the *bourgeois* Parties were able to push them out from their original position of predominance in the affairs of the new Parliamentary Democracies of the post-war world. Stage by stage the Social Democrats found themselves pushed back all along the line, until the coalitions which at first they had led collapsed, and they were reduced to the status of an opposition unable even to oppose with all its strength for fear of upsetting the democratic constitutions which had been gained, and of provoking a powerful offensive alliance of all the *bourgeois* and reactionary forces.

From the Communist point of view this constitutes a "betrayal" even if the leaders of the Social Democrats remained throughout wholly honest according to their lights. They thought doubtless that they were acting for the best and in the interests of the working class when they made their original decision for the policy of compromise and coalition and against revolution. And, when once this initial decision had been made, it was extraordinarily hard for them at any subsequent stage to reverse it and adopt a different attitude. For each step seemed to follow logically upon the last, and to the bitter end the "defense of the republic" has appeared to most of them a justification for the continuance of the original policy. The more their own forces become weakened by the long succession of compromises and retreats, the greater the need for rallying to the defense of the republic against the reactionaries is apt to appear, so that Social Democracy, steadily losing ground in the countries in which this policy has been followed finds in every loss of influence a fresh reason for maintaining its previous attitude. Its leaders have been, and remain to-day, emphatic in asserting with perfect sincerity that they have acted throughout in the interests of Socialism. But the fact stands out beyond question that their policy has not prevented Socialism, which seemed on the eve in 1919 of a prodigious conquest, from having to retreat precipitately all along the line.

These considerations apply in the form in which they have just been stated only to the Social Democrats of those countries in which, in the period immediately after the war, the definite choice between the two policies of compromise and revolution presented itself in a definite and immediate form. In the Allied countries, which emerged victorious from the war, the situation was radically different, because no revolutionary situation there came into existence of itself as a consequence of defeat, and the opportunity for revolution, if it was to exist at all, would have had to be deliberately made by the method of mass agitation. The Socialists of Germany and the Succession States made a conscious choice between the two policies because they were confronted with a situation in which they had to choose. The Socialists of the Allied countries, on the other hand, were for the most part not conscious of choosing at all. They did not have to choose because they were not actually confronted by a revolutionary situation. They chose only in the sense that, under the changed conditions of the post-war world, they merely modified and did not radically alter the gradualist policy which they had been pursuing in the generation before the war. It never occurred to them, or it occurred to very few among them, that this policy could be altered, or at any rate that a respectable case for altering it could be made out. Even the possibility of a British or a French revolution in 1919 was barely considered. British Labor and French Socialism simply carried on, stiffening up their programs with fresh demands in accordance with the changed temper of their followers, but not contemplating at all the idea of a revolution *à la Russe* or even *à l' Allemande*.

For some time this constitutional policy seemed to be achieving a fair amount of success. Socialism in both France and Great Britain emerged from the war much stronger in electoral influence than it had ever been before. The change was far more marked in Great Britain because there the collapse of the Liberal Party and its sharp division into opposing groups gave the Labor Party after 1918 the chance of becoming the principal factor in the opposition, and the only possible source for an alternative Government. In France, where the political situation was radically different owing to the existence of a large number of independent groups instead of the traditional great parties of British politics, French Socialism became an important influence on the left wing of Radicalism and was instrumental in the return to power of the Radical Socialists under M. Herriot both in 1924 and in 1932. The French Socialists did not, indeed, like those of some other European countries, accept actual coalition with *bourgeois* parties of the left or center in the Government, but in both 1924 and 1932 they were largely responsible for keeping the Radical Socialists in power and were able to exert a substantial influence on policy in both home and foreign affairs. There was, however, no sign that this collaborative position was bringing them any nearer the ultimate attainment of a Socialist majority in the French Chamber, or indeed that a clear majority for any party or group was at all likely to be possible within the working of the existing political system.

In Great Britain the policy of constitutional political action carried the Socialists a good deal further, for, as we have seen, the virtual extinction of Liberalism as an effective political force made the Labor Party, which could after the war be counted definitely as a Socialist body, the only possible alternative Government. Thus the wave of liberal feeling which brought the Radicals to power in France in 1924 resulted in Great Britain in the formation of a Labor Government. This Government had indeed no majority of its own behind it; it depended on the support of the weak and divided Liberal Party, and its tenure of office was precarious and short-lived. But even after its overthrow at the end of 1924, when Mr. Ramsay MacDonald's bungling of the Russian situation gave the opposition a useful pretext for turning it out, it was left as the official opposition with every expectation of a return to office within a few years. The British Socialists had indeed more hope, though even they had no assurance, of winning within a comparatively brief space of time a clear majority in the House of Commons; for Great Britain has as strong an inclination toward a two-party system as France has toward the multiplication of political groupings, and it seemed plausible to suggest that before long the final extinction of the Liberal Party would leave the field clear for a concentration of all "left" opinion round the essentially moderate and evolutionary policy of the Labor Party.

How these hopes were to be disappointed is now a matter of history. Labor came back to office in 1929, still without the clear majority for which some of its supporters had hope and still accordingly dependent on the ambiguous support of the Liberal rump. It continued in its second tenure of office to pursue the essentially moderate and temporizing policy which it had followed in 1924, but on this occasion the luck turned far more decisively against it. For the coming of the world crisis raised up problems demanding courageous action which a half-hearted Government with no independent majority of its own was exceedingly ill-fitted to take, and internal divisions in the ranks of British Socialism further complicated the position.

In most continental countries the Socialist forces had been severed clean across into Communist and Social Democratic fractions, and Communism had been successful in detaching from orthodox Social Democracy most of the elements which were by temperament or policy definitely on the left. This, however, had not occurred in Great Britain, where the Communist Party had remained an impotent faction commanding no solid measure of support amongst the working classes. Large elements of left-wingism accordingly remained within the ranks of the Labor Party, and the extreme constitutional evolution-ism of Mr. Ramsay MacDonald and his immediate associates could by no means be regarded as the accepted policy of the party as a whole. All through the period of office of the second Labor Government there were loud rumblings of discontent both in the rank and file of the party and in the government itself, and there was no cause for surprise when, in the event, the fall of the Government came about at the hands of its own leader, who repudiated the great bulk of his followers and broke away to form a coalition with the Conservative and Liberal Parties. Indeed, the extreme paucity of the following which Mr. MacDonald and his immediate friends carried with them into the National Government of 1931 showed clearly that the general opinion of the Party members had been against the policy which, under Mr. MacDonald's leadership, the Labor Government had pursued.

The futility of the Communist Party in Great Britain and the extreme feebleness of its following stands in sharp con-trast to the rapid growth of Communism in most of the Con-tinental countries. This difference is explained in the main by two things—first and foremost by the comparative stability of the British economic system even during the post-war years, the comparatively high standard of living of large sections of the British working class, and the comparative absence of class-war feeling which is the result of these peculiarities; but also in some degree by the difference of tradition between British and Continental Socialism. For whereas Continental Socialism has been for the most part throughout professedly Marxist, making regular use of Marxian phrases and familiar with the essential Marxian doctrines, British Socialism grew up in almost complete ignorance of Marx, and far more as a department of middle-class victorian radicalism than as a theoretical growth based on the conception of class conflict. It was far more an extension of the notion of social reform to include the Socialist control of industry, as a means to reform, than a new doctrine consciously basing itself on the class struggle and the materialist conception of history. Thus, whereas the doctrines of Communism based on the interpretation of the Marxian "scriptures" were in no way unfamiliar, save in the new deductions drawn from already accepted premises, to the Socialists of Germany and France, they were thoroughly alien to the insular tradition of British Socialist thought. British Communism had to start absolutely *ab ovo* and to build up Marxism as a doctrine before it could hope to create Communism as a deduction. Accordingly the British working-class movement is still in the stage of slowly assimilating the fundamental Marxian concepts and has not yet even approached that of drawing the consequential Communist conclusions.

It has, however, become abundantly clear that, whether the constitutional Socialist Parties are operating under Continental or under British conditions, their methods offer no prospect of any speedy or drastic transition to a Socialist system. The pace of their advance toward Socialism, where there is any discernible advance at all, is quite extraordinarily slow, and their positive achievements are in the field of democratic social reform rather than of Socialist reconstruction. In this field they have indeed made important gains, but only to be confronted with the increasing difficulty of reconciling their claims for a progressive policy of social reform, based on the redistribution of the national income, with the continued successful working of the capitalist system. For as constitutional Socialism presses further its demands for Insurance Benefits, Old Age Pensions, measures of public health and housing and the like, it is confronted with a double difficulty. In the first place, can this policy be pursued without trenching dangerously upon the funds

which must be left for investment in the hands of the rich if
Capitalism as a system is to continue to do its work? Is not
there a limit under Capitalism to the taxable capacity of the
rich; and has not this limit almost been reached in the countries
where social reform has made the longest strides? Secondly,
while international commerce continues to be conducted under
the capitalist condition of competition between one country
and another, can any one country afford to get much out of
step with the rest by raising its wages or increasing its social
burdens much beyond those accepted by its competitors? Can
it, at any rate, do more than keep just as far ahead as its comparative efficiency as a producer allows it to go without sacrifice of competitive power? These questions were pressing even
before the coming of the world slump; and since the slump
came, with its inevitable result of intensifying enormously the
competition between country and country to hold a share in
the diminishing total of world trade, the dilemma has taken
an even more disquieting form. For it is now no longer a question of how much further the policy of social reform can be
pressed without endangering Capitalism, but rather of en-
quiring how much of the reforms already gained it is possible
to retain in face of the international pressure to bring down
the costs of production.

The combination of these conditions has rendered the so-
called "gradualist" policy of social reform as it existed preëmi-
nently in Great Britain suspect among a large proportion of
the adherents of Socialism. For the new conditions have made
men realize, far more clearly than before, the difficulties in the
way of reconciling the continued existence of Capitalism with
either a rising standard of life for the mass of the people *or* conditions of international coöperation and security over the world
as a whole. Capitalism in depression throws men out of work
because it does not pay to employ them. "Rationalized" Capitalism in prosperity throws them out none the less because it
pays better to employ machines. The workman is caught between the upper and the nether millstone; and, while the immediate effect may be to make him press more than ever for
the alleviations of social insurance, he is driven step by step to
realize that while he continues to work within the capitalist
order he is fighting of necessity a losing battle against forces
that are too strong for his aspirations.

This sense of the necessity for a definite decision and a defi-

nite choice between the two rival systems of Capitalism and
Socialism is now, I believe, sinking deep into the consciousness
of the European working class—in Great Britain as well as in
most of the Continental countries. But it has to encounter,
especially in the more advanced countries and in those where
capitalist civilization has attained to a large measure of stability, very powerful psychological reluctances. For men are profoundly unwilling, as long as they have anything to lose at all,
to recognize the necessity for a fundamental change in their
way of life and a dragging up by the roots of all the familiar
social institutions which form their environment. They will
believe to the last possible moment that things can be put right
by some less fundamental change—by something that will not
require them to modify and even to turn upside down all their
established habits and ways of living. They fear the unknown
as well as the difficulties of transition to it, and in this fear they
are inclined, before accepting the conclusion that really far-
reaching change is the only way out of their difficulties, first
to blame other people for mismanaging their affairs and, when
they realize that mere recrimination gets them nowhere, to
attach themselves for a time to quack remedies which promise
to cure all the ills of society by means of some simple operation
performed upon only one part of the social organism.

Most inclined of all are they to blame the monetary system
for their troubles, largely because they understand it least,
and to suggest that a few simple changes in the management of
the monetary machine would cause Capitalism to grind out
blessings as fast and as efficiently as it grinds out curses to-day.
But the popularity of these quack panaceas is mainly among a
small articulate minority which at any rate thinks it has grasped
the essential secret of the money magic. The main mass of the
working-class movement, as it comes to realize the failure of
gradualism and the prospect of a continued depression in its
standard of life, turns straight to more radical remedies—from
blaming Capitalism as a whole to the formulation of schemes
for its complete replacement.

Over most of Europe there has not yet been time for this
ferment to work itself out. For in the years between 1924 and
1929 European Capitalism appeared to be making a remarkable recovery from the disasters of the war. As the published
figures of the League of Nations show, the production of foodstuffs and of raw materials and the development of industrial

resources were proceeding during these years even faster in Europe than in the world as a whole. The European countries seemed to be resuming the place which they had lost in the old system of world exchange, and there was some recovery in the European standard of life, especially as the various European currencies settled down more nearly to a fixed international value and a large proportion of the old debts were successfully written off.

Great Britain, it is true, did not share by any means com-completely in this European recovery of the years preceding the slump, but that was mainly due to her own inconceivably stupid mistake in returning to the gold standard on the basis of the pre-war gold parity of the pound sterling. For this over-valuation of the pound, in relation to the internal levels of prices and incomes in Great Britain, imposed a fatal handicap on the British exporters, and lost Great Britain a large part of her share in the returning prosperity of the following years. What she gained as creditor and debtor—for she gained in both ways—by the revaluation of sterling, she far more than lost by condemning herself to a continuance of industrial depression.

It is easy now to see that the prosperity of Europe during the years between 1924 and 1929 was in fact largely artificial. The recovery of Germany, for example, which was to a great extent the key to the entire recovery of Europe, was made possible only by the huge-scale borrowing from America, with the aid of which the rapid rationalization of the German economic system was carried through. A large part of what Germany borrowed from America, moreover, spread itself over the rest of Europe by means of the reparation payments which it enabled Germany to make. Over Europe was poured *via* Germany a share of the abundant wealth of the United States, and as long as the United States was willing to go on pouring out money without any real chance of ever getting it back the prosperity was able to continue. I say without any real chance of being able to get it back because, although it is possible to conceive conditions under which the United States might be successful in recovering this money from Europe, these condi-tions involve a far more drastic reorganization of the American economic system than American public opinion, with its strong belief in a protected home market, seems in the least likely to contemplate. To all intents and purposes between 1924 and 1929 the Americans were making Europe presents with the same unintentional liberality as they had shown during the years of war.

It was soon, however, to appear that internal economic conditions in the United States were themselves thoroughly unstable. This became manifest some time before the Wall Street crash, in the period during which share values were still skyrocketing while production was beginning to slacken off and the number of the unemployed was steadily increasing owing to the progress of rationalization, and the distresses already in existence among the farming sections of the community. For American prosperity was essentially dependent on a steady and rapid expansion in the home demand for consumers' goods proportionate to the steady and rapid advance of productive power. But this condition was by no means satisfied. Wage rates rose but slowly, and there was an actual contraction in the volume of employment, so that the total wages bill was probably decreasing for some time while Wall Street was continuing to discount the anticipated profits of future years of economic prosperity. Moreover, with prices kept deliberately stable by the policy of the Federal Reserve System, the situation could not be relieved by an increase in the purchasing value of each unit of money distributed in wages. The demand for consumers' goods was therefore bound to fall off, and as soon as this fact was realized there was bound to be an almighty crash in the stock markets. Moreover, the boom in America had already caused a sharp fall in the American export of capital to Europe, and some attraction of European capital to America in the hope of sharing in the high profits of the stock exchange boom. American prosperity thus withdrew the prop on which Europe's recovery had largely rested, and trade in Europe was already sagging when the stock market crisis in America and the ensuing contraction of American demand for exports gave it the *coup de grace*.

Since then universal depression has made men far more receptive to thorough-going Socialist doctrines. For though there was for a long time a wide-spread disposition to regard the crisis as no more than one of those recurrent breakdowns in the functioning of Capitalism with which the experience of the nineteenth century had made men familiar, before long there was increasing doubt in most men's minds whether recovery could come as it appeared to have come in previous crises, automatically, by the mere effluxion of time and the

unguided operation of economic forces. Men began to scru-
tinize more carefully the history of past depressions and to be
more critical of economists who wrote about a rhythmical movement which they called the trade cycle. They wondered more
and more whether it were really true, as those economists told
them, that the economic world was a switchback on which the
further down you went the higher would the subsequent
momentum carry you up again.

They began to see that no past depression had been like this
one in that none had been to the same extent world-wide, and
to ask whether the recovery from previous depressions had not
in fact come about as a result of forces originating somewhere
outside the area of the depression. Had not some external event,
some discovery of a fresh market, or a supply of gold, something at all events beyond the mere lapse of time and the internal rhythm of the trade cycle, caused recoveries in the past?
And was there any outside area from which relief could be
expected in the present case? Was not the whole world now
bound together in one system and sharing in the common disaster? Men began to see that, if there was to be recovery, they
would have to make that recovery for themselves and make it
by international action extending over the whole area affected
by the crisis. It would not do simply to wait in the hope that
things would recover of themselves. It would not even do to
rely on merely national remedies.

But there still remained the question whether, if men had
to take positive steps to engineer a recovery, they should do
this by an attempt to set Capitalism again on its feet, or by a
concerted move to substitute for it a quite different system—
in effect Socialism, for there is no other alternative in the field.
Either policy appeared to present very great difficulties. It
could be said against the attempt to institute Socialism that
there seemed to be no hope of getting it instituted at present
by united world action. Socialism, moderate or extreme, possesses little strength in the United States. It has been laid prostrate in Italy by the Fascist dictatorship, and in France it seems
to have no prospect of getting the majority of the people on
its side. For France, even after her industrial accessions as a
result of the war, remains predominantly a peasant country—
but a peasant country with so high a degree of civilization and
so large a *bourgeois* class as not to be open to the allurements
of agrarian Communism. Germany might go Socialist, and if

she did, join her forces with those of Russia. If that happened, a good many other countries would probably go Socialist too. Great Britain might go Socialist, though after the Socialist *débâcle* of 1931 it would obviously take time to rebuild the working-class forces on a more constructive Socialist foundation. But suppose Germany wanted to go Socialist, would France let her? France had the military whip hand in Europe. But could France stop her if she really did take her own way? A second Ruhr occupation would hardly be popular among the mass of the French electorate, and it would be an adventure upon which even the most chauvinistic French Government would hesitate to embark.

Still, in face of these uncertainties the possibility of a concerted move towards world Socialism looked doubtful, and Capitalism in the years after 1929, and especially as the slump dragged on through 1932, showed itself possessed of an unexpected degree of toughness and resisting power. The absolute collapses which had been predicted as the consequences of the dwindling of world trade and the dramatic rise in unemployment did not come about, or were at least delayed. Even countries like Austria somehow staggered on, aided by doles from their richer neighbors. Capitalism might possibly be on its last legs, but these last legs seemed likely to be able to stagger along for a good while yet.

On the other hand, the prospects of any successful world action for the reconstruction of Capitalism seem singularly small. At Lausanne in 1932 the late Allies did take the first realistic step toward clearing away the tangle of dead wood left behind by the war. They did, though in a hesitant and conditional form, cancel reparations, having realized that there was not even the smallest chance of reparations being paid. But this one act of collaboration stood alone, and in every other field international disunity and economic nationalism still prevailed. Great Britain abandoned Free Trade and took not very successfully to the policy of Empire consolidation inaugurated at Ottawa. All over the world tariffs rose more sharply than ever, and embargoes on imports, quota systems, and restrictions on foreign exchange spread in an ever-widening vicious circle.

Politically the handling of the Manchurian problem by the League of Nations did much to undermine such belief as men had in the potency of that diplomatic instrument of world unification, and finally in the matter of financial policy, which

seemed to offer the best hope of joint action by the leading
countries, opinion remained hopelessly divided between those
who saw the one chance of promoting recovery in concerted
action to raise the level of prices by monetary reflation, and
those who believed that salvation lay in a drastic scaling down
of incomes (especially wages) and a return to the conditions of
laisser-faire. The World Economic Conference, announced for
the autumn of 1932 and then again for January, 1933, was
repeatedly postponed, and there is even now no assurance of
its meeting. The capitalist world may be tough, it may have
shown an unexpected power of resisting the forces of dissolution, but no one can say that it has so far shown any power of
acting internationally in order to stimulate recovery.

So the world hovers still uncertainly between the two possible alternatives, and most men who give thought to economic
problems probably still do not clearly know which side they
are on. They would prefer to see Capitalism reconstructed, if
it can be successfully reconstructed, for most men are conservatives by temperament; but they are becoming more and more
doubtful whether such reconstruction is really possible at all,
although they may admit the possibility of temporary and partial revival. For they are coming to see that the present slump is
not simply the result of post-war dislocation or of some temporary departure from economic sanity by the people of the
United States or of any other country, but the product of causes
deeply rooted in the capitalist system itself. Briefly, the situation is that men's power to produce goods has been expanding
in recent years faster than ever before in the history of mankind. But the expansion of productive power is only useful
if there is a corresponding expansion in the effective demand
for ultimate products—nay, without this corresponding expansion it is positively disastrous, in that it is bound to lead to a
severe economic crisis of so-called "over-production."

In the past the individual countries in which a similar rapid
expansion of productive power has occurred have solved the
problem by disposing of a large part of the additional product
in the form of exports based on the loan of capital to the less
developed areas of the world. They have thus been able to
maintain the stability of Capitalism in face of increasing production without a corresponding expansion in the consuming
power of those particular people among whom the increase in
productivity has taken place.

It may be said that this remedy is still open to the capitalist world, because there remain to-day vast areas needing to be exploited and a vast need for new capital equipment in order to set up as advanced countries nations which are at present still in a primitive stage of economic life. But in the first place, any resumption of foreign lending by the advanced countries on the requisite scale is out of the question as long as there hangs over the world the enormous burden of preëxisting debts, largely unbacked by existing productive assets; for the credit of the less developed countries is so heavily mortgaged in respect of these debts as to make fresh loans on a large scale obviously unsound. Secondly, the insecurity created by the war, by the rise of Socialism, and by the development of national sentiments in the less advanced countries, has made investment in these countries a far less securely profitable business, for it threatens the safety of the invested capital. And thirdly, the industrialization of the less developed parts of the world has now reached a stage at which, while it aids certain of the constructional industries in the older countries to dispose of their products, it threatens a far larger number of industries producing chiefly consumers' goods with the extinction of their existing markets.

The old outlets for the surplus products of advancing Capitalism are therefore increasingly blocked; but in face of these obstructions Capitalism can no longer prosper unless it can find increasing markets at home. This, however, it cannot do as long as it continues to engage in a competitive struggle of one national capitalist group with another, for home markets can be increased only by raising wages, and to raise wages in any country is, under present conditions, to handicap that country in its struggle with the rest. Capitalism has thus reached an *impasse,* and formidable as may be the difficulties in the way of the alternative Socialist solution, it seems likely that men will be driven in the end to face them—not willingly, for it is doubtful if any people ever made a revolution by its own will, but perforce as the result of an ultimate though it may be long-delayed paralysis of the existing social order.

It is indeed possible that whereas what is really needed is a world transition to Socialism, brought about by concerted international action and based on ordered international planning of the world's economy, what will really happen is a disorderly breakdown of the capitalist system in one State after another, followed by a distressful and damaging period of transition out of which will emerge, to the accompaniment of a truly terrific amount of unnecessary suffering, the basic institutions of the new Socialist order. Russia, in her isolated attempt to lay the foundations of Socialism, is now in the pangs of this transition, and maybe the world will in its tragic plight reproduce Russia's painful experience on a grander scale. But this need not be; for, difficult as the task is of bringing together the Socialist movements of the different countries into a concerted drive toward international Socialism, there is at least Russia to serve as a rallying point for the now scattered and disorganized forces of the world's working class. Russia, indeed, has at present too many internal difficulties of her own to be able to extend positive help to others; but her existence as a Socialist country is a guarantee that, if other communities do take the task of constructing a Socialist system seriously in hand, they will not find themselves isolated in a capitalist world. Moreover, Russia as a primarily agricultural State is in a position to collaborate to best effect with those more highly industrialized countries in which the great experiment of Socialism is most likely next to be made.

RUSSIA POINTS THE WAY

RUSSIA needed the Bolshevik revolution. It saved her from economic and political slavery.

We do not know the laws of revolutionary conception, birth and development. That is still an embryonic science. But it appears that no virile and viable state was ever destroyed by revolution. Only debilitated governments succumb to the virus of mass revolt.

It does not follow, of course, that all existing states are healthy. Long after growth has stopped and deterioration sets in, a system of society may remain in power by reason of inertia or its enemies' lack of organization. Although the social organism, like the human body, generates the poisons which ultimately lay it low, an outside agent, apparently, is required to administer the last blow. Revolution is a means of dispatching a régime which has outlived its usefulness but refuses to die.

There comes a time when the class that dominates a given country is incapable of performing its normal duties to that country, of solving its current problems, and of insuring it a measure of future progress. That was the situation in March and November, 1917. Neither the Czar nor the Provisional (Kerensky) Government which succeeded him had the will or the power of averting Russia's internal collapse. And more immediately, neither could muster sufficient determination to take Russia out of the World War and thus save her from ruin.

Russia's pre-war record of moral disintegration, poverty, administrative folly and mounting indebtedness was bleak indeed. But the utter paralysis of the system was brought more fully into view by the heavy demands of war. The army began to melt away in 1915. "By January, 1917," writes Alexander Kerensky, "more than a million deserters were roaming about in the rear of the army." Petrograd suffered hunger all through 1917. Other cities were in a similar plight. Workingmen went on strike against chronic under-nourishment and the political ineptitude of the régime. In 1915, 156,000 laborers participated in political strikes; in 1916, 310,000; in January and February, 1917, 575,000.

How did the Czarist Government behave in the face of the approaching catastrophe? Rasputin, a drunken, licentious monk exercised dictatorial prerogatives by reason of his psychic hold on the hysterical Czarina and her pusillanimous husband. Because loving parents believed he could cure an invalid crown prince, Rasputin was allowed to appoint cabinet ministers, veto military plans, and determine national policy. The state had reached the end of its resources. In 1916, when the critical condition of the country and the conduct of the war called for a leader with ideas and energy, the Czar appointed the hoary Ivan Goremykin as Premier. On that occasion, Rodzianko, the president of the Duma, said to Goremykin: "How could you, Ivan Loginovich, at your advanced age, accept such a responsible position?" "Ah, my friend," Goremykin sighed, "I do not know. But this is the third time they have taken me out of the moth balls." Subsequently, when Prince Golytzin succeeded Goremykin, Rodzianko put a similar question to Golytzin. "I agree with you completely," the noble prince answered. "You should have heard what I told the Emperor about myself. I declare, if a third person had said such things about me I would have been forced to challenge him to a duel." Here Rodzianko, who wrote excellent memoirs but was an equally bad politician, sadly adds: "Was order possible under such conditions?" It was not.

The situation grew rapidly worse. In the capital, during February, 1917, bread became critically scarce; hunger riots multiplied. Kerensky delivered a violent attack on the government in the Duma on March 9th. The speech was not printed. But the Czarina petulantly wired to her royal husband at staff headquarters: "I hope that Kedrinsky [she did not know his real name. L. F.] will be hung for this horrible harangue."

The next day, a general strike broke out in Petrograd. Cossacks fired on the unpopular police. What great statesmanly act did the Czar interpose to improve matters? He sent a telegram to Khabalov, chief of police in Petrograd. "I command," he wired, "that no later than to-morrow all disorders in the capital cease. They are intolerable at this difficult time of war with Germany and Austria. Nicholas II." The waves paid more attention to Canute.

Within four days, a tempest of protest would sweep the monarchy into the ashbin of history. The entire working class of Petrograd was on the streets. Policemen, janitors and special constabulary fired on the angry crowd from rooftops. A regular man-hunt for police had commenced. But on the morning of the 10th, the Czarina informed her husband by telegram that "all is calm in the city." By eventide she had changed her mind. "Things are rather bad in the city," she wrote him. "The workers should simply be told that they must not arrange strikes. If they do, they must be punished by being sent to the front." There was no front any more. And the workers had ceased to listen to the Czarina, Rasputin, and the unhappy Nicholas. On March 11th, nevertheless, he dissolved the Duma, the only institution which could have saved the throne for him.

The Czar did not even see his approaching doom. Rodzianko wired him on March 12th: "The situation is worse. Immediate measures indispensable, for to-morrow will be too late. The last hour has arrived when the fate of the fatherland and the dynasty will be decided." "Again that fatty Rodzianko," was the Czar's only comment, "has written me a lot of nonsense. I will not even answer him." The Czar merely reflected the blindness of his entourage. When fatal disease attacks a régime, the first organs affected are the eyes. They lose the power to read the signs of the times.

It is significant that the men who overthrew the monarchy actually did not intend to do so. They wished to perpetuate it. The March or so-called "Kerensky" revolution in Russia was in no sense conceived as a republican movement. Its fathers urged Nicholas II, on March 12th, to abdicate, appoint his invalid son, Alexis, as supreme ruler, his brother Michael, as regent, and Prince Lvov as Premier. Three days later, Nicholas, acting on this suggestion, pronounced Michael his successor, and signed a decree making Prince Lvov the head of the new government.

There was, thus, an obvious continuity between the Czarist régime and its successor. The continuity, indeed, was more than formal. Grand Duke Michael, to be sure, knew better than to accept the proffered honor, for its very announcement in the streets of Petrograd had whipped the resentment of the masses to fever heat. Miliukov, the Foreign Minister, and Guchkov, the War Minister of the Provisional Government, tried to persuade him to stay. He refused. Yet the personnel of the new, "Kerensky," Government showed that little had changed except the façade. Prince G. E. Lvov, Premier and Minister of Interior, was a big landowner; Konovalov, Minister of Trade and Industry, was a well-known textile manufacturer; V. N. Lvov, Procurator of the Holy Synod which the "revolutionary" Government did not abolish, owned a landed estate; Tereshchenko, Minister of Finance, operated sugar factories and held an interest in several banks; Guchkov, Minister of War, and a prominent Moscow merchant, had earned national repute as a militant monarchist while Miliukov, Minister for Foreign Affairs, shared Guchkov's ardent advocacy of the dynasty. With the exception of Kerensky, Minister of Justice, who was the most radical member of the cabinet, the remaining ministers exercised little influence. It was, essentially, a government of land barons and capitalists who might have held offices under the Czar, who had been appointed, in some cases, by the Czar, who retained Czarist generals at posts of political importance and not merely as military specialists, who wanted no social revolution, who subsequently supported monarchist adventurers like Kornilov (V. N. Lvov, for instance) and Kolchak (Tereshchenko, for instance), and who, above all, insisted on the continued prosecution of the World War with a view to territorial aggrandizement by Russia.

The Provisional Government declared a broad amnesty and freed many important political prisoners. It commenced to break down the Czarist bureaucracy and thus too furthered the Bolshevik cause. The weakness of its administration and its failure to solve village problems encouraged peasant violence and the seizure of estates. The Kerensky régime, in other words, did perform its services to the revolution. Yet but for the rising ferment of the disaffected masses, the Provisional Government would have been a supremely reactionary government. In April, for instance, Paul Miliukov sent a note to the Allies reiterating Russia's designs on Constantinople and the Straits.

On May 1, he informed Paris, London and Rome that the
March revolution would not entail "any slackening on the
part of Russia in the common struggle of the Allies." To disprove these words, 40,000 armed troops marched through the
streets of Petrograd on May 3rd bearing banners which read
"Down with Miliukov," "Down with Conquest," "Down with
Imperialist Policy," "Miliukov Must Resign." That evening
Miliukov delivered a speech. "I affirm," he said, "that the Provisional Government and I as Minister for Foreign Affairs will
keep Russia in such a position that nobody will dare accuse
her of betrayal. Russia will never agree to a separate peace."
But the next day, the anti-war demonstrations continued. The
civil population as well as the army demanded Miliukov's
scalp. On the 15th he resigned.

Kerensky soon took the office of Minister of War. He did
not, however, read the pulse of the nation. The Miliukov incident was a portent which none understood. Instead, Kerensky
prepared for a grand offensive against the German-Austrian
armies in Galicia. The Russian army was a seething cauldron.
The soldiers who had not deserted were in open mutiny, shooting officers, disobeying commands, and refusing to fight. Under
such circumstances, the June offensive, calculated to "galva-
nize" the army and the nation, actually became a massacre. It
was Russia's last wartime effort. It sealed the fate of the Provisional Government. The Russian bourgeoisie needed economic reform. Russia needed political renewal. But above all
the Russian people needed peace. Czarism failed in this supreme pressing task, and so did Kerensky. Peace, on the other
hand, was the Bolsheviks' first achievement, and the keystone of
their further success. When the Communists came to power, Sir
George Buchanan, the British ambassador in Petrograd, suggested to his government that Russia be released from her international obligations and allowed to negotiate a separate
peace with Germany. "Every day we keep Russia in the war
against her will," he wired, "does but embitter her people
against us." He spoke too late. The Bolsheviks had acted without his advice. He should have given it to Miliukov and Tereshchenko.

The Czar had tried to bring about a separate peace with
Germany in 1916 and conducted secret negotiations with that
in view in Stockholm. But court influences were divided, and
Allied pressure was heavy. The monarchy had the wish but not

the power to meet the emergency. In the same manner, many far-seeing Russian capitalists urged upon Kerensky a bourgeois solution of the land question. Too large a section of the Russian capitalist class, however, was too interested in estate ownership and petty trade to adopt the advice of its advanced section of heavy industrialists. After the propertied classes of Russia had brought the country to an impasse in the war, the March, 1917 revolution offered them an opportunity of continuing their rule with less compromised and more modern methods. But they could not avail themselves of the opportunity. This double failure was Russian capitalism's death sentence. History thereupon summoned Bolshevism to carry out the verdict. A single false move by the executioner might have prolonged the life of the condemned system and given it still another chance to return to power. A virile philosophy and a group of able leaders, however, prevented the revolutionists from faltering. Lenin merely had to reap. The ground had been prepared for him by Russia's capitalists who did infinitely more than he to destroy Russian capitalism.

The so-called Kerensky period of the Russian revolution (March-November, 1917) has gone down into history as an interval of bourgeois democracy and liberal capitalism. But it never really assumed the pure form of either of these. During the first few months of its tenure, the Provisional Government shared sovereignty with the monarchists. Later, it became a condominium of the bourgeoisie with the radical labor and peasant parties. First it leaned to the right on the feudal monarchy. Then it leaned to the left on the Soviets which, at the same time, it tried to crush. Never did Russian democratic capitalism rise to the heights of independent existence. It apparently did not possess the vitality necessary for self-contained life or for the work which history summoned it to do in a difficult hour.

The Bolsheviks, consequently, experienced few hardships in sweeping the bourgeoisie out of power. Their revolution was no secret. The date had been officially set in advance. Lenin insisted that the Soviet revolution was "not a conspiracy but an insurrection." It had none of the characteristics of a palace putsch or a coup d'etat. It therefore involved little bloodshed.

A minority never made a successful social revolution without mass approval. The Bolsheviks would not have acquired or retained power had not the overwhelming bulk of the peasantry joined with the workers in supporting the new régime. The Soviets could not have won the Civil War had not the peasantry sided, at least for a time—and in crucial times—with the Bolsheviks. This coöperation by the village was due to its interest in a national, anti-feudal revolt against the landlords and the landlord governments of Nicholas II and Prince Lvov. Lenin once said that in November, 1917, the Bolshevik revolution was a bourgeois revolution. The paradox is only apparent. For from the point of view of the peasantry, the chief goal of the revolution was the ousting of the estate owners so that the small holder might acquire land for himself. If the partially feudal character of the Kerensky régime had not prevented it from reacting to this truth by carrying out a sincere small-holders' agrarian policy (and if its essentially capitalist nature had not prevented it from breaking faith with the Allies in order to give peace to the peasant army), its fate might have been very different.[1] Kerensky's failure enabled the Bolsheviks to win the help of the peasantry. The Soviet revolution, the peasant hoped, would further his own private capitalistic or bourgeois interests. He trusted the Bolsheviks because he knew they were enemies of feudalism. In a sense, he was disappointed. The Communists did not believe that the solution of Russia's land problem lay in the substitution of one form of private ownership with another less odious though equally anti-socialist form. Yet the peasantry persisted in its pro-Soviet attitude even after it had failed to attain its own social and bourgeois ends. It did so for a good reason. Lenin has said that in the ten weeks between November 7 and the dispersal of the Constituent Assembly on January 5, 1918, the Bolsheviks finished the bourgeois-democratic phase of the revolution by cleansing the "Augean stables of Feudalism" in Russia. The peasants, however, could not agree that the cleansing was final, and their fears were well founded. For from 1918 to 1921, the landlords fought side by side with the counter-revolutionary white armies and hoped to be reinstated in their former status. By supporting the Soviet Government, the peasants shattered this hope. If they failed to erect their own private capitalist structure on the ruins of land-

[1] In Latvia, Esthonia, and other new states, a stronger and more cultured capitalist class, employing newly-stimulated nationalist sentiments as a lever to dispossess foreign (mostly German) estate owners, laid the foundations of a relatively rich peasant or "kulak" class which has served as an effective check against Bolshevism.

lordism, they at least liberated themselves from crushing debt and from the possibility, even, of incurring further debts. They likewise paved the way to collectivization which, all its trials notwithstanding, is a long step toward the final solution of Russia's agrarian problem.

The golden opportunity of winning millions of peasant adherents which Russia's backwardness presented to the Bolsheviks, would be missing in a highly industrialized country where feudalism had ceased to exist or to dominate politics, and where the capitalistic farmer class, therefore, would not readily lend a hand to the revolution. For this reason a social revolution in a Western country would be forced to follow an altogether different strategy. The Communists in the Soviet Union as well as the Trotzkyists agree on at least one point: that the majority of the working class, and even a majority of the whole population in decisive industrial and railroad centers must be brought under the banner of Bolshevism before a Soviet upheaval could take place in England or France or Germany. It is highly probable, moreover, that a large section of the petty bourgeoisie would either have to be directly proletarianized or else neutralized by despair and poverty, and that the pauperization of the farmer would have to make considerable progress. The same type of reasoning brought the Communists to the conclusion, long ago, that the capitalist Powers might also be crushed by an attack in the rear, so to speak— in their colonies. The "infantry of the East," they contend, the millions of hungry, hopeless coolies and rayots would join the "cavalry of the West," the proletariat. Asiatic colonies would then play the same role in a revolution in an advanced capitalist nation as the Russian peasantry did in a less progressive one.

The inceptions of the Bolshevik revolution partook of a bourgeois-democratic character and therefore attracted a large non-proletarian following. But a revolution in the West would have to be socialist from the very beginning. The world has not yet seen a socialist revolution. The Soviet Union is only now entering upon its socialist phase. If and when a socialist overthrow does take place in a Western country, therefore, it will not adhere closely to the pattern of events in Bolshevik Russia. It will, however, benefit by the mistakes committed by the Soviet revolution.

Lenin, and with him all Communists, recognized that the

application of the Marxist program would vary with every country. Lenin said: "In no sense do we regard the Marxist theory as something complete and unassailable. On the contrary, we are convinced that that theory is only the cornerstone of the science which Socialists must advance in all directions if they do not wish to fall behind life. We think that it is especially necessary for Russian Socialists to undertake an independent study of Marxist theory, for that theory provides only general guiding principles which can be applied differently in England, for instance, than in France, differently in France than in Germany, and differently in Germany than in Russia."

Differences notwithstanding, however, all Soviet or socialist régimes would, in the Bolshevik conception, have much in common with the Soviet system as it has maintained in Russia: the proletariat must rule; private capitalism must be banished; and the ownership of land, industry, transport, and natural resources must be vested in the state or the community but never in an individual or group of individuals working for private gain. The moral of Soviet Russia's experience is that such a system is possible, and that, despite innumerable errors and endless foreign hostility, it can make progress. The establishment of this single principle marks an epoch in world history.

Soviet affairs are followed with such keen interest abroad not merely out of curiosity or because capitalist nations wish to adopt Bolshevik methods or yet out of any real apprehension lest the U.S.S.R. becomes an immediate physical menace, but rather because Soviet success testifies to the proposition that a nation can prosper without capitalists. Hence the importance which Russians and outsiders attach to the record of Bolshevik achievements.

The revolution first achieved by destroying. The initial pressing task of Bolshevism, according to Lenin, was to "annihilate the remnants of medievalism, to sweep out every one of them, and cleanse Russia of that barbarism, of that disgrace, of that greatest obstruction to all culture and all progress in our country."

"What," Lenin goes on to ask, "were the chief expressions, the chief remnants of serfdom in Russia in 1917?" He gives his own answer: "The monarchy, social rank and titles, land ownership, the manner in which land was used, the position of women, religion, and the oppression of the national minorities." In ten weeks, Lenin affirms, the Bolsheviks did more to banish these evils than the bourgeois-democrats, liberal Cadets and petty bourgeois Socialist Revolutionists and Mensheviks did in the eight months of the Kerensky interregnum. Indeed, Lenin claims, the Bolsheviks accomplished more in this respect than the Western nations which had completed their bourgeois-democratic revolutions decades ago but where vestiges of these feudal institutions nevertheless remain to this very day. Absented landlordism, royalties for subsoil wealth, bourgeois marriage and divorce codes, discrimination against racial groups, and at least the temporal rôle of the church are a few of the things Lenin had in mind.

For the Bolsheviks, the removal of those feudal vestiges was a "by-product." They performed that service to Russia on the run, so to speak. It was incidental but a necessary preliminary to their socialist tasks of eradicating private capitalism and establishing a new society. The anti-capitalist phase of the Bolshevik revolution set in simultaneously with the bourgeois-democratic phase. By the end of 1918, the institution of private ownership in land, industry and finance had practically ceased to exist. Under the pressure of Civil War, the Soviets then made the mistake which Lenin, with characteristic honesty, subsequently took upon himself, of attempting to introduce purely Communist forms of city rationing and an almost moneyless economy based, chiefly, on merciless requisitioning of peasant products. The New Economic Policy of March, 1921, was a retreat from this excessively advanced position to a synthesis of state capitalism in the city and of private capitalistic molds on the countryside which, however, were lacking in stability because land, industry, transport and banking were nationalized and because the ultimate consumer of the mujhik's surplus was the anti-capitalistic proletarian.

The inauguration of agrarian collectivization and the establishment of state farms in 1929 marked the painful inception of the "socialist offensive." Russia thereupon became much more exciting, interesting and revolutionary. Concurrently, the Five Year Plan of rapid large-scale industrialization intensified the hardships and struggle which were bound to accompany the wholesale attack on the private capitalistic village implied in collectivization. Throughout 1930, 1931 and 1932, the Soviet Union rocked in this gigantic battle. The issue is clear, yet the fighting continues. The Bolsheviks cannot lose, but they have not won.

Throughout the years that have elapsed since 1917, varying Soviet policies have of course influenced the daily lives of people and general conditions. But the forces released by the revolution have continued to operate in the most dissimilar circumstances; they transcend decrees, changing strategy, and the trend of current events. The Bolshevik revolution is affected by the size of any given year's harvest, by the percentage of industrial growth, by food shortages and goods scarcity, by security pacts and diplomatic demarches, and by political alignments. The significance of the revolution to Russia and the world, however, is not determined by these factors. It is independent of them and bigger than all of them. The revolution made a new nation out of Russia, and even if the inconceivable happened and the influence of the revolution were withdrawn, Russia would remain a different, a richer and a younger country than she was in 1917 or 1914.

The Soviet revolution was called upon in the first place to perpetuate the achievements of the bourgeois-democratic phase of the Bolshevism and to infuse them with socialist content. Thus the anti-religion of the Communists consisted not merely of negative destruction—the disestablishment of the church, the disfranchisement of the clergy, the dethronement of superstition, the closing of churches, etc., etc.,—but of positive changes such as the domination of science in philosophy and political policy and the spread of materialistic education. Likewise, the new status of Russia's national minorities first required the removal of all earlier legal and social disabilities. But formal equality having thereby been achieved, a further step was undertaken with a view to the economic development of the regions, usually peripheral, inhabited by the minor races. For under Czarism, the Empire's outlying districts had served as colonies which produced raw materials for the factories of the central motherland. The Russian capitalist class was not interested in the progress of its subject nationalities when progress would have meant the rise of a local bourgeoisie with natural inclinations towards economic independence or competition and political separatism. The pre-revolutionary system, therefore, condemned scores of races and millions of people to planned backwardness. The Bolsheviks, on the other hand, have commenced to build up a textile industry in Turkestan where cotton grows; the distant Caucasus is becoming a new industrial center. Complicated, oriental scripts calculated to prolong the cultural sleep of Russia's Asiatic peoples have given way to Latin alphabets which quickly wipe out illiteracy, make for westernization, and evoke a desire for advancement.

Freedom was the necessary companion of every one of the changes wrought by bourgeois-democratic revolution. Freedom is their logical result. Recently, Benedeto Croce, an Italian Senator, wrote an article [2] entitled "On Liberty" wherein, without devoting a single word to the repressions of his own Fascist régime, he attacked the Soviet Union. " . . . the Russian Communists," he wrote, "have not solved, nor will their violent and repressive methods ever enable them to solve, the fundamental problem of human society, the problem of freedom. For in freedom alone can human society flourish and bear fruit. Freedom alone gives meaning to life: without it life is unbearable. Here is an inescapable problem. It cannot be eliminated. It springs from the very vitals of things and stirs in the souls of all those countless human beings whom the Communists are trying to control and reshape in accordance with their arbitrary concepts. And on the day that this problem is faced, the materialistic foundations of the Soviet structure will crumble and new and very different supports will have to be found for it. Then, even as now, pure communism will not be practiced in Russia."

Now it is perfectly true that communism does not exist in Russia; no intelligent person ever made such a claim. But for the learned Senator to prophesy that it never will exist in Russia or, by implication, anywhere else, is to venture on ground where angels have hitherto feared to tread. Moreover, the fundamental problem of human society is not freedom but the purposes which freedom can serve. Absolute freedom is the license of the drunkard or of the criminal who runs amuck. Man does not treasure the freedom to starve or to be unemployed or the freedom of his rulers to send him to war. That is scarcely an ideal which makes for culture and civilization.

Here it may be fitting to juxtapose Lenin and Croce. Lenin wrote: "As long as social classes have not been destroyed, all talk of freedom and equality in general is an illusion. . . . As long as classes continue to exist, one must, in any discussion of freedom and equality, put the question: freedom for which

2 "Foreign Affairs" Quarterly. New York. October, 1932.

class? and for exactly what use? equality of which class with which? and what exactly is to be the relation of the one class to the other? . . . The slogan of freedom and liberty, if accompanied by silence on these questions and on the question of private ownership of the means of production, is a lie and a hypocrisy of bourgeois society which employs the formal recognition of freedom and equality to cover the actual absence of freedom and equality for all workers, for all toilers and for all those exploited by capital, that is, for the overwhelming majority of the population in all capitalist countries."

Tendencies toward high tariffs and state capitalism have superseded nineteenth century *laissez faire* in all Western countries, and liberty therefore fares increasingly worse. The world economic crisis and the consequent unrest in Europe and even in America have resulted in the introduction of more rigid measures of supervision. When Croce suggests that Lenin built on the foundation of "the good old autocratic tradition" of Czarism, he forgets, for a moment, that nations far more advanced than Russia have surrendered their freedom to dic-.ators, and that in Germany, perhaps the most civilized of European states, freedom of the press, parliamentarism and freedom of assembly are now submerged in an arbitrary terror which respects neither the individual nor the law. In Russia, on the other hand, there is a new liberty. The freedom for national minorities has produced a high flower of culture. Suppressed races are acquiring their own individuality. Women enjoy rights undreamt-of in the Czarist Empire, rights more real than the vote in democratic countries. The enthronement of science on the site where superstition and dark ecclesiastical reaction ruled supreme has released a nation's mind for new thought and new intellectual growth.

Freedom is indispensable to the maintenance of these triumphs of the bourgeois-democratic phase of the Bolshevik upheaval. The socialist features of the revolution, on the other hand, intensified the class war; and war brings strict administrative control. The destruction of Russia's largest and most tenacious capitalistic class—the private peasantry—did not begin in earnest until 1929. Until then, the natural desire of the peasant to grow rich and remain a capitalist aroused his resistance to a socialist program, and that attitude accounted not alone for Russia's relatively slow progress along the road of revolutionary development, but also for the policy of dictatorship. The peasants' capitalist leanings created a complementary class of city capitalists, and inspired considerable sections of the urban intelligentsia and even of the Communist party with heterodox ideas against which the authorities felt called upon to employ the weapon of terror. Collectivization and the social phenomena which accompanied it broke the back of capitalism in the U.S.S.R. without, however, completely eradicating it. Even old agricultural specialists who never believed that the Bolsheviks could conquer the private property instinct of the Russian mujhik now admit that they erred. A decade from now, with the perspective of passing years, the world will probably evaluate the great psychological revolution which commenced between 1929 and 1932. The hardships are many. But it is significant that, in 1932, despite short rations, the masses were more pro-Soviet than ever before. Everyone realizes to-day that there is no way back, and that the road ahead promises welcome improvement which is already almost within grasp. The intelligentsia too has turned over a new leaf, and the old "wrecker" engineers who sabotaged and attempted to weaken the Soviet state now stand in the front line of the builders. The time is coming when the Kremlin will be in a position to loosen the tension and allow a greater measure of economic democracy and political initiative than has hitherto existed. If indeed, as the Bolsheviks boast, the classless society is approaching, then the class war and repression can be relaxed.

I have felt for some time that, partly on account of the existence of a clumsy, stupid and stubborn bureaucracy, the Soviet Government is ruling with a firmer hand than the safety of the régime and the execution of the socialist program require. Petty officials and fearful leaders lend themselves to methods which have become unnecessary and which hamper initiative and dampen the ardor of the masses. In this connection, one must note an embryonic change of far-reaching consequence: the encroachment of the party on the prerogatives of the state. Whereas in Fascist Italy, the government under Mussolini has grown more potent and the ruling party weaker, Stalin has brought the Communist party to the fore until it today occupies itself with many—in fact, too many—problems of administration and execution formerly the strict province of governmental commissariats. Needless to say, the future of the state must determine the fate of state capitalism and socialism, and of the stern police methods of the Bolsheviks. In 1932, an unprecedented wave of tolerance and liberalism made its appearance in the Soviet Union which, logically, will gain ground when the current economic difficulties and consequent strain and the exaggerated war scare shall have been at least partially dissipated. This new spirit of tolerance reflects the destruction of opposition in the party to Stalin's policies. On the other hand, Stalin's victory and the resultant concentration of authority stifle discussion and induce a barren ideological unanimity in which bureaucracy and disrespect of rights tend to flourish.

The Bolsheviks, however, never ruled with the crude, thick mailed fist. They used a thin glove of steel (Stalin said: "A revolution cannot be made with silk gloves") which could strike a hard blow but was fine enough to allow the hand to build, to mold human nature, to educate, and to found a new society.

A radical change in human nature, I should say, is the greatest achievement of the Bolshevik revolution. I do not wish to suggest that all Soviet citizens are pure idealists. They are far from it. The tense struggle for existence and the political severity of the régime even foster some very ugly traits of character. But one thing is certain: the mad race for private gain is disappearing among the older generation and of course among the youth. Only ignoramuses still believe that it is impossible in Soviet conditions to earn big salaries and to own furniture, books, a home, an auto, et cetera. Only the naive will suppose that the Russians are so puritanic as to despise the comforts which come with possessions. That is not the point. But the central principle of life is no longer, "What can I get out of it?" It is difficult to grow rich in the U.S.S.R., and wealth has value up to a certain limit—the limit of one's own consuming capacities. Beyond that it ceases to attract and to stimulate effort, for wealth cannot be converted into capital and used to produce further wealth in agriculture, industry, or trade. This tends to create other standards. Money return becomes one of several forms of compensation. A social incentive enters into play. Individualist philosophy is disfranchised.

If this were not so, it would be difficult to explain the great burst of energy which the revolution has released and which is now engaged in an orgy of industrial upbuilding unprecedented in world history. What is it that has transformed Russia, the Russia of the lumbering, lethargic mujhik, the Russia of an effete and morally bankrupt ruling class, into a dynamic nation tingling with the will-to-do, to produce, to march forward, into a state pulsating with ideas, resourcefulness, and creative impulses? Russia is the most active, the most alive country on the face of the earth. Despite her technical and cultural backwardness, she is building more than any other nation. How did it all happen? How is one to explain this throbbing passion of a whole people to perform and achieve in a society where the prospect of personal enrichment is minimal? If only private initiative produces economic activity, how explain Russia's industrial progress in the last few years? The pioneer in America and the founders of economic enterprises everywhere suffered privations in the expectation of material compensation. But the thousands of Bolsheviks and non-Bolshevik enthusiasts who sacrifice themselves that Russia may develop know that their only reward will be national or local appreciation plus undermined health from overwork. Yet even foreigners like Colonel Hugh Cooper, Dr. A. Hirsch and John Calder are sometimes caught by the spirit which moves the Russians.

Various factors contribute: an urge, conscious and unconscious, towards better living standards and towards urban life which forces the Bolsheviks to build; a potent public opinion, skillfully manipulated, which compels the slackers to enter the ranks; a highly centralized leadership guided by a set of dominant principles; the romance, the scope, the imagination of Soviet construction which make work its own reward; the rise to power of young, unexhausted, unspoiled classes long separated from light and sun by a thin stratum of nobility, aristocracy and capitalists, and now reveling in their new influence and the capacity to mold their own destiny; and finally that social incentive which appears the moment the stimulus of personal gain is eliminated.

Russia has experienced nothing less than a national renaissance since 1917. The destruction of the rights of property and the introduction of a new social content into the individual's life have tapped sources of energy heretofore unsuspected in Russia or in any other nation. Every Soviet citizen feels that what the workers and all the so-called lower classes get under capitalism is merely the by-product of arrangements made by and for the bourgeoisie, but that what he gets is the result of a concentration of attention on his interests and needs. He is therefore prepared to forgive the Soviet Government a great deal, and to bear with it under very difficult conditions. He knows that he will rise with the community and he is ready to sacrifice and contribute more to the improvement of society as a whole. All this is only another way of saying that private property has been abolished and that Soviet workers work for themselves when they work for their employer the state. There is no one else for whom they could be working; the capitalists are gone. To be sure, they toil extra to pay for unnecessary mistakes. They protest when such errors become too numerous and stupid. Yet the principle remains that a new social sense has been evoked by the socialization of the means of production in Russia, and that that social sense is being harnessed to tremendous building and cultural programs which are changing the face of the country beyond recognition.

Under the socialist system in the U.S.S.R. the workers are exploited for the future and by themselves but never by another hostile class. They therefore tolerate exploitation. On the other hand, the disproportion between effort and compensation in the acquisitive world arouses the resentment of those who suffer from it; when living conditions grow bad, that resentment is directed against the owners who benefit from it. Equality then becomes an ideal through which the disproportion can be removed. Actually, however, equality can only be achieved in the Communist millennium, if then. The more immediate purpose of the intervening socialist stage is the elimination of undeserved privilege, the abolition of glaring inequalities, and the entrenchment of a system of payment in strict ratio to service. To the extent that the Bolsheviks have countenanced the return of certain privileges they weaken their moral position. For this denies the essence of Soviet democracy and consequently weakens the enthusiasm of the masses for their government.

A thorough application of the principle of compensation according to service implies the withdrawal of the profit motive. This does not signify that each individual economic enterprise does not endeavor to work efficiently and profitably, but rather that labor is not a commodity and that money moves not to the place where it earns most but where it is most useful to the community. This, undoubtedly, infringes upon many laws of bourgeois economy; it makes the state an expensive affair; but the nation benefits, and, in the end, the individual.

Control over the movement of money is not attained by the nationalization of banks but by the elimination of profit. Without money control there can be no planning. Without government ownership and operation or—as in Soviet agriculture to-day—government guidance, to put it mildly, there can be no planning. A planned economy postulates an upward economic curve. A plan must include production, relatively the simpler part of economic activity, as well as distribution. And distribution can only be planned if wages and other incomes are a fixed charge instead of the result of chance. There are some absolute limitations on planned national economy: international influences and weather conditions, for example. The Soviet plan, moreover, suffers from lack of experience, cultural backwardness, technical inefficiency, and over-concentralization of executive functions. Nevertheless, the fact is that a plan was never undertaken under any other than a socialist system because only that system is compatible with planning.

Planned economy is responsible for the tremendous progress achieved in the Soviet Union since 1928. From a poor though potentially rich country, Russia has reached fifth place among the nations of the world in the production of electricity, fourth place in chemical and coal production, second place in pig iron, machinery and oil, and first place in tractors, agricultural equipment and peat. Part of this relative rise is explained by retrogression in other countries, but it also represents a vast amount of construction, the building of scores of cities, the erection of dozens of industrial giants unequalled in Western countries, and the introduction of 5,500,000 men and women into productive industrial employment between 1928 and 1932. The Bolsheviks feel that this progress will continue even though its direction may change, its rate decrease, and its quality improve. There is in Russia to-day a certainty of success, a unity of purpose and a consciousness of power which are lacking in the rest of the world. While the bourgeoisie is torn by doubts as to the wisdom of its own methods—hence the groping for new policies such as planned economy, political reform, autarchy, Fascism, et cetera,—the Bolsheviks are convinced of the justice, strength and ultimate victory of their cause.

The first Soviet Five Year Plan was devised to build the foundation of a new heavy industry which, in turn, would subsequently enable the Bolsheviks to concentrate attention on the production of consumers' goods. That foundation is now partially laid. Thanks to the world economic crisis, and the food and goods shortage that naturally resulted from the huge capital investment incident to the first Five Year Plan, the Soviet Government in 1932 began, slowly, to shift the emphasis from the foundation to the superstructure, from the production of machines which make machines to the production of commodities which make men better-fed, better-clothed, happier, and healthier. To-day, every evidence of Soviet progress is surrounded by evidence of Soviet poverty. To-morrow, the Bolsheviks hope, further Soviet progress will remove that poverty. The task will be complicated and extended, but it is interesting to note that the maneuvering powers inherent in planned economy give almost immediate effect to the Soviet Government's decision to "shift emphasis." One actually sees and hears the gears shift from heavy to light industry, and in villages as well as cities, one sees the result in the shape of goods.

To the Soviet citizen, the availability of consumers' goods is of course a matter of considerable importance. It is also of prime significance to the world communist revolution. The Soviet Union has two things to contribute to the cause of international social change: a socialist economy and genuine prosperity.

There is only one real reply to Trotzky's charge that Moscow is doing nothing for the world revolution: Moscow is establishing a socialist state. "Socialist," to be sure, is a term of convenience. Elements of state socialism or state capitalism mingle with socialism and even pure communism as well as crippled capitalism. The struggle against capitalist economy and capitalist psychology are far from finished. Yet capitalism is not viable in the Soviet Union; it certainly lacks political influence. The basis, control and inspiration of the system are socialist. This circumstance is a stronger lever for world revolution than all the propaganda which the Third International might undertake.

Communism has gained some ground in foreign countries during the last two or three years. But compared to the intensity of the capitalist economic crisis, the millions of unemployed and the helplessness of bourgeois leadership the gain, except in Germany, has been trifling. Capitalism still has at its disposal large reserves of material, men, money, and hope. The last is perhaps more effective than any of the others. People will not take steps to destroy the present system as long as they hope that it will some day again yield the comparative plenty of the past. People, moreover, hesitate to tilt their lances against the present as long as the future remains uncertain. Soviet Russia is a test of that future. If all Soviet citizens lived comfortably and beautifully and worked under perfect conditions, workers and farmers who suffer under capitalism might be less inhibited in their revolutionary tendencies. It is not enough to demonstrate the theoretical supremacy of Communism, or the advantages of planned economy, or that Russia has been moving rapidly forward while the rest of the world stagnates and retrogresses. These are partial proofs. Final conviction can come only in the shape of a nation so happy and prosperous that arguments and words about superiority become superfluous. Otherwise, the revolt against capitalism must wait until capitalism's reserves are exhausted and hope yields to despair.

When it becomes clear to the naked eye, so to speak, clear beyond the slightest doubt that Soviet socialism is superior to capitalism, no one will be able to suppress the truth, and the end of capitalism will be in sight. That capitalism is already on its guard, that it grows frantic without sufficient cause when the danger of communism looms dimly in the distance indicates that Russia has made progress and that her enemies admit her promise of further progress at least to themselves.

Given peace, the quiet economic competition between capitalism and communism may last many years. International disarmament, accordingly, is necessary to the very life of capitalism. The painful conversations at Geneva seem to show that the Western world is aware of this fact. Czarism was equally aware of the need of peace, and the Provisional Government of the imperative necessity of solving the land problem. The effectiveness of those League of Nations debates, however, may prove that knowledge alone offers no salvation.

War would assuredly hasten the downfall of the capitalist system, and it is somewhat paradoxical at first sight, that the Soviet Government which ought to be most interested in that collapse is loudest in its demand for peace and disarmament. Be that as it may, the truth remains that the fear of revolution inspired by Russia's example will continue to be a potent influence toward world peace—if the Powers can help themselves. The very existence of the Soviet state, therefore,—altogether apart from Moscow's thoroughly pacific policy—is a compelling factor against war.

In the absence of war, the co-existence of the two rival economic systems is conceivable. Indeed, that co-existence is now eleven years old. Russia as well as the rest of the world have benefited from this symbiosis which neither desired and to which both are partially reconciled. The final outcome of the passive struggle between them will depend on events in the Soviet Union and in capitalist countries. The danger point for the latter may be the spot where their descending economic curve is crossed by a rising Soviet economic curve. Then, in other countries only Fascism and terror could delay a social upheaval. In such a conjuncture, the Russian example plus the compulsion of domestic conditions would constitute a menacing combination, though the speed of developments might be less than the impetuous would desire. Obviously, since Russia acted without a model in 1917, the Bolsheviks in any other nation might precipitate their revolution if there were no Soviet Union. Russia's experience is merely an encouragement; it tells radicals throughout the world that their efforts may succeed and that the system they propose to establish is viable. A few are already convinced by Soviet history. Every unit of Soviet progress, especially if attended by a capitalist crisis, turns still others towards the goal for which the Soviet Union is striving.

ENGLAND CONFRONTS A NEW WORLD

I

THE problem of representative democracy has been altered in a final way by the events of the post-war years. It is improbable that anyone will again defend its superiority over alternative forms of government in the terms which would have satisfied either Jefferson or Jeremy Bentham. It is obvious that any view which places confidence in the power of universal suffrage and representative institutions, unaided and of themselves, to secure a permanently well-ordered commonwealth is seriously under-estimating the complexity of the issue. Such a view not only gravely exaggerates the power of reason over interest in society; it also misconceives the dynamic nature of the purpose which representative democracy is seeking to secure.

Looking back now, at a generation's distance, upon the success of representative democracy in the nineteenth century, it is plain that this was due to the coincidence of quite special conditions. The vast expansion of material well-being which scientific discovery effected made possible the concession of an improved standard of life to the working-classes without any negative effect upon the standard enjoyed by their masters. The main character of the purposes it was sought to realize by governmental action was largely negative also. Privilege was overthrown in the realms in which it was established by law upon the assumption that liberty of contract was the inevitable parent of social equality. The establishment of things like popular education, a wide franchise, religious toleration, and

63

the like, conferred upon the masters a profound sense of satis-
fying emancipation without involving any of the tragic consequences which the opponents of those changes had predicted.
The relatively narrow sphere of governmental regulation,
moreover, made the issues of policy largely non-technical in
character; and it was possible for political discussion to be
followed by the multitude in a way which made representative
institutions themselves effective organs of popular instruction.
Nor had the ideal of national independence yet assumed a form
in which its economic expression seriously hampered the relation between states; the development of capitalization had not
yet come to imply such an intensity of international interdependence as made the national state a dubious unit of sovereign
authority. Emigration to America was unrestricted; and all
over the world there were great areas of capital investment in
which the taking of risk without coördinated plan still seemed
to offer a high and assured return. The Far East still accepted
domination by Europe and America without sign of serious
revolt; and the opening up of Africa offered the prospect of a
wealth unhampered by the limiting demands of social regulation. Anyone who observes the history, say of Great Britain
between 1815 and 1914, can hardly help concluding that the
prestige of Victorian parliamentarism was the outcome of quite
special economic circumstances of which there seems no reason
to expect a repetition.

Anyone who compares the complacent optimism of fifty
years ago with the institutional *malaise* of our own time cannot
fail to be impressed by the contrast. The Marxian socialists
apart, it was well-nigh universally admitted that the road was
clear to the triumph of representative democracy at least in
Western civilization and, as it was thought, all over the world,
as the process of education completed its task. Things like freedom of speech, judicial impartiality, freedom of migration,
were highly prized; the statesman seemed the master of the
forces it was his business to dominate. Taxation was low; and
the legend was still accepted that liberty of contract had established equality of opportunity. There was little left of that
pessimistic denunciation which, in the 'forties, was the keynote
not only of Marx and Engels, but of men so different as Carlyle
and the young Tories to whom the Sybil of Disraeli seemed a
prophetic utterance. The trade unions had nowhere won a
position of primary significance in the state. The men who

really counted in the making of the public opinion seemed to differ only on the incidentals of social philosophy. If there were national rivalries there seemed no reason to doubt that the main lines of institutional development had been laid down in a final way.

No one has that confidence now. What alone can be said to remain of the Victorian political ideals are the final eclipse of aristocracy and the recognition that no Church can dominate the life of a nation. The advocates of *laissez-faire* have been driven to admit that liberty of contract has no meaning in the absence of equality of bargaining power. The national state has become, as a sovereign entity, completely incompatible with the existence of a highly intricate and inter-dependent world-community. The price of social peace has become a volume of costly social administration which overwhelms national legislatures and has transferred effective political power to the executive of which parliament has become little more than the organ of registration. The subject matter of legislation has become so highly technical that much of its meaning is unintelligible to the multitude; and its extent is so great that there is rarely time for its essential principles to be illuminated by public discussion. The East is in revolt against tutelage. The breakdown of currency, and the ideal of economic self-sufficiency in the national state, has everywhere ended freedom of trade and migration. Taxation is everywhere so high that every new social experiment necessarily alters the way of life of the little minority who, in every state, control the basic sources of economic power. In many countries, the ideal of representative democracy has been frankly abandoned; and that feeling for liberty which was characteristic of the Victorian period is everywhere at a discount. Socialism in Western Europe has, almost universally, become the essential opposition to the bourgeois parties; and its emergence to that rank is significant, above all, because its conception of society is antithetic to the ideal that it challenges. If European trade unions have not achieved the scale and power which seemed possible in 1919, their growing immersion in politics is a vital expression of changed conditions. And it is urgent to realize how completely the foreign policy of the nation-state has become a way of expressing the major capitalist interests by which each political community is controlled. Oil, coal, steel, high finance, are empires which utilize political mechanisms for the expression of the single

purpose of profit that they embody; and because their operations are world-wide, no state remains outside the orbit of their
influence. International relations have become a function of
the habits of economic imperialism. If war superficially represents nation-states in collision, behind the legendary symbols
it is a struggle between competing groups of capitalists for access
to economic power.

Representative democracy seems to have ended in a *cul-de-
sac*. And few of the remedies for its difficulties that were put
forward by the thinkers of the nineteenth century seem in the
least degree adequate to its cure. That the best men do not enter political life, that it is dangerous to enfranchise the unedu-
cated, that our methods of voting are illogical or absurd, that
we need more experts, or better information, that parties sub-
ordinate the national to functional interests, that there is too
much government, or too little—none of these explanations
even begins to scratch the surface of the problem. Who are the
best men? What is an educated person? Who can say that the
strict logic of Germany's voting system makes the results of her
governance more adequate than those of Great Britain? Who
can tell, by any objective criteria, when a party is hostile to the
interests of the whole community? Is there a single vital theme
of government policy—the tariff, disarmament, currency, wage-
standards—upon which the experts speak with a united voice?
Better information we all may proclaim as desirable. But in the
presence of interests so profoundly conflicting as those which
divide the modern state, who is to interpret the information in
a way so disinterested as to command widespread assent for the
policy in which it is to issue? Men speak of institutional reorganization. But it is useless to reorganize institutions unless the
community is agreed upon the purposes for which they are
intended. The demand either for more or for less government
is meaningless unless it can specify also the kind of society it is
proposed to build. All schemes of greater or lesser social regulation must be built upon a clear view of public policy; and that
is largely absent from the affirmations of either side.

II

To anyone who, like myself, accepts the ideal of a democratic
society as preferable to any alternative, the social fact which
emerges from the present situation is that the conditions are

not present in which such a society can function. I mean by a democratic society one in which the incidence of policy is not biased in the direction of any particular group in the community—in which, therefore, the interest of any individual in the operation of the state is approximately equal to that of any other. I believe, with Tocqueville, that the evolution of society represents a perpetual struggle for the establishment of this equality; and, therefore, that the source of the *malaise* we are witnessing is the inability of the principle of equality to find expression in a framework of institutions which deny it the possibility of effective entrance. I propose to illustrate this position by analyzing the situation of democratic institutions in Great Britain—mainly because I am most familiar with them— and to draw therefrom some general inferences.

The British position is inherently simple. Great Britain became the leading industrial nation in the world during the nineteenth century by being the first people to profit by the results of the revolution in manufacturing technique. Until the 'eighties of the last century, her predominance was unchallenged; and her business men were able to afford all the concessions demanded from them by organized labor without losing their power to underbid their competitors in the world-market. But that position grew steadily weaker as rivals emerged, as protective tariffs made it increasingly difficult to enter new, and retain old, markets. Universal suffrage demanded an ever-growing volume of social legislation as the price to be paid for the favors of the electorate. The post-war period merely clarified a situation the outlines of which could be decisively seen under the Liberal government of 1906-14. It was that, with a heavy burden of debt and a shrinking market for its exports, the standard of life attained before the war could be maintained for the community as a whole only if the owners of property were prepared to surrender their privileged position and agree that their income should be increasingly taxed to offer amenities to those without property which the latter could not afford from their wages alone.

The decline of Liberalism and the rise of the Labor party have been due to the fact that those who dominated the Liberal party were themselves the owners of property who found themselves threatened by the demands made by Labor on the state. The increasing tendency of Liberals to join the forces of Conservatism arose from the realization that both alike were threatened by the rise of a socialist party; and that, if the latter had its way, the vested interests of a capitalist society would be attacked at the root. Liberals were prepared to disagree with Conservatives upon matters of incidental significance so long as both were agreed upon the fundamental character of the society —that fundamental character being the private ownership of the means of production upon the basis of profit-making by the entrepreneur. As soon as socialism became the alternative government in the state, Liberals joined with their historic rivals to protect this system of private ownership from an attack made upon it in the name of equality.

This alteration in the disposition of party forces is likely to have important results on the constitutional position. The success of the British parliamentary system has been built upon the fact that the major parties in the state could agree to accept each other's legislation, since neither altered the essential outlines of the social-economic system in which the interests of both were involved. With the emergence of the Labor party as the alternative government, a different position has come into view. The Labor party aims at the transformation of a capitalist into a socialist society. It seeks, therefore, directly to attack, by means of Parliament, the ownership of the means of production by those classes which constitute the foundation of Tory and Liberal strength. Its principles are a direct contradiction of those of its rivals. It denies the validity of the whole social order which the nineteenth century maintained. Is it likely that it can attain its objectives in the peaceful and constitutional fashion which was characteristic of the Victorian epoch?

No one not a Communist is likely to prophesy these matters with any certitude. He will note, indeed, that so comparatively small a change as that involved in home rule for Ireland brought Great Britain, in 1914, to the verge of civil war. He will be influenced in his judgment by the fact that the transference of power from king to Parliament in the seventeenth century involved a civil war and a revolution before it was complete. He will remember that the dispossession of a governing class has rarely been effected without violence. A change in the essential methods of production, such as the Labor party envisages, involves changes in the legal and political institutions which are literally fundamental. However generous be the compensation to established expectations, the interference with vested interests which the policy predicates is momentous in amount. Are the owners of property likely to accept the peaceful destruction of their position in the state?

Nor is that all. Even if it takes a considerable period for the Labor party to secure power, the position in which the Conservative forces find themselves is not an easy one. The last thirty years have brought into being the social service state; and the cost of its maintenance is high. The burden of war-debt, the shrinkage of the export trades, the growth of the demand for self-government by India—all intensify the weight of that burden. If Conservatism is to maintain the predominance of those who control its policies, it must be at the cost of the standard of life built up by the working-class in the last generation. To economize on things like the social services is to risk a Labor victory; not to economize on them is to jeopardize the power of British capitalists to produce at a cost which enables them to penetrate foreign markets. Alternative sources of economy—armaments, for example, are likely to be small for a considerable period simply because the disturbed state of Europe and the Far East does not offer that feeling of security out of which disarmament can come. The drama of a currency crisis, as in 1931, may steel the nation to temporary sacrifice; but that merely postpones the discussion of equality and does not abandon it. Sooner or later, Great Britain has to face the issue of whether it will adjust its economic and social constitution to the political democracy upon which its legislative constitution depends.

The observer who seeks to analyze the prospects of this position must realize that, on any showing, thoroughgoing institutional adjustment is unavoidable. The position of the House of Lords is incompatible with the aims of the Labor party. The procedure of the House of Commons is utterly unsuited to the necessities of the positive state. The reconstruction of the areas and functions of local government is an urgent matter if efficient decentralization is to be possible; and, without efficient decentralization, no reform of Parliament would leave it adequate to its tasks. The whole machinery and principles of the common law, moreover, are conceived in terms of concepts which deny the very essence of an equal society; their reformation is unescapable if its realization is to have meaning. No one, in a word, can visualize what is involved in the transformation of the existing institutional structure without realizing how gigantic is the task involved in its reconstruction.

Nor must we omit the international aspect of the matter. Not only is Great Britain involved in a world-economic system by the standards of which she must set her own. She is involved also in a world-political system the rivalries of which at every point affect the character of her policy. A German revolution, a Franco-Italian war, an attack on Russia by Japan, an Indian revolt, may alter altogether the position in which she finds herself. And her economic adjustments are peculiarly costly by reason of the deep-seated social habits they disturb. Laissez-faire, in the Victorian sense, is dead. Modern forms of regulation involve problems for her which go to the very root of that curious combination of political democracy and aristo-plutocratic social control to which she has so far entrusted her destiny. All her essential habits—toleration, absence of deliberate plan, leisureliness of adjustment—are threatened by the rapid changes in economic technique which the scientific revolution in modern industry is compelling.

The very nature of those rapid changes, moreover, gives decreased significance to historic representative institutions; it leads one to inquire whether political democracy has not, so to say, arrived too late upon the scene to control the total process by which it is confronted. For the leisurely processes of parliamentary debate are far too slow for the requirements of economic decision. They tend merely to register agreements arrived at outside the legislative assembly. Parliament could not have controlled the bankers in 1931; the movement of finance had determined the course of events before ever it could be summoned to grapple with its implications. No one supposes that Parliament, either, could charge itself with the control of the detailed processes of industry; at the most it must confine itself to the largest general issues. And this raises the question of whether, if the movement toward an equal society on socialist principles gains momentum, the public which is now represented in the House of Commons is not going, from the very nature of its problems, to find itself dissolved into a series of special publics much more loosely integrated by the political process than is the case under the price-mechanism of a capitalist society.

Or, it may be, the evolution may not be in the direction of an equal society. In that case, the disproportion between the political democracy and the economic oligarchy will be even more striking than now. For only the advent of some sudden and unexpected economic prosperity will enable that oligarchy to satisfy the wants of the political democracy. The characteristic of capitalism tempered by spasmodic regulation, especially in a protectionist society, is everywhere the same. It means special privilege in terms of the power at the disposal of the different groups. It means, where foreign investment is concerned, the use of the state by the investing class, where it is significant enough in wealth or size or skill in propaganda, for the usual purposes of imperialism. The courts and the legislature are utilized to protect what privilege obtains from the vantage-ground of its inequality from the assault of the unprivileged. The implication of such a society is necessarily conflict.

From all this, I conclude that the success of the British parliamentary system was due to the privileged economic position gained by Great Britain in the course of the Industrial Revolution, and that it is rapidly becoming dubious as that privileged position disappears. It is, no doubt, true that the tenacity of British constitutionalism will give it a better chance of survival than is the case in countries where the tradition is less deeply rooted—in France, for instance, or Germany, or Italy. But that success, as I have argued, was the outcome of the facts (1) that the concessions demanded were mainly negative in character, (2) that they could be made without serious cost to those who conceded them, and (3) when the mass of the population were not being organized into parties divided by final differences of economic outlook.

None of this is true to-day. The position of privilege is gone, and there is no reason to expect its return. The concessions demanded fundamentally alter the position of the class which dominates the economic system; they can make them only at the price of their eventual disappearance. Increasingly, again, the division between parties is determined by a vital difference of view upon matters of economic constitution; they have moved to the fundamental debate upon the rights of property in the community. We have been warned on high authority that under such circumstances the classical traditions of British politics are likely, in the very nature of things, to be jeopardized.[1]

---

[1] Bagehot, The English Constitution (World's Classics edition), preface by Lord Balfour, p. XXIIf.

III

This analysis of the British position may reasonably be extended into a wider generalization. For a state to realize the common good, it is necessary that it should be built upon the conditions which make possible the emergence of that common good. Where the claims of its members upon the results of the social process are seriously unequal, conflict can be postponed only so long as those whose claims receive less satisfaction have the constant sense that the differences which exist are clearly referable to the needs of that common good itself. Once that sense ceases to be widely present, there is absent from the society that agreement about fundamental principles which makes possible the effective working of representative government.

All over the world, in the nineteenth century, political democracy succeeded because it associated the abolition of privilege with increasing economic welfare for the masses of the population among Western nations. It was widely believed that as the masses became, through representative institutions, the masters in their own house, the operations of the state would increasingly represent the general advantage. Men did not realize how special were the conditions of this success. They depended upon the increasing economic returns of America and the imperialistic exploitation of the colored peoples. Once the saturation point had been reached in America, and the East became unwilling to submit to white domination, the conditions were changed. It became clear that to improve the condition of the masses meant an attack on economic privileges, and a consequent reorganization of the economic order. But the terms upon which political privilege had been abandoned were that the way of life of those who owned the effective sources of economic power should not be altered. The new movement—which the war of 1914 rather threw into striking relief than started—challenged precisely those terms. Representative democracy became unstable because there was no longer agreement between the governing classes and the mass of the people, either upon the ends it should seek or upon the ways in which it should seek them.

The position in which we find ourselves was startlingly seen by Tocqueville in a passage to which too little attention has been paid. "The people," he wrote,[2] "had first endeavored to help itself by changing each political institution, but after each change, it found that its lot was in no way improved, or was only improving with a slowness quite incompatible with the eagerness of its desire. Inevitably, it must sooner or later discover that that which held it fixed in its position was not the constitution of the government, but the unalterable laws that constitute society itself; and it was natural that it should be brought to ask itself if it had not both the power and the right to alter those laws, as it had altered all the rest."

That is the question put squarely to modern civilization by socialism, and, of course, with peculiar and dramatic intensity by the Russian experiment. The *malaise* of representative democracy is due to the fact that the governing classes are not willing to alter the essential characteristics of capitalist society to their disadvantage. That unwillingness can be maintained only upon the basis of a capacity to secure economic improvement at a rate which satisfies the demands of the workers. Such a capacity is unattainable under modern conditions. For it depends upon the ability of a capitalist society to work its assumptions without constant interference from non-economic ends. A society able to make its adjustments in terms of a purely objective price-mechanism might ignore considerations, especially ethical, of a subjective kind. There is no such practicability in Western civilization. State-policy meets demands for a non-economic kind to which it is continually bound to pay deference. Politicians dare not offend a powerful group of manufacturers; they are driven by public opinion to regulate prices, or wages, or the hours of labor; they must seek to protect society from the dangers of monopoly. Whatever be the causes, the free play of the market will no longer control the results with which we are confronted. The abandonment of laissez-faire means the necessity of social control.

But with the admission of that necessity, there is no escape from the problem of economic equality. So long as there are differences in the return to effort, and privileges in the attainment of those differences, men are bound to inquire into the causes of the difference and the justification of the privilege. They are bound to ask why social control should be so exercised as to benefit only a few; and there is certain to be increasing

2 Recollections (Eng. trans.) p. 99.

insistence that it should be exercised in the interest of the many. Such an exercise, of course, means a transvaluation of values; it involves the response to wants in other terms than effective economic demands. Representative democracy, at this stage, is, briefly put, asked to solve the problem by paralleling the political equality it achieved with a similar economic equality. To do so constitutionally, it has to call upon the holders of economic power voluntarily to abdicate from their position of dominance. So far-reaching a demand is not welcome; and, no doubt, to most of those to whom it is made, it seems like an attempt to overthrow the natural foundations of social order. The forces of prescription are on their side, and it is psychologically intelligible that they should be prepared to fight rather than give way.

In any society, in fact, the state belongs to the holders of economic power; and its institutions naturally operate, at least in the main, to their advantage. But by establishing political democracy they offer to the masses the potentiality of capturing the political machinery and using it to redress the inequalities to which the economic régime gives rise. Where that position arises, they are asked to coöperate in the abolition of the advantages they enjoy. Such coöperation has rarely been offered deliberately or with good-will; and it has been necessary, as a rule, to establish by force a new legal order the institutions of which permit the necessary adjustments to be made.

It appears likely that we are approaching such a position at the present time. It is significant that the rivalry of competing economic nationalisms appears to make impossible the attainment of that political security which is the condition of any economic equilibrium. The absence of political security, especially in the aftermath of recent war, makes necessary a volume of expenditure upon debts and armaments which hinders the prospect of material improvement. For it reduces trade; it lessens the essential capital accumulation; and it involves such a scale of taxation that social services are threatened at their foundation because of the cost to the governing class of their maintenance or development. The reduction of trade, moreover, means unemployment; and the world is confronted by the spectacle of a vast army of workless men who, sharing in political power, are inevitably tempted to use it for their protection against want. In such a condition, the differences between men become final in character; the prospect of solving them in terms of reason instead of terms of power becomes a matter of extraordinary difficulty. But the thesis of representative democracy is precisely the willingness to accept the verdict of that reason which is able to win a victory at the polls. It may be that, aware of the dangers which now attend the application of violence to the solution of social problems, our generation will act differently from its predecessors. It is as yet difficult to scan the horizon of politics and discern there hope that this will be the case.[3]

<h2 style="text-align:center">IV</h2>

"A specter is haunting Europe—the specter of Communism." Eighty-five years have passed since the Communist Manifesto opened with those fateful words. It is little less since Tocqueville predicted that the democracy, weary of the inadequate results of their political emancipation, would one day turn to the destruction of the rights of property as the condition precedent to their economic emancipation. "In matters of social construction," he wrote,[4] "the field of possibilities is much more extensive than men living in their various societies are willing to imagine."

After the breakdown of the revolutions of 1848 there was little disposition among the statesmen of Europe and America to take the growth of socialism with any profound seriousness until the epoch of the war. A moment of horror at the events in Paris in 1871, a sense that the abortive revolution in Russia of 1905 might be the prelude to a vaster drama, exhausted the sense of doubt about the foundations of the social system. Neither the experience of France nor of Germany seemed to point to the likelihood of Socialist governments; and as late as 1908, President Lowell, reflecting upon the English position at the close of his famous treatise,[5] concluded that "unless the Labor Party should grow in a way that seems unlikely" there was no protest of a class-division in English politics in the near future. Lord Grey, indeed, on the very eve of the war, was troubled by a sense that its prolongation might result in a repetition of 1848; but the universal welcome which greeted the

3 Reprinted, with the kind permission of the *Political Science Review* (August, 1932).
4 "Recollections," p. 101.
5 "Government of England," II, p. 534.

March Revolution in Russia did not suggest that men had any doubts about the foundations of a capitalist society. At no time in American history prior to the war had the socialist movement made any profound impact upon American life.

The Bolshevik Revolution wrought an immediate and fundamental change in the perspective of public opinion. The very fact that Marxian principles could assume the guise of action made it evident that the foundations of capitalism had nothing like the security that had been assumed. As Lenin consolidated his position against both the attacks of the Allies and the impact of civil war, the Russian Revolution began to reveal itself as the profoundest change in the mental climate of the world since the Reformation. The proletariat in a state of one hundred and thirty millions had not merely challenged the rights of property, it had overthrown them. Before five years had passed it was obvious that the Russian Revolution was not, as its enemies hoped, a temporary portent. It had affected the psychological fabric of all civilization. Ideas like the class-war, the dictatorship of the proletariat, the expropriation of the capitalist, had passed at a single bound from books to action. What seemed in 1914 an underground and unimportant conspiracy had become, ten years later, a state. And it was obvious that the fact of such a state's existence, the knowledge that it could survive and grow, had turned men's thoughts into new directions. For the first time in history, a proletarian state was an actual, and not merely an ideological, inspiration; and for the first time in history, also, capitalist society met a direct and thorough-going challenge.

The impact of Russia upon the old world and the new cannot be expressed in simple terms. Certainly there were few thoughtful minds whom it did not compel to a revaluation, or, at least, a reassessment of the basic principles of politics. The pre-war state-system emerged from the great conflict far more shattered than was apparent in the mood of vindictive triumph embodied in the Peace of Versailles. It had to grapple with a *damnosa hereditas*. The necessities of war had given an enhanced status to the working-classes of the belligerent countries; and it was necessary to satisfy their new claims. National feeling had been profoundly inflamed by the conflict; and since nationalism took the form of an intense revival of neo-mercantilist doctrine, a community of states emerged whose political practices were increasingly at variance with the objective needs

of the world-economic market. The problems created by debts
and reparations, the control of imports and migration in the
interest of the several states, the new levels of taxation rendered
necessary by the demands of social legislation, the refusal of the
Far East any longer to accept the domination of Western Europe and America, all implied the futility of believing that
the old laissez-faire was compatible with the attainment of social
good. It had become clear to every careful observer that it was
necessary either deliberately to plan the post-war civilization
or to perish.

For a brief period, the sudden prosperity of America (though
much more confined than was generally realized) concealed
from many the realities of the situation. It was argued that the
condition of Russia was a special one; that, elsewhere, the
problem was rather one of dealing with the excrescences of the
capitalist system than with capitalism itself. As late as 1928
President Hoover felt able to announce to an awe-struck world
that America had (under God) solved the problem of poverty.
Two years later, it was clear that his announcement was prema-
ture. The world (including America) was caught in the grips
of a depression more intense and more widespread than any
recorded in history. The unemployed could be counted in millions in capitalist countries. The mood of pessimism was universal; men spoke gravely of a possible collapse of civilization.
At a time when science had made possible a greater productivity than in any previous age, the problem of distribution seemed
insoluble. All the nations demanded the removal of barriers
against world-trade; despite pious recommendations, like those
at Geneva in 1927, they did not seem able to remove them. All
the world agreed upon the necessity of disarmament; the conference at Geneva to attain it would have been farcical if it had
not been tragic. The dislocation of currency methods deprived
commerce of that automatic measure of value upon which the
life-blood of trade depended. Thirteen years after the end of
the war, the perspective of capitalist civilization revealed an
insecurity, both economic and political, which made justifiable
the gravest doubts of its future.

Russian development was in striking contrast. The Five Year
Plan gave it an integrated and orderly purpose such as no
capitalist country could rival. Productivity increased at a remarkable rate; unemployment was non-existent. If the standard
of living was low compared with that of Great Britain or the

United States, its tendency was to increase and not to decline. The whole population was united in a great corporate effort at material well-being in which there was the promise of equal participation. Where Europe and America were sunk in pessimism, the whole temper of Russia was optimistic. The authority of its government was unchallenged; its power to win amazing response to its demands was unquestionable. Granted all its errors, no honest observer could doubt its capacity both to plan greatly and, in large measure, to realize its plans. No doubt its government was, in a rigorous sense, a dictatorship. No doubt also it imposed upon its subjects a discipline, both spiritual and material, such as a capitalist civilization would hardly dare to attempt. No doubt, again, its subjects paid a heavy price for the ultimate achievement to which they looked forward. Yet, whatever its defects and errors, the mood of the Russian experiment was one of exhilaration. While the rest of the world confronted its future in a temper of skepticism and dismay, Russia moved forward in a belief, religious in the intensity of its emotion, that it had a right to ample confidence in its future.

V

No one can understand the character of the communist challenge to capitalism who does not grasp the significance of this contrast. A hundred years ago the votaries of capitalism had a religious faith in its prospects. They were, naturally enough, dazzled by the miracles it performed, confident that the aggregation of its individual successes was coincident with the social good, happy in a security about the results of their investment which seemed to entitle them to refashion the whole world in their own image. The successful business man became the representative type of civilization. He subdued all the complex of social institutions to his purposes. Finance, oil, coal, steel, became empires of which the sovereignty was as unchallenged as that of Macedon or of Rome. Men so different as Disraeli and Marx might utter warnings about the stability of the edifice. Broadly speaking, they were unheeded in the triumphs to which the business man could point.

But those triumphs could not conceal the fact that the idol had feet of clay. The price to be paid for their accomplishment was a heavy one. The distribution of the rewards was incapable of justification in terms of moral principle. The state was driven increasingly to intervene to mitigate the inequalities to which capitalism gave rise. Vast and costly schemes of social legislation, militant trade unionism, a nationalism of pathological proportions, imperialist exploitation with its consequential awakening of nationalism among the peoples exploited,[6] were all inherently involved in the technique of a capitalist civilization. Nationalism meant imperialism; imperialism meant war; in the struggle for markets there was involved an inescapable threat to the security of the whole structure. That became finally evident in the Great War and its aftermath. A world of competing economic nationalisms could not avoid inevitable conflict.

Nor is this all. The condition for the survival of an acquisitive society is twofold. There must be no halt in its power to continue its successes; and it must be able so to apportion their results that the proletariat do not doubt their duty to be loyal to its institutions. This condition has not been realized. Economic nationalism has given birth to a body of vested interests which impede in a fatal way the expansion of world trade. On the one hand, the power of productivity makes the ideal of self-sufficiency incapable of realization; on the other, the capture of foreign markets means commercial warfare which issues into actual warfare. The individual ownership of the means of production is incompatible with the kind of planning necessitated by the interrelations of a world reduced to the unity of interdependence.

The failure to maintain the allegiance of the proletariat, though different in degree in different countries, is, nevertheless, universal. Its danger was foreseen by Tocqueville nearly a century ago. "The manufacturer," he wrote,[7] "asks nothing of the workman but his labor; the workman expects nothing from him but his wages. The one contracts no obligation to protect, nor the other to defend; and they are not permanently connected either by habit or by duty. . . . The manufacturing aristocracy of our age first impoverishes and debases the men who serve it, and then abandons them to be supported by the charity of the public. . . . Between the workman and the master there are frequent relations but no real partnership."

6 See my "Nationalism and the Future of Civilization" (1932).
7 "Democracy in America," Part II, Book II, Chapter XVIII.

Everything that has happened since Tocqueville wrote has combined to give emphasis to his insight. The decay of religion has intensified the appreciation of material well-being. The growth of education has made working-class resentment at the contrast between riches and poverty both keener and more profound. Universal suffrage has made necessary a far wider and more costly response to the demands of the proletariat; and the perfection of party organization has made the struggle for political power one in which the offer of bread and circuses is an essential part.

Men, in short, accept a capitalist society no longer because they believe in it, but because of the material benefits it professes to confer. Once it ceases to confer them, it cannot exercise its old magic over men's minds. "It has become," writes Mr. Keynes,[8] "absolutely irreligious, without internal union, without much public spirit, often, though not always, a mere congeries of possessors and pursuers." Once its success is a matter of dubiety, those who do not profit by its results inevitably turn to alternative ways of life. They realize that the essence of a capitalist society is its division into a small number of rich men and a great mass of poor men. They see not only the existence of a wealthy class which lives without the performance of any socially useful function; they realize also that it is inherent in such a society that there should be no proportion between effort and reward. They see this when the decline of capitalist prosperity makes the payment of the price demanded for their allegiance to the system one it is increasingly difficult to pay without destroying the position of advantage which the rich enjoy in society. The social service state can only be maintained at a level which satisfies the worker in a period of increasing returns. Once its benefits have to be diminished, the moral poverty of capitalism becomes apparent to all save those who live by its preservation. There arises an insistent demand for economic and social equality—such a distribution of the social product as can rationally be referred to intelligible principle. Resistance develops to the normal technique by which capitalism adjusts itself to a falling market. The growth of socialism in Great Britain, the dissatisfaction with the historic parties in the United States, the rise of Hitlerism in Germany, the profound and growing interest, all over the world, in the Russian

[8] "Essays in Persuasion," p. 306.

experiment, are all of them, in their various ways, the expression of that resistance. Men have begun to ask, upon a universal scale, whether there is not the possibility of consciously building a classless society in which the ideal of equality is deliberately given meaning.

It is not, I think, excessive to argue that the experience of this generation leads most socially conscious observers to doubt the desirability of relying upon the money motive in individuals automatically to produce a well-ordered community. It is at least a matter of universal recognition that the collective intelligence of society must control all major economic operations. But the translation of that recognition into policy encounters difficulties of which the importance cannot be overemphasized. For it asks men to part with power on an unexampled scale. It changes a system of established expectations profoundly rooted in the habits of mankind. It disturbs vested interests which are well organized, both for offense and defense, and accustomed by long tradition to have their way. No governing class in the history of the world has consciously and deliberately sacrificed its authority. It has gone down fighting, as in France and Russia; it has coöperated with the *novi homines* of the industrial revolution, as in England or Germany. But the call to socialism, which the anarchy of capitalist society has produced, is, at bottom, a demand for economic egalitarianism in which the possessors are invited to sacrifice their power, their vested interests, their established expectations, for the attainment of a common good they will no longer be able to manipulate to their own interest.

The socialist parties of Western civilization have conceived a simple formula upon which to place reliance. They will win a majority of the electorate to their side; and they will proceed, by legislative enactment, gradually to introduce the socialist commonwealth. Possessing themselves of the constitution of the state, they assume that they can operate the machinery to their own purposes. They argue that if the pace is not too violently forced, the instinct for law and order will enable them to consummate their revolution with good-will because their policy will proceed by reasonable stages. That has been the policy of the two Labor Governments which arrived in office, a little accidentally perhaps, in Great Britain; and in their different ways it has been the policy of such socialist governments as have held office elsewhere. Of them all it is not unfair to say that they nowhere made any essential difference to the foundations of capitalist society. Of them, also, it is true to say that if they showed signs of seriously compromising those foundations, they were driven to surrender power to their rivals. And in that event it was the bankruptcy, rather than the success, of gradualist change which became apparent.

In this context, what is important is the underlying assumption of socialist gradualism: it builds upon the persistence of constitutional democracy. But not only—as Italy, Jugoslavia and the rest make plain—is that persistence a dubious matter in practice; the persistence of constitutional democracy depends upon the further assumption that men are agreed upon the fundamental principles of policy. In a broad way, this was true as between Liberals and Conservatives in the nineteenth century; experience has demonstrated how little ground there is for believing that it is true when the choice is between a capitalist and a socialist way of life. No one who meditates upon the prospect of large-scale socialist experiment can conclude that it is likely to go into operation without grave challenge. No one, either, can argue that such a challenge will permit the principles of constitutional democracy to survive unimpaired.

VI

It is at this point that the communist hypothesis becomes of such overwhelming importance. It points to the inherent contradictions of capitalist society. It denies that there is in it any longer the power to resolve those contradictions within its assumptions. It insists that no socialist government can attempt seriously to put its principles into practice without encountering determined resistance which will issue in civil war. To maintain socialist principles, in short, socialists will be driven to become communists or to betray their socialism. If they become communists, they will find themselves involved in the grim logic of Leninism—the dictatorship of the proletariat, the drastic suppression of counter-revolution, the confiscation of the essential instruments of production, the building of the state, in a word, upon the principles of martial law until the security of the new order is firmly established. The transformation of capitalism into socialism means revolution, and that implies an experience akin to that through which Russia has passed.

I do not see how it is reasonable to deny the possibility—to put it no higher—that the communists are right. The threat of war is implicit in our society, and war means revolution all over the world. Even if that revolution assumed a Fascist form, communism would be its inevitable antithesis; and, in that event, sooner or later communism would move to the assault. To avoid the threat of war, the degree of self-reformation which capitalist states must undertake would leave them unrecognizable as capitalist. The observer of England, of America, of France is entitled to doubt whether there is in the possessing classes of any of them that will to self-reformation which would make it effective. The change of heart required would involve a transvaluation of all values, the supersession by agreement of money as the dominant motive to action. It is only the acceptance of new values with an intensity almost religious in character which could effect that supersession; and that possession of a body of alternative values held with religious intensity is, to put it quite bluntly, practically a monopoly of the communists at the present time.

That, indeed, is the secret of its strength. Its devotees believe in it with a faith so absolute that there is no sacrifice they are not prepared to make in its name. Communism has succeeded in Russia for the same reasons that brought triumph to the Jesuits, the Puritans, the Jacobins in an earlier period. Willing the end, the communists have not shrunk from the application of any means likely to attain that end. They have consistently opposed an unshakable will to the resistance they have encountered. They have disdained both compromise and hesitation. In the service of no other social system in the world today can it be said that these qualities are enlisted. No one defends the acquisitive society save in the most mitigated terms. No capitalist society could attempt experiment on the Russian scale without risking the willingness of the working-classes to observe the demands of law and order. Not even the most intense propaganda in capitalist countries has prevented the working-classes from feeling a proud interest in every success the Russian experiment can show. "Perhaps," wrote Mr. Keynes,[9] "Russian communism does represent the first confused stirrings of a great religion." That is a widespread and growing feeling among all who are disturbed by the contradictions

[9] "Essays in Persuasion," p. 309.

of capitalism; and it is an emotion far more profoundly diffused among the workers than is realized by the rulers of alternative systems.

The unity, in fact, of capitalist society has been broken. No
country is prepared to pay the price which its simple rehabilita-
tion demands; and to attempt the enforcement of that price
would involve disorders of which no one could predict the outcome. That is the significance of the point made earlier in this
essay that the Russian revolution shapes the perspective of
men's thoughts. Lower the standards of life, whether by de-
creases in wages or by economies in social legislation, diminish
the worker's security, sharpen the contrast between poverty
and wealth, and it at once comes into the worker's mind that
in Russia, if the standard is low, it is rising, and that the hope
of still greater rises is profound, that all social legislation is in
the proletarian interest, that the contrasts between poverty and
wealth are largely without meaning. A state has been built
upon the exaltation of the common man; it is inevitable that
the common men of other states should have its existence and
its possibilities increasingly in their minds.

Capitalist society, in other words, is running a race with
communist society for the allegiance of the masses. The terms
upon which the former can be successful are fairly clear. It has
to solve the contradiction between its power to produce and its
inability to distribute income in a rational and morally adequate way. It has to remove the barriers which economic nationalism places in the way of an unimpeded world-market. It
has to remove the fear of insecurity by which the worker's life
is haunted. It has to end the folly of international competition
in wage-rates and hours of labor; it has to find ways of saving
Western standards from the slave-labor of the East. It has, not
least, to cut away the jungle-growth of vested interests which
at present so seriously impair its efficiency. Even a capitalist
society will not long endure the spectacle of the cotton and coal
industries of Great Britain or the power-trust in the United
States. Above all, perhaps, it has to find some way of removing
from the clash of competing imperialisms those structures of
armed power which, clothed in the garb of national sovereignty,
make certain the perpetual threat of insecurity and, born of
it, the advent of war.

Let me emphasize again that to meet successfully the challenge of communism a capitalist society has to show itself im-

mensely more successful than the former. This does not, of course, mean that communism, in its Russian expression, does not confront its own grave problems. Broadly, they are of two kinds. It is necessary, by economic success, to maintain the exhilaration, the enthusiastic will to sacrifice, of the first great period of striving; and it is necessary, in the second, to relate Russia more adequately to the conditions of the external world. For, in the context of the first condition, it must not be forgotten that Russia was to some extent fortunate in her situation. Not only was she dealing with a people accustomed to the psychology of an autocratic discipline; she was also able to take advantage of a profound patriotism engendered by external attack. The Soviet State cannot go on perpetually demanding the postponement of consumption for the sake of a future which does not arrive. They must come to a point where the maintenance of enthusiasm for the new régime is the outcome of having conferred tangible benefit. Nor will it be possible over any considerable period to maintain the dominating grip of the Communist Party over the whole political life of Russia. That grip has been acquiesced in because of the social circumstances confronting the new régime; no acquiescence in a dictatorship is ever permanent in character. There must, that is to say, not only be economic success in the new Russia; there must come also a time when restriction is relaxed and room is found for the admission of freedom. The permanence of communist society depends upon its ability to meet these issues creatively. For any new social order that seeks to become universal must be able to correlate its economic advance with spiritual growth.

No doubt, of course, spiritual growth, and especially that temper of tolerance which is the groundwork of all intellectual achievement, is, in its turn, dependent upon economic advance. Periods of revolutionary poverty rarely synchronize with periods of great scientific or literary production; for the atmosphere of dictatorship, the preoccupation with material well-being, are stifling to that atmosphere of experiment upon which intellectual advance depends. It is not accidental that neither the Puritan nor the French Revolution has left behind it a great cultural impact upon the mind of the world; the spiritual fruits of each were gathered after men could in leisure and in safety seek to probe their implications. It is therefore reasonable to argue that the success of Russian communism depends upon the maintenance, at least for a considerable period, of world peace. For if Russia becomes involved in any serious military conflict the transformation of its energies will dangerously impair the prospect of its economic policy. More than this, the intensification of the dictatorship involved in war might easily, if the struggle were at all prolonged, result in the kind of internal conflicts within the Communist Party which, in the French Revolution, made ultimately possible the emergence of Napoleon.

It would be folly to deny the possibility of Russia becoming involved in war within the next decade.[10] The clash of interests with Japan in the Far East is a grave one. The fear of the effect of Russian exports of butter, timber, oil, coal and wheat on a depressed market already gives birth to those economic reprisals out of which war has so often come. The instability of Europe is fed by Russian propaganda; and the very fact that communism expects a world-revolution to come by way of war gives to that propaganda the psychological perspective which so easily makes expectancy fact. The failure of disarmament, the dissatisfaction of minorities, the intensity of social revolutionary movements in the East, all of these point to that kind of collapse in the system of international regulation which is the prelude to conflict. And it is useless to deny that there are, all over the world, important interests which would welcome an attack on Russia before its success is beyond question as the surest way of ending that implicit challenge to capitalist society which it represents. Certainly militant communism and militant capitalism cannot exist side by side, especially in a period of serious economic stress. It is important that Moscow is the Mecca of the discontented and disinherited of the whole world; it is not less important that Moscow is ideologically driven to the encouragement of their hopes. No one who surveys at all objectively the relations of Russia with the external world can possibly be optimistic about their outcome.

I do not think that a war against Russia would destroy communism there though I believe it would enormously increase the price of its accomplishment; but I do believe it would be fatal to the maintenance of capitalist society at least in Europe and the Far East. Probably its cost would be a period of anarchy

[10] On this see Mr. R. D. Charques' admirable résumé, "The Soviets and the Next War" (1932).

comparable to the Dark Ages, with every sort and kind of dictatorship emerging to supply for brief periods an uneasy semblance of order. Ultimately, I think, Russia would be the first state to emerge from that chaos with something like the hope of recovery; and its authority, under those circumstances, would be far more compelling than it is to-day, its challenge more direct and explicit. In the long run, in a word, the price of challenging communism to military conflict would be not its defeat but its victory.

VII

The future of communism is a function of the capacity of capitalist society to repair its foundations. The success—despite the appalling cost—of the Russian experiment has made it the one effective center of creativeness in a world which, otherwise, does not seem to know how to turn its feet away from the abyss. Capitalist society since the war has adopted every expedient of self-destruction. The Peace of Versailles, the tangled mess of war-debts and reparations, the struggle for power concealed beneath the myth of national sovereignty, the failure to respect the League, all of these were implicit in its ultimate disrespect for moral principle. The social habits of its votaries, its literature with its insistent note of cynical skepticism, its philosophy which sought refuge in mysticism and impulse to shut out the still small voice of reason, a press which (not least notably in its dealing with Russia) could make miraculous propaganda but could not tell the truth, its religions in decay, its political and economic institutions hopelessly remote from the realities they confronted, its leaders like straws caught in the eddies of an ever-quickening stream—it is not in such a society as this that one looks for the spring of a new hope. On the credit side, no doubt, there was a science more renascent than at any time since the seventeenth century; but it was also more dangerous because the formula seemed lost by which it could be bent to social purposes.

Such a society cannot meet the challenge of communism, because its faith in itself is not sufficient to give it a victorious destiny. It may postpone defeat; it cannot finally elude it. For in the conflict of ideologies victory always goes in the end to men who are willing to sacrifice material power for spiritual conquest. Communism interests the new generation because, alone among the welter of competing gospels, it has known how to win sacrifice from its devotees in the name of a great ideal. It offers the prospect—the clew to the success of all the great religions—of losing one's life in order to find it. There is poverty, there is intellectual error, there is grave moral wrong; but there is also unlimited hope. These have been characteristic of all great religious movements. They do not seem to disturb their power eventually to triumph.

The chance for a capitalist society in contest with communism lies in its ability to remake its own creed. Its danger is the ease with which it attacks the symptoms of communism instead of its causes. It is afraid of the propaganda of the Third International instead of the conditions which make that propaganda fall on fertile soil. It is afraid of the bold imagination which underlies the Five Year Plan; but instead of planning more boldly and more imaginatively itself, it spends its time dourly foretelling its inevitable failure. It attacks with passion the outrageous injustices of which communism has been guilty, its stifling of initiative, the reckless cruelty of the Ogpu, the relentless attack on the Kulaks. But it does not stay to remember that its own Sacco-Vanzetti case, the Polish treatment of minorities, the dreary wastage of its own unemployment, bear the same lesson to the masses, and that for them the costs of Russia are expended for the advantage of the many, while the costs of the capitalist society are paid for the profit of a few. There is an uncomfortable sense in the world that what is happening in Russia may be the prelude to a renaissance of the human spirit. There is no such prophetic confidence in capitalist society. Its very leaders look less like great adventurers than men who scan a gray horizon without confidence of a dawn.

The principles which govern capitalist society are, in fact, completely obsolete before the new conditions it confronts; and it seems to lack the energy to bend itself to their revision. It needs a new scheme of motivation, a different sense of values. It needs the power and the will to move from the era of economic chaos to a system which deliberately controls economic forces in the interests of justice and stability. To do so there are required far more pervasive international controls, on the external side, and far greater equality in matters of social constitution, on the internal. To find equilibrium by the blind adjustment of competing interests is simply to court disaster.

Yet, generally speaking, the men who govern the old world can think in no other terms.

It is true there are men about us who voice a different philosophy. Rathenau, Keynes, Salter—these have endeavored, as best they could, to insist that the way to survival lies along the road to profound reconstruction. They have seen that a temper is required which gives new significance to the claims of the common man, which recognizes the dangers inherent in a system which identifies self-good and social. They admit the need for sacrifice as the price of reconstruction. They see all the cost involved in a clash of ideologies which seek to test their respective strengths in terms of power. But theirs, if I may say so, is an aristocratic approach, a cool and skeptical impatience of dogma, a passion for the rational solution of questions in their nature essentially rational, of which the appeal is by its nature a limited one. They underestimate the inertia of the existing order, the irrationality with which men will cling to vested interests and established expectations even when their title to response is no longer valid. Given something like a geological time, such rationalism might prevail against the passions which stand in its path. The tragedy of our present position is that the voice of the Mean is unlikely to win attention until humanity has been sacrificed to the call of the Extreme.[11]

[11] This second part is reprinted with the kind permission of *Foreign Affairs* (Oct. 1932).

H . N . B R A I L S F O R D

INDIA'S RESURRECTION

ON a first glimpse of the misery and discontent of the Indian population one supposes that it must be ripe for instant and irresistible explosion. On closer study one swings to the opposite extreme: the balance of forces in this complex social structure is such that one doubts the bare possibility of movement. And yet it moves. So much, in the end, one believes on evidence: but dare foresight gauge the pace at which this movement will gather momentum, and cut its way through history?

The fact of discontent assails the white traveler at his first contact with this people. Race stands mobilized against race. For loyal support the British Government can reckon on the feudatory princes, the great landlords, the more wealthy and conservative leaders of the Mohammedans, its mercenary troops and police, and on no one else. Virtually the whole Hindu population forms an irreconcilable opposition, and with it are many of the younger and better educated Mohammedans. Since the World War this opposition, which had been confined to the literate *intelligentsia,* has spread to the masses, invaded the factories, enlisted the peasants and fired the women with self-sacrificing enthusiasm. The evidence of one's eyes will suffice to support this statement. There are districts where nearly every man and boy wears the white Gandhi cap, though this emblem invites the hostility of the police and may bring its wearer a beating. The bitterness of feeling, as one talks to the better educated Indians, seems to have no limit: it is a wound in their souls: there is hardly a suspicion too crude for them

90

to cherish against rulers whom they regard with dislike, yet with a blending of respect and fear. With rare exceptions they see in British rule the cause of all that is amiss in India. Nor has the promise of qualified self-government done anything to lessen their hostility, for if one of Mr. MacDonald's hands extends to them a constitution, the other wields a *lathi*.

For this national attitude of opposition there are many explanations. Foreign rule is an injury to India's self-respect, an affront to her pride. It lames her energies, forbids her self-expression, and makes the mental ill-health which always attacks a fettered will. Indians of the present generation are rarely willing to admit the many benefits that are the by-products of conquest, while they are acutely aware of its economic evils—the costliness of a white garrison and civil service living on a scale of expenditure far above their own, the drain of wealth in pensions and interest payments on debt which are spent in another land, the high rewards which British engineering, shipping, banking and industry draw, doubtless for services rendered, but always in the form of a tribute enjoyed beyond her shores. To all this one must add the sense of neglect, which grows increasingly among the more thoughtful members of the educated class. Something, indeed, has been done by these foreigners for education, for health and for the development of the resources of the country, but so slowly and on so small a scale that it has hardly touched the root evils of illiteracy, under-nourishment, disease, and poverty in the typical village.

None of these explanations accounts, however, for the bitterness of Indian feeling. That is instinctive, almost physiological. It is the reaction of the gentlest and most courteous race of mankind to the contempt which Englishmen feel for its color. There are, of course, exceptions—sensitive men who respond to the grace and romance of this nation, scholarly men who steep themselves in its history and literature, humane men who labor to relieve its sufferings. These are the minority. The attitude of the average Englishman in India is one of aloof superiority, scarcely qualified by curiosity, which turns to active dislike, if he lives among the quicker-witted branches of this race. The well-bred civil servant may conceal it under the mask of a stiff official manner. The better type of army officer is often a kindly father to his men. It is the ill-educated business man, the clerk and the foreman who display this racial insolence in its most offensive and brutal forms, while white women of all classes are notoriously less kindly, less courteous, and more ignorant than the men. The relationship improves in proportion as Indians are simple-minded, given to sport, and endowed with the martial virtues, as are the Punjabi Moslems and Sikhs: it is at its worst when they possess quick wits, as Bengali Hindus do, a keen critical faculty and the gift of articulate speech, combined with a sedentary habit of body and a poor reputation for physical courage. There are few Indians of the educated class who have not experienced at some time of their lives some gross physical insult, which has shown them the unbridgeable gulf that divides the two races. Though there has been in recent years some improvement in English manners, and a self-conscious effort to promote social intercourse, the broad fact is still that out of business hours the English in India live in a closed world of their own. It is the realization that neither rank nor education, neither good manners nor a perfect command of the English tongue, no, not even the profession of the Christian faith, can ever atone for the original sin of color, that has made rebels of Indians, when they are not sycophants.

The contemporary phase of Indian nationalism began with Mr. Gandhi's leadership of the National Congress movement after the war. Congress had been, up to this point, a movement which kept its agitation within constitutional limits. Its outlook was in the main that of English liberalism: it struggled for civil and political rights, and its objective was not to end the British connection, but to check the bureaucracy, and replace it, very gradually, by representative self-government on the European model. Its leaders were men whose outlook and habits of mind and speech had been formed by their Western secular education. They talked English and they thought English. Mr. Gandhi, though he studied law at the Inns of Court, has remained Hindu in thought. He is neither a rationalist nor a liberal, though one might call him a humanitarian, and his outlook on religion, economics, and politics is that of a medieval, ascetic mystic, who has added to his Indian heritage a single Western idea—nationality. His nationalism has, however, little in common with the usual middle-class attitude which goes by this name in Europe, though at times it approaches Mazzini's creed. It means primarily the assertion against Western capitalism and materialism of the traditional Hindu values. The British yoke is an obstacle to a return to an Indian rule of life. How far Mr. Gandhi has accepted Western democracy it is difficult to say. He would retain caste, though in a mild and purified form. The ancient village community is the one vital thing in his conception of political structure. The State, as he conceives it, is the loosest framework around innumerable villages, each of them, as nearly as may be, economically self-contained. He seems to be more deeply interested in creating a dynamic party than in building an Indian State. The Congress movement, as he has shaped it, follows spontaneously the model of the sovereign party which one may see at work in Italy, Russia, Turkey and China. It is a State within the State, even, as the English rulers of India complain, a rival State. It will on occasion conduct quasi-judicial enquiries, and set up its own arbitral tribunals to replace the British courts. It has its corps of unarmed but drilled and uniformed volunteers, who act on occasion as an unofficial police. Rarely, if ever, has it used its voting power in the legislative councils, central or provincial, to inspire any positive policy: it enters them only to obstruct, but as often as not, it has preferred to boycott them and to abstain from elections. It works outside the official machine of government, creating and organizing a disciplined public opinion which will act, both positively to realize Gandhi's ideas, and negatively to undermine the British fabric of government. Foremost in its positive program stands the revival of hand-spinning, which is his chief expedient for relieving the poverty of the villages. In this forlorn hope he has won a surprising measure of success. Next to this one must rank his work to raise the "untouchables" and to banish alcohol. The basis of his doctrine is a rigidly ascetic ethical discipline founded on absolute chastity, unflinching truthfulness, universal love, and non-violence (*ahimsa*). The disciples who have adopted this rule of life are within the broad Congress movement what the Communist Party is in Russia, shock troops, an ironside brigade. But far beyond Mr. Gandhi's personal sphere of influence, Congress had made itself the one universally diffused vehicle of Indian opinion, the only party that has a mass organization and possesses its pervasive centers of propaganda in the villages as well as the towns. In Bombay, before the repression attained its height, it dominated life so absolutely that the British officials and police seemed interlopers in an Indian city. Its national tricolor flag flew everywhere: its patriotic and often satirical songs, sung in the streets by organized parading bands of youths, were always in one's ears:

its uniformed patrols controlled the market so completely that no cart could move a bale of goods without its printed permit. Its suppressed Bulletins were distributed everywhere. It could with a word close virtually every shop and factory in the city on a day of protest and mourning *(hartal),* or by a whispered summons, running from mouth to ear through the bazaar, assemble any day of the week a crowd of at least forty thousand demonstrators in defiance of a police prohibition.

Such is Congress, shaped and dominated by the personality of this gentle, unassuming saint, whom the populace has all but deified. It is drawn from all classes, as befits a national party. Millionaire bankers and mill-owners contribute to its funds, partly no doubt because its policy of economic nationalism, *(swadeshi),* suits their interests, but chiefly, I think, because their skins are brown. It includes some of the leading lawyers of India, and many Brahmin aristocrats, but also a vast mass following of peasants. Its active workers and volunteers come chiefly from the clerk class, the semi-educated intellectual proletariat, scourged in India by unemployment. Mr. Gandhi is far from being a Socialist. Utterly opposed to the class struggle, his outlook is ethical, and his economics medieval. None the less he is obsessed by the burden of Indian poverty, and draws from the indignation with which it fills him most of the ardor and passion of his campaign. He goes all but naked, that nothing may distinguish him from the poorest of the poor. He has scant respect for property, and at the Round Table Conference hinted that he would, if he had the power, subject all titles to land to a searching scrutiny on ethical grounds. Congress has, indeed, a Left Wing under Jawaharlal Nehru, who is an avowed Socialist, and an ultra-Left Bengali section under Subhas Bose, which is "redder" still. Doubtless, if India's freedom were won, it would break into divergent fractions. Its main tendency is populist rather than Socialist. One knows it as a militant movement of revolt. One can imagine it as a sovereign party, controlling India under a dictatorship, as the Kuo-min-tang controls China. I find it difficult, however, to imagine it working contentedly as one constitutional party among several, under a British Viceroy, within the framework of a Federation modeled on Western patterns. Whether for destruction or creation, it is a revolutionary force.

To the strategy of revolution Mr. Gandhi has made an original contribution of the deepest interest. His object is to render

British rule in India impossible, and to this end he uses two forms of pressure, the moral and the economic, though both may be described as "civil disobedience." Morally he requires an absolute rejection of British authority, an inward emancipation from its yoke, which will in action result in defiance and disobedience. One must not suppose that he is thinking here in terms of tactics. His purpose is first of all to liberate the mind of India, so that it shall will itself and think itself into freedom. This is at bottom a mystical conception, though it may have highly practical effects. India may achieve inward freedom, though British regiments still cumber her soil. Hence his insistence on acts of rebellion which are hardly more than symbolical. One cannot hope to shake King George's throne by boiling sea-water in a kettle, but even if the loss to the revenue from this practice of making contraband salt is negligible, it serves to affirm the will to be free. It leads to prison, and there a man, though fettered, proclaims by deeds his rejection of an authority which his moral sense condemns. By holding meetings or processions which this authority has forbidden, by facing the *lathis* (heavy metal-tipped staves) of the police and courting imprisonment, Gandhi's followers prove with passive but enduring courage the firmness of their will. India stands in such ordeals erect, disdaining to recognize, even to notice the physical force of her conquerors. This the volunteers will often literally achieve: for they will squat motionless under a rain of blows until they drop unconscious. Under no provocation may the rebel use violence. He is bound by the rule of *ahimsa,* which forbids the taking of life or the infliction of injury, and should also mean, as Mr. Gandhi interprets it, positive and universal love.

Several effects upon the mind of the Imperial Power are anticipated from this strategy. It can transport to its prisons a thousand tons of human substance, but it cannot change men's minds, or command obedience. Must it not become demoralized, and finally recognize its own impotence? It may also be softened by the spectacle of this innocent passivity, this gentle self-restraint under its violent assaults. Will it not grow ashamed, and allow itself to be overcome by love?

The economic side of Mr. Gandhi's strategy may be less original, but it is not less important. He uses two methods. Firstly he aims at starving the revenues. If contraband salt could be substituted for the monopoly article, if no alcoholic liquor were consumed, and licenses became unsaleable, gaping holes would be torn in the budget. In some districts the people were organized to refuse to pay the police rate: in others, notably Gujarat and the United Provinces, the peasants resisted the land tax, which in the latter case involved also non-payment of rent. The second method was to boycott foreign but especially British goods, above all cotton cloth. This is an attack on the customs revenue, and the intention is also to encourage home industries, and to put pressure on the British producers and merchants, more especially on Lancashire.

If this strategy could be applied over the whole of India and maintained indefinitely, doubtless it would make British rule impossible. But Congress is not everywhere equally strong: all but supreme in Bombay, it is powerful throughout the Center and the North, but it is weak in the Punjab, and in the South the population is not easily roused to active militancy and is more readily cowed. Though the peasants of Gujarat showed amazing stubbornness in their resistance to the land tax, their example was not generally followed. The campaign against alcohol and the boycott of British cloth—both enforced by picketing—were adopted all over India: the revenue shrank and imports suffered a heavy decline. It was, however, difficult to distinguish between the effects of the boycott and those of the slump. In any event revenue would have fallen and imports diminished. Even without Mr. Gandhi, peasants, with the prices of rice and wheat falling catastrophically, would in fact have dropped into arrears with their taxes, though they might not have ventured a defiant refusal. The sight of whole towns in which no shopkeeper dared on a day of *hartal* to sell became explicable, when one learned that on other days surprisingly little business was transacted. In India the unrest of the masses suffering under a cruel slump took the form of a nationalist movement inspired by a very peculiar local ideology. But was it not at bottom the same economic disturbance which made *pronunciamientos* in South America, a republican revolution in Spain, and the "Nazi" movement in Germany? The shrewder minds in the British bureaucracy were well aware of this economic background, and resolved to hold on till a trade revival should bring relief. The decline in revenue led to savage economies at the expense of the social services and in all constructive work, including even the upkeep of the roads, but there was money enough to maintain the army and the police, and

civil servants' salaries were cut only by 10 per cent. The most
ominous symptom was that in the first year of civil disobedience loans had twice to be raised in London to meet current
expenses.

The moral effects of Mr. Gandhi's movement answered to
his expectations on the Indian side. The mind of the whole
population was exalted: it felt a certain subjective liberation:
it gained in self-confidence and self-respect. But I doubt
whether the Imperial people was moved in the same degree. It
was not ashamed. It was not "converted by love," and indeed
only a very subtle enemy could have discerned the love latent
under the trade boycott. The officials and police actively engaged in repression were hardened and coarsened by their experiences: in some of them sadistic instincts were aroused. As
for the general public in England, its imagination was never
touched, and its newspapers took care that nothing should be
printed which might have set it questioning. The trade boycott
assuredly did disturb it, but there were evident limits to any
possible compromise. India is bent on protecting her own industries, so that the concession even of virtual independence
might not avail to restore Lancashire's trade.

None the less, this revolt of Hindu India did powerfully affect British calculations and British policy. Toward the close
of 1929 the Cabinet and the Viceroy, faced with the threat of
Congress to resort to civil obedience with Independence as its
watchword, promised a Round Table Conference, and declared
that Dominion status was the goal of British policy. None the
less in the negotiations at Christmas the Viceroy could not give
Mr. Gandhi a plain assurance that at the Conference the British Government would offer self-government at the Center, albeit with safeguards. The revolt thereupon was proclaimed.
Throughout the early months of 1930, public opinion in England, if one may judge by the press, was ready to go as far as
the Simon Commission proposed, but not a step further. It
would grant Home Rule in the provinces, but it would make
no change at the Center. Yet when the Round Table Conference met in the Fall of 1930, even the Tories and the Liberals
were ready to concede what the Labor Government had not
dared to promise a year earlier. Nine months of civil disobedience had wrought this remarkable change. It was no doubt the
boldness and unanimity of the speeches of the Indian moderates and the Princes which impressed the governing class, but

the attitude of these usually timid people was itself the direct reflection of the revolt of the masses. It was realized at last that India's claim to self-government could not be resisted. It must be conceded at the national Center as well as in the Provinces. The sole problem was to render the concession as harmless as possible. So much Congress had achieved, not specifically by tax-resistance, or trade boycott or by the sufferings of its sixty thousand prisoners, but broadly by the proof that a nation's mind was bent on freedom.

An Empire in such a situation will repress while it can, concede when it must, and all the time it will endeavor to divide. This tactic of division has found the flaw in the Indian Nationalist movement. Hindus and Moslems have been united only twice in their struggle against British rule—during the Mutiny, and for a short time after the War, when the Moslem Caliphate agitation joined forces with Congress. Habitually and instinctively the main body of the Moslems, rather poorer than the Hindus and much below them in education, follows its wealthy, conservative leaders in an attitude of relative loyalty toward British rule. For this the Imperial Power is not ungrateful, and traditionally the governing class and the Tory party lean with a sense of comfort on Moslem support. Mr. Gandhi has a numerous following among the younger generation of the Moslem *intelligentsia*, while the North-West Province, dominated by the "Red Shirt" movement is enthusiastically for him. None the less the liberalism of the older Congress movement furnished a more natural basis of union than his mysticism, drawn as it is from Hindu religion. The clash of these two antagonistic views of life is sometimes as evident today as it was when the first Moslem iconoclasts smashed the Hindu temples at the conquest. Socially, people of these two creeds have never blended. Where there is neither intermarriage nor a common culture, does nationality exist? Alien rule has, indeed, begotten a somewhat negative substitute for it, a bond of color, a sense of a common humiliation and exploitation. Each creed, none the less, fears and mistrusts the other. The Hindus have an obvious motive for desiring national unity, since in any representative national assembly they must form the majority. The Moslems on the other hand have their own compact area where they predominate—the North-West Province, the Punjab, Kashmir and Sind, while in Bengal also they have a bare majority. Their older generation feels a communal and local rather than a national patriotism, and some leading Moslems would rather create a Mohammedan State in the North-West than join an Indian federation. This mutual fear and antagonism, breaking out in occasional riots which often end in indiscriminate slaughter, has increased in our generation. Undoubtedly it has been aggravated by the system adopted as the basis of India's political organization, when Lord Morley introduced the first scheme of elected consultative councils. On the plea that minorities must not be swamped, Moslems, Sikhs and Hindus were enrolled as voters in distinct communal electorates, each electing a fixed number of representatives of their own faith. The result was to stereotype Indian politics on a basis of religion. No party with a secular program could come into existence: the ordinary divisions of democracy on lines of interest, class or opinion were effectively prevented. Inevitably a candidate must recommend himself by his devotion to the creed of the isolated electorate, an arrangement which fostered bigotry. Once established, this system turned religion into a vested interest, for the communal parties concentrated upon the division of the spoils. The Congress Party is indeed an exception, since it stands for the national idea and includes men of all creeds, though Hindus greatly predominate. But it will not take office and sometimes boycotts the elections. British statesmen have unanimously condemned this system, but as unanimously they refuse to abandon it till the minority (meaning in effect the elder, conservative Moslem leaders) freely renounces it, which for obvious reasons it will not do. For not only does it serve as a barrier against nationalism: it also keeps the Moslem peasants and workers (in so far as these have votes) immune from the infection of Hindu radicalism. Democracy cannot function till it disappears, and one may doubt whether the British ruling class ardently desires that it should function in India. A simple expedient would secure the representation of minorities without separate electors. A fixed minimum number of seats may be reserved for those candidates of a given creed who secure the highest votes. On this plan Hindus may vote for Moslems and *vice versa:* the bigot is at a disadvantage, and secular parties may combine to support candidates of both faiths.

In this wretched system lay the formula for perpetual division. Mr. Gandhi, all the Hindus and the younger Moslems realized that India would never be a nation while it lasted, but the Mohammedan magnates stood firm for their privileges. In his absence, locked in prison, Mr. Gandhi had dominated the first session of the Round Table Conference. Present in London but disarmed by a truce, he failed to influence the second session in the Summer and Fall of 1931. The atmosphere had changed, for Labor had fallen, and the ruling Tory party fell back on its traditional policy of division. The Moslems, ardently backed by the Tory press, formed an anti-Hindu block with all the smaller minorities, which refused to abandon communal electorates. To it rallied the nominated spokesman of the "Untouchables," Dr. Ambedkar, though it is doubtful whether he represented more than a small section of their forty millions. He too demanded a separate electorate, and so a new gulf yawned across Indian national unity. The Moslems refused to take part in any discussion of the central problem of the Constitution—the "safeguards," through which the British Government proposed for an indefinite period to withhold from the future parliament of federated India control over the army, foreign relations, the budget, banking and currency. In fact these issues were hardly debated. India presented the spectacle of apparently incurable disunion, and pressure for genuine self-government came only from the Hindus. The Government seized its chance, as it saw it, broke up the Conference, entered again by still more drastic ordinances on a period of coercion, re-arrested Mr. Gandhi on his return, and declared its resolve to crush the Congress Party once for all. It would, indeed, continue to prepare the reforms and to consult selected Indians. India—under safeguards—should govern herself, provided that the British power held her leaders in its prisons, muzzled her press, and smashed the one political organization that her masses trusted.

Midway in this revolutionary struggle it is not easy to reach a confident estimate of the efficacy of Mr. Gandhi's methods. The repression has certainly failed to crush Congress, though it has driven it under ground. No organized mass party of Indians retains its faith in a Constitution prepared amid coercion, though the Liberal moderates, a small group of distinguished but ineffective individuals, after refusing their coöperation for some months, have been persuaded (though they still protest against the measures of coercion) to renew it. Some of these ordinances have meanwhile been made permanent. On the other hand Mr. Gandhi, by his fast in prison, has frustrated the design of isolating the Untouchables politically, and Mr. MacDonald has withdrawn his decision which gave them a separate electorate. That arrangement, while rendering national unity still more difficult of attainment, would also have split the Indian proletariat, and postponed the time when it can be organized for political action. Divided by these communal electorates, the laboring mass of peasants and town workers cannot learn to act as a class. Mr. Gandhi, by his brave and unworldly sacrifice has hastened the removal of a ghastly blot on Hindu civilization, but he may have done even more. He has shaken the Moslems in their reliance on the tactics of division, and brought appreciably nearer the abandonment of their separate electorate. If and when that happens, the whole aspect of the Indian struggle will be changed. Mr. Gandhi's chief mistake has been to overestimate the power of Congress. It is, indeed, the only dynamic mass organization in India, but it lacks one thing to become irresistible. If it could enlist the Mohammedan masses, shoulder to shoulder with the Hindus, no Government could stand against it.

The Federal Constitution, as it now stands, vague and unfinished, in rough draft, measures what the Imperial Power will concede to Hindu pressure alone, while it still can trust the calculating loyalty of the Moslems, who form two-fifths of the population, but claim a third of the representation. To count by heads is of course to underestimate its power, for it includes some of the best fighting material in India. If to this third, we add the feudatory princes and the great landlords, we have measured the support on which the Imperial Power relies. The Constitution reflects its reckonings. It makes assurance doubly sure through an uncertain period of transition, by the "safeguards" which reduce the range of action of the federal Parliament to narrow limits. Some restrictions were doubtless inevitable, until the native Indian army can be provided with Indian officers, a Staff and an artillery capable of assuring defense and order without a white garrison. But the proposed limitations, especially on finance, are so far-reaching that no radical nationalist party could accept them in advance, or refrain, if it did accept them, from a continuous effort to infringe them. To guard against this risk the Constitution is a model of conservative precaution. The franchise for British India entrusts the vote only to 2 per cent of the population. The princes will enter the Federation as oriental despots, who will nominate their representatives as they see fit. None of the rights, civil or political, which the Constitution may establish for the inhabitants of British India will necessarily accrue to their subjects. These princes, whose autocracy is tolerated within wide limits, must submit in their relations with the Paramount Power to a strict discipline which ensures unswerving loyalty and a seemly subservience towards the higher bureaucracy. Within the federal Parliament they will form a reliable block of loyalist voters, as trustworthy as the old nominated official contingent, which disappears, and psychologically more valuable, since they look like Indians. In this Parliament the masses of India, the working peasants, can have no representation whatever.

Secure in its control of finance, banking and the army at the Center, the Imperial Power makes an apparent, perhaps a real surrender of authority in the provinces, which control the social services, the land, local Government and the police. The Governors have, however, under the Viceroy, wide powers of veto. The franchise, though more liberal than that of the central legislature, still rests on property and education, and includes only 14 per cent of the population, while special franchises give heavy and disproportionate representation to capitalist interests and to the landlords. If the communal electorates survive, self-government in some provinces will be wholly thwarted, though in others, where Moslems are not numerous, the middle class may, if well led, engage with a better hope of success in the struggle for power. I cannot, however, envisage the Congress Party operating within such a framework, save as a party of fundamental opposition bent on smashing it. No other popular party exists as yet, vital and spirited enough to win its way against the bureaucracy. The average Indian Minister at present earns office from his white masters, and gives no trouble when he gets it.

The obscurity of the future turns, as I try to peer into it, on the question whether within such a Constitution as this, the propertied classes, the lawyers and the rising capitalist element, who are to-day strongly nationalist, partly for economic reasons, and partly because their brown skins hide a perpetual blush of racial humiliation, will feel on both counts sufficiently satisfied to form a capable Indian conservative party, which will ally itself with the much less nationalist landlords, and attempt to govern India for property and the British crown, trusting to the limited franchise and the efficient police machine which the British have created. It is presumably on this reckoning that the bureaucracy and the British ruling class rely. These in their cynical way are often shrewd and realistic judges of a situation, but with some diffidence I incline to think them mistaken. I doubt if they will concede enough to the economic nationalism of Indian capitalists to buy their full support. I doubt if they allow enough for the personal ascendancy of Gandhi. Finally, I question whether the Indian propertied classes have as yet sufficient reason to fear an awakening of the masses or the radicalism of the Left Wing of Congress, to betray the national cause at this stage. For an Indian Conservative Party must assume responsibility for the maintenance of order, and use the British-built machinery of the police and the Ordinances to repress the patriotic mass of the population. The structure of Indian society, in which the immense patriarchal family and beyond it the organized caste press overwhelmingly upon the individual, even when he holds an exalted position, seems to me to forbid it in the predominantly Hindu provinces. On the whole, then, I doubt whether this new constitution will ever function smoothly, or bring the revolutionary unrest finally to an end, though doubtless there will be pauses. It is barely conceivable that Congress can maintain its agitation indefinitely at the pace set during 1930 and 1932: there must be close seasons and truces, but it is not the policy of the predominantly Tory Government now in power to assist it by negotiating truces lightly. If and when Congress flags in its resistance, or compromises, it is certain that the terrorist campaign will spread beyond Bengal, where it is already strong among the younger *intelligentsia*. They can exasperate their conquerors: I doubt if they can do more. But prediction is futile, for one cannot foretell the economic conditions that will govern Indian politics in the next decade. India is an item in a world-wide financial system. If one knew at what price the Indian peasant will sell his rice and wheat two or five years hence, one might also be able to guess whether he will fling the weight of his numbers into a revolutionary movement. The necessary doctrines and ideas, mystical or materialist, Hindu or Western, will always be invented by saint or agitator, when economic suffering has made the life of the masses unendurable. I incline to think that any widespread revolt must conform, more or less, to Gandhi's pattern. Pacifism seems innate in these frail Indian bodies, and it has behind it thousands of years of religious brooding and discipline. These people do not instinctively strike from the shoulder, but they know how to fold their arms tight.

For my own part, the ultimate question that I address to any Indian political movement goes back to the fundamental fact of the poverty of this suffering population. Has it the will and the intelligence, if it succeeds, to make a hopeful beginning in transforming the economic and social conditions under which these millions multiply and starve? When one attempts to analyze this poverty, it is true that much must be laid to the account of the British Empire. It swamped the traditional handicraft economy with its machine-made products, and deliberately delayed the industrialization of India: it lessened the Malthusian checks on population, war, pestilence and famine, yet took no adequate steps to render the labor of the increasing population more productive: its fabric of administration, coercion and defense is relatively too costly, and its whole system of investment and enterprise tends to drain away wealth. Finally and chiefly, merely because its rule is alien, it has lamed the collective will of this people, and checked its ability to react to the economic and social demands of the modern world. But when all this is said, and the conclusion drawn that only an Indian Government inspired by a dynamic ambition can deal with Indian poverty, the fact remains that its graver causes are imbedded in the structure and beliefs of Indian society itself. Throughout the North the working peasant is mercilessly exploited by landowners who perform no social or economic function whatever. When the landlord has reaped, the usurer gleans. There can be no progress till these parasites are removed.[1] But the main problem is to render labor in the villages productive. Agriculture, with insignificant exceptions, still follows the methods of the Bronze Age; the work of these peasants could be performed by a mere fraction of their numbers. The rest must be drafted into industry and services. All this might be done, perhaps, very gradually, by coöperation and education, in the course of a century or more. But can India stand still, living at her own sub-normal pace, while the rest of the world changes its aspect? She cannot

[1] On this subject the reader will find fuller information in my little book "*Rebel India.*" (*New Republic* dollar books.)

live as an anchorite peninsula: she is in the stream of world
events. If any country calls for an intensive plan of social transformation and economic development, carried through at a
rapid tempo by a party which the masses will trust when it
dictates, it is India. A foreign bureaucracy could not do it, even
if it had the will.

Congress has set this mass in motion. It has disturbed the
apathy and quietism of countless centuries. It has taught the
teeming towns and even the villages the power of solid numbers. It has turned popular thought, however unscientifically,
to the problem of poverty. Stumbling, hesitating, and only half-
conscious of what it did, it has started a class-struggle, of work-
ing-tenant peasants against landlords, in the United Provinces,
and in one district at least of Bengal. In short it has begotten
the revolutionary temper, and has, albeit by accident, begun
the agrarian revolt. It has the necessary dynamic will. It knows
how to organize. Some of the essentials of revolutionary leadership it possesses without a rival. No Indian Socialist Party
exists, though a little group of Socialist intellectuals has formed
a nucleus in the Punjab. The Labor Unions may in time constitute themselves as an effective party of the urban workers,
but at present they are absorbed in their internal dissensions,
and are everywhere overshadowed by Congress, which contrives
to interest the factory-hands by its genius for drama. The peasants in several regions have already a militant organization
which concerns itself with their economic interests, and aids
them in their perpetual struggle against a grasping and parasitic
landlord class. But as yet these peasants' leagues work under
the wing of Congress. It has shown an understanding of mass-
psychology unique in India. But when one looks forward to
its rôle in the future, it is difficult to believe that it can transform itself, and pass abruptly from the national to the class
struggle. To-day it includes every man with a brown skin who
is ready to march to jail under Gandhi's leadership—usurers
and debtors, landlords and tenants, capitalists and workers,
Brahmin lawyers and untouchable sweepers. It passes at its
Conferences sweeping resolutions on social questions, which
seem to Indians extremely radical, though they would hardly
disturb the average middle-class pillow in Europe. But the
bankers and mill-owners who contribute handsomely to the
funds of Congress may disregard these symptoms of militancy.
They can have no practical effect while the white bureaucracy

is still firmly in the saddle at Delhi. But what will happen if
Congress should participate in the elections, notably the provincial elections, after the reformed Constitution comes into
effect? For the purposes of the contest one supposes, not too
confidently, that its leaders will be released from prison and
its propaganda tolerated. In several provinces it should have
a majority. Will it accept office? I cannot imagine it in that
situation. But if it keeps up the revolutionary struggle, for
how long will its propertied element remain with it? Sooner,
if Gandhi should retire from politics or wear out his frail body
in his efforts for the untouchables, later, if he should retain
his leadership, the younger generation must grow impatient
with his medieval economics. India's problems of production
and distribution cannot be solved by reviving the spinning-
wheel. Each in its own way, the capitalist element and the
radical proletariat element in the ranks of Congress will inevitably break away from his unworldly inspiration. When
they face the real problems of usury and landownership, in-
fallibly these two sections, which unite to-day to idolize him,
will be confronting each other in an incipient class struggle.

The poverty of the Indian village, in those Northern provinces, at least, where landlordism prevails, cannot be cured
without a social upheaval. To sweep the parasitic landlord
away would be merely a beginning. To organize credit without
the usurer would be only a partial reform. The root cause of
this poverty is the incredible waste of labor, for Indian peasants
must devote forty days of toil to raising an acre of wheat, where
an American farmer with his machines would spend less than
a single day. Finally this inefficiency is aggravated by the vetoes
and scruples of Hindu religion which by their refusal to take
life render any balanced agriculture or any economic management of the cattle impossible.

Where, in India, is the popular force that could undertake
this work of fighting orthodoxy with its left hand and smashing
class privilege with its right? Can one conceive a combination
of the gift of popular leadership that could win and keep the
allegiance of the peasants, with the genius for economic organization that could work out the details of a constructive plan?
The first of these Congress possesses. The second it never can
develop while it lives in Mr. Gandhi's world of faith and
renunciation. Some attempt at this immensely difficult task the
ablest and most magnetic of the younger leaders of Congress,

Jawaharlal Nehru, may one day make, if his health survives British prisons, and if he can emancipate himself from Mr. Gandhi's spiritual legacy. But Congress, if ever it dares to evolve on these lines, will cease to be an all-inclusive national party, and must shed both its propertied and its orthodox adherents.

The chances, I confess, that Indians can create, without aid from abroad, a dynamic party of the working masses, capable both of the ruthless destruction and the scientific construction that alone can end her poverty and stagnation, seem to me slight. There will come a day, I believe, when the militant Communism that is battling for the peasantry in Southern China, will find its way, in spite of Indian priests and English policemen, through the guarded passes of the Himalayas. A Five-Year Plan will sweep away the boundaries of the tiny fields; tractors will hurry where the humped bullocks dawdle to-day: electricity will irrigate the fields, and under the banyan tree where the village gathers, the radio will carry men's minds across the centuries that separate Benares from Moscow. Some beauty, some tranquillity of soul, some gentleness and dignity will be swept away with the bullocks and the gods, the humiliation and the hunger of present day India. It will not happen to-morrow, and when at last it comes it will be with agony and bloodshed. With vision and courage India's gentle saint is leading her past the first obstacle to freedom. He has taught her to fear her white conquerors no longer. But how in this twentieth century this strayed child from an elder world should build her home amid the restless engines—that was not his to teach.

SPAIN'S SWING TO THE LEFT

I

TOWARD REVOLUTION

THE climax of eight years of dictatorship in Spain paradoxically brought to the Spanish people the first opportunity they had ever had to express their will freely. The stirring events which followed their overwhelming vote against the monarchy are well known to the outside world. Yet the underlying causes of those events, and the probability that the same social forces will produce yet other exciting events in the not distant future, are little understood and appreciated by those not intimately conversant with the Spanish people.

In the following brief résumé I shall attempt to analyze the real factors back of the revolution, and to show that one of the most significant tendencies has not as yet reached its peak, and that when it does so, the present republican form of government will go the way of its predecessors.

There is no need to elaborate upon the superficial stages by which the revolution was achieved. Following the popular vote against the monarchy, the king fled, a republic was proclaimed without bloodshed, a provisional government was named, and elections to the Constituent Assembly were held, resulting in the selection of more than three hundred Republicans of various political shades, together with 115 Socialists and a bare handful of priests, monarchists and other reactionary elements.

The world, long accustomed to judge this nation by the character and actions of its rulers, was astonished at the strength mustered by the liberal and radical elements in a country that had been under the yoke of crown or dictatorship from time immemorial.

However, for those who know the real Spain, these developments were not surprising or unexpected. The Spanish people had paid heavy taxes for the support of the church and the crown, but not willingly. It was a daily commonplace for the truly patriotic and devout Spaniard to vent his feelings in open criticism of the greedy representatives of these institutions of "divine rights" and special privileges. Even those who remained loyal to the Catholic religion were continually irked by the exactions of the clericals all of whom were supported by state subsidies, and many of whom used their sinecures for the most selfish and domineering ends. History records many popular attacks on churches and convents.

The Spanish people have never been such voluntary and diligent church-goers as one finds among the people of most other Christian countries. Moreover, there are a very considerable of intellectuals in Spain who are outspoken atheists. In fact, the great majority of Spanish intellectuals are either atheists or agnostics. In the present government there is to be found only one Catholic, that is, the President. All others are atheists or agnostics.

The very mildness of the revolutionists in their dealings with the church can be traced in part, at least, to the fact that the people had already achieved a separation between church and state in their own minds, so that what remained to be wrought was not an act of sudden and passionate revocation but only a cool and business-like acknowledgment in outward form of a cleavage between clericals and general public that had long since taken place within the hearts of the people. At any rate, the Constituent Assembly, although voting for separation of church and state, displayed no harsh or fanatical reaction against the priesthood, but provided for their immediate necessities in a very fair and humane manner. Their state grants were allowed to continue for a two year period with gradual reduction.

But these arrangements do not alter the fundamental truth that the present separation of church and state is the product of a long existing spiritual alienation. Only such a spiritual revolt could explain the moral severity of the step the Republic has taken in appropriating every foot of ground, every building, and every form of chattel property possessed by the Catho-

lic churches in Spain. The churches can now use these properties only with the permission of the state. Ownership remains
with the state. It should be remarked that the powerful Jesuit
Order was one of the first to be dispossessed and disbanded.
No priest or nun in Spain may engage in any profitable work,
not even agriculture. Such support as the clergy derive in the
future must come from fees paid for their strictly religious
services.

Spain has no official religion to-day. But there is freedom of
worship—as much as there is in any country—and much more
than in some regarded as being very progressive, but which
enact laws against "blasphemy." In matters of religion, in short,
Spain is now thoroughly up-to-date.

II

THE NEW STATUS OF WOMEN

Spanish women like their Italian sisters and, to some extent
those of France and Latin-America, have been kept in a very
backward condition. The Spanish law hardly recognized them
as having any rights. "The husband should protect the wife and
the wife obey the husband. . . . The husband is the manager
of the estate. . . . The husband is the representative of his
wife. . . . She cannot, without his permission, appear in a
trial by herself or through an attorney. . . . Nor may the wife,
without the permission or a power of attorney from her husband, acquire or sell her property" . . . etc.[1]

As may be seen from the above as well as from common observation of actual life, man was the absolute master of the
home. Spain was a "man's country." For all the prattle about
the chivalry of the Spanish "caballero" toward the ladies, it
was only a surface gesture and limited to romantic courtship.
Stuffed with narrow and stupid prejudices derived from the
illiberal education of the clericals, the Spanish gentleman hardly
considered woman, as wife, to be anything more than a breed-
ing-machine. True, there was afoot, especially in the larger
cities, a movement for the emancipation of women. But this
trend was restricted to small intellectual and radical circles.
The peasant woman, who constituted the bulk of the female

[1] Civil Code.

population, remained, to all practical purposes, a mere beast of burden, submissive, ignorant (the percentage of illiteracy among the Spanish women is appalling), the helpless victim of the conjoined selfishness of the church, capitalist exploitation, and man.

One of the first laws enacted by the Republic was the divorce law, conceived on an eminently broad and fair basis. Other laws provide for the equal treatment of women, including their right to vote.

Let it be said, then, to the credit of the Spanish Republic that the Spanish woman of to-day is advanced to full equality with man, politically and socially. Hence, a new era is dawning for Spanish womanhood. She is eagerly taking advantage of the new privileges given her by her erstwhile enslaver and exploiter. Her warm, inherent beauty will be enhanced by the added charm of a liberal education and the freedom to live her life unshackled by ecclesiastical superstition and repression.

Another great forward step has been taken in the field of education. The illiteracy in Spain has been about 40%; but it should be understood that most of the illiteracy was found among women and in the agricultural regions. Most men in the cities and in the industrial regions have known how to read and write. Let it also be recorded to the credit of the Republic that general education in Spain, especially elementary education, has made such rapid strides that in less than one year and a half under the Republican régime over 10,000 new schools have been opened, with a much larger number listed for opening in the near future.

There is reason for the friends of culture and enlightenment to feel elated at the development of education in Spain, not alone by reason of the many new schools being opened, but also because of the fact that the system of education has been considerably revised and improved. Indeed, the curriculum has gone through a great change. No religion of any kind is taught in government schools; elementary education is obligatory; the teacher has been given a new freedom, and, in general, the Spanish schools, if nothing interferes with their present development, will soon equal the best in Europe. As Fernando de los Rios, the Socialist Minister of Instruction puts it, "Every school is a new fort."

It is not too much to say, therefore, that present Spain, all things considered, is on a level with the most politically emancipated and socially advanced countries,—woman, education and religion having been dealt with in a most satisfactory manner from the point of view of the prevailing standards of Europe and America.

III

LABOR—RADICAL AND CONSERVATIVE FACTIONS

In the labor field, the constitution and the laws have gone quite as far as laws usually go for the protection of labor in *capitalistic* countries. The first article of the Spanish constitution reads: "Spain is a democratic Republic of workers of all kinds, which is organized as a régime of Liberty and Justice." In this connection, it should be noted that the Minister of Labor, Largo Caballero, is a Socialist. The same is true of the Minister of Education, Fernando de los Rios, and Prieto, the Minister of Public Works.

The Spanish socialists are not different from their brothers in England, Germany or France. Largo Caballero, holding the Labor portfolio, is also General Secretary of the Union General de Trabajadores (UGT). This is the labor union controlled by the Socialist Party. During the time this former stucco worker has been in the Cabinet he has had many opportunities to show his partisanship and has acted quite openly in favor of the UGT and against the National Confederation of Labor (CNT), the rival anarcho-syndicalist labor union.

Out of his socialistic devotion to the concept of a dominant government he devised a labor law containing such provisions as obligatory arbitration by a mixed jury composed of delegates of the government, the employers and the workers, the filing with the government of the names and addresses of the officials of every labor union local, the giving of two weeks advance notice to the government and employers before declaring a strike, etc. The great majority of the workers considered this as a scheme injurious to their freedom of action and branded it as an attempt on the part of Largo Caballero to destroy the rival National Confederation of Labor. The opponents of the law labeled it the "fascisti law," and openly declared that they would refuse to abide by its provisions and declare a general strike of protest if an attempt to enforce it should be made.

Such a storm of protest arose throughout the Spanish labor ranks, including a number of locals of the socialist unions, and so ugly was the temper of the advanced workers that the government considered it inadvisable to attempt enforcement for the time being.

In the meantime the National Confederation of Labor (CNT) the union of the anarcho-syndicalists had been forging ahead, organizing the industrial workers, the farm hands who, in the South were virtual peons, the railroad workers, the house-maids, the municipal workers, etc. Its membership has increased by leaps and bounds, and quite a number of the locals of the UGT have broken away from the socialist ranks and joined it.

The present membership of the National Confederation of Labor is set at nearly one million and a half, which figure is disputed by some, but it is generally admitted that the CNT has at least one million members.

As the growth of the CNT has continued, once more an attempt was made to enforce the "labor law," and September first (the first attempt had been April 8th) was the date set. But the protests of the revolutionary workers, now more numerous and better organized, were so violent, their meetings were so threatening, and the menace of a national general strike was so ominous in its possibilities that the government once more backed down and the law was put aside indefinitely. It is significant that great protest mass-meetings were called in every city. The one held in Barcelona, a city of one million inhabitants, was attended by one hundred thousand people, the biggest rally of any kind ever held in that city by any labor or political organization.

Why did the workers protest against the "fascisti laws"? Because, as the anarcho-syndicalists claimed, the purpose of the law was the destruction of their union; its provisions meant the tying down of the workers by the decisions of bureaucrats and job-holders; because it required that the labor unions should furnish their enemies (the police and the employers) with the names and addresses of their officials, and in short, because it was a cheap trick on the part of Largo Caballero to gain power for his unions at the expense of the anarcho-syndicalists.

The labor field in Spain is divided mainly into two sections: the Socialists on one side, and the anarchists or anarcho-syndicalists on the other. There are also some unimportant Catholic

unions, independent unions, and a few Communist unions.
But none of them is a vital factor in Spanish social or political
life. The Socialists, being a part of the government, look with
apprehension on the activities of the anarchists, and seldom support any strike declared by the latter. On the other hand, whenever the socialist unions declare a strike, the anarcho-syndicalist
unions always offer them their unconditional support which
the strikers accept sometimes, over the protest of their Madrid
leaders. Such was the case with the strike in the Ferrol ship-
yards; the anarcho-syndicalists offered the UGT strikers their
unconditional support, and when that offer was accepted, over
the protests of Caballero, the general strike was declared
throughout the four provinces of Galicia, resulting in victory
for the shipyard workers.

However, there is sometimes a clearly united front, as in the
instance of the putsch of General Sanjurjo last August in Seville. When Seville awoke one fine morning to find that Sanjurjo had captured that fair city, the CNT immediately declared
a general strike and published a manifesto urging the workers
to fight against Sanjurjo; the strike was one hundred per cent
effective. The communists also responded and declared a strike
in the port of Seville, which they controlled. The socialists also
did their duty, and in the industries that they controlled either
totally or partially, they struck to a man. The soldiers refused to
fire on the demonstrating workers, and in a jiffy the Sanjurjo uprising went up in smoke. It was a great lesson both for the Monarchists and the workers. The former learned how weak they
were, the latter, how strong!

Immediately after Sanjurjo had escaped and the government
troops had entered the city, the workers marched on the jail
in an impressive demonstration and demanded the release of
a number of anarchists and other extremists imprisoned there.
The prisoners were released. The next day, however, socialists,
communists, and anarchists were again fighting among themselves, though closely united on one particular point, namely,
that no monarchy or military dictatorship would be permitted.

Before the Sanjurjo revolt the government was rather timid
about tackling the agrarian question where it concerned the
big land-holdings (latifundios), notwithstanding its pre-revolutionary promises to the landless peasants. After the Sanjurjo
fiasco, the common people became more insistent. They would
wait no longer, and in a great many instances they went ahead

and took the land themselves, just as the Russian peasants did, but with this significant difference. In quite a number of cases they took the land and decided to work it in common, instead of dividing it up, as was the case in Russia. This communistic attitude on the part of a portion of the peasants was perfectly in accordance with the resolution of the Congress of landless peasant unions, affiliated with the CNT, which had been passed a few months previously. This resolution demanded from the government the expropriation of the big land-holdings to be turned over to the various peasant labor syndicates so that they might work the land in common.

After such events and the growing popular demand for action, the government decided to move, and expropriated the land of the grandees, and, later, the land of the monarchists involved in the Sanjurjo revolt. From that time the government felt somewhat safer in the saddle; it felt that it need have little fear of the weakened right, and that the left would be quiet for some time to come after this expropriating gesture!

The Republic continued on its regular course, with minor "incidents," riots and such happenings here and there, the civil guards killing protesting workers just as in the good old days of the monarchy. In this connection it is interesting to note that in one year and a half of the Republican régime over 250 workers were killed by the civil guards, soldiers, and assault guards, the last named being a body created by the Republic for suppressing disorders, riots, etc. This figure does not include the casualties sustained in the last anarchist uprising in January 1933, which are estimated at 48 killed and hundreds wounded. The anarcho-syndicalist paper "CNT" of Madrid had three consecutive issues confiscated in one week; once because it published those figures, another time because it attacked the Socialists, and the other because of an article attacking the government for making these seizures.

The Spanish Republic is not safe. There is a great menace hovering over the Republican régime. At this writing (Jan. 1933) Spain has 600,000 unemployed. There is no dole; only inadequate municipal relief. Yet the unemployed must eat. Forceful expropriations are a daily occurrence both in the country and in the cities. In the daily press we read continually of groups of unemployed entering large estates and taking a number of sheep or hogs and dividing the "loot" among themselves. Or, of urban unemployed workers attacking flour mills or bakeries or groceries and carrying the goods away before the arrival of the assault guards, or fighting with them for the possession of them when caught.

The 600,000 unemployed, already radically predisposed because of communist and anarchist preachings, find little comfort in the cautious words of the socialists who, being a part of the government, are more conservative than previously. The socialists are called "enchufistas" (a name applied to politicians holding various paying jobs simultaneously), hypocrites, fakers, and so on. Thus, while the membership of the Socialist Party has been swelled with new recruits from the "better classes," who hope to secure some of the many offices provided by the Ministry of Labor, such as members of Labor Juries, Labor Inspectors, etc., the anarchists, and also the communists to some extent, are increasing their followers by the thousands from the ranks of the real proletariat.

As a point of information, which will assist the reader in the understanding of the Spanish social problem, it should be noted that of the 24 million inhabitants in Spain, there are, according to the figures of the German Statistical International Office, 2½ million workers employed in industry and 4½ millions employed in agriculture. Let us now glance at the relative strength of the three main social schools that are now fighting for the hegemony over this Spanish proletariat of 7 million souls and their family dependents.

The Socialist Party claims a membership of 100,000. In addition, they control the Union General de Trabajadores (UGT) with an estimated membership of approximately half a million. Next come the communists of the Stalin faction who claim 10,000 members. The communists have also some following in scattered localities among organized workers. They control the port of Seville, and a section of the miners in Asturias. The Asturias miners have three unions—socialists, communists and anarchists—the largest faction being in the UGT (socialist). In addition to the official Communist Party there are other communist factions such as the Workers and Peasants Bloc, led by Maurin; the Trotsky faction, and some others of negligible importance, numerically speaking. Then, come the anarchists or anarcho-syndicalists, who claim a membership of one million and a half.

I shall not stop to describe the program of the socialists because they are regular social-democrats; and as I have already shown, they act very much like their brothers in other countries. As far as the communists are concerned, they are also very much like those in other countries. In fact, they are all astonishingly alike in their ethics and actions.

There is one item of interest in connection with the communists, however, which will throw some light on the attitude of the Spanish worker, or at least of a certain section of Spain, toward communism. Recently, for the first time in centuries, elections were held in Catalonia to elect the first Catalonian Congress following the approval of its "Estatuto" (constitution) by the Spanish Congress. The anarchists and syndicalists who, during the first elections that caused the fall of the Monarchy, had not campaigned against voting, though that practice is contrary to their ideology, made strenuous efforts in this particular election to keep the people from the polls. As a result less than 50% of the voters cast their ballots. The communists, on the other hand, believe in voting. They put up their own candidates, with the following results: The Official Communist Party (Stalin Faction) supported by the Trotsky faction, polled 1,500 votes in Barcelona, and the Maurin faction (the Peasants and Workers Bloc) polled 3,500. This, in one of the most revolutionary cities in the world.

It is obvious that the ideas and aspirations of the anarchists in Spain deserve careful study since they constitute one of the largest revolutionary groups. Moreover, they stand alone and apart from the rest of the advanced labor movements in other nations, where, with the exception of Argentine, and possibly a couple of small Latin-American Republics, the revolutionary proletariat is following the teachings of the communists.

Why, one naturally wonders, is the Spaniard so inclined to anarchism when the current of the world revolutionary movement is decidedly toward communism?

In the first place there is the element of racial characteristics. The Spaniard is very individualistic. But this individualism of the Spaniard, or of the Spanish worker at least, should not be confused with the selfish individualism—the "rugged" capitalist individualism—which aims at the attainment of material advantages at the expense of others, even at the price of crime. The Spaniard's love of independence concerns itself mostly with questions of personal conduct. It is an individualism that hates imposition from above. And as far as the proletariat is concerned, this assertion is conclusively proved by the multiplied examples of solidarity among workers who do not hesitate one moment in joining in a protest against an injustice. This same sympathetic and coöperative individualism is demonstrated in the many nation-wide, regional or local strikes that Spain has had in the last forty years.

Again, Spain has been traditionally the land of anarchism from the time of the First International. When Bakunin split with Marx, Spain was the country where Bakunin found a most decided support. The Spanish section of the First International had at one time over fifty thousand members, which is a high figure since Spain at that time had probably less than 15 million inhabitants and hardly any industry. The Spanish internationalists even attempted a social revolution in Jerez de la Frontera, and nine of their leaders were hanged in the public square of that town. That event was then referred to by the press and the government as "The Black Hand Conspiracy."

Anarchism in Spain has undergone some changes, like all social philosophies, in the course of its development. During the early years the Spanish anarchist was a great believer in propaganda by deed or "attentats." This is explained in part by the fact that the anarchists were continually persecuted and their press suppressed. Of late, however, the Spanish anarchists have forsaken such tactics, and have gone in more thoroughly for education and the organization of the masses into powerful autonomous, federated labor unions. In this respect, the Spanish anarchists have been acting quite differently from those of other Latin countries, especially France. Whereas in France many anarchists refused to participate in the organization of the workers because of the danger involved in job-holding by anarchists, the Spanish anarchists went ahead and organized the workers, evidently convinced that even at the risk of losing some good comrades to conservatism and reformism, it would be better so than to lose the great masses of workers to the politicians and governmental reformers. As seen from the results the Spanish anarchists were right. For the French anarchists, having chosen for the most part to remain aloof, have to-day little influence among the masses.

Through constant efforts, and despite relentless persecution, imprisonment, exile and executions, the Spanish anarchists succeeded in infusing the masses with the free spirit of militant anarchism. Consequently, whenever an unusually harsh tyrant arose, they did not hesitate to give their own lives for the lives of the tyrants. Premier Canovas del Castillo was killed by Agiolillo in 1898, Canalejas was killed by Pardinas in 1913, and Dato by a group of three anarchists in 1921. Not one of the ministers or governors or men high up in the government who distinguished themselves for cruelty in persecuting the workers in general and the anarchists in particular, was spared in the terroristic attacks by the anarchists. Maura, the assassin of Francisco Ferrer, the anarchist educator and founder of the Modern School, was attacked three times and wounded twice by anarchists.

Previous to the *coup* that put Primo de Rivera in power as a dictator, when the National Confederation of Labor was declared illegal and disbanded, a great reign of terror had been instituted in Spain in order to put down anarchism and syndicalism. Bands of gunmen in the pay of the government would lie in ambush for the anarchist and syndicalist leaders who would be "put on the spot" by the police. In this manner were killed Salvador Segui, Eugenio Boal, Layrent (the latter a crippled lawyer who used to defend anarchists and syndicalists in court); and in this fashion over 200 militant workers in Catalonia, mostly in Barcelona, were killed by bands of gunmen in the employ of the government. Some were killed right in their homes, others in the streets, and still others (the most noted) were slain at night after having been "put on the spot" by the police. The procedure was as follows: The man intended for the victim was arrested and held in jail for a few days or weeks; one night, in the late hours, he would be released and told to go home, and then killed en route. General Martinez Anido, the man responsible for this régime, was named Minister of the Interior in the Cabinet of Primo de Rivera. When the Republic was proclaimed he was indicted for the murder of Layrent and others; he felt that he would be lynched if caught, and fled to France.

While in Barcelona and the rest of Catalonia the anarchists and syndicalists were killed outright as we have just seen, another method even more cruel had been devised by the then Premier, Ed. Dato. He established the punishment of "conducción" which meant the deportation of militants from one end of the country to the other, on foot. They were accompanied by mounted civil guards, who would beat them whenever the prisoners, tired and hungry and thirsty, would collapse by the wayside. Many died while en route, others succumbed later, in consequence of these tortures. It was at that time that Dato paid with his life for the tortures and deaths of these anarchists and syndicalists.

In fairness, one may conclude that the terrorist methods of the Spanish anarchists were a measure of self-defense, for they never made any attempt on the lives of rulers who governed with any degree of justice.

IV

THE ANARCHIST RIGHT WING

Let us go back now to the question of the organizations of the anarchists comprising the great labor unions. It usually happens that whenever a labor organization becomes powerful it turns conservative. However, this has not been the case with the CNT in Spain, although the tendency did appear among some leaders, as the French anarchists had predicted. But the structure of the organization, being entirely decentralized, on a federative basis, with local and regional autonomy, as well as the large number of the militant anarchists in the ranks, did not permit conservatism and bureaucracy to thrive.

There were, in connection with the CNT, several capable and fearless leaders, such as Pstaña, Peiró, Clarat, Fonells, etc., who for many years had gone throughout Spain preaching the gospel of anarchism and syndicalism as represented by the CNT. They had all won recognition through hard work and sacrifices. These men, recognized leaders of the CNT, never ceased to call themselves anarcho-syndicalists, but they apparently were tainted or spoiled by official positions, and subtly at first, then more and more boldly, they began to flirt with politics, thinking perhaps that they could change the course of the CNT into some sort of political body, although in fairness it must be said that they never advocated parliamentary methods. This aroused the anger of the ranks and grave accusations were made against them. In August, 1931, hardly six months after the proclamation of the Republic, and before the government had organized the corps of assault guards and while the army was demoralized, with over 350,000 workers on strike in Catalonia and a great revolutionary ferment throughout Spain, it seems that a great number of anarchists and syndicalists wanted to take advantage of the opportunity and start a social revolution. But the above-mentioned leaders and others of the same opinion to the number of thirty, published a Manifesto, signed by every one of them, which appeared in "Sõlidaridad Obrera" of Barcelona, the daily organ of the CNT, in which they attacked the "hot heads" who wanted to start a revolution, which they branded as untimely.

The "Manifesto of the Thirty" as it has been called ever since, has become a very important issue in the history of the Spanish revolutionary movement, and as some of the points discussed therein are of considerable interest for the student of current history, I shall translate some of its most salient paragraphs. It runs in part:

"Some people say that revolutions have always been made by audacious minorities who have impelled the masses to go against the established authorities. And that it is sufficient for these audacious minorities to want it, and in situations such as the present one, the destruction of the established régime, and of the defensive forces that support it will become an accomplished fact.

"A rudimentary preparation, a few elements of assault to begin with, they say, is sufficient. They depend for the triumph of the revolution on the courage of a few individuals and the problematic assistance of the multitudes which will follow them when they are on the barricades.

"It is not thought necessary to foresee anything, or to take account of anything—it suffices to rush out on the street and fight and beat the State.

"To reflect that the State has formidable elements of defense, that it is hard to destroy, so long as its source of power, its moral dominion over the people, its economy, its justice, its moral and economic credit, are not broken by scandals and stupidity, by the immorality and incapacity of its leaders, and by the weakening of its institutions; to suppose that, unless this sort of breakdown takes place, it will be impossible to destroy the State, is but to waste time, to forget history, and be entirely ignorant of human psychology. Yet all this is being forgotten now—even the very revolutionary moral is forgotten.

"Everything is left to chance; everything is expected from the unforeseen; we believe in the miracles of Saint Revolution as though the revolution were a panacea and not a stern and cruel fact which man must forge with the suffering of his body and the pain of his mind."

The Manifesto goes on to say that this way of regarding the revolution is the demagogic way, the way which the old political parties have cultivated, but that this is not and should not be the way of the anarchists. They say also that an uprising at that time would inevitably end in defeat and Republican fascism, that the preparation should not be merely a matter of fighting elements, but that it should be also, and more urgently, an affair of moral elements, the element which is to-day stronger, more destructive, and the hardest to overcome. They argue further that a revolution now, even if successful, without the moral development of the masses, will inevitably make dictators of their leaders whether such leaders be anarchists or anything else. And then they continue with this significant paragraph:

"We are revolutionists, yes, but not cultivators of the revolution myth. We want capitalism and the State, be it red or white, to disappear, not to be replaced by another one, but in such manner that when the economic revolution is made by the organized working class, this same working class will be able to prevent the establishment of any other state power, no matter of what color. We want a revolution born out of a deep desire in the people, like the one which is now in gestation, and not a revolution made to order and crammed down our throats by a few individuals. For, if such a revolution came, these same individuals, no matter what they may call themselves, will inevitably become dictators the day after the triumph of their revolution."

When the Manifesto was published there was a great protest among the anarchists. Insults and charges of all kinds were hurled at the 30 signers. They were called traitors, reformists, "firemen" and so on. Regardless of whether they were right or wrong in their appreciation of the situation, it is evident that they did not have the rank and file of the CNT with them, for immediately Peiro, one of the signers, who was editor of the daily "Sõlidaridad Obrera," the official organ of the CNT, was removed and replaced by Felipe Alaiz, a "left" anarchist. In the course of a few months, practically every one of the 30 signers had been removed from the official position they held in the CNT. Naturally they had some followers too, and things have not been very quiet in the ranks of the anarcho-syndicalists. There have been violent factional fights resulting

in casualties. The followers of the 30 in Sabadell, outnumber-
ing the "lefts," refused to abide by the decisions of the Regional
Congress, and were expelled from the CNT. A serious split has
been narrowly averted in the CNT.

V

THE ANARCHISTS AND THE INTELLECTUALS

It should be pointed out that the CNT is not the only organization of the Spanish anarchists. The CNT is principally
the economic organization. But they have also the Iberian
Anarchist Federation, composed of some 500 anarchist groups
throughout the Peninsula which includes Spain and Portugal.
This anarchist federation deals with ideological questions and
such matters which for obvious reasons cannot be treated in the
CNT. The anarchist federation is composed of anarchists only,
whereas the CNT, being a labor organization, admits everyone
who is a worker. In this connection let me remark that a worker
is considered anybody who does any sort of useful work and
does not exploit another man. Hence, the CNT has the "Union
of Intellectual Workers" for writers, newspaper men, etc., the
"Union of Technicians" for engineers, and the like. The CNT
is making great efforts to enroll in its ranks the technicians and
the intellectuals. They realize that when the revolution comes
they could hardly get along without them, and therefore their
coöperation is sought.

The CNT aims at revolution and the establishment of Anarchist Communism, as repeatedly proclaimed in the various
regional and national Congresses, and as openly advocated in
their press and literature. It has two daily official organs in the
press, "Sōlidaridad Obrera" of Barcelona, and "CNT" of Madrid. In addition, there are scores of weekly and monthly
papers, organs of the various local, trade or regional federa-
tions, which are also anarcho-syndicalist. There are also purely
anarchist papers and magazines, such as "Tierra y Libertad,"
"El Luchador," "El Libertario," and magazines such as "La
Revista Blanca," "Estudios," etc. Leaflets outlining the aims
of the CNT and the structure of the future society are published and distributed by the hundred thousands, the same
being true of books on tactics, studies on the resources of Spain,
—industrial, agricultural, etc.,—and in general a wide educa-

tional campaign is being conducted by the anarchists and syndicalists.

It is erroneously believed by many otherwise well informed people that the anarchists have no clear conception or even an outline of the organization of the new society,—that they have no plans for the day after the overthrow of capitalism. Whatever the degree of truth there might be in such a notion as applied to the anarchists of America, it is certainly false as regards the Spanish anarchists. They intend to arrange the new order of society by means of the various unions or labor syndicates which serve as the basis for the economic life of the country. Through the labor unions, federated and confederated, locally, regionally, and nationally, with the assistance of cooperatives which will be organized for the purpose, and by the establishment of Free Municipalities or Communes in the villages and small towns, they intend to carry on the necessary industry of the country. On these broad and free foundations the anarchists in Spain intend to build the edifice of the new Society.

They have made quite a thorough study of the national economy with a view to the possibilities of supporting themselves without the aid of the outside world, in the event that they are boycotted after the successful anarchist revolution, as they expect to be. They feel that Spain has enough coal for home and industrial purposes, enough agricultural products, and more than they need of practically all metals. They lack, however, oil and its by-products, such as gasoline, heavy oils and lubricants; also rubber, cotton, machinery and paper pulp. They realize that the lack of these products will be a great handicap, but feel that they will be able to overcome this difficulty. They will develop the industrial distillation of coal and lignites, and extract therefrom oil, benzol and its by-products. Cotton is already grown in Andalusia and the Levante. It would not be easy sailing during the first years but they feel equal to the task.

It would be an incomplete picture of revolutionary Spain if I gave you only the proletarian side of the revolutionary forces. For in addition to the CNT and the FAI (Iberian Anarchist Federation) there are the intellectual groups which are more or less mixed in politics, such as the Federal Republicans, followers of Francisco Pi y Margall, the great Spaniard who was president of the First Republic in the seventies, but who resigned when he felt that he could not be an executive part of such an unjust social system.

These Federals, with Major Franco (the noted aviator), Barriobero, Soriano, etc., are a great help to the anarchists and syndicalists, their political and social ideas being the nearest approach there could be to anarchism in a political party.

These various politically advanced revolutionists publish the daily paper, "La Tierra", which enjoys a very wide circulation throughout Spain. The columns of "La Tierra" are filled with articles from the best anarchist pens and news about the anarchist and syndicalist activities.

Before going further, I shall relate an event which will throw more light on the ideas and actions of the Federals as compared with those of the Socialists. In January, 1932, there was an anarchist uprising in the Upper Llobregat, Catalonia. The rebels captured several towns, proclaimed and practiced Anarchist-Communism and held the towns for several days. The revolt was noted for its humane character, the victorious rebels, who were more than justified in being vindictive because of the cruel treatment which had forced them to take this step, contenting themselves with disarming the "somatenes" (a sort of home guard), the priests, the judges and the mine superintendents, and allowed their enemies to remain in their own homes, with guards posted around the town to prevent a surprise attack. When they were overpowered by the arrival of troops with artillery and airplanes from Barcelona, a number of the rebels were rounded up and together with other anarchists and some communists from the industrial centers, especially Barcelona, making a total of 119, were deported to Villa Cisneros, in equatorial Africa. The case came up to the Constituent Assembly for its sanction, and only the Republican Federals and four other deputies, making a total of 16, voted against the deportation, the 115 Socialists either voting for the deportation or abstaining from voting.

A clearer idea of the stand of the Federals may be derived from an article by one of their leaders, Mr. Canovas Cervantes, editor of "La Tierra," in connection with a controversy with the CNT who feared that "politics" might enter into the Confederation because of such a close coöperation with this political group.

Says Canovas Cervantes in a signed editorial: . . . "The tactics of the CNT are perfect. The press in charge of defending those confederal organisms fulfills its mission of being non-political. But the intelligent leaders of that organization must agree with me that the National Confederation of Labor, although it is the principal basis of the revolution, is not the revolution itself; that ouside the anarcho-syndicalist field there are other factors which the CNT must take in, stimulate and direct, and that it is not its mission to intervene in these fields of the revolution."

A further clarification of the position of Senor Canovas Cervantes will be obtained from the following statements he made in a lecture: "No doubt," says Canovas Cervantes, "that the bourgeois democratic revolution has arrived too late in Spain, as it comes at a time when the capitalist régime does not find anywhere a place for itself and is dying through exhaustion.

"The production system has broken down entirely, because wealth is in the hands of a few, and these few, who are neither intelligent nor generous, deny the people their due, and do not help them as they should in justice and fairness, thus arousing in the hearts of the humble and the poor an aspiration that is plainly and clearly an earnest communistic desire. This fact has more importance in Spain, because the Spanish capitalist is still less intelligent and less generous than the capitalists of other countries.

"There are two kinds of communism: State communism and libertarian communism. The latter is the product of peoples that have already evolved to a higher state of development, of those who, having gone through revolutions, can rise to that degree which we may call super-life. In Spain it finds the ground prepared by its history and because of the Spanish idiosyncrasy, fundamentally individualistic.

"The State communists, whose good faith and sincerity I recognize and proclaim, must agree as to the correctness of this reasoning. The Spanish revolution will not be one manufactured according to the patterns of other countries, but a revolution of our own, original, for no doubt these movements are always a genuine product of the race that makes them. I hope that the State communists, who are a very valuable element, after having studied the problem dispassionately, will admit that in Spain there is a more complete basis for Libertarian Communism than for State Communism."

There is also a deep-rooted background in the intellectual field. Pio Baroja and Blasco Ibáñez (to mention only the best known), the former indisputedly the best Spanish contemporary writer, and the latter, the best known Spanish novelist throughout the world, have done much to enlighten the people on the true meaning and purpose of anarchism and anarchists. Pio Baroja, himself an anarchist, though not orthodox at present, has in "The Red Dawn" and "La Ciudad de la Niebla" (The City of Fog) portrayed anarchist types with a master hand; and Blasco Ibáñez has done likewise in "The Shadow of the Cathedral" and in "La Barraca."

Even Miguel de Unamuno, who because of his intellectual pranks is not taken very seriously now, has written many anarchistic pages in his long literary and philosophical career. The same is true of Ortega Gasset, another great philosopher and nominal Republican. They are all truly Spanish types, individualists to the core, not to be confused with the bourgeois materialists, nor with the selfish and corrupt individualism all too evident in this and other capitalistic countries.

In short, the Spanish people are permeated with the spirit of anarchism. They are anarchists by nature, so to speak, having a long tradition of anarchism dating back to the late sixties. They have drunk of the fountain of freedom contained in the works of Francisco Pi y Margall; they have emulated the fighting spirit of the brave and tireless Bakunin and Malatesta, have absorbed the sacrificing, Christ-like idealism of the great and loved Fermin Salvochea, and the serene and scientific reasoning of the learned Anselmo Lorenzo, and other noted Spanish as well as foreign libertarians.

The anarchist seed has taken root in Spain because it found there a virgin and fertile soil for its exuberant growth. From this soil may come a harvest of world-wide influence.

While studying Spain and the Spanish people, we are witnessing events that are laden with ulterior possibilities. The advance guard of the Spanish revolutionary proletariat, as represented by the National Confederation of Labor and the Iberian Anarchist Federation, wants to do away with a social system whose right to exist has long been challenged.

For the past fifty years Spanish martyrs have shed their blood generously to hasten the downfall of the present order and to open the door to a larger liberty and a freer evolution for all the people.

We may soon hear the news that Spain is no longer a capitalist country, that modern, constructive anarchism—anarchist

communism—has won a chance to put its philosophy to the
test, and that the conception of a society built upon human
solidarity and the widest range possible of voluntary coöperation—the ideal with which the names of Godwin, Josiah War-
ren, Emerson, Thoreau, Proudhon, Bakunin, Kropotkin,
Reclus, Ferrer and many another spiritual pioneer have been
associated—is privileged at last to prove its virtues to an unbe-
lieving world.

ARNOLD ROLLER

WHIRLWINDS OF REBELLION IN SOUTH AMERICA

THIRTY revolutions, revolts and civil wars have taken place in fifteen countries below the Rio Grande since the Wall Street crash of November, 1929.

Indo-Afro-Ibero-America or, what we usually call Latin America, is a melting pot of new races formed by all possible combinations in the interbreeding of Indians, Spaniards, Africans and Portuguese, and lately also of Yugoslavs in Chile and Peru, Germans in Brazil, and Jews and Italians in Argentina. It presents a veritable sociological and anthropological museum of human societies living in all stages of economic organization or disorganization. All political forms are there: from the tribal systems of head hunting Indians in the jungles of Brazil and Ecuador to the highly industrialized state of São Paulo; from the sanguinary personal despotisms in Venezuela and Cuba to modern, liberal Uruguay.

The countries of Latin America present more variations climatically, racially, economically, geographically and politically than Europe. Class distinctions in South America are often emphasized by racial differences. Several of these nations live near the equator, some extend to arctic temperatures. A few live in altitudes of 8000 to 12,000 feet and others in tropical lowlands. There are regions engaged almost exclusively in mining, others derive their livelihood from the exports of agricultural and pastoral production. Two countries are landlocked, and in other republics the capital can communicate with the rest of the country only by sea. Due to impassable mountain ranges, communication between and within many countries is extremely difficult—a condition which has given rise to conflicting regional interests and separatist tendencies. In Brazil, which is larger than all Europe, and has less than one-tenth of its inhabitants, as well as in the South of Colombia and Venezuela, there are still large, unexplored tracts in which Indians roam with arrow and bow. In a few countries Spanish is spoken only by the educated upper strata, while the aborigines speak various Indian dialects and do not understand the language of their masters.

The various underlying geographical and geological conditions have produced different political groups and forms. In the Argentine pampas, a powerful aristocracy of cattlebreeders has arisen; in Brazil the coffee barons of São Paulo ruled; while Chile's policy is shaped by the nitrate magnates. In a few countries the Church, as the largest landowner, has been the preponderant economic and political power.

Nevertheless, there is a tendency to ascribe this wave of revolution, comparable in its sweep to that of Europe in 1848, to some particular racial psychology common to all "Latin-Americans." Revolutions below the Rio Grande began to be regarded as the state of normalcy, and the more sophisticated dismiss them as typical *opéra bouffe* stunts of the mythical General Caramba of Mexico, who started revolutions every six months, but tearfully envied the "gringo" general who could make 4000 revolutions a minute—General Electric of Schenectady.

Though the revolts in South America took on various aspects and were divergent in form and aspirations, according to the economic situation and the classes controlling the different countries, there were several common denominators which accelerated their outbreak. The principal underlying cause was the world economic crisis and the decline of the prices of coffee, copper, tin, nitrate, sugar, wheat, silver, cotton, rubber—to sometimes less than one-third of those prevalent three years ago and often to the lowest in history. These products are the basis and the life-blood of Latin American economy. The collapse of the prices brought bankruptcy to the middle classes, budget deficits to the government, unemployment to the workers and general discontent and bewilderment.

The existence of several dictatorships simplified the problem.

The dictators became the visible target of the discontent, just as Hoover was often blamed for all the ills caused by the capitalist system in the United States. Most of these dictatorships were supported by American loans which enabled the dictators to maintain themselves in power by keeping and paying large armies of soldiers, policemen and spies. The breakdown of Latin American economy which preceded the North American collapse, was accentuated by the sudden stopping of the gold stream from American investors, which had flowed to South America at the rate of a million dollars per day. With the reduced income from export taxes, with the stoppage of the gold flow from American bank vaults, budget difficulties began to tell. Soon the salaries of the government employees had to be reduced over and over again, and later stopped altogether, or paid after great delay. The salaries of the army officers and the police were maintained the longest. For it looks as if no dictator need fear a political revolution so long as his budget allows him to pay the army and the police.

But in the countries where the salaries of army officers and police finally had to be reduced or stopped, no bulwark remained between the ruling clique and the wrath of the rest of the population. The loyalty of the armies, which absorbed from 25 to 40 per cent of the budget, could not withstand the test of the budget deficits. With the collapse of copper, tin, wheat and nitrate prices, the breakdown of the budget, and the vanishing of the pay envelope, vanished the loyalty of those hired to defend the dictators. With the collapse of the loyalty of the army, the régime also collapsed. The machinery of the army ceased to function and the thrones of these peculiar republics toppled over as soon as American gold stopped greasing the native bayonets. Gentlemen and officers cannot be expected to die for a boss who cannot pay.

Another feature common to all these revolts of the various classes in different countries and for various purposes, were their similar slogans. As almost all the régimes ousted by these revolutions were dictatorial and able to cling to power thanks only to American gold, the rebels, who did not share in the gold stream, were usually opposed to American imperialism. They declaimed against the "Yankee peril," and the financial and political control of their governments by American imperialism. All rebellions were started with protests of righteous indignation against the suppression of civil liberties, the violation of the constitution, the self-perpetuation of the presidents in office, etc. In their outspoken demands they rarely went beyond those raised by Europe's revolts in 1848. Only in Chile, with a stronger communist labor organization, representing a desperate unemployed working class, was the situation different. There the rebellious middle class "outs" felt compelled to use socialist slogans and promises for the first time in South America. In other countries the new rulers elevated by revolts decided to do something for the masses who fought and died for them, by incorporating the word "revolucionario" into the name of the new ruling party. Thus, the party of the ruling Calles generals in Mexico is the "Partido Nacional Revolucionario," and that of General Sanchez Cerro, the sanguinary military despot of Peru is "Unión Revolucionaria."

In some of the countries of Latin America, still chiefly engaged in agricultural or pastoral production, and ruled and owned by feudal aristocracies of big landowners, the revolts did not involve divergent political principles or ideals. Their object was a change of persons or cliques; they were mere struggles—often undisguised—of the "outs" against the "ins."

The contest for power in such cases has often been fought between the "best families," who arrogate to themselves dynastic rights to rule their country, and the struggles have usually assumed the form of military *coups* arranged by generals. Thus, the Errazuriz in Chile, the Chamorros in Nicaragua, the Jiminez in Salvador, the Uriburus in Argentina have for decades "given" their countries their presidents, prime ministers, ambassadors and archbishops. (Not to be outdone by Central America, we now have in the United States the Roosevelt family.) The sons of the Catholic archbishops—as the story goes—which means of the best families, have become generals and admirals, and commanded the armies and the navies. But other feudal families, jealous of the prestige and profits of power, wanted their turn at the throne and the treasury. Hence many of the first struggles and "pronunciamientos" of generals. These struggles were sometimes even below the level of clique contests, when, as in Salvador, two related families, the Molinas and the Quiñones, fought for many years for power by ballots and bullets. The epic struggles finally ended when it was agreed that if a member of the Molina branch is president, a Quiñones must be vice-president, and vice versa.

From the family quarrels for power, most of these countries

graduated to clique struggles, when larger groups of the ruling classes representing certain divergent interests began to take part in public life. They were then compelled to assume party names. In the beginning these were very simple. Thus in Uruguay, two groups of landowners fought each other for fifty years in bloody civil wars and revolutions, under the party designation *Colorados* and *Blancos,* the Reds and the Whites, and these party names remain to this day. But the red of the Colorados was only on the collar of their uniforms, from which they gained the name; the Blancos got theirs from the white collar of their uniforms. Only much later did the Colorados of Uruguay become the Liberals and the Blancos the Conservatives. In Paraguay the same party names originated from the uniforms worn during its civil wars, but there the Colorados —the Reds—became the Conservatives and the Blancos the more or less Liberals. But the "Colorados Radicales" (the "Red Radicals") of Uruguay are a section of the Conservative Party. Later these names were simplified into Schereristas, Gondristas, Jaristas, etc., in Paraguay, or Batllistas, Riveristas, Vieristas, etc., in Uruguay, after the name of the party leaders. In very few cases do the party names in Latin America, such as "Republican Unionists," "National Unionists," etc., describe their divergent aims—if any—better than our denominations of "Democrats" and "Republicans." In most cases the "Liberals" in Latin America are the party opposing the power of the Church. In every other respect, however, they are Conservatives. In Argentina, in several provinces, the "Liberal Party" is the name of the Conservatives who oppose the anti-clerical "Radical Party." In Cuba the "Liberal Party" is the party of Machado, the most bloodstained despot the island has had in its history, while the "Conservadores Ortodoxos" lead the revolt against the dictator . . . with the slogan of "return to constitutionalism."

In many cases it would be difficult to decide if distinct party names were adopted to designate the divergent principles, postulates and economic interests of the various groups, cliques or strata,—or if certain divergent principles, postulates and promises were formulated *ad hoc* by cliques aspiring to attract a following.

Typical clique struggles were those in Guatemala, when—in December, 1930—the revolt for the presidency gave the country three presidents within one week and five within one month—

all generals. Another instance was Costa Rica where—in February, 1932—cousins fought for the conquest of political and electrical power and the profits both would produce.

In some countries, where foreign influence is stronger than local interests, and dominates the policy of the country, revolutions are made to order to suit that particular foreign country. Thus in Panama, the obstreperous anti-American liberal president Arosomena had to be removed by the "revolution" of January, 1931, when he refused to ratify treaties signed in Washington. In these treaties, Panama "agrees to consider herself in a state of war in any conflict in which the United States would be a belligerent," and to turn over to the United States control of radio communication and air-craft, as well as "the direction of all military operations in the Republic of Panama during actual or threatened warfare." The night after Arosomena signed a bill abrogating the American monopoly of radio communication he was deposed by a revolt and Panama's minister in Washington assumed the presidency.

Among the first struggles to go beyond narrow family and clique strife, were the revolts against the Church. No mere uprisings against the spiritual and even political power of the priests, these revolts were, and still are, very pronounced economic struggles. In many countries of Latin America, as in Mexico, Peru, Ecuador and Colombia, the Church was the largest landowner. In some of them it owned as much as one-third of the whole inhabited or cultivated land. When, with the growth of the population, the demand for land in accessible regions became more insistent, the more intelligent landowners among the ruling classes favored "liberal" or "radical" movements which demanded the expropriation of the Church lands. This was to provide land for their growing families, and partly also to divert the covetous gaze of the landless from their own estates. The development of an educated middle class in the cities contributed to the creation of anti-clerical parties. For many years it was possible to offer the priest as a scapegoat to the workers to divert their attention from attacks against their direct exploiters, the manufacturers. In recent years, in Spain and in several Spanish-speaking countries, the first anger of the revolting masses has often been vented upon churches and convents. The number of Jews was not sufficiently large or conspicuous in Latin America to serve the same purposes as in some European countries, though Mexican and Argentine politicians have recently begun to imitate their European brethren in this respect.

On the other hand, however, revolts of the "Cristeros" (from their battle cry, "Viva Cristo Rey—long live Christ the King") and the recent bloody revolt in Ecuador were attempts of the dispossessed Church to regain its power.

In August, 1932, the reactionary garrison of Ecuador's capital, Quito, revolted and proclaimed as president the clerical conservative president-elect Neptali Bonifaz, whom the anti-clerical congress had disqualified after his election. Situated in the interior, Quito is without commerce or industry, but full of churches and their dignitaries, government job-holders, absentee landowners, pensioned officials and officers, politicians and aspirants to political jobs. Consequently, it has different interests from those of anti-clerical, anti-bureaucratic Guayaquil, the port and the largest city of the country, with its commerce and industry, its middle class and organized labor movement. The federal army, stationed outside of Quito, remained under anti-clerical control. It reconquered the reactionary capital like an enemy city, and machine guns and artillery were used on both sides, with a loss of more than 400 lives. Monks and priests took part in the fighting for the defense of Quito, and monks directed the pious artillery fire from the belfries of the churches.

Finally, after six days of fighting, the federal army overcame the Quito garrison, and a Liberal was proclaimed provisional president.

Thus, what to all appearances was only a military revolt, or a civil war between various sections of the army, really represented political, regional and economic conflicts. It was the attempt of the Church and the landowners to wrest power from the liberal bourgeoisie which had won it some twenty years before.

In 1919, Peru's dictator, Leguia, officially "dedicated Peru to the sacred heart of Jesus," in order to increase the power of the clergy. The students protested, staged violent demonstrations in the streets of the capital and seized the university. After bloody clashes with the police and the monks, who fired on the students from windows of the convents and monasteries, Leguia was compelled to abandon his "dedication to Jesus." For that, however, he dedicated Peru to the American bankers.

But the military revolt of 1930, led with slogans of political liberties and constitutionalism, only replaced the civilian dictator Augusto Leguia,—who ruled with jails and deportations—by the military despot Sanchez Cerro, who rules with the firing squad.

Thus far, most of the revolutions in Latin America had been made by or with the army. As long as only generals made "revolutions," accompanied by grandiloquent declarations, these military *coups* were patriotic "pronunciamientos." However, few of the revolts of the past three years were merely old style "pronunciamientos" of one aristocratic clique against another. The revolts descended one step in the social scale when, aided by factions of the army, commanded by subaltern officers, or even non-coms, various strata of the middle classes started to rebel. The revolts thereupon lost their aristocratic name and became simply "cuartelazos"—barrack revolts. The aristocratic generals were no longer the revolutionists; the plebeian revolutionists became the generals.

Agricultural countries based on small property can remain peasant countries for centuries, with scarcely a change. But countries in which the system of large landed estates, latifundism, prevails, and particularly in countries cultivating only one or two crops, carry in themselves the germs of the transformation or destruction of their economic systems. Monoculture on large plantations demands exportations on a large scale. This in turn requires continuous improvement of import and export facilities, followed by the rise of a merchant bourgeoisie, a maritime and port proletariat, and later, a large working class population in the growing cities and ports. Thus, Argentina, the wheat and cattle producing country, has inevitably developed a large middle class and proletariat.

Various new strata and classes are formed. The clique struggles expand into class struggles. They become more articulate with the slogans, ideals and postulates often formulated or imported by progressive, socialist, anarchist, syndicalist and communist immigrants. In fact, there is no political party, revolutionary labor movement or sect which has not its counterpart in South America, particularly in Argentina. The latter is a complete museum of European revolutionary sects, with its two socialist parties, three communist factions, six anarchist sects, and the syndicalists, each of them publishing its own newspapers, and bitterly fighting the others.

In the recent revolutions in South America, the workers still played a rather unimportant rôle. In most cases the various cliques of the parasitic classes fought their battles without attempting to drag the workers into their political struggles. In Bolivia and Peru, some strikes of the workers preceded the political revolts. In Chile alone, for the first time in South America, workers and sailors revolted for their own interests. But their day had not yet come.

The peasants, almost all Indians and more oppressed than any other class, are entirely outside of all political and economic struggles, like the slaves in ancient Rome. They are inarticulate, unorganized and stultified by the Church and perpetual coca chewing or strong alcoholic drinks. There have been occasional Indian peasant revolts, but they were sporadic, unorganized and unconnected. Their resentment against feudal oppression vented itself in burning down the houses of some of the more hated white landowners, and in killing their families, after which they escaped into the hills.

The students, on the other hand, played an important rôle in most of these revolts. In many ways the South American students can be compared with the rebellious Russian students under the Tsarist régime, or the European students of 1848. The economic conditions of these countries are in some respects similar to those which prevailed in Russia under the Tsar, or in Europe before 1848. The students hail mostly from the middle classes, which became bankrupt as a result of the economic crisis.

There is an overproduction of professional men and other intellectual workers, with little hope for jobs or income under a régime of landowners, who reserve all available positions for their own families. The rebellious students are the sons of families belonging to classes coming to the fore and demanding their share of power and profits. The students have no outlet for their surplus energy. There is no baseball or football in South America to absorb their physical energy and spiritual enthusiasm, as in America or in England. There is not even the possibility of killing time by drinking, as the German students do. The Latins seem physiologically disinclined to strong drink. The students cannot even kill their time pleasantly with love-making or flirting, because in Latin America, as in the mother country Spain, love is still only to be had either in the nuptial bed or in the brothel. Their discontent with the hopelessness of their future is not diverted or "sublimated." So they play politics and revolutions.

The technique of the revolts has varied somewhat. In a few countries, particularly in Central America, a certain ritual of legality in the revolution had to be preserved to obtain the recognition of the United States. A treaty instigated by the United States and signed by the five Central American republics binds each one of them not to recognize any other Central American government which has come to power by revolution. Therefore, a few revolutions in Central America were made perfectly constitutional by forcing the president at the point of a gun, to appoint—before "resigning"—the leader of the rebels to the vice-presidency or such a post as would automatically make him the acting president upon the resignation of the incumbent.

However, in one country, Salvador, where the vice-president and minister of war overthrew his chief to become president himself (after which he distinguished himself by massacring a few thousand Indian peons who revolted against starvation), he was not recognized by the United States. This was really a reward, because it enabled him to ignore the American fiscal representatives who had up to then controlled 70 per cent of the customs in order to deduct the amounts necessary for the payment of the American loans. He defaulted all bond payments and was thus able to pay his army and to keep the loyalty of the officers and himself in power.

All these thirty revolts and revolutions were staged by or for the various strata of classes lording it over the workers and peasants. In a few cases, the result was the consolidation of the power of the bourgeoisie or the middle classes against a feudal régime or a military or civilian dictatorship exercised in the interest of high finance—mostly foreign. In Argentina the revolt reëstablished the rule of the former feudal landowners' régime and destroyed—for the time being—the rule of the middle classes.

The revolutions in Argentina, Bolivia, Brazil and particularly Chile were so complex and characteristic, that though none of them brought any improvement to the masses, they were of sufficiently historical significance to deserve a more detailed survey.

I

BOLIVIA'S FLASH IN THE TIN PAN

In South America the wave of revolts during the world crisis began in the least accessible of all American countries, in Bolivia, where Indian peasants labor in tropical jungles and near the glaciers of the Andes, and miners toil at altitudes of 15,000 feet.

Few countries in the world were so deeply affected by the world depression as this remote country, despite the fact that for probably 80 or 90 per cent of the population—illiterate Indian peasants—the world ends at the ridges of the Andes. Bolivia is neither an agricultural nor an industrial country. It neither produces enough food nor manufactures enough products for its population, but lives almost entirely on the tin produced by its mines. Tin forms about 75 per cent of the total exports of the country, and it is estimated that about 80 per cent of the population depends for its living directly or indirectly on the production or exportation of tin. At least 40 per cent of the government revenues is derived from the taxes on the export of tin.

Bolivia's tin is of extreme importance to the United States. Tin is indispensable for war purposes. Most of the food transported for the armies is packed in tins. Large, modern cities cannot exist without tinned foods. As more than half of the world's tin mines are in the British colony, the Malay States, and almost 60 per cent of all tin is used in the United States, the British statesman who said that without British tin the United States would starve to death, did not exaggerate.

The international tin trade is still controlled primarily by British interests as almost all tin ore is smelted and refined in England. The lack of fuel and the difficulties of transportation to the altitudes of the mines makes smelting in Bolivia almost impossible. The development of oil lands and oil production in Bolivia is the prime condition for the emancipation of the United States from the control of British smelting and refining plants because cheap oil could supply the necessary fuel for American-controlled smelting plants in Bolivia.

In 1930 the price of tin in the world market dropped to £137. per ton from £300. per ton in 1926. The demand de-

creased to such an extent that more than half the workers in
the mines were dismissed. The wages of the remaining workers
were reduced 30 to 50 per cent. The government revenues
dropped sharply. Until 1929 the regular deficits and a large
part of the government expenditures were covered by repeated
borrowing, mostly in the United States. In 1920 the external
debt of Bolivia amounted to only slightly over $4,000,000; in
1930 it was already more than $60,000,000, most of it contracted
through American bankers. The orgy of borrowing began after
the revolt of 1920, which overthrew the Liberals and brought
to power Bautista Saavedra, the leader of the conservative big
landowners. When the over-borrowing of South American
countries became apparent, Hoover, at that time Secretary of
Commerce, demanded that henceforth loans should not be
granted to Latin American countries for military purposes, but
only for productive ends. Nevertheless, shortly thereafter the
American bankers Dillon, Read and Company made a loan to
Bolivia of $23,000,000, part of which was immediately spent in
the purchase of arms and munitions from Vickers Ltd., London, and part in building military roads to the Chaco Boreal,
the territory disputed with Paraguay. This "productive" purpose was to open the way—by war and conquest—for the Standard Oil Company, which owns seven and a half million acres
of oil lands in Bolivia, to a navigable part of the Paraguay river,
in Paraguayan territory. When Bolivia applied for that loan,
experts of the U. S. Department of Commerce advised against
it. But, according to the statement made before the Senate
Finance Investigation Commission in 1932 by an official of the
Department of Commerce, the State Department approved the
loan, despite the objection of the Commerce Department: "because at this time our Latin American relations were upset"
and the United States did not wish to antagonize Bolivia during its conflict with Paraguay. At that time the State Department needed Bolivia's signature to the Kellogg Anti-War Pact.

The racial differences in Bolivia accentuate the class differences. The white or semi-white ruling class of about 400,000,
who own about three-fourths of the land, rule the rest of the
three million Indians and Mestizos of the country. The half-
breed Mestizos (the *cholos* as they are called in Bolivia) are the
foremen, overseers, small tradesmen or artisans and the skilled
workers. The pure Indians are the landless or poor peasants,
agricultural laborers, unskilled workers. They live in a perpet-

ual state of semi-starvation, semi-slavery and semi-stupor produced by undernourishment and the constant chewing of coca leaves from which cocain is extracted. They do not vote and do not participate in the political life of the country, which is the monopoly of the whites and semiwhites. The whites speak Spanish, the Indians speak Quechua or Aymara and rarely understand Spanish. The *cholos* who are in general the intermediaries between the two classes, usually speak both Spanish and one of the Indian languages. Thus the classes are distinguished in Bolivia by dress, language and color. In addition to this the ruling class fosters racial antagonism between the Quechua Indians and the Aymaras, the aborigine inhabitants of these lands which were conquered by the Incas, the rulers of the Quechuas. There are very few "free peasants" owning land left in Bolivia. They are being rapidly expropriated in favor of the large landowners and mining companies.

Despite the crisis which caused the government to reduce the salaries of its employees and officers by 20 to 30 per cent and to remain in arrears for many months, the government spent in these last two years, according to a report of the League of Nations, about $20,000,000 in the United States and Great Britain for arms and munitions. For 1931 the total revenue was estimated at not more than $7,000,000, 44 per cent of which was destined for war purposes.

Finally, when no more money was obtainable from investors in the United States, since the bankers do not lend their own money, the crisis came to a head. The deficits could not be covered by the usual methods of more borrowing. The government employees, the teachers, the university professors and the officers had to wait for their salaries. Indirect taxes could not be increased further. The cost of living had increased enormously. The price of a box of matches was increased from 15 to 50 centavos (17 U. S. cents), that of a yard of cotton goods from 15 to 75 centavos. To maintain himself in power, President Siles suppressed the press and all civil liberties, exiled all political opponents and ruled with a permanent state of siege, relying solely on the police and the army, whose Chief of Staff was the German General Hans Kundt, contracted by the previous president to protect him and to train the army for war.

Siles had been elected president in 1925 as a compromise candidate between the Liberals and the Conservatives, when it became apparent that the previous reactionary dictator, Bautista Saavedra, who had ruled in the exclusive interest of the big landowners, would be overthrown by a revolution. Saavedra's brother Abdón was elected vice-president, to leave the family near the seat of power where it could control Siles. Siles had previously signed a document promising to execute Saavedra's orders, if elected president.

Siles now proved himself more Christian than the Spanish Conquistadores, the Knights of the Cross. He became the greatest knight of the double-cross. After having secretly double-crossed his Liberal Party friends, Siles now openly double-crossed the Saavedras. He exiled Bautista to Europe on a "diplomatic" mission and deported his brother Abdón. But when Siles also began to rule in the manner of all other dictators, suppressing all opposition, exiling his enemies into the jungles of the interior, these perpetual gyrations left him without friends in Bolivia.

When finally Siles announced his intention of prolonging his dictatorship, dispensing with the formalities of an election, the time for a revolt had arrived. Liberals, Conservatives, the army, the workers, the students—the whole people were now against Siles.

In June, 1930, a group of political exiles, headed by Roberto Hinojosa, an Indian radical agitator, who, at the age of 26, had been the president of the South American Student Federation, crossed the frontier from Argentina with a small armed group, and began to arouse the Indians with such demands as nationalization of mines, oil wells and principal industries, confiscation of the large estates and all church property and their distribution to the Indians, abolition of all forms of peonage and forced labor.

The double-crossed politicians and the unpaid and disgruntled army had accounts to square with Siles. They saw now that they had to make their revolt quickly to prevent the revolution of the masses. They could not permit the participation of the Indian peasants and workers in the settlement of the destinies of the country.

But, as usual, they sent the students and the workers into the first fire. A demonstration in the streets of La Paz on June 22, 1930 led to bloody clashes with the police. In the meantime, General Blanco Gallindo, a Conservative, assembled about 3,000 troops in Oruro, an important railroad center south of La Paz. At the head of these troops he entered La Paz, deposed

Siles, who escaped to a foreign legation, and proclaimed himself provisional president.

General Gallindo appointed a cabinet of generals and colonels, but the under-secretaries in the cabinet were civilians. Among the members of his cabinet were the lawyers of the Standard Oil Company of New Jersey and lawyers of tin mine and other foreign corporations. When in the subsequent constitutional election Daniel Salamanca, the leader of the old-time constitutional parliamentary conservatives, was elected president, he solved part of the country's problems by defaulting all foreign bonds. He could now use all this money to pay some of the back salaries of the army and to prepare better for the war with Paraguay, to make the Chaco safe for the Standard Oil, and to free the American tin industry from British control.

II

ARGENTINA'S REVOLUTION
OF THE GENERALS FOR FEUDALISM
AND THE STANDARD OIL

Very few revolts in Latin America, if any, met with so much sympathy and approval in the press of the United States as Argentina's "Revolution" of September 6, 1930. Recognized authorities on Latin America hailed it as "in every sense a popular and democratic bloodless revolution" and "no barrack uprising, but a spontaneous movement of the people at large." It was particularly praised for having been "the only urban revolution in which street car service functioned and the taxis ran as in normal times." A new criterion of what constitutes a really popular and good revolution had thus been discovered: a parallel to that dictatorship which is admirable because the trains run on time.

This revolution was no barrack uprising. On the contrary, it was concocted in the officers' casinos by a conspiracy of generals belonging to the "old families." Its aim was to bring back to power the feudal, landed aristocracy, to protect it against the growing demands for agrarian reforms and land distribution and to strengthen the economic power of the Standard Oil Company of New Jersey.

Argentina's economy is based on agricultural and pastoral production on a large scale. It is one of the most important

wheat producing, cattle raising and meat exporting countries
of the world. The big feudal landowners of the interior had
ruled supreme by means of a parliamentary system based on
a very restricted suffrage until 1916 when, after an energetic
campaign of the growing middle classes and the workers of the
cities, the government was forced to grant universal suffrage.
In the following election the newly created anti-clerical, liberal
Unión Civica Radical, known as the *Radical Party,* elected
Hypolito Irigoyen to the presidency.

The economic power of the large feudal landowners was,
however, never broken. Thus, in the province of Buenos Aires
alone, the most valuable and fertile part of Argentina, one
thousand persons own more than 38,000 square miles, or a territory as large as Belgium, Holland and Switzerland together.
Fifty families of Basque origin own ten million acres worth
about half a billion dollars; and so on. Argentina which covers
an area almost one-third of Europe with its 470 million inhabitants, has only eleven million people. Though 75 per cent
of this immense territory is arable, only 10 per cent is in
cultivation. The largest landowners are not wheat growers, but
cattle breeders.

They are not interested in the increase of the population by
immigration. Populous cities eventually result in demands for
distribution of the land to the landless.

As a larger population is in the interests of the middle classes,
the *Radical Party* favored immigration and agitated for subsidized colonization in the interior and for sale of land to tenant
farmers. But the landowners refuse to sell. Nor will they reduce
their exhorbitant rents, although the prices of farm products
in the world markets have decreased by more than half.

Irigoyen rarely repressed civil liberties. Labor newspapers
and organizations were permitted, and the workers were pla-
cated with occasional concessions.

After an interval of a presidental term, Irigoyen was again
elected president in 1928 with an enormous majority. But he
had the misfortune to come back to power when, due to the
overproduction of raw materials and foodstuffs, the crisis had
already begun in Latin America. In the closing days of his
first administration Irigoyen had drafted a bill providing for
the expropriation of lands adjacent to railroads and highways
and their distribution among tenant farmers. In September,
1919 he had submitted to Congress a bill which set aside large

areas of oil lands for government exploitation, empowering the president to expropriate private property. In 1927 and 1928 the Chamber of Deputies accepted Irigoyen's proposal, but in both cases the Senate, in which the conservatives retained their majority, vetoed the bills. The Standard Oil Company was antagonized by the Argentine fiscal policy in the oil fields.

When wheat prices dropped 50 to 60 per cent and the principal government revenues, based on the export taxes decreased accordingly, salaries of government officials were not paid. In 1930 exports had decreased 36 per cent. When, in order to pay the service on the foreign bonds, gold was exported and the Gold Conversion Institute closed, the peso depreciated considerably. Unemployment increased. Wages and salaries continued to be paid in depreciated pesos worth half the previous amount.

The crisis caused the greatest suffering among the small farmers and the workers. But, by his fiscal policy, Irigoyen antagonized even more, both economically and politically, the large landowners, big business and American interests. Yet he held on to power with all the means at his disposal. Whenever in the provinces local administrations were elected which opposed Irigoyen, he "intervened" by dismissing the governor and local legislature, and by appointing federal governors. His *Radical Party* gradually became a sort of Tammany Hall, using its political power for the creation of a job holding monopoly and extensive graft. Discontent increased in all classes. The provinces in which he had "intervened" showed signs of revolt. These provinces were the fiefs of the big landowners, and members of their families were the generals and colonels in the army.

Under these conditions a number of generals and colonels connected with the provincial landed aristocracy organized a military conspiracy under the leadership of General Augustin P. Justo and General José Francisco Uriburu, the nephew of a former president Uriburu. An open revolt began with the demonstration of students demanding Irigoyen's resignation. In that demonstration one student was killed by the police. Finally, Uriburu marched into Buenos Aires at the head of 1400 soldiers and 300 armed civilians. The sons of the best families and the cadets joined the revolt. After a short encounter between the police and various other detachments of the police and the army, in which a number of soldiers and civilians were killed, the police declared its neutrality. Irigoyen was arrested, Uriburu proclaimed himself provisional president, immediately declared a state of siege over all Argentina and ruled over the country by courts martial and deportations.

Without delay Uriburu began to carry out the aim of the "revolution." All labor organizations and labor publications as well as those of the *Radical Party* were prohibited. All active communists, anarchists, syndicalists, the leading socialists and all leaders of Irigoyen's *Radical Party* were arrested and their party organizations dissolved. Hundreds of militant workers were deported to the icy Tierra del Fuego. Uriburu immediately decreed increases in the duties on foodstuffs by five to fifty per cent. He prohibited the importation of *hierba maté* tea, which all Argentines deem indispensable with a meat diet —almost the only diet the poor have in that cattle country. All *hierba maté* from now on had to be bought at more than double the price from the owners of the immense *maté* lands in the North of Argentina. 10,000 government workers and employees were immediately dismissed. All provincial governments held by members of the *Radical Party* were dismissed and staunch conservatives put in their place. Uriburu appointed a cabinet consisting exclusively of old-time conservatives, all members of rich, feudal families. All were connected with large, capitalist enterprises as directors, presidents or corporation lawyers. Sanchez, the Minister of the Interior, was the lawyer of the Standard Oil Company in Argentina. The Minister of Public Works was Chairman of the Board of Directors of the Andine Petroleum Company, which is controlled by the Standard Oil Company. Uriburu himself controlled large concessions of petroleum lands in the North of Argentina which he had obtained from Irigoyen as late as 1929.

It surprised no one when less than a year later Uriburu dissolved the Youzhamtorg, the Soviet Trading Corporation of South America. He accused it of "endangering national and foreign oil interests" by offering to sell oil to the Argentine government below the price at which "foreign companies"— that is, the Standard Oil Co.—were selling oil in Argentina. Several Argentine newspapers wrote openly that the dissolution of the Youzhamtorg was in the exclusive interests of foreign oil concerns and against the interests of the people, as two-thirds of all Argentina's oil requirements must be imported anyhow. The Youzhamtorg had proposed to sell oil to the State,

which could resell it at a profit to the consumers. As one of the
first acts of Uriburu was to dismiss and arrest the Director
General of the government oil lands, who had had repeated
conflicts with the Standard Oil Company, it became apparent
that well oiled indeed had been the wheels of that "revolution."

During Uriburu's régime the Minister of the Interior and
Police introduced the most ferocious and incredible tortures
against workers and opponents of Uriburu. These tortures in
all their details and horrors were revealed under Uriburu's
successor in open sessions of the Argentine Congress; the newspapers were full of these revelations. But not one American
newspaper wrote a word about it! It appears that just about
that time American bankers were discussing a new loan for
Argentina.

Uriburu finally agreed to call legislative and presidential
elections. Irigoyen's *Radical Party,* as well as the communists,
were not allowed to present their candidates. General Justo—
Uriburu's candidate and co-manager of the "revolution"—was
elected president.

Though 43 Socialists were elected out of a total of 152
Deputies, the Conservatives again obtained full power in the
Senate. Justo established a moderately conservative régime,
outwardly not so savagely reactionary as that of Uriburu. That
little has been changed may be surmised from a recent report
that political prisoners in two prisons in Buenos Aires simultaneously attempted a mass suicide. 57 men slashed their ab-
domens with razors and several died.

In Paris, cancer removed Uriburu, the hero of Argentina's
"Revolution", shortly after the election of his successor, and
thus the anarchists were saved the trouble. But the Standard
Oil and the "best families" are again safely in the saddle on
the backs of the Argentine people.

III

BRAZIL'S CIVIL WAR FOR THE COFFEE POT

The elimination of the power of the coffee barons of the
State of São Paulo, the "Paulistas," who have ruled Brazil since
the overthrow of the Monarchy in 1889, was the purpose of
the revolution of October, 1930. It was a civil war of the poorer

states for the conquest of Rio de Janeiro against the Paulistas who held the capital and the power over the whole country. The armies of the different states fought against the central power with infantry, cavalry and artillery, and with such effect that several generals in Rio de Janeiro, recognizing the ultimate outcome of the war, preferred to accelerate the result and secure for themselves the continuation of their military posts and power. On October 24th, 1930, a number of generals of the federal army arrested President Washington Luis and a few weeks later shipped him off to Europe. A Committee of two generals and an admiral proclaimed themselves the provisional government until the arrival of Dr. Getulio Vargas, who, having been defeated in the presidential elections as the candidate of the *Alianza Liberal,* had started and led the revolt.

The presidency of Brazil had hitherto been held in rotation by the governors of the three states of São Paulo, Minas Geraes and Rio Grande do Sul.

At the elections in 1930, however, the São Paulo coffee barons, anxious lest a new president from another state might not maintain their coffee-protection policy, broke the ancient custom and decided to elect Dr. Julio Prestes, governor of the State of São Paulo, although the incumbent president, Washington Luis, was also a former governor of that state.

This disregard of Brazil's political etiquette and elimination of the politicians of Rio Grande do Sul and Minas Geraes precipitated a split in the ruling party, the only party then in existence, which had hitherto appointed all presidents. The conservative *Republican Party* split into the *Concentração Conservadora* and the *Alianza Liberal,* and the latter nominated an opposition candidate for the first time in the history of the Republic. There was, however, also a profound divergence within the ruling party on the policy concerning coffee, the basis of Brazil's national economy. Coffee constitutes 78 per cent of Brazil's total exports. The whole financial policy of Brazil had been shaped exclusively in the interest of the large coffee growers. To maintain the high price of coffee, in spite of its continuous overproduction, became practically the sole aim of the policy of the conservatives.

The enormous profits derived in former years from the sale of coffee had stimulated coffee growing in Colombia and Central America. The price reduction which would have resulted naturally from this foreign competition was prevented by the "valorization" or "coffee defense" systems of the Brazilian Government. Millions of bags of coffee were stored by the Government, which even bought up large quantities in foreign countries to prevent their being thrown on the market. The coffee growers were given advances on unsold crops. To finance this protection of the coffee interests, large loans were contracted in Great Britain. These loans were guaranteed by the value of the stored coffee and partly or indirectly by the revenues of the nation.

The Liberals opposed the forced "valorization" of coffee. They maintained that artificial support of high prices favored further development of coffee plantations in foreign countries which cannot produce as cheaply as Brazil. They favored allowing the price to drop to the level determined by the demand and opposed the reckless borrowing which was mortgaging the country to foreign, especially British and American financiers.

The rule of the Paulista policy of monoculture on large plantations perpetuated the semi-slavery and starvation of three-fourths of Brazil's forty million inhabitants. Their inability to buy prevented the development of native industries and business. Brazil's Director of Public Health, Belisario Penna described the situation in the following statement published in the conservative newspaper *A Noite*: "Thirty million human beings without any earthly possessions are dying slowly in Brazil from hunger, syphilis and malarial diseases." These thirty millions are small peasants or landless rural laborers, mostly mulattoes, who own nothing besides their ragged shirts and trousers which they have on their bodies. The average wage of the skilled workers in the cities is about twenty-five cents per day, in the smaller towns about half that amount. Agricultural laborers and share-croppers earn no more than the equivalent of about twenty-five to sixty dollars per year.

The opposition to the Paulista régime was supported by the middle class in the industrial sections of the country, and the farmers producing commodities other than coffee, such as oranges, sugar, cocoa, rubber, silk, meat, who, overburdened with taxes for the benefit of the Paulistas, fought against being sacrificed to the coffee interests, the chief beneficiaries of the loans and the financial policy of the government.

The program of the *Alianza Liberal* included general amnesty for all participants in previous revolts against the Paulista régime, secret ballot, right of workers to organize, the "right of the people to select their own Chief Executive without inter-ference from the President and the politicians in power," and similar promises. For this Getulio Vargas was accused by the federal government of leading a "bolshevist revolution."

Vargas' "bolshevism" consisted in promising "to introduce similar corporation laws and organization of the classes as those promoted by the fascist régime during the period of creative renovation through which Italy now passes. I shall follow that same principle in the supreme administration of the republic if I am elected." He kept his word. Shortly after he assumed power, all labor newspapers and organizations and opposition groups were prohibited as under Washington Luis, and Vargas showed no intention of calling elections for a constitutional president. Pressed very hard, he promised to call elections in 1933.

Brazil now tries to solve its economic problem by dumping a million tons of coffee into the sea. So far, more than twelve million sacks of 132 lbs. each (about 1,600,000,000 lbs.) have been destroyed. But it still has in its warehouses about a million more tons of coffee—or almost as much as the whole world con-sumes in two years.

In July, 1932 a new revolt broke out in the state of São Paulo. The slogans of the rebels, who called themselves "constitucion-alistas" were again reëstablishment of the constitutional ré-gime, speedy presidential elections, civil liberties, etc. The rebels fought for the return of power to the old conservative Paulistas, whose political power had been broken two years before by the "liberal" revolt of Getulio Vargas, who had used the same slogans against them.

As the whole machinery of the state of São Paulo and its local army and police were in the hands of the Paulistas, the revolt was from the beginning a civil war of that state against the federal power of Rio de Janeiro, which controlled the rest of Brazil. This was not a vulgar revolution—on the contrary it was civilized warfare with bombing airplanes, poison gas, artillery, etc. Finally, after three months, when the supply of food of the state of São Paulo was exhausted and it appeared that the other states were unwilling to join and fight for the reëstablishment of the power of the reactionary coffee barons, the revolt col-lapsed and the federal power was reëstablished in São Paulo. About 15,000 forcibly recruited poor devils were killed or wounded . . . all for the price of a cup of coffee.

IV

CHILE'S NITRATE REVOLUTIONS
AND SYNTHETIC SOCIALISM

In Chile a series of revolts, revolutions and counter-revolts brought to power successively the liberal middle class, the return of the feudal aristocracy, the moderate liberals, followed by a military dictatorship of Ibañez, overthrown in 1931, then a conservative bourgeois régime, followed in July 1932 by the "socialist revolution" of Ibañez' former ambassador in Washington, Carlos Dávila. After a week in power Dávila was overthrown by Colonel Marmaduque Grove who promised a still purer socialism than Dávila. After a few days Dávila, at the head of another army group, crushed what he called Grove's "communist régime," and came back to power for three months to be in turn overthrown by revolting army groups. Then, for several weeks, revolts and counter-revolts of various army cliques became a daily routine, until in October 1932 the election of the lawyer Arturo Alessandri brought back to power the moderately liberal middle class.

This closes the cycle of the political changes which had kept the country in turmoil for more than ten years, since 1920, when the hitherto uninterrupted rule of the feudal aristocracy was challenged by the election of a liberal president, the same Arturo Alessandri. It marked the progress from the rule by generals and landowners to the rule by lawyers, the attorneys of the bourgeoisie.

As long as Chile's nitrate ruled the world markets, unchallenged by foreign competition, the nation was fairly prosperous and the workers were employed. Chile's trouble came, so to speak, from the air when, during the War, the Germans began to extract the nitrate from the air which they had formerly bought mainly from Chile. At the end of the War Chile, of course, expected to get back its old customers; but instead those customers had become Chile's strongest competitors. Chile lost the basis of its prosperity, the world monopoly of nitrate,— the riches it had wrested from Bolivia by a war of conquest for the nitrate lands, more than fifty years ago.

Until 1920 Chile was ruled by the "old families" and a few thousand big landowners who own 51,684,000 acres or 89 per

cent of the whole farm land of Chile. They considered the
presidency, political power and the nitrate fields as their private domain. When nitrate prosperity began to decline, the
middle classes, the intelligentsia, and the workers began to be
interested in politics and elected the liberal Alessandri to the
presidency. Alessandri's program included the separation of
State and Church, laws for the protection of the workers, an
income tax to stabilize the budget, a reduction of the army and
navy.

The "old families" had ruled with the help of the navy,
which was officered by their sons, and with the aid of the
Church, which was one of the largest landowners in the country.
In this long, stretched country, in which every important town
can be bombarded from the sea, the navy, the main support of
the aristocracy, was the pampered child. In 1924 a military
coup headed by General Altamirano overthrew the régime of
Alessandri to reëstablish the "old families" in power. A Junta
of admirals and generals—all members of the landed families—
ruled the country for a few months, until in January 1925 the
younger officers in the army, drawn from the rising middle class,
the young intelligentsia and the anti-clericals, in another military coup, overthrew the Altamirano Junta. It was a sort of a
class struggle of the bourgeois army officers against the feudal
navy officers.

Among the leaders of the revolt of the younger officers against
Altamirano was Carlos Ibañez, colonel of the gendarmerie. He
became Minister of War. Alessandri resumed the presidency in
March 1925. Soon the new Alessandri-Ibañez régime was again
threatened by another revolt of the navy. But now a class revolt
within the navy itself prevented the success of the higher officers. The engineers and engineering officers who came from
bourgeois families, revolted against the revolting aristocratic
navy officers and sealed the doom of feudal rule. After the
expiration of Alessandri's term, Colonel Ibañez remained Minister of War under the new President, a moderate liberal. In
the meantime, the economic condition of Chile was getting
worse. In 1926, of 142 nitrate plants 128 had to close and the
remaining 14 plants announced that they would close at the
end of the year.

In 1927 Ibañez, whose power was steadily ascending, forced
the government and the president to resign—by the mere threat

of a military coup. Upon assuming dictatorship, he began to solve Chile's problems in his own way.

He arrested, imprisoned and exiled all his opponents, and suppressed the opposition press. Disregarding parliamentary immunities, he arrested and deported Conservative as well as Liberal and Communist Deputies and Senators and completely ignored the protests of the Supreme Court. Ibañez not only struck at the workers and the feudal interests of the landed aristocracy, but also at certain liberals representing the native financial and nitrate interests.

The nitrate situation was disastrous for the Government. The export taxes on nitrates formed usually more than half, and in 1916, 80 per cent of all government revenues. But the estimated production for 1927 would have netted the Government not more than 17 per cent. In 1890 Chile supplied 80 per cent of the world's nitrogen and only 20 per cent in 1926. There was the additional danger that the salaries of the Government officials and the army could not be paid. Ibañez' Minister of Finance made a statement in which he attacked the native nitrate magnates, accusing them of having forced the nitrate industry to a crisis in order to compel the Government to reduce or eliminate the export tax.

In the same breath the minister declared that "the Government was fighting a political oligarchy which thrives on public misery" and that it was "necessary to save the country from the bolshevist danger and put an end to the governing class, which through its methods made the people eager recruits to the communist cause."

Ibañez undertook to "save the country," the pay of the army and power for himself, by the expropriation of the native and British nitrate landowners by means of fiscal measures and by handing over the control of Chile's main industry and national riches to the American Guggenheim interests. The Guggenheims bought some nitrate tracts from the Chilean Government for $3,500,000, promising to pay the export tax, which the other companies said they were unable to pay.

All labor organizations were destroyed to prepare the ground for the unhampered exploitation of the country by American capital. Ibañez increased the strength of the gendarmerie so that it became numerically larger and better armed than the army. He had thus a permanent, pretorian guard for the protection of his personal power and of the interests of the Guggenheims against the nation and even against the army.

In March, 1931, the Chilean Government made a new arrangement with the Guggenheim interests to combine and absorb all the nitrate producing properties in Chile by the creation of the Compañia Salitrera Chilena, known under the name Cosach. This new company was capitalized at about $360,-000,000, comprised 36 Chilean nitrate producing companies, and represented more than 95 per cent of the nitrate productive capacity of Chile. The 3000 shares of the new company were equally distributed between the Chilean Government and the Guggenheims. Chile contributed the state nitrate lands, including those which it expropriated from the former owners. In addition to this, Chile undertook to contribute $120,-000,000, which it was to obtain by a loan in New York, for the special purpose of financing the new combine. The Guggenheim interests contributed, for their equal share in the combine, the Anglo-Chilean Nitrate Corporation and the Lautaro Nitrate Corporation, and their improved process of nitrate refining. This theoretical half share which gave them control of the $360,000,000 combine cost the Guggenheims merely the original outlay of $3,500,000, the amount for which they had bought some nitrate lands a few years before! On the basis of these properties they raised money on the New York Stock Exchange by issuing bonds and preferred stocks, printing several million common shares whose total amount was soon quoted at nearly one hundred million dollars. One of these bond issues, the $32,000,000 loan of the Lautaro Nitrate Corporation, sold to the public in 1929 by a syndicate of American bankers, at 99% of the par denomination, was quoted only a short time later at one-fourth of a cent to the dollar. Thus, the Guggenheims got control of Chile's nitrate deposits and many million dollars, and the investors got some beautifully engraved paper.

Finally, however, despite all the frantic attempts to postpone the collapse, the nitrate situation became such that, even after the Government had defaulted on all foreign bonds, amounting to about $500,000,000, there was not enough money for the most necessary disbursements—the army and the gendarmerie. The interest on Chile's debt amounted to about one-fourth of the total revenue of the country.

In the early summer of 1931, Ibañez made several attempts to create civilian cabinets that would solve the crisis without reducing the expenses of the army and gendarmerie. Within three weeks he forced out three cabinets. Students in Santiago occupied the university and demanded Ibañez' resignation. The illegal underground communist Chilean Federation of Labor proclaimed a general strike. Doctors, lawyers and even judges announced that they would support the movement. The general strike was complete. Clashes in the streets between gendarmerie and cavalry on one side, and the workers and students on the other, lasted for three days; about 150 were killed and 2,000 injured on both sides. When, finally, the army refused to take part in the repression of the demonstrators, Ibañez fled to Argentina.

Esteban Montero, a "constitutional conservative," assumed power in August, 1931. He promised to abolish the gendarmerie, to disband the secret police, to grant full liberty of the press, the right to organize, etc., etc.

The substitution of Ibañez by Montero did not solve Chile's problems. At the beginning of November, 1931, 5000 sailors, including the whole Chilean navy, the largest in Latin America, revolted against proposed wage cuts and arrested the officers. Petty officers took command and held the naval bases of Coquimbo and Talcahuano. Soon afterwards, coast defense forces, two regiments of Valparaiso and a general strike of the workers in the cities, joined the movement. The sailors demanded the division of the large estates among the poor farmers, a capital levy from the rich, and unemployment relief. The government declared martial law, arrested all active communists and mobilized the artillery, constabulary and air forces against the navy. The press reports spoke of 500 killed in the battles between the mutineers and the rest of Chile's armed forces. Finally, the mutineers surrendered, whereupon their leaders were condemned to death. The fear of a general revolt was, however, so great that they were not executed, and when two of the imprisoned leaders were later elected by the workers to the Chamber of Deputies, their sentences were commuted to life imprisonment. On the American continent, it is interesting to note, this was the first united revolt of workers, soldiers and sailors without bourgeois or intelligentsia leadership and with revolutionary demands of their own.

Montero's régime hardly lasted a year. In turn it was overthrown in June, 1932 by a military revolt, when he could not bring Chile "back to prosperity," when nothing was done to allay the dissatisfaction of the lower middle classes, the former owners of the nitrate fields, and the workers, nor for the 250,-000 unemployed.

The revolt against Montero was led by quite heterogeneous elements. The principal leaders were Carlos Dávila, Ibañez' former ambassador in Washington, who made it his special business, while in Washington, to learn socialist phraseology; and Marmaduque Grove, the former head of the aviation corps, who had once attempted an unsuccessful revolt against Ibañez. Dávila became provisional president. He promised everything to everybody: no unemployment within three months and the establishment of "pure socialism." Grove became Minister of Defense and it seems that he actually sought to inaugurate certain reforms demanded by the lower middle class, to make concessions to the workers and to impose higher taxes on the profits of Chilean and foreign capitalists. This, however, was not the intention of Dávila. Within a few days after the new government took power, sharp conflicts broke out between Dávila and Marmaduque Grove. Grove, supported by workers and students, ousted Dávila and ordered him exiled.

A few days later Dávila, who did not leave Chile as ordered, and who all the time had the support of the gendarmerie, the favored troops of Ibañez, suddenly attacked Grove with the gendarmes, a few aviators and a part of the army. He deposed and exiled Grove who, among the armed forces, had only the support of part of the air force and a part of the navy and the army.

The American and British newspapers, which at first protested against the threatened "bolshevism" of Dávila, soon recognized that he would do nothing detrimental to foreign capital.

Immediately after reassuming power he announced that in place of Grove's "communistic" régime which, he said, was leading the country to "anarchy," the new government would establish "pure" socialism which would "satisfy all classes." For this purpose he proclaimed martial law throughout Chile; gendarmes and marines were sent everywhere to suppress the strikes which protested against his return to power. Five hundred communists were arrested, trade unions were suppressed and labor headquarters raided.

The new "socialist" government—as it was called by the whole press—announced that the death penalty by court martial would be meted out for every form of "communistic activities." Almost all foreign governments hastened to recognize the first "socialist republic" in South America, maintained with machine guns and martial law against continuous revolts of the students and the workers.

But, alas, this peculiar "first socialist republic" on the American continent hardly lasted three months. The régimes which followed each other in quick succession were now counted by days. In September, 1932, a General Blanche who, under Montero, had organized a few attempts to bring back Ibañez, overthrew Dávila. A group of aviators forced out Blanche, another group put Blanche back in power. After two weeks he was again overthrown by a military revolt in the North—the nitrate districts—of Chile, which demanded the return of civilian rule, that is, of the former nitrate owners. The Chief of the Supreme Court became provisional president, to call the elections. A few weeks later, Alessandri was elected president with 183,754 votes against 60,065 for Grove. The middle class in Chile is back in power—for the time being.

CONCLUSION

These revolts or revolutions have neither inaugurated a new era in Latin America nor have they improved the lot of the workers and peasants. Yet they are symptoms presaging important changes in the economic and political systems of the countries below the Rio Grande.

The collapse of prices and the permanent overproduction of South America's staple products undermined their economic basis and shook the feudal systems of these countries. International competition and the growing of similar crops in other countries destroyed the virtual monopoly which a few Latin American countries held in certain products, such as nitrates in Chile, coffee in Brazil, sugar in Cuba, etc. Trade restrictions through high tariff walls further reduced the possibility of exports, and hence of imports, forcing many Latin American countries to consider abandoning their monoculture system and introducing diversification of crops and products. Abandonment of monoculture will in turn reduce the profits of the large landowners, forcing them to sell or rent parcels of their land to farmers. This is bound to reduce the economic and political power of the large landowners and to bring about a gradual abandonment of the semi-slavery of the peonage system still prevailing in mines and plantations.

Having defaulted all foreign bonds these countries will be unable to borrow abroad for decades to come. This will force them to stand on their own feet and strive for economic independence. With smaller exports and imports and lesser reliance on and influence by foreign capital, all these countries will have to resume and accelerate the industrialization interrupted by the World Crisis. Industrialization and crop diversification are the basic conditions of the rule of the middle classes. Exchange restrictions established by many Latin American countries to prevent the export of gold caused many foreign interests to reinvest their credits by establishing in these countries new industrial and commercial establishments. The dividends derived from them may later be taken out of the countries, but the factories remain, further contributing to the reduction of imports and the industrialization of the countries and giving employment to more native workers. Industrialization must bring about and presupposes a certain degree of education of the workers. A better educated and large working class will bring more forcefully to the fore its own demands, first for higher standards of living and finally for socialization. The future struggles will no longer be mere contests for power among various cliques and strata of the exploiting classes, comparable to the conflicts among the slave-owning classes of antiquity, in which the slaves did not participate. History travels faster under capitalism than under feudalism. The South American peons of to-day, and industrial workers of to-morrow, will disprove Bülow, the late German Chancellor, who wrote that the workers are like horses who may occasionally kick but, nevertheless, are destined to carry their masters for all time to come.

With the growth of the population the revolts represented more and more the interests and the aspirations of larger strata. Where the revolts went beyond simple clique struggles, they became revolutions for stratified emancipation. One group or class after another emancipated itself from the domination of the classes above. When the revolutions are no longer the privilege of generals and the ruling classes, stratification in emancipation is accompanied by the democratization of revolution. The revolts of the old families against each other were followed by the revolts of the patrician bourgeoisie to overthrow the landed aristocracy. The middle class, aided by the workers, attacked the power of the upper classes. The lower middle class, aided by the intelligentsia and the workers later fought the rest of the bourgeoisie, allied now with the aristocracy. Then the workers and the declassé intelligentsia fought against all other classes. Finally, as in Chile, the workers and sailors fought alone for their own demands—against the whole pyramid above them.

In these countries which are potentially rich beyond all dreams, the workers and peasants, who are poor beyond description, have witnessed so many revolts and revolutions that they will not deem them possible only in distant countries or remote times. Industrialization and socialization may there come about even sooner than in already highly industrialized countries, where the middle classes have had time to consolidate their power. Such a thing has happened. Industrialization, the revolt of the working masses, and socialization will bring out all the untapped riches of these countries, for the benefit of the producers.

THE SHIFTING SCENE
IN MEXICO

THE seven lean years are upon us, and though we filled our granaries during the fat years, we are starving apparently because the granaries are full—ironical commentary upon the intelligence of a great productive nation. Now that our tail-feathers have been plucked during our Coolidge ostrich-head-in-the-sands prosperity, our Tories glibly tell us panics are inevitable, to be born stoically with the due ration of uneatable optimism; God will not only give us heaven but new radios—by and by. The idea that a nation might plan its national life to avoid catastrophes, is akin to Bolshevism, lèse majesté against the basic concepts of rugged individualism.

This is a great hour for prophets with panaceas, from Communist programs for revolution to demeaning doles. Lacking a panacea, you can blame Europe, à la Hoover. The magazines bristle with bated breath cagey articles by sweetness-and-light professors and liberals on the necessity for a five-year plan; or Owen D. Young suggests a fishless-fowlless coalition dictatorship—we are not quite without illumination these dark days.

In this discussion of democracy or dictatorship, planning or non-planning, revolution or non-revolution, the essential question of planning *by whom and for whom,* if dictatorship or revolution—by whom and for whom—is largely sidestepped.

We have always had planning for private profit. The rugged individualists have always planned, personally and collectively. The Teapot Dome scoundrels did their planning. The men who have bled this country dry with fancy loans to South

American dictators did their planning, and the corner dentist who bought Peruvian bonds that Leguía might give mistresses pearls, is holding the sack of blissfully penurious monogamy. After the record of Mooney, Sacco and Vanzetti, Gastonia, West Virginia, the bonus marchers, etc., etc., we are not entirely convinced that we are devoid of dictatorship. And the period of American life since the Spanish-American War represents a radical and violent change in our mode of living, the structure of our government, and our attitude toward over-seas imperialism that is perhaps the most astounding and chaotic revolution in our history, a brutal impact upon the *mores* and organization of our country. Thus there is nothing really revolutionary in discussing national planning, dictatorship, or reconstruction through revolution. We merely wish to know who are to be the high priests of the great God Prosperity and just whom he elects for his paradise.

This abusive preamble has definite bearing upon my topic —Mexico. In 1911 the Mexicans decided they had had enough prosperity and tyranny and drove Porfirio Díaz into Paris exile. Everybody around the lot began shooting at tyrants, stars, cactus, Chinamen, white foreigners, trains, oil-derricks; a few pot-shots were taken at God himself. The Díaz government, though it affected belief in laissez faire, had done a great deal of planning; the revolution did very little. The planning was done by a small claque of *Cientificos* (Scientists), who believed that they alone possessed the knowledge and ability to run government scientifically: in reality a scientific method of stealing, through monopolizing government funds and cornering handsome rake-offs by dishing out generous concessions to foreign capitalists. The brilliant leadership of the Cientificos was justified by a few statistics on railroads, extravagant public buildings in bad taste, diplomatic jobs to aristocrats, petty jobs to all the middle-class literate, and serfdom for the Indians and lower classes. It was a white Creole government, modeled along colonial conquest lines. At the second Pan-American congress held in Mexico City shortly after the turn of the century, Finance Minister Limantour ordered that all uniformed attendants must have white skins—this in a nation of dark-skinned people. Mexican life was excellently planned—for the large landowners, the Catholic hierarchy and the bureaucratic camorra.

This central despotism was buttressed up by all-powerful

state dynasties. The Terrazas clan, which had arbitrarily seized all the cattle of the vast state of Chihuahua, owned eight million acres and had held the life and death of Chihuahua citizens in its hands for over sixty years. Another dynasty ruled Campeche for nearly a century. The Torres clan in Sonora, enriched by selling Yaqui Indians into slavery and stealing lands, ruled over thirty years, Governor Cahuantzi of Tlaxcala twenty-six years. The story was the same in nearly all the states, a well-planned, self-perpetuating system of exploitation run by aged and cynical men.

Francisco Madero—spiritualist, vegetarian, wearer of queer clothes, rachitic, with a funny pear-shaped head—had been told by the planchette he would be president. Along with all these idealistic variants so obnoxious to the standardized acquisitive mind, Madero, in addition to listening to spooks, *believed in democracy*. Part of his belief in democracy was the idea of non-reëlection of presidents—Díaz had ruled a third of a century. By the ballot and limiting the duration of power, the people would get a new deal.

But he forgot realities, forgot that any enduring régime does not rest upon democratic rights but upon definite economic factors. He forgot that eighty-five per cent of the Mexican population was illiterate, that nearly two-thirds lived in serfdom, that the entire literate portion of the country, save the few members of the bureaucracy who had jumped on the revolutionary band-wagon, were against him. He had less reason for existing than Miliukof. Lacking any organized social backing, he tried to govern by goodness.

With the aid of Ambassador Henry Lane Wilson, who represented not so much the American government as the Guggenheim interests, goodness was shot in the back in 1913 by Victoriano Huerta, the Indian general, who butchered his way into power—and between flagons of cognac in El Globo cafés welded together his military dictatorship, rallied the remnants of the Científicos and the aristocrats to his side, made an alliance with English capital, and pretended to govern with terror to the plaudits of all resident democracy-loving Americans.

But Huerta was doomed. The 1910–11 Madero revolution had been almost an accident; but it had broken the iron bonds; and a gale soon whipped up from the hinterland which swept Huerta into exile in 1914. The peasants were growing more conscious, were demanding lands; labor was organizing; a religious struggle was impending.

The white-bearded, blue-spectacled Carranza led the new hosts. He was a practical, obstinate politician, representing the small middle-class group. He had been a Díaz politician, a small rancher—and under Díaz the small ranchers had suffered from the encroachments and competition of the large hacendados. But though he knew the country did not want Huerta, he had no concrete conviction what the country really did want.

This was the dilemma of the revolution. Most revolutions have been the chicks of recognizable ideological hens. Marx and Lenin hatched out the Bolshevik revolution. Pareto, Sorel, Corradini, Croce, Gentile and others, provided Mussolini his pedestal. In Mexico the Científicos had justified their rule by Comte, Spencer, and John Stuart Mill, but the Madero-Carranza revolution that ensued, had no comparable philosophical background.

Carranza soon found himself hedged in by the inarticulate peasant Indianism of Villa, the peasant movement of Zapata, the Red Battalions of Vera Cruz and Orizaba, the militarism of Obregón and others. The inevitable ensuing break-up saw the marching and counter-marching of weary hordes, the tearing up of railway tracks, the shooting up of trains, the splatter of machine guns—a wild orgy of blood-letting apparently without other purpose than lust for power, looting, and the free play of long-suppressed brutal passions.

Carranza won out through a hypocritical alliance with the militarism of Obregón, the Red Battalions, and the Socialistic henequén coöperative of Yucatán, in the hands of that fantastic son of Utopia, General Salvador Alvarado, who filled the Carranza Constitutionalist war-chest with many millions. But the program Carranza presented at the 1917 constitutional convention was more reactionary than that written into the 1857 Reform Constitution; no nationalization of sub-soil, no anti-church code, no labor code. He was beaten in the final drafting of the Magna Charta by the more radical proletarian forces and by other elements to be mentioned presently.

Most of the provisions of this disconcerting document, which now gave him the right to rule as legal President, he made no attempt to enforce. He did emphasize the nationalistic phases, bucked Wilson and the Monroe doctrine, bucked the oil companies, bucked the Vera Cruz occupation, bucked the Pershing expedition, but along with this anti-foreignism, he also bucked the peasant movement—his General, Pablo González, assassinated Zapata; he bucked the Red Battalions and the growing labor movement, bucked Obregón whose military genius had seated him on the cactus throne. To do this, Carranza had to junk constitutional methods and depend upon an ever narrowing clique of militarists, all the most disreputable of the upstart generals.

Sounder military elements won out. The bulky, one-armed Obregón, also a small rancher, saw that a reaction was coming against Carranza, just as it had come against Huerta, and making an alliance with the peasants, and a rather reluctant alliance with the proletarians, swept into power in 1920, sending Carranza scurrying to a loathsome death in the Puebla sierras.

Madero, still ringed around with his Científico family, had tried to straddle between peasants and the reactionary Catholic landed aristocracy. He hoped that a mild reform in political practices would lead finally to a tolerant and juster regeneration of his country. Carranza had represented the Mexican middle class, and though a white creole, was the representative of the mestizos, the men of mixed blood. Though he made a temporary alliance with the peasant and labor forces, it was not a grateful alliance; he broke it as soon as possible. Thereby he cut the economic roots of his power.

Obregón definitely linked up the middle class and the more proletarian elements, especially the peasants, shut the brakes on nationalism and tried to conciliate Washington. His successor, the lantern-jawed ex-school-teacher Calles, coming into office in 1924, ran definitely as a Labor Party candidate—shift from peasant to industrial worker, again a false move in a non-industrialized country basically rural in tradition and habit. Even more than Obregón, he stressed his alliance with middle-class elements, stressed the need to build up a national, non-foreign economy, with Mexican entrepreneurs. Obregón had already begun to make his peace with foreign capital; but Calles broke the reconciliation, started a new petroleum struggle. His very nationalistic tenets also precipitated a bitter Church-State struggle. But before he was through, Calles, like Obregón, made his peace with the United States and Morrow; i.e., he made his peace with definite American-capital groups —telephones, General Electric, and New York City banks—at the expense of other American interests. He broke with labor, declared the agrarian program a failure.

In other words, himself now an extremely wealthy man, he agreed to slice the melon between certain definite foreign interests and certain national capital interests—chiefly those of his own narrow political clique.

Obregón, in 1927–8 saw cannily that with leadership he could cut Calles' ground from under his feet. He also had become a wealthy entrepreneur. Definitely allied with the Standard Oil Company of California and other smaller American business elements, largely in the west, he saw the danger of severing all basic native support. While he went even further than Calles in disrupting the labor movement, he swung back to an alliance with the peasant.

Calles' program, before he finally broke with labor, revealed definite inconsistency. He had been tinkering with the idea of promoting native capitalistic development while at the same time battling for the cause of the industrial worker—better hours, higher wages, and a complicated system of regulation which bound industry hand and foot. Thus the nationally controlled industry he basically desired to promote was caught in the cogs of foreign competition—vast capital which had the power to ignore or circumvent the new labor legislation, punitive labor tactics, and the ferocity of the native bureaucracy, which can invent more ways to fleece legitimate business than any similar group in the world. Only Calles' and his friends' stakes, well-protected by their iron-clad control of the state and all the political machinery, have prospered.

Calles, by supporting the industrial worker, elevated his standards far above those of the peasants, and created a proletarian division that made of the industrial worker—a few hundred thousand in a nation of sixteen millions—a species of parasite on the peasant. The CROM, the official Calles labor organization battening at the tables of power, pretended to have peasant support, but in reality never had a single bona fide peasant leader among the members of the Grupo Acción, the inner camorra which ran the organization.

Obregón then utilized this peasant-worker split as a means to return to power. But he was assassinated in 1928, and the régime which he originally founded in 1920—now with only one outstanding leader, Calles—went on to another phase, that of unification. The basis for unification was laid by Portes

Gil, Provisional President from 1928–30. He had been a demagogic governor of Tamaulipas, whom Calles lifted into the presidency to conciliate the Obregónistas and to perform various disagreeable tasks, and then threw on the junk-heap. Portes Gil, who when Governor had presented all the peasant and workers' leagues of his state with pictures of Lenin, now, in power, used the Communists, syndicalists and other labor groups to smash the conservative CROM, now grown into an obstacle for Calles' purposes; then before the new radical elements could gather strength, Portes Gil ruthlessly smashed them with the police-power.

To replace these and other political organizations was founded the official "closed-car" National Revolutionist Party (PNR), an organization which monopolizes all the political activities of the country, a very chauvinistic, nationalistic, exclusivist corporation.

Before analyzing the present situation with the PNR at the helm, it is necessary to retrace our steps and consider more in detail the confused social forces, without a knowledge of which it is impossible to understand the whirling kaleidoscope of events during the past two decades.

1. THE ARMY. This is the most direct political power. During the hundred years of Mexico's independence, it has been the feudal cast which has clung most jealously to its prerogatives. Never a patriotic national organization, it has been built up around personal loyalties. In times of foreign crisis, it has usually betrayed the fatherland, and it has served chiefly as an instrument with which to assault the power—the Praetorian guard tradition. Mexico has more generals than any other country on the face of the globe, and with few exceptions, though occasionally political and social considerations have weighed in the balance, their main motives have been greed for power and wealth. All governments (those of Madero and Lerdo de Tejada less obviously so) have been military dictatorships.

2. THE CHURCH. The Church, though shorn of direct political power, still exerts great influence. But recently it kept five states in armed uproar, and it consistently fights the educational efforts of the government.

3. THE BUREAUCRACY. The Mexican bureaucracy, for the size and population of the country, is a top-heavy group, largely reactionary however much it mouths the revolutionary phrases of the moment. Like the army, it is treacherous, ideologically undefined, constantly intriguing. Ever its ear is to the ground, and its plots are usually the pivot from which swing governmental crises. Lerdo de Tejada, many years ago, called it "the most wolfish in America."

4. RACIAL ELEMENTS.

a. The Indians. Variously estimated at from thirty-five to fifty per cent of the population. Eighty-five per cent of the population revolves in the rural Indian habitat. The revolution, because of the need for security of life and property, has accelerated urbanization. The Indians are villagers, hacienda peons, parish priests, workers in a few industries.

b. The mestizos. The mestizos for the most part are mixed Spanish and Indian, predominantly the latter. They are small ranchers, army officers, bureaucrats, city priests, minor employees, white-collar slaves, teachers, lawyers, doctors.

c. The Creoles. Native born descendants of pure-blooded foreigners. They make up the aristocracy, the large proprietors, formerly the high offices of the Church (now passing into mestizo hands), the diplomats, and they occupy an occasional cabinet post. They are conservative, even reactionary, often fanatically Catholic, anti-foreign.

The descendants of foreigners other than Spanish, are known as *New Creoles,* because most of the English, American, French, German and other nationalities arrived after Independence. The New Creoles are usually mild Catholics, fairly liberal, with the psychology of modern *laissez faire.* They made up the bulk of the Científicos, intent upon attracting foreign capital; and many of them participated first in the Juárez reform movement. Quite a few of them were found on the side of the recent revolution.

These three race groups, located at different economic levels, complicate the pattern, and their cultural and economic conflicts, while often obscured by other issues, is constantly operative.

5. ECONOMIC FACTORS.

a. The Landed Aristocracy. This group achieved its maximum power at the close of the Díaz rule. Now broken and scattered, it is recovering some of its energies. A new landed group, headed by the successful men of the revolution, Calles, Saenz, Portes Gil, Amaro, Almazán, and others, is arising.

b. The Middle Class. An unformed group, largely mestizo,

slavishly imitative of European and aristocratic practices. With
the revolution it has become increasingly nationalistic.

   c. *The Peasant Movement*. Unorganized, inchoate, its aims
undefined at the beginning of the revolution, it gained military
leadership with Zapata, and finally with Obregón's aid, civilian
organization in 1920. It has enlisted under various banners,
has never really achieved national cohesion, and is now split
into many factions.

   d. *The Labor Movement*. Originally anarchistic and syn-
dicalistic, it began to organize under Madero, continued doing
so more or less unnoticed under Huerta, achieved military
significance in Carranza's 1915 struggle against Villa. It was
swung over from syndicalism to American Federation of Labor
standards in 1919 under the leadership of Morones into the
Regional Confederation of Mexican Labor (CROM). While
all trends of labor thought have at one time or another found
organized expression in Mexico, the bulk of the movement—
the CROM—crystallized behind Calles in 1924. The railway
workers remained independent and pro-Obregón. The CROM
was smashed by Portes Gil in 1928–9. Subsequently he smashed
the other organizations. They are now skeletons.

   e. *Native Capital*. This is beginning to show a shift toward
industrial activities, chiefly in the hands of the political leaders
of the revolution, Calles, Saenz, Almazán, etc., who have been
aided by their control of the State, thus able to favor themselves with special dispensations, secure exaggerated tariffs,
special rulings and concessions.

   f. *Foreign Capital*. Most of the wealth of the country is still
controlled by foreign capital, American and English leading.
The revolution has greatly curtailed the prerogatives of foreign
investors. Foreign enterprise is in the doldrums. Little new
foreign capital has come in, although apparently as an aftermath
of a personal pact between Calles and Morrow, the Electric
Bond and Share Company has acquired most of the light and
power resources of the country. The National City Bank and the
Chase National Bank have made their appearance; also a new
telephone company allied with I. T. and T.

   In this welter of conflicting interests and the resultant armed
turmoil, it now becomes clear that the tendency toward the
rise of a native capitalist group with exaggerated nationalistic
feelings, has won the upperhand. Labor has been thrown concessions, which little by little have been rescinded; the peasants

have been given some land, a more meager allotment than all
the furor might have indicated; popular education has been
extended, though many another Latin American country can
show a better record.

The new governing group is not powerful enough to control
the country without alliances, and Calles has played a masterly
game of making concessions to various conflicting elements,
but it cannot be said that the final results are yet clearly discernible. The old alignments still persist in rather nebulous
form. The northern native entrepreneurs, represented by Almazán, Saenz, Pérez Treviñá, centering largely in the industrial center, Monterrey, keeping company with the iron and
steel interests of that city, represent the major tendency we
have described. But Cedillo, military commandant of San Luís
Potosí, Tejeda, Governor of Vera Cruz, Cárdenas, Governor
of Michoacan, Canibal, Governor of Tabasco, and some others,
still make a strong bid for radical support.

General Amaro represents the military elements, and the
present cabinet is dominated by army elements, who are holding the balance of power between the factions. Calles, for all
his constant talk about laws, institutions, and the overthrow of
government by military *caudillaje,* has never lost sight of or
control of the major political factor—the army.

Thus while the scene is still turbid, the outlines of a strenuous Fascist régime are clearly discernible. While parallels are
always dangerous, there is much similarity in the development
of the Mexican régime and the Fascist rule in Italy. Fascism
was compounded of four major elements: the *arditi,* or demo-
bilized shock-troops, the syndicalists, the middle-class punitive
squadri, and the extreme blue-shirt nationalists. In Mexico,
the revolutionary régime rode into power through the military,
a labor and peasant alliance, and the middle-class bureaucracy,
and in it was ever latent a violent nationalistic reaction against
the lavish concessions made to foreigners by the Díaz régime.

This last needs some comment. The Mexican revolution has
been credited with being more radical and more proletarian
than at any time it ever was. In most respects it was a decidedly
reactionary revolution. The false impression of kinship with the
Russian experiment has been carried abroad because of ignorance of the Mexican legal and social structure. For the Mexican revolution, having a strong anti-foreign virus, attempted
to reëstablish many native laws and systems which the Díaz

government had radically overthrown. In the question of minerals, the Spanish law had always distinguished between surface and sub-soil rights; and the sub-soil always belonged to the Crown, a conservative and age-old system rather than modern or socialistic. Díaz overthrew this ancient sub-soil concept with regard to petroleum; the revolution partially restored it. The restoration of the *ejidos* or village commons, enclosed since 1857, is another example in point—an attempt to reëstablish a system that existed even before the Spanish conquest. This has been done without too much regard for local needs, large-scale crops, or the wisest regard for rounded national economy.

That proletarian and socialistic doctrines became entangled with these efforts is significant but not of too much moment. Essentially the Mexican revolution has been Fascist, with trimmings of socialism and French revolutionary sophisms.

The machinery for channelizing these Fascist manifestations was late in appearing, not until the 1928 National Revolutionary Party (PNR), founded by Calles, Portes Gil, and Saenz. While many of the revolutionary symptoms have appeared from below, this organization was imposed from above by Calles, aided by the revolutionary barons, by the militarists and the bureaucrats, much in the style that Primo de Rivera founded the Union Patriotica in Spain, composed of feudal landed proprietors, a few industrialists, Catholics, and aristocrats. The PNR is, however, a much more official organization than even the Fascist Party in Italy. It is sustained by forced contributions from all government employees—arbitrarily collected from their payrolls. Thus it is like the Holy Roman Empire of Bryce, neither holy, nor Roman nor an Empire, but merely a governmental bureau of political control. The leaders, imposed from above as in Fascist Italy, discipline the members, purge all local organizations, and determine who shall control them. It is a very artificial group, both for the reason given above, and because of the fact that the real political factor remains the army.

Yet the PNR has developed a maximum of centralized power. Every governor must be a member. The Chamber and Senate are one hundred per cent PNR bodies; no representatives of other parties or points of view are seated. (One Laborite was seated this last session to give the appearance of legitimate opposition.) The press is carefully throttled. Political opponents are eliminated, the extreme measure, aside from occasional assassination, being seizure by the military authorities and shipment without trial to the penal islands. In other words the PNR monopolizes all political expression. This means that the régime in power, which means Calles, finances and directs the party. Such is the present political situation.

In other words, the new ideology of the group in control is enforced by traditional Mexican political methods, which were wrought to their highest perfection under Díaz. Whatever its aims, the PNR does not differ from the Científico group under Díaz, save that it represents a more definite and obvious machine than Díaz ever devised.

I have already indicated the veiled Fascist origins of the Mexican revolutionary movement. In both organization and aims it has ended up in an exaggerated and scarcely veiled Fascism. In organization, as we have seen, it is more Fascist than the Fascisti; in aims, however much it stresses rabid nationalism, it falls short of Italian Fascist practices, for the Fascist there, while he believes in the hierarchical system, seeks, theoretically at least, a complete and full expression of all the classes in the social life of the country, subordinated to the needs and purposes of the strong state—Prussianism savored with emotional mysticism. While the present Mexican régime stresses nation-autonomy and national rights and anti-foreignism on every and all occasions, rather is the state an instrument for protecting not so much the emerging Mexican bourgeoisie as the new political elements who have recently entered the bourgeoisie folds. The state is thus used for their attempted monopolization of the economic life of the country. The progress they have contributed toward the introduction of modern industrial enterprise is offset by its monopolistic character and the strangling of native enterprise not within the political fold of the elect.

Thus, while the cry of national autonomy and economic independence and the throwing off of the yoke of foreign capital has a legitimate basis, this is far from being, under the circumstances, a bona fide patriotic expression. On the one hand, it has degenerated into a narrow boxerism, a hatred of all things foreign, on the other it serves to protect the new economic interests of "the barons of the revolution"—a phrase not original with me, but coined by Francisco Bulnes, to designate the new economic and military overlords who emerged with the Tuxtépec revolution when Porfirio Díaz came into power. Thus, the present exaggerated nationalistic propaganda in Mexico is a smoke-screen to hide the failure of the revolution on the more popular side, the failure of the agrarian program, the baulking of proletarian aspirations, the decline in interest in popular education, the usurpation of all political activities by a narrow clique.

Everything foreign has become inimical to Mexico. Not only have the immigration bars been put up so strictly as practically to exclude all outsiders, but an incessant barrage is kept up in the newspapers against the *Ausländer*. Foreigners, resident and visiting, are harassed in every possible way, and a definite campaign has been waged against them. Small to begin with, it is hard to see how the foreign colonies could endanger the cultural independence of Mexico—an attitude as boneheaded as that of the Californians toward the Japanese. The Chinese, the largest group next to the Spanish, have been bitterly persecuted, especially on the west coast. They have been robbed, assassinated, driven out of the country in droves in the most illegal and arbitrary manner, most unfortunate, because the Chinese have been beneficial, hard-working, sober, modest in their living standards. But the treatment of Austrian nationals in the Tyrol by the exalted Fascisti has been tame compared to the treatment of the Chinese in northwest Mexico.

A similar campaign has been carried on against the Jews, originally invited by Calles to come and settle in the country. They have been mobbed and their business sacked, despite the fact that they have made many valuable contributions to Mexico's economic life.

In other words, the shift of American policy from Kellogg's browbeating to Morrow's kindly smile, however desirable from the standpoint of decency in foreign relations, has given the Mexicans a bit of swellhead. Since Morrow's arrival they have been wallowing in an orgy of self-important nationalism.

It is very desirable, I suppose, for a weak nation to discover its self-importance, its own resources and capacities, to feel it can run its own destinies. But it is not wise even for a powerful nation to become too dazzled by its own importance, but such headlines as "Mexico asked to settle Manchurian dispute," because a Mexican is given a seat on the futile Geneva committee borders on the ridiculous, and indicates the pride-before-the-fall trend of all Mexican news these days. In other words, the political *nouveaux riches* of Mexico have given the country the bright bauble of national hatred instead of tools with which to take advantage of the present moment of national integration and thus become truly independent.

And Mexico needs tools, needs technical knowledge, capital, sanitation, if it is to carve out its economic independence upon which any enduring system of social justice must rest. The goal is still far distant, and it is not brought nearer by anti-foreignism fostered by the present leaders attempting to monopolize as much of Mexico's national wealth for themselves as possible.

Thus we come back to our original thesis—revolution *by whom and for whom?* Mexico has been afraid to face that question and has fallen into the pit of a narrow Fascist nationalism which will cost her dear. Revolution by reconstruction! Revolution, dictatorship—its inevitable concomitant—is a costly and cruel experiment for any nation. But when greed and political blindness shove a nation headlong into such a course, it is well that the people of that nation know beforehand the answer to the question—dictatorship *by whom and for whom.*

Dictatorships are the order of the day, as they have always been throughout human history whenever an older economic order was breaking down. Democracy was born with the rise of the capitalist system and proved a workable instrumentality so long as the rapidly developing capitalist productive methods offered more political and economic freedom for the masses than the previous feudal system. The eighteenth century dictatorships which protected the bourgeoisie in their control of the state measured out rations of political liberty to the masses in return for their support against the medieval barons. The new bourgeoisie, through dictatorship, later through democracy, perfected their economic and social control. To-day, not democracy, effectively directed by press, radio, and job dispensations, menaces the existing order, for even where a definite labor party assumes power, the MacDonalds are soon attracted by the industrialist and leisured classes and become serviceable instruments for patching up the broken parts of the existing system. The Socialists—who lost their moral significance in 1914—serve admirably as shock absorbers for the upward thrust of the proletariat, and only when they fail in this rôle are they cast aside—as in Italy, confronted by the factory seizures when Mussolini rode into power.

Both Socialists and Fascists are holding outworn ramparts of nationalism and as they advance in political influence become increasingly nationalistic. They serve to hold the national ramparts while international capitalism reforms its ranks along a new and more indestructible line. The revolutionary enemy remains divided, bickering over national concerns, while the new world empires of production and distribution are being formed largely quite beyond the power of the present political systems even to control.

Roughly speaking, two types of dictatorships have appeared since the War—Communist and Fascist. The communist dictatorship has resulted from the complete failure of the capitalist mechanism in a country in which immature capitalism was utilizing older feudal relationships. The Soviet system in Russia has made a clean sweep of the older economies.

The Fascist dictatorship represents a last resort to salvage the existing order through discipline, the substitution of a class-conscious proletarian organization with a national syndicalist group willing to make sacrifices to preserve a state which remains in bourgeois hands, yet which through stern measures prevents much unemployment and by state aid continues the expansive tendencies of capitalism.

A variant of these two types appears in colonial countries such as Cuba, Mexico, Venezuela, and elsewhere, where capitalism utilizes its ancient feudal enemies and provides the new native bourgeoisie with a share of national wealth in return for holding proletarian forces in check. The political and economic situation in such countries is still further confused by racial and cultural conflicts. Our theory of Nordic superiority also tends to throw our support to the white Creole oppressors of Latin America, who are largely of European origin and hence more akin to our own conceptions of capitalistic organization.

So long as Obregón and Calles showed indications of making their alliance with proletarian and Indian forces rather than with feudal and foreign capitalistic forces, recognition was withheld their governments; only when they became members of the new native bourgeoisie and turned back to the original democratic slogans of the 1910-20 revolution, abandoning their more radical programs of social amelioration of the masses, did they find favor in Washington. Morrow's task, by that time, became quite simple, and his success preordained.

The super-nationalistic propaganda of the present Mexican

régime has not prevented the Electric Bond and Share Company from absorbing practically all of the light and power resources of Mexico, has not prevented the penetration of the National City and Chase National banks, the international telephone corporation, nor is it likely to hold in check any of the enterprises now forming their international lines of defense.

Calles thus becomes no more than the Mexican version of MacDonald fulfilling the historic rôle described above. Ideologically he is indistinguishable from his more brutal, less imaginative contemporaries, Machado in Cuba and Gómez in Venezuela. He merely represents this century instead of last century, is less feudal and pays more obeisance to the gods of democracy.

The Calles tendency has already found more than local expression in Latin America, and it is bound to be recurrent against more brutal past-century dictatorships, as was that of Díaz in Mexico, as was that of Leguía in Peru. The latest Madero-Obregón-Calles apostle in Latin America of outstanding significance has been Haya de la Torre of Peru, who founded the so-called Apra organization—a nationalistic, anti-imperialistic, pseudo-Socialist, pseudo-Fascist organization, based upon class collaboration, stressing democracy.

To-day, Haya de la Torre is suffering an unjust imprisonment in Peru; the more brutal type of dictatorship has won out again. But Haya represents the inevitable trend of Liberal socialistic movements in colonial America, which begin with an intellectual endeavor to combat foreign capitalism by a left alliance with the submerged native races and classes, a greater stressing of economic reforms, education, and democracy, but which are soon reabsorbed by the native bourgeoisie, usually with an opportunistic alliance with some phase of foreign capitalism. Haya happens to have lived in England, and the right wing of Aprism, which he now represents, has made an alliance with British capital, in fact Haya's fare was paid back to Peru by such interests. Had he lived in the United States, capitalist rivals would have equally supported him in his recent struggle.

Thus such tendencies as Aprism and Callism, while resulting in far more liberal and progressive types of dictatorship, inevitably become—realistically speaking—but bartering, nationalistic leverages for the greater participation of the new native bourgeoisie in the capitalistic expansion. It serves for a minor widening of national economic autonomy, but no solution of native problems.

It is too soon yet to designate this type of dictatorship, which Washington now shows a tendency to recognize as opposed to the Machado-Díaz-Gómez types, as Aprist dictatorship, especially as in Peru that tendency has been temporarily defeated. But some new phraseology should be invented to designate modern colonial dictatorships from Fascist or Communist forms.

From the foregoing it can be appreciated why the fundamental objectives of the Mexican revolution were doomed to abortion. The proximity of Mexico to the United States, feudal and military evils inherent in the Mexican social structure, the confusing ethnic and cultural conflict, the immaturity of industrial development and its subordination to American control all were determinative. Another factor was the small size of the factory worker bloc. The factory proletariat, for all practical purposes, allied themselves with the military and bourgeois elements at the expense of the peasant. Naturally this contributed to the more rapid junking of the agrarian program, a process already under way when Morrow arrived and which his presence hastened to completion.

Mexico, far more than Russia, must decide between rapid industrialization or a development of a peasant-controlled rural economy. The former inevitably means the opening of the doors to foreign capital on a large scale, for the leadership, wealth, and bases are lacking for autonomist industrial expansion, not to mention lack of knowledge. Neither proletarian or state-capitalist programs are likely to be successful however idealistically invoked. Furthermore the economic dependence of Mexico upon the United States is too great.

The labor of socialization in Mexico should begin rather at the peasant end. The mass of Mexico's population sleeps on home-woven straw *petates,* makes sandals out of rawhide, wears home-made hats, and requires—thanks to the climate—but a few yards of cheap *manta* cloth a year for clothing. These people—Indians or mestizos in the Indian habitat—are not users of civilized goods; and in the case of rapid industrialization, they provide a mass of ignorant labor easily exploited, for they are then dislocated from their native environment.

But in relation to their native environment, they are far more hardy, self-reliant and wise. They are soil-conscious and know their true relation to the soil in a productive and economic sense. They were the first to take up arms under Villa and Zapata; they were the last to lay down arms; and they achieved temporary national organization in the National Agrarian Party and the Mexican Agrarian League. They are further united by a deep-seated racial consciousness against their economic and political exploiters. Nor do their demands run so immediately foul of foreign capital and the American State Department. And for this reason, their gains have been more permanent, and what is left of the original political movement which overthrew Díaz, still exhibits itself in rural education and other efforts in behalf of the peasant.

The technological efforts of Manuel Gamio, as exhibited in Teotihuacán, to scientifically adapt the native peasant environment to the shock of the machine-age and permit him to protect his culture and elevate his standards while the process was going on, have terminated; but they are still being carried on in some small degree in diluted form by the rural schools and the efforts of Moisés Saenz in Michoacán. And about a million heads of families have a new economic leverage in the reëstablishment of the village *ejidal* or communal economy. And in the reopening of large tropical agrarian enterprise, the Indian peasant, more in a proletarian rôle, has learned to protect himself despite the destruction of his national organization by the Calles régime—by local organization and if necessary by the use of arms. Until the peasant becomes more potent, more politically conscious and with higher standards of education and living conditions, anything other than an Aprist dictatorship in Mexico is impossible.

It is fascinating to note that the only cultural products of the hybrid revolution in Mexico which has now ended up in Aprism, has been concerned with the proletarian, peasant and Indian renascence. While literature, except for a few writers such as Maples Arce, Lizt Arzubide, Cruz and others, who have grasped the sociological implications, has been concerned with chronicles of the mass military movements, particularly in the north, as set forth by Azucla and Guzmán, painting, the major product of the revolution, has definitely concerned itself with the deeper racial and class struggles. Diego Rivera, José Clemente Orozco, David Siqueiros, and the other most forceful painters of the new epoch, began their work as members of a painters' labor syndicate and have alternated between the pen, the rifle and revolutionary politics. In the aggregate it is perhaps the most vital and original painting in the modern world. With this has gone a revitalizing of the native handicrafts and a strengthening of the artistic potentialities of the former hacienda serfs. When the forces which generated these two great tendencies are really released, a vast reservoir of ancient but defiled creative purposefulness will be purified and drawn upon for an artistic reinterpretation of life and human freedom which will be completely lost to the world if Mexico's fate is to be crushed under the heel of imperialism and crammed into the mold of a foreign culture.

PART TWO

THE AFTERMATH OF THE
GERMAN REVOLUTION

THE German Revolution began on the 16th of October, 1918. What followed was but the inevitable consequence, November 9th but the climax of forces set in motion on that fateful day, when the Reichstag—against the opposition of only the Conservative Party—amended Art. 15 of the Reich Constitution with the significant clause that "every official transaction of the Chancellor must be presented to the Reichstag for approval," that the "Chancellor shall be responsible for every political act of the Emperor within his rights and privileges under the Constitution," and that "the Chancellor and his representatives shall be responsible to the Bundesrat and the Reichstag for all official acts." The right to declare war and make peace was transferred from the Emperor to the Reichstag. The Emperor was removed as Chief-in-Command of the Army and Navy by the provision that appointments and dismissals of navy officers must bear the signature of the Chancellor, those of army officers the signatures of the War Ministers of the state army contingents. The latter were made directly responsible to the Bundesrat and the Reichstag in all matters pertaining to the administration of their contingents.

It is important for an understanding of the aftermath of the German Revolution to appreciate the full portent of these changes. Under the monarchy the power of the Reichstag had been more figurative than real. The army and navy had been under the absolute control of the Emperor and his military advisors. His had been the power over war and peace; the

181

Reichstag met at his pleasure and governed with a Cabinet of his choosing that was responsible to him alone. In 1848 Prussian Democrats had fought and Prussian workers shed their blood in vain for full and equal suffrage and democratic rule. Now, seventy years later, democracy fell into the lap of the people as a gift from its military rulers, was forced on a surprised and reluctant bourgeoisie as an emergency measure by Ludendorff, General Quartermaster of the army and virtual dictator after September 1916, when no one else dared accept responsibility for the armies at the front.

True, this change in the Constitution was but the means to an end. The Allies had made it clear that they would deal only with a "democratic Germany." Ludendorff's and Hindenburg's insistence on a new régime were therefore necessary preliminaries for armistice negotiations. The military camarilla never for a moment doubted its ability to regain its abandoned positions. Certainly nothing in the attitude of the Reichstag indicated anything but a pathetic eagerness to continue in implicit obedience to the military machine.

But, once started in their course, events moved much more swiftly than these generals had foreseen. The Allies proved less tractable than the deluded Germans had imagined so that both Ludendorff and Hindenburg were prepared to break off negotiations and to "fight to the last man." Fortunately for Germany their word had ceased to be law. Prince Max von Baden, appointed Chancellor by the Emperor, with a Cabinet in which were represented the Social Democratic Party (Scheidemann and Bauer), the Centrist Party, the Progressive Party and the Left Wing of the National-Liberal Party, accepted the proffered armistice terms and put an end to the World War.

The General Staff had resisted submission to the demands of the Allies for another reason: it trembled before the social revolution at its doors and hoped to avert it by a last desperate rallying of the country's forces against the enemy to drown the threatening insurrection of the masses at home and the army at the front in a paroxism of patriotic intoxication. In his *Journal,* under the date of October 31, written under the impression of an interview with the new Cabinet Ministers, Ludendorff admitted this with utmost candor: "Clearly the Government was determined to give up the fight. It was prepared to sacrifice everything—to accept any terms, even the most outrageous—as a price for peace. To a number of gentlemen who interviewed me after the meeting I could only say that all seemed lost and that I believed Bolshevism inevitable."

At the insistence of Prince Max, Ludendorff was replaced by Groener. Hindenburg remained. He played the game astutely, using his tremendous popularity—a popularity that was merely heightened by his apparent compliance with the will of the people—to work slowly but surely for the restoration of monarchy and military supremacy.

It was in no small degree due to his influence and that of other Conservatives who had been left in high government office that the new order changed so little in the life of the nation. At the head of the new "government of the German people" stood a Hohenzollern Prince. The state of siege that had laid the country in chains during four long years of war remained in force. Public affairs continued to be administered by local Generalkommandos. The Reichstag, instead of exercising its power, adjourned. In mortal fear of the labor masses it dared not use the power that had fallen into its hand; even the Social Democrats shared Ludendorff's fear of the Bolshevist menace.

This state of affairs was revealed in its full significance when the High Seas Fleet, penned up at Kiel since the naval defeat at Jutland, received secret orders from the General Navy Command to put to sea. This order had been issued without knowledge of the government, to prevent the discontinuance of U-Boat warfare and to make one last attempt to forestall humiliating defeat by a daring surprise attack on the British fleet. The crew saw through the mad intent of their officers before the fleet was ready to leave the harbor. Fires were drawn and the men refused to obey orders. This mutiny saved thousands of lives and years of bloodshed, yet 600 of their number were thrown into jail to quell the uprising. Great demonstrations in Kiel and Hamburg followed. The first Soldiers Council was elected; the dock workers struck in sympathy with their comrades on the ships and elected Workers Councils that made common cause with the mutineers; Kiel was in the hands of revolutionary workers.

Thus far the national government had allowed matters to take their course. Now it sent the Social Democrat Gustav Noske and Conrad Hausmann of the German Progressive Party to Kiel to bring about an understanding that would prevent the conflagration from spreading, sent them with instructions from State Secretary Scheidemann that were astonishing in their naïveté. "Tell the soldiers and workers . . . that exemption from punishment shall be granted to all who have committed breaches of discipline . . . provided the men return to their usual duties and surrender all arms and ammunition seized by them." On November 6th, Hamburg too was in the hands of the revolutionists. The uprising was spreading from city to city —all Germany stood in arms against the old régime. Berlin alone held back, although it had been for months the hotbed of the revolutionary movement and its workers were deeply embittered. Their leaders hesitated, however; they knew that Berlin, the stronghold of the military, would not be taken without a struggle and they wished to be prepared before striking the first blow. Social Democratic functionaries were being admonished by their leaders to remain calm—to prevent bloodshed. The Emperor would abdicate within a few days. The military Kommandant of Berlin, General von Linsingen, issued a proclamation "forbidding the organization of Soldiers and Workers Councils as illegal." Plants and factories were guarded; soldiers patrolled the streets; labor leaders were arrested, but too late to check the rising tide. Still the Social Democratic Party hoped that the abdication of the Emperor and the Crown Prince would save the October Constitution and the Constitutional Monarchy.

But the flaming up of the Revolution in Bavaria with Kurt Eisner at the helm under the leadership of the Independent Social Democratic Party, which had seceded from the SDP in 1916, made further procrastination impossible. The Berlin factories were already electing Workers, and the garrisons, Soldiers Councils. The latter placed themselves under majority socialist leadership and refused to go with the Spartacus group which, together with the group of the "Revolutionary Foremen" (Obleute), who were strongly influenced by Anarcho-Syndicalists, had up to that time conducted the propaganda for the Revolution.

By such incidents is the fate of nations decided. The stand of the Soldiers Councils in Berlin determined the course the German Revolution was henceforth to take. From that time on it moved increasingly in Social Democratic paths, away from social upheaval, in the direction of bourgeois reconstruction that left the economic foundation of the capitalist system unchanged. As yet the fate of the nation hung in the balance. The Emperor was still at Spaa, torn between the conflicting advice of his military counselors. At the urging of his Cabinet, who saw the masses getting beyond control unless some decisive action were taken at once, Max von Baden forced the Emperor's hand by announcing the Kaiser's abdication two days before it actually occurred, and appointed Fritz Ebert Chancellor in his own stead, refusing to comply with the latter's request, however, that he assume the Regency. The Majority Socialists found themselves in an unenviable position. The time for compromise was past and the Party faced the alternative either of declaring a Socialist Republic and, together with the Independent Social Democratic Party and the Spartacus group, forming a revolutionary government, or of establishing a bourgeois Republic which would leave the governmental and economic system of the nation essentially unchanged. Consistent with its attitude during the entire war, it chose the latter.

The Berlin Workers and Soldiers Councils comprised that portion of the population which participated actively in the Revolution. The latter consisted, in the main, of men who had had no contact with the labor movement and had neither sympathy nor understanding for its aims. It was a foregone conclusion that they would oppose the efforts of the Workers Councils—those workers who had been intimately connected with the class conscious organizations of labor, to effect a radical change in the social and economic structure of the nation. The Soldiers Councils were the products of a military revolt that had its beginning at Kiel and had spread to the armies at the front. They were motivated by war weariness and discouragement, their program: immediate peace and the destruction of the power of the officers of the Imperial army. They were not interested in social theorizing and became a hindrance to revolutionary development. The union of the Soldiers with the Workers Councils decided the fate of the Revolution. It set very decided limits to the possibilities for its development toward the Left, and none at all to coöperation with bourgeois society.

The congress of the Soldiers and Workers Councils on November 10th, elected a Council of Commissars which it entrusted with the formation of a new government. It consisted of Ebert, Scheidemann and Landsberg (SPD) and Haase, Dittmann and Barth (ISDP). Karl Liebknecht, who at first expressed his willingness to participate and together with Scheidemann signed the first Governmental decree, withdrew on the same day on the urgent advice of Rosa Luxemburg and Leo Jogiches who convinced him that the new creation was not a representative Socialist Government but a reincarnation of the old Reichstag majority. Centrists and Liberals were being left in control of the most important Ministries. The Centrist Secretary of State Erzberger was conducting armistice negotiations and Dr. Preuss of the Progressive Party continued as Minister of the Interior. The country's foreign and national policies were being actively influenced, if not actually determined, by hold-overs from the old régime while the People's Commissars bore responsibility for their actions.

The Independent Social Democratic Party had entered the government with great misgivings to save as much as possible for the Revolution, but resigned at the end of December. It was the hesitating and often confused policy of this Party that was partly responsible for the failure of the revolutionary elements to gain the upper hand. The Party consisted of widely divergent elements, pacifists like Ströbel, Dittmann and Crispien and social revolutionists and whole-hearted supporters of the Russian November Revolution like Ledebour, Haase and Zetkin. It was this lack of a homogeneous conception that left this promising movement without the force that only unanimity of purpose can give.

The Spartacus group, under the leadership of Rosa Luxemburg, Karl Liebknecht, Paul Levi, Franz Mehring, Dr. Ernst Meyer, Paul Froehlich, August Thalheimer and others, had seceded from the Independents in protest against their vacillations, and on December 30th, 1918, established the Communist Party of Germany. Had the Minority Social Democrats, who were very popular with the masses, taken their stand with the Spartacus group in the critical month of the German Revolution, the power of the military camarilla might have been broken and the apparatus of the old line bureaucracy eliminated. As it was they consented, with much unwillingness, to the calling of a Constitutional Convention, although it was evident from the start that, with the political complexion of the people and the influence of the Church and the capitalist press, the election for such a convention must produce a bourgeois majority.

To place the responsibility for the collapse of the Revolution on the Majority Socialist leaders alone would ignore the forces that were at work in post-war Germany. The working class had just learned from the Russian Revolution that a comparatively small but aim-conscious minority can lead a proletarian revolution through its first stages to political power. Why, then, did it pursue exactly the opposite course? The answer is not hard to find.

The Russian worker, before the 1917 Revolution, was almost wholly without working-class political experience. He went into action blindly, sweeping ever-increasing masses into the fight with the elemental force of his enthusiasm. He hated the bourgeoisie as the merciless oppressor with a hatred that neither reasoned nor philosophized. He had lived a life of want and degradation and still bore the chains of a serfdom that was legendary in Germany's most backward East Elbien provinces. To him the famous words of Marx: "You have nothing to lose but your chains," had a very tangible meaning. Moreover their experiences in the Revolution of 1905 were a compass that directed their leaders in 1917. Theirs was a wild revolt that expressed itself in numberless spectacular and dramatic encounters—a revolution in keeping with their entire historic background.

Conditions in Germany were fundamentally different. After the Franco-German War, capitalism had advanced with mighty strides. The Social Democratic Party as the representative of a mass movement arose in Germany and gained official standing sooner than in any other country. It brought forth a trade union movement which, particularly in the first decades of its existence, achieved outstanding success in the industrial struggle for a higher standard of living. The German worker was the most thoroughly schooled worker in the world. He was what Bebel called "der Arbeiter in gehobener Lebensstellung." That he should feel himself an integral part of the capitalist state which gave him a fairly comfortable existence—though he still used the Socialist phraseology—is humanly understandable, particularly if we remember that both his unions and the Social Democratic Party became less revolutionary and more reformistic as the years went by. Economically and emotionally the German worker had become a petty bourgeois who used revolutionary phrases but combined them with no concept of revolutionary action. The doctrines for which Eduard Bernstein had almost been read out of the Party in the early nineties had supplanted the theories of Karl Marx and Friedrich Engels.

The German worker came to look upon strikes as something to be avoided because they depleted the treasury of his organization. He carried this Cunctator Fabius policy into the political movement, trembling at the idea of open conflict that might bring defeat. It is quite comprehensible that the irresolute evasiveness of such tactics should appeal to the masses so much more strongly than the contumacious methods of Spartacus. Those most glorious martyrs of the German Revolution—Karl Liebknecht and Rosa Luxemburg—actually found it impossible to secure mandates to the crucial Congress of the Workers and Soldiers Councils in Berlin and were refused the floor when they appeared there to address the meeting.

Yet it would be insufficient to explain the inadequacy of the German proletariat in its great hour without saying a few words concerning its Socialist leadership. Unless we comprehend the motives that compelled them, the attitude of their Party must remain unaccountable. More or less consciously their politics had been based on the firm conception of the German people as an entity and was, in that light, bourgeois and anti-marxian. They fought for the people, not for a class. They were convinced—and in this were at one with Democrats of all shades of opinion—that the German people is the arbiter of its destiny and that it will find its way through parliamentary political action to a socialized state. An invincible faith in the effectiveness of its educational work in the political field and in the essential democracy of industry that will ultimately evolve society from the capitalist to the socialist state was its dominant characteristic.

The Weimar Constitution was the fruit of this perverted conception. Unquestionably it represented an advance over the Germany of the Kaiser. It put an end to state particularism with its outgrowth of reaction. It gave every citizen of Germany the possibility of participating in political life and simplified control over parties and party leaders by the public. But the organized workers who had hoped for socialization of at least the basic industries, received stones for bread. Instead of economic relief they were given democratic reforms which the possessing class soon learned to use as shrewdly as they had safeguarded their interests in the days of the Hohenzollern. That political self-reliance which is the life-blood of democracy had never been developed in the German people, and its middle class lacked the democratic traditions of the English and French.

To appreciate the hold that reaction has always had, and has to-day, on a large part of the German population, it is necessary to deal briefly with the somewhat hackneyed subject of German militarism as the impulse that has been so powerful a force in the history of that people. German schools were and are, with the emphasis they place on their nation's military grandeur in the past, and its military impotence in the present, hothouses of jingo-patriotism. German home life was, and frequently still is, a monarchy within four walls. At an age when the normal youth cuts loose from school and family domination, generation after generation of young Teutons were conscripted into military service. Two years of unquestioning obedience and mental dependence, two years in which social consciousness found its only outlet in the stultifying apparatus of a mechanized nationalism, two years in which the weal and woe of the individual depended on the whims of his immediate and remote superiors, could not but leave an indelible mark on the national character, a mark that the fourteen years since conscription was abolished have not been able to erase.

Obviously the bourgeoisie was not interested in combating a system that so completely served its interests, particularly when so large a part of the working class population had imbibed a love for the "Kaiser's Rock" with their mothers' milk. Nor was the labor movement free from its taint. After two years of standing at attention, discipline becomes a fetish to all but the unconquerable soul. Without the inbred respect for authority that dominated every phase of life, the split in the Social Democratic movement of Germany would have come long before the war robbed its leftist element of the chance to carry on constructive propaganda for a secession movement.

Efficient capitalist production is possible only where class differences are normally subordinated to the immediate interests of production and distribution. Similarly democracy can function only so long as the fiction of a unity of class interests can be maintained. Class differences destroy the very essence of democracy. But class harmony presupposes the satisfaction of at least the elementary needs of the exploited class. The success of the German Republic as a democracy, therefore, and its continuance as a capitalist state, demanded a period of rising prosperity as the indispensable preliminary to the harmonious coöperation of all elements in the country. That it did not materialize was a potent factor in the unrest of the years that followed.

It has often been said—and not without justification—that social revolution in Germany was jeopardized by the belligerence of the Socialist groups toward one another. To us it has always appeared that the failure of the people to cash in on the promises of the 9th of November was attributable in a much larger measure to the failure of the Majority Socialists to comprehend the full potentialities of their own, albeit equivocal, socialization promises. Those who followed Socialist leadership, and a large portion of the middle class as well, expected and were prepared to accept a fundamental change in the structure of the nation. Had the post-revolutionary Government of Ebert and Scheidemann made a serious effort to put into practice the promises of their party that the basic industries would be made the property of the state, the masses would have applauded and the middle class would have submitted to the inevitable. But they had no stomach for experiments. True, they continued to speak of socialization as the end and aim of revolution. When disturbances threatened the torpor of the Republic, gaudy signs appeared with the caption: "Socialization is on the march!" A Socialization Commission was appointed. The fruits of its work are buried in government archives. Its recommendations were never taken up.

In the end capitalism was to prove, for the workers, the more costly experience. For socialization of the heavy industries would have mitigated the disastrous effects on business of Germany's reparation burden and the world economic crisis. The tendency of periodic crises of increasing intensity inherent in capitalism might have been checked and ameliorated by the nationalization of the basic industries which are the point of departure of every economic crisis on the one hand and of recovery on the other. Shackled by the terms of the Versailles Treaty and by the limitations of the Weimar Constitution business recovery became more and more unlikely. The former burdened the country with a mandate for enormous production and deprived it of its markets; the latter gave official recognition to the rights of the worker and made it impossible to impose its obligations on the underdog by the curtailment of social services and by wage cuts. These realities the Social Democracy failed to take into account. It refused to recognize that existing forces are more powerful than theories of government and persisted in a vain endeavor to ward off the impending conflict between capital and labor by endless concessions to its class enemy. Yet with its fundamental conception of the impulses that determine social phenomena it should have foreseen that the German bourgeoisie with its veneration for "Blut und Eisen" in government, would sooner or later arrive, driven by the stern logic of economic distress to reaction and Fascism, away from the essentially alien philosophy of democracy. To-day the German bourgeoisie stands once more on native soil, hoping to succeed through the Fascist Party of Hitler and the bonapartiste reaction of Hindenburg-Papen-Hugenberg where democracy failed.

Far from recognizing the intrinsically reactionary nature of all capitalist democracy, the government in 1919 and 1920 gave to the embryonic counter-revolution the weapons that are dealing the death blow to the Weimar Constitution to-day. Under its eyes, with the tacit consent of its Defense Minister, Gustav Noske—Oberpraesident of Hanover and the only Social Democrat in high office who was not removed from his post by the Papen government—volunteer troops under officers of the old Imperial army were organized throughout the length and breadth of the land. Without the knowledge of their colleagues of the Independent Social Democratic Party on the People's Commissariat, Ebert and his comrades were in constant and intimate contact with the General Staff, the very heart of the counter-revolution.

The Reichswehr, the official army of the Republic, was created during the Weimar Convention and placed under the command of former army officers. Thus the military camarilla was restored to prominence, not only in the army but in the government and the nation as well, a condition that was to become startlingly manifest during the Kapp Putsch in March 1920. In this revolt of reactionary militarists the commanding officers of the Reichswehr maintained a watchful passivity— deserted by those whom it had looked upon as its sole support, the government had fled from Berlin in a panic and made no attempt to protect the Republic. Not until the latter, thanks to a general strike of organized labor and the Socialists, was able to establish its supremacy once more, did the Reichswehr advance against the feudal rebels.

During this period the forces of the Right had been gaining

in consequence and number. They organized their so-called secret societies with impunity. Monarchist sentiment was publicly nurtured by veteran organizations that boasted powerful political connections. The "Reichsbund der Frontsoldaten" which later became the Stahlhelm, the semi-military backers of the present government, was founded in September 1918 by George Seldte, a Magdeburg manufacturer, and for years carried on an active campaign for the "liberation of the German people from the servitude of the Versailles Treaty" and against the "debauchery of the Revolution." The Republic was soon to reap the fruits of its indulgence. An organized crusade generally known as the "Feme" for the murder of prominent Republicans and traitors to the monarchist cause set in. Matthias Erzberger, leader of the Centrist Party, the man who had, at the urgent demand of Hindenburg, signed the Armistice agreement for Germany and had, as the first Minister of Finance of the Republic tried to bring order into its chaotic finances, was one of its first victims. A year later, in June 1922, Walter Rathenau, Minister of Foreign Affairs, was shot. An attempt to assassinate Philipp Scheidemann failed through fortuitous accident. The Bavarian Independent Social Democrat Gareis was less fortunate and paid with his life for his devotion to the cause of the workers.

This pressure from the Right induced a unification of the Majority and Minority Social Democratic Parties although the last named had been decisively weakened by the desertion, at the Congress in Halle, of a strong minority to the Communist Party. The German Communist movement suffered a blow from which it has never recovered when the murderers of Liebknecht and Luxemburg deprived it of its most clear-headed, courageous and beloved leaders. The men who took the helm possessed neither their popularity nor their independence of thought and strength of character. After a temporary standstill, the movement was reorganized under the guidance of the Communist International. Karl Radek was charged with its supervision and under his direction it prepared for a revolutionary uprising in March 1921, though the majority of the Central Executive Committee—among them Heinrich Brandler, August Thalheimer, Jacob Walcher and Paul Froehlich—doubted the wisdom of such a course. When it became apparent that the venture would fail because of the weakness of the organization and the lack of revolutionary preparedness of the

masses Secretary Brandler countermanded the orders already
sent out to the Party Subdivisions, too late, however, to reach
Hamburg in time to avert an uprising that ended in death and
failure. Paul Levi, the Party Chairman, a young lawyer of
independent means, a recognized Marxian scholar, one of the
founders of Spartacus and an intimate member of the Lieb-
knecht-Luxemburg circle, had opposed the March uprising
from the start. He now came out openly in denunciation of the
practice of grafting methods and tactics successfully employed
in the Russian Revolution mechanically on Communist Parties
in other countries, a course that was substituting Party action
for class action everywhere.

The fight with the Left Wing of the Communist Party that
followed ended with his expulsion, a decision which was upheld
at the next International Congress. Though Lenin and Trotsky
agreed with Levi's analysis of the situation in Germany, they
sided with the majority of the delegates and the German Party
in condemning him for the injury he had inflicted on the
German and the international movement by the publication of
his critical pamphlets and by his speeches.

The Central Committee was now placed under the control
of Ruth Fischer, A. Maslow and the Left Wing whose policies
still more completely isolated the Party from the daily struggle
of the masses. Levi, after maintaining an independent Communist group for a time, joined the Social Democratic Party
in 1924 in the hope of making it the purveyor of a revolutionary but realistic ideology based on German conditions and in
accord with the economic and political development of that
country. He failed miserably in this attempt. The friends who
followed him into the Social Democratic Party seceded from it
in 1931—Levi had died several years before—after they had
learned from experience that new wine cannot be filled in old
bottles, that the strong influx of middle class elements into the
SPD and the influence of trade union and coöperative society
officialdom more than offset whatever influence they themselves
may have gained with their revolutionary teachings. In the
years that followed, the German Communist Party weathered
several crises and splits—Right Wing Communist Opposition
and Left Wing Trotsky Opposition—before it secured a firmer
foothold in the masses. To-day its members number about
150,000. The Communist vote on November 6th, 1932, had
risen to almost 6 millions with 100 deputies in the Reichstag.

The Social Democratic Party which reached its high-water mark in the Reichstag election of May 1928 when it polled more than 9 million votes and won 152 deputies, fell to 7,-200,000 votes and 121 deputies in the November election. The decline of the Social Democrats has run parallel to the growth of the Communist movement. Indeed it appears as if the latter were more and more to become the political expression of the masses. However, this increase in the popularity of the Communist Party does not necessarily indicate a mere radicalization of the masses. Much of its popular appeal may lie in the nationalistic attitude it has taken since the National Socialists, with their chauvinistic clamor, became an important factor in German political life. Ever since Karl Radek proposed that the execution of the German "patriot" Schlageter by a French military court during the Ruhr occupation be used as a propaganda issue, and initiated this new policy in a newspaper debate with the Fascist Count Reventlow, the German Communist movement has played variations on the nationalist theme, from a light pianissimo to a very emphatic forte in the November election under the immediate impression of Germany's declaration of independence from "foreign domination."

In the post-war period there were several occasions when German Labor could have made a determined fight for power. After the Kapp-Putsch popular disgust with the cowardice of the Ebert régime and the unreliability of the Reichswehr would have brought success to a movement determined on a complete break with Germany's capitalist and militarist past. The trade unions had conducted the general strike with commendable vigor but as so often before, the inability of the two wings of Labor to unite for a common purpose prevented this splendid action of the working class from bearing positive fruit. When inflation brought even a ruined middle class to the verge of rebellion, when strikes in Middle Germany and in the Ruhr District inflamed the workers to a white heat of resentment, the German proletariat might have followed its Russian brothers, had the distrust and enmity engendered by years of warfare between the two Parties not made a solid phalanx impossible. The tragedy of this state of affairs is only just becoming fully manifest. In the face of a Fascist offensive that threatens the very existence of the labor movement, neither of the parties was able to find a way to a common ground.

The dualistic trade union and organization policy of the

Communists contributed materially to the widening of the breach. They created their own sport units, their relief auxiliaries, their freethinker and cultural organizations, their cooperatives, and, most important of all, their own trade unions. Wherever labor congregated, they forced splits in the ranks, developing an antagonism that not even the present crisis has been able to overcome.

It has been one of the great drawbacks of the Communist movement everywhere—and this is particularly true of Germany—that it was always an annex to Soviet Russia, the immediate interests of which superseded those of the working classes in the respective countries. The maintenance and development of the Soviet Union is an important premise for world revolution. But the fact that the tactics of the different national Communist parties are so often determined by political and economic considerations for Russia and its momentary international relationship, has kept them from taking advantage of favorable opportunities in their own countries.

The stronghold of the Communist Party in the early days of the Revolution lay in the Ruhr district, the home of the heavy industries, where it was able to conduct successful strike campaigns. When the French and Belgian Governments occupied that region, because Germany was unable to deliver the coal it had promised as part of its reparations obligations, the Communists led the workers in a passive resistance movement. They opposed the tactics of the conservative Luther Government which subsidized the mine and mill owners to conduct a campaign of sabotage against the invaders. This struggle was financed by the issuance of fiat currency. The result was a convulsive inflation that will be remembered for generations for the cataclysmic rapidity with which it wiped out all monetary standards. Agricultural traffic came to a standstill, the farming population refusing to accept worthless paper in exchange for its commodities. Barter took the place of money transactions. Business was in a state of chaos. In January 1920 a gold mark was worth ten marks in paper, on July 3rd, 1922, 100, on October 21st of the same year 1000, on January 31st, 1923, 10,000, on July 24th, 100,000, on August 8th, 1,000,000 and on September 7th, 10,000,000 marks in fiat money. German industry and high finance, with its fear of taxes, had brought about a complete demoralization of its finance economy. The price was paid by the small shareholder and the middle class whose savings were wiped out, and above all by Labor and petty officialdom from whose wages and salaries the by far greatest portion of the national income tax was deducted by means of the hated "Steuerabzug." The inflation was not entirely undesigned; it was undeniably a part of the well laid plan of German business to rid itself of old obligations to facilitate the erection of a new production apparatus. It was an ingenious attempt on the part of the moneyed bourgeoisie to recuperate by inflation what it had lost in the War. To the masses it meant intense suffering. They had no debts to discharge, but were forced to buy bread and potatoes, clothing and milk for their children with scrip that depreciated from hour to hour. For them inflation meant stark hunger and the disintegration of family relationships.

The German bourgeoisie looked beyond a momentary advantage with its inflation policy. Having reconstructed its productive apparatus on modern lines, it hoped to regain its position in the world market. It overlooked the fact that the War had come because the world market was no longer adequate to satisfy the needs of international capital. All over the world the post-war boom had produced a swollen, highly efficient mechanism, the usefulness of which had broken down since there was no public that could buy, no consumer with the necessary purchasing power. German business was the first to succumb. It was unable to find a market for the products of its distended output.

This unfortunate situation had a malign influence on the German people. Where formerly a strong bourgeois minority had opposed the super-nationalist sabre-rattling of its Junkers, the republican parties now—in so far as they did not belong to the class conscious workers—stood foursquare behind a foreign policy that held out only disaster for the nation. It began at the moment when Chancellor Hermann Müller affixed his signature to the Versailles Treaty. It persisted, logically in the "policy of fulfillment," as Cabinet after Cabinet, with more or less ill grace recognized the demands of the Allies. The willingness of the governments to meet their obligations became more and more doubtful as the concealments adopted by German business to protect itself against industrial paralysis and the evasion by its financiers of their national responsibility by investing capital abroad, undermined Germany's ability to pay. The protests of the Communist Party, which, from the first day, vigorously opposed the Versailles peace and the fulfillment program, fell on deaf ears. It went to such extremes in its opposition that it was more than once accused—and not entirely without justification—of stealing the thunder of the National Socialists who were beginning to attract attention with a program of chauvinistic propaganda against the "hereditary foe." Not until public opinion had been aroused by Hitler's propaganda, did the republican elements forsake their conciliatory attitude in international affairs.

Marked social changes are taking place in the Germany of the strong middle class and the subaltern officials. These middle strata are vanishing rapidly. With the exception of the thin upper layer of a numerically decreasing wealthy bourgeoisie, the great mass has been proletarianized. The middle class which was represented by 166 deputies in the Reichstag after the Weimer Convention, to-day, little more than a decade later, has well-nigh vanished from political life. Big business, which at first showed no inclination to fight organized labor actively on the political field, has taken its place. The National Socialist movement which, under the leadership of the Austrian Hitler, made its first public appearance in Munich on the 8th of November, 1923, in the famous Hofbräuhaus Putsch, was its initial venture in this direction. On the ruins of the Deutsch-Völkische Partei and with the active coöperation of General von Ludendorff and the Bavarian Minister of the Interior, von Kahr, Hitler had collected a following of disaffected militarists and monarchists about his standard. They prepared to overthrow the government of the Bavarian state as the first step to national control. The Munich uprising degenerated into a sort of comic opera revolution after von Kahr and Ludendorff, sensing defeat, deserted the more audacious Hitler and later turned against him when he was charged with insurrection. Hitler was condemned to four years in prison, serving nine months. Upon his release he found his Party decimated. With remarkable energy and an undoubted talent for organization he set to work once more. Six years later he had made of it the strongest political party in the country.

National Socialism is definitely committed to an anti-parliamentary dictatorship in the interests of the bourgeoisie and propagates an imperialistic super-nationalism which emphasizes military power as a world issue and Teuton racial purity at home. Its supporters come from every strata of the German population, uniting groups that are not and can never be brought together in a congruent program, that have no common Weltanschauung. It was possible to weld them into a political organization only because all Germany was clamoring for a new deal and had lost confidence in the ability of the old parties to effect the desired changes. Chiefly the movement is recruited from the ranks of the impoverished middle class and a peasantry groaning under low prices and accumulating indebtedness. To these have been added the multitude of *declassés,* those men and women of uncertain means who were thrown out of an assured livelihood and a well defined existence by ten years of industrial crisis, and numerous workers, particularly of the younger generation, who have lost faith in the labor movement. The National Socialist German Labor Party is, in a sense, a reservoir, holding these heterogeneous elements together without possibility of permanent amalgamation. But so great was the desire of the German people for stabilization and Ordnung, that, with sufficient financial support to spread its message of a better future and to organize its adherents, success was practically assured.

The finances were willingly supplied by the great industrialists who saw the possibilities of the new party as an instrument for the suppression and ultimate annihilation of the labor unions and by the Junkers who hoped to reinstate a monarchist state on the back of the Nazi movement. The heavy industries, through their outstanding spokesmen came out for the Hitler Party and opened their plants wide to its propagandists. With such open-handed assistance from the wealthiest elements in the nation, it was possible for the Hitlerites to assemble in half a decade more than a million members and to establish a uniformed military auxiliary organization—the Storm Troops—of five hundred thousand men. Many of these belong to the army of the permanently unemployed and are housed and fed in the Nazi barracks and supplied with a not too niggardly pocket-money as well. Here as in Italy the ascendency of the Fascist movement was possible only because it enjoyed the subsidies of the heavy industries and the patronage of the banks and the aristocracy.

The phenomenal growth of the National Socialist movement is without equal in German history. It swept cities and communities. It won majorities in the provincial Landtag and state elections, until it seemed only a matter of months before it would hold the government of the Reich in its hands. The national administration was unable to cope with this political giant. On the contrary, it receded before its relentless advance. But a new political alignment, as yet concealed, was taking form in the background of political events. The large industrialists and the Junkers sensed uneasily that the National Socialists might yet represent a danger much more incalculable, and certainly much more immediate than either Socialists or Communists. It dawned on them that Hitler's organization to win, must have the confidence and support of a large part of the working population, which would be possible only so long as it maintained the appearance of representing their interests. If the Nazis come to power, these masses will demand payment on their political promissory notes. There is a real danger that the National Socialist masses may stride over the heads of their Hitlers, their Strassers, their Göbbels and their Feders if the latter should attempt to take their stand with the possessing classes against the pauperized workers. On the other hand, the trinity of heavy industries, aristocracy and bureaucracy cannot and will not fulfill the social-economic promises of the Hitlerite leadership.

This alone can explain the change of front of the Hindenburg following that precipitated Brüning's removal. They had perceived, before it was too late, the deeper currents that were sweeping Hitler and his generals into power. Chancellor Brüning was sacrificed, not for his silent coalition with the Social Democratic Party, but because of the weakness of his position and the imminence of his downfall. Hitler would have been his logical successor. This had to be prevented under all circumstances. Documentary proof has recently been published showing that Groener, Brüning's Minister of Defense, was persuaded to dissolve the Sturm Abteilungen by the very cliques which immediately afterwards used this act as a petard on which to hang Brüning and Groener as well. The Papen-Schleicher Cabinet was waiting behind the scenes. Every detail of what followed had been prepared. The dissolution order of the Nazi Storm Troops was at once repealed to win the National Socialists as an appendix to the Junker government. The ambitious Hitler was willing enough to accept the Vice-Chancellorship Papen offered. But his lieutenants were more wary than their ingenuous leader. They did not walk into the trap, but forced the German "Duce" instead to take up the fight against the Junkers and the industrialists.

The Monocle Government proceeded to exploit the situation to its full advantage. The first of its victims was the Majority Socialist-Centrist-Democratic Government of Prussia—the last bulwark of Social-Democratic power in Germany. A stroke of Hindenburg's pen—that same Hindenburg for whose reëlection the German working class sacrificed so many ideals and material advantages—ousted the Prussian government with its host of Socialist officials and filled the posts that were vacated, with the Junker nobility.

Since the Reichstag election on August 30th, the German labor movement has had to recede from post to post before the onslaught of a determined reaction. After a barren victory, when it adopted its nonconfidence vote with a 90% majority, the Reichstag was dissolved. By a system of emergency decrees the Papen-Schleicher Government set the national stage for dictatorship. An autarchy of sorts was established in the interests of the great landholders by forbidding the importation of certain foodstuffs; wage agreements between labor unions and manufacturers were set aside, wages reduced, strikes forbidden and labor unions threatened with dissolution and indemnity suits under a One Year Plan that threw billions of marks into the lap of German capitalism for the reanimation of industry. The entire oppositional press was persecuted to a degree that was unequalled even in the days of Bismarck's anti-Socialist Law. Radical papers were forbidden for periods varying from one week to three months. Even the cautious "Vorwaerts" was twice suppressed. The November election brought a deflation of the National Socialist danger, but changed nothing in the actual outlook. Whatever may be the composition of the government that the industrialists and their Junker allies will decide upon, it will be just as determined to deprive labor of its weapons as the heterogeneous band of Hitlerites, just as determined to restore the monarchy and to abolish equal suffrage, that last "great achievement" of the democratic Revolution. To the working class the methods of these reactionaries should be a liberal education in revolutionary tactics. From them it might learn that a democratic code becomes a scrap of paper in the hands of a capitalist class fighting for self-preservation.

In a radio speech on the evening of September 12th Chancellor von Papen proclaimed the end of "formal democracy." The "Deutsche Allgemeine Zeitung," the recognized representative of the heavy industries and the semi-official organ of the present régime, that paper which, as the "Norddeutsche Allgemeine Zeitung" under Bismarck was known as the "Regierungshure," announced on the following morning: "We stand in a dictatorship." Thus, without ceremony, the Weimar Republic was borne to its grave.

What took its place? The dictatorship of that class which was ousted from political power on the 9th of November, 1918, but remained firmly entrenched in the social and economic vantage points of the national apparatus. Its logical evolution is toward the restoration of monarchy—a monarchy adapted to the hazardous conditions of this post-war world. The monarchy of William II rested on a capitalism unshaken. It ruled with bourgeois parties with a semblance of constitutional forms. The Papen-Schleicher government existed as the last line defense of a capitalism shaken to its foundation, as the unwilling forerunner of a Fascist dictatorship.

The conception so popular in the American press that German Fascism had passed its zenith and that the Hitler movement would dwindle into insignificance even more rapidly than it rose to power, was but another example of the persistent inability of the American correspondent to view the German political picture as the logical outcome of historic forces. He saw in Hindenburg the savior of German democracy and forgot that he was the product of that most undemocratic class in the world—the German Junker. He looked at the ridiculous mustache and theatrical make-up of Herr Hitler and refused to take seriously a movement that was born out of the need and suffering and despair of millions; looked again, first with unbelief and then with amazed respect at the growing force behind this political charlatan, promptly revised his judgment of this "coming man," and presented him to the American public as the embodiment of this new "WILL" that was to lead Germany out of its slough of despond. By a political maneuver, the dishonesty of which was hardly mitigated by its supreme disdain of the people as a political force, Hindenburg, advised by the Machiavellian Schleicher and the unscrupulous Papen, succeeded in checkmating the covetous Hitler just as success seemed about to fall ripe into his outstretched hands. And again the American press, with its facile logic in all matters

European, decides that the Fascist movement is dead and that
Papen and Schleicher have come to stay.

But the feudal Herrenklub knew only too well that a military dictatorship in Germany has little outlook for permanence,
particularly when, as was the case with the Papen government,
it had so signally failed to win the support of an organized
counter-revolutionary movement of commanding proportions.
The government was not impelled to call for a new Reichstag
election by some almost atrophied sense of public duty. It
could not for a moment believe that the Reichstag to be elected
in November would vary essentially from that which it had so
arbitrarily dismissed, or that its standing with the German
electorate had been appreciably improved by the reduction of
wages, the demand for military preparedness and conscription,
its plans for a compulsory labor service and its ruthless reduction of social protection. The election therefore resolved itself
into a futile gesture, an expedient by which the Junker monarchists hoped, perhaps, to wear out their opponents while
they laid the foundation for the subjugation of the German
people to the interests of its monarchists, its militarists and its
industrial and financial overlords.

The November election brought no surprises. What the National Socialists lost—2,000,000 votes and 29 seats in the Reichstag—was recaptured by Hugenberg's German Nationalist
People's Party, the reactionary German People's Party and the
Economic Party. The losses of the Social Democracy corresponded roughly to the gains of the Communist Party, so that
the balance of power between Left and Right in the Reichstag
remained practically unchanged. Papen retired for the time
being and was replaced by Kurt von Schleicher who took over
the entire Papen Cabinet. We have already described the fateful rôle this man played during and after the Revolution. Here
again he relied on his old tactics, on his ability to play group
against group to solve this impasse, as he had solved so many
others before. He tried first to make connections with the
leaders of the National Socialist Party, who had always treated
him with great restraint in their attacks on the Papen government. After weeks of fruitless negotiations first with Hitler
and then with Gregor Strasser, the head of the more "practical"
opposition, he turned to Prelate Dr. Kaas, the Chairman of the
Centrist Party and to Theodore Leipart, President of the
German Trade Union Federation, in the hope of uniting a ma-

jority of parliament behind his government. The Centrists were willing to join hands with the Chancellor, provided the Social Democratic Party could be persuaded, through its labor unions, to a policy of neutrality and toleration. Just as success seemed assured, the Fascist secessionist movement under Strasser, upon which Schleicher had counted for the 20–30 votes necessary to produce the desired majority, collapsed. On the other hand Hitler's position was strengthened by his success in the Lippe state and a number of municipal elections. With the beginning of the new year the Nazis inaugurated an anti-Schleicher campaign that further demoralized the efforts of the government. After 67 days in office, the shortest Ministry in the history of republican Germany was forced to resign and the second "authoritative" Hindenburg government went the way of the first. Hitler as Chancellor and von Papen as Vice-Chancellor were instructed to select a new Cabinet.

The appointment of the Nazi chief, after he had been eliminated from the picture by the European and American press, created a perplexing situation. The inclusion of Papen, Hugenberg, leader of the German Nationalist People's Party, and Seldte, Commander of the "Steel Helmet" in the Ministry, was looked upon as a guarantee that Hindenburg had once more safeguarded Germany's constitutional rights and checked Hitler's dictatorial powers. But actualities told a different story. Against the opposition of Hugenberg and Seldte, who demanded that the government put an end, once and for all, to the "senseless game of parliamentarism," Hitler, for purely tactical reasons, forced the dissolution of the Reichstag and the calling of a new election for March 5th. Though the National Socialists held only two other Ministries in the Cabinet, they were the strategic posts most concretely representative of real power, the Ministry of the Interior which dominates the police and makes all official appointments in the Reich, and the acting Ministry of the Interior for Prussia, with full control of the police and gendarmerie of that state.

Hitler was manifestly determined from the beginning to use the Junkers as a scaling ladder to power. With this purpose in view he insisted on immediate Reichstag, Prussian Diet and Prussian municipal elections. The election returns proved the political wisdom of this seemingly futile gesture, for as the days went by even those most loath to recognize that democracy had breathed its last in Germany were forced to admit that the out-

come of the election would in no way influence Hitler's determination to remain in control of the nation. The National
Socialists received 17,300,000 votes, the Nationalists only 3,000,-
000, the two parties fifty-two per cent of the total vote, the
largest ever cast in Germany, and a firm majority in the Reichstag. A week later the Junkers were forced to submit to the
inevitable; two important posts in the Cabinet were given to
National Socialists, the posts of police presidents in all large and
industrial cities were filled with Hitlerites and the state governments in Bavaria, Baden, Hessia, Saxony, and in the smaller
states of Hamburg, Bremen, Lübeck, etc., all of them hitherto
controlled by other parties, were summarily placed under Reich
control with Fascist Reich Commissars. With the removal of
Vice-Chancellor von Papen as dictator of Prussia despite his
complacent acquiescence in the terroristic methods of the Nazis,
and the appointment of Hitler to that post immediately after
the election, the Chancellor showed his utter contempt for the
pretensions of his allies of the German Nationalistic People's
Party. In the Reich government the Hugenberg Nationalists
are to-day the tail to the National Socialist kite.

Schleicher's overthrow had been brought about chiefly by
the Rhenish-Westphalian heavy industries when his readiness
to come to terms with the trade union movement became apparent. Between the remote danger of rampant Hitlerism, now
that the more radical elements had been subjugated, and the
immediate problem of a possible fortification by Schleicher of
trade union rights, there was but one choice. Hitler was more
than willing to take up the fight against organized labor. Immediately after his accession to power, his government laid the
foundation for a system of labor conscription that would force
all young men to render compulsory service to the state for a
stated period in return for pocket-money, food and shelter. It
promulgated a plan for economic recuperation that was based
on lower wages, the abrogation of existing wage agreements
and the reorganization of labor arbitration courts. To the
farmer it promised tariffs on farm products which still further
increased the cost of living. It recognized national self-sufficiency as a governmental policy and put into effect rigorous
limitations on imports. Its demand for a popular militia paved
the way for the coming of general and compulsory military
service "to restore the nation to the place it had once held
under the glorious rule of the Hohenzollern." Its first official

act was the appointment of a Secretary for the development of a national air force. In its job-producing campaign, the slogan "Germany for the Germans" played an important rôle with the deportation of immigrants and the suppression of many thousands of poor Jews and Jewish intellectuals. With the Jews of great wealth, Hitler, Hugenberg and the other professional Jew-baiters in the German Cabinet will come to terms as did the anti-Semitic von Bismarck in an earlier epoch.

Hitler's ascendency marks the beginning of a new period in Germany's political life. Democracy came to the German people at a time when it had almost outlived its usefulness in many capitalist countries. In Italy, and to a degree in Finland, Poland, Rumania, Hungary, Bulgaria, Yugo-Slavia and Lithuania, Fascism, in some form or other, has replaced democratic government and parliamentary supremacy. Its victory in Germany will give added impetus to the movement in Austria and Czecho-Slovakia, where already strong Fascist organizations exist.

To the labor movement the Reichstag has long ago lost the significance it once possessed. Parliamentarism holds out no solution for its problems and elections have meaning chiefly as an opportunity to mobilize its forces for extra-parliamentary action. It may be that the new régime will pave the way for the coming of a united mass organization of labor with but a single aim: the organization and training of the proletariat for the social revolution by a relentless campaign against bourgeois dictatorship and suppression. The latest secession from the Social Democratic Party, known as the Socialist Workers Party, which has drawn numerous recruits also from the Communist opposition groups, points the way for such a development. Among its leaders are men and women like Georg Ledebour, Max Seydewitz, Kurt Rosenfeld, Anna and August Siemens and Georg Walcher and Paul Froehlich, two of the founders of the Spartacus Bund. The Party has remained numerically small because it came into being in a period rendered unpropitious by overwhelming political issues, but is bending its every effort toward unification of the proletarian forces to the neglect, frequently, of its organizational growth. That the labor parties, after a campaign in which all Socialist and Communist papers and meetings were suppressed and 7000 functionaries were arrested, fell so little below their November returns—the CP. lost one million of its six million votes, while the SPD. gained

300,000 votes—shows the organizational soundness of the German labor movement and its inherent possibilities in the coming struggles. As we are writing these lines the cables report that Communist deputies will not be allowed to take their seats in the Reichstag and the Diets, and that the party itself will be outlawed, while the Social Democratic Party will be permitted to exist for the time being only as a party of the second class with limited propaganda possibilities.

Capitalism has discarded democracy, pacifism and parliamentarism as excess baggage from an outlived era. For the working class, at the present stage, it is an unsubstantial chimera, a phantom deity at whose feet of clay it once sacrificed its high aims. There is no easiest way out of this fetid morass of capitalist decomposition. The proletariat must choose between two alternatives—spiritual and physical starvation and mental slavery OR revolution.

REVOLUTION AND REACTION
IN FRANCE

IN the summer of 1931 there was held in Paris an exhibition of the resources and achievements of the French Empire. Visitors to this exposition, particularly those from the United States, were astonished not so much at what they saw as by the fact that such an exposition could be held in France. In Great Britain, yes; for Great Britain was an empire and made no bones of it. Or in Berlin in the days of the Kaiser. Or in Rome, if such a thing were possible, under Mussolini. For these two, we had been told, were the natural sons of the Cæsars, hungering for world conquest. But in France! Yet there it was. And neither Paris nor France seemed aware of anything incongruous in the situation. From the four corners of the earth, tributary peoples, black and yellow and brown, had been assembled, and round them lay the products of their lands, a colorful display arranged as much to flatter the French populace as to impress the colonials with the wealth and power of France. Never in all her history, not even in the days of the Grand Monarch or the First Napoleon, had Paris seen such an exhibition.

Is this a new France which has risen since the Great War or the France of the ages? Seen from Europe, undoubtedly it is the latter. But so far as the United States of America is concerned, it is a new France, totally different from the one we have always known. The France we knew was the France of Europe, not the France of the world.

The explanation, of course, is that we have been living in

207

the days of our Revolution, refusing to see with our own eyes, accepting an appraisal of France handed down from the days of Jefferson. The French were still the French of their Revolution, a nation of the ideal, thrifty and home-loving, rivals of other nations in the field of the arts, passionately devoted to their own country, satisfied with France. Yet always to be counted on coöperation in the advancement of liberty in any part of the world. This was the France, the only France we knew. Or cared to know. We refused to look either before or after. We saw, therefore, only the Republic. We did not see the Empire stretching away on either side, an enduring fact of history, shattered one moment by the Revolution, then coming together again and pursuing its interrupted course.

Undoubtedly it was because France was a republic. We had inherited and accepted from our Colonial fathers their conception of a republic. It was something radically different from an empire, the creation of a free people who saw in their own liberation a prelude to the liberation of the world. Empire, in its colonial aspect, was a projection of monarchy, an extension of the denial of self-government to peoples of foreign countries. Empire increased its power by conquest; a republic, through the development of its citizens. Empire was founded on force; a republic, on the rights of man. With this principle, which sooner or later was to possess the earth, our Colonial fathers saw France intimately associated. This it was that drew the two nations together. At a time when legitimate successors of the Cæsars were occupying thrones throughout the lands of western civilization and taking over, as the mood seized them, the territories of weak peoples, America and France stood forth, lone antagonists of the Old Order of Force, advance guards of an era when conquest should be no more.

These were the thoughts that came back to Americans visiting the Colonial Exposition in Paris in the summer of 1931. They recalled the charges, frequently made since the Great War, that France was imperialistic. And the passionate denials of France. Yet here, too plain to be disguised, was a glorification of conquest obviously staged to kindle the pride of the French people and win support for imperial policies. It seemed to say, "See what a world power France has become, how mighty she is and envied of nations. War pays. How else could we have had all this?" Which was France, the Republic or the Empire? The Declaration of the Rights of Man or this exhibition of subject peoples? To-day the world is asking this question, for it is one which concerns not only Asia and Africa, but Europe and the Americas, North and South.

No one acquainted with the territorial acquisitions of France during the last half century can fail to realize that the appraisal of France handed down from our fathers is woefully inadequate. We are face to face not with a republic, self-contained and self-sufficient, but with a world power of the first magnitude. In strange contrast to other powers that have achieved glory and dominion, battling their way noisily now in one part of the world and now in another, Imperial France has come quietly upon the stage and taken her seat with the mighty, unscarred by conflict and untouched by criticism. Miraculously, as compared to other powers, France's colonial possessions have fallen into her lap, unnoticed by the world. Our eyes were elsewhere, upon Great Britain, conquering in South Africa; upon Russia, enlarging her Siberian dominions; upon Japan, in Formosa and Korea; upon Germany, shaking her mailed fist now over South Africa and now over Asia Minor, at Tangiers and in far off China. Meanwhile, behind the scenes, France was quietly adding to her dominions areas of enormous extent, with no hue and cry in any part of the world. The blusterings of a single Hohenzollern attracted more attention and evoked more opposition than this whole achievement of France.

But why the astonishment, now that this achievement has been discovered? Solely because of the manner in which it was accomplished. Conquest itself was no new thing in the history of France. Our Colonial fathers, in the flush of their enthusiasm, may have been content to disregard the centuries of that history, but we surely are far from all that.

Consider the geographical position of France in its bearing on the development of military power. On three sides are open seas. At her four corners are four nations, powerful all of them at one time or another, Italy, Spain, Great Britain, Germany, products of the long war traditions of Europe. Successively and, it would seem, under some biologic compulsion, as plants put forth leaves at certain stages of their development, these nations have risen and gone forth to achieve by force of arms glory and dominion. And inevitably the imperial vision has embraced France. First, Italy of the Cæsars; then Spain of the Saracen and the Hapsburg; then England, returning with her

Norman Kings; and finally Germany, late comer into the family of conquerors. These are the neighbors of France, rivals through the ages for dominion, competitors for the hegemony of Europe.

France, therefore, more than any other nation, is a product of war. Her very survival is proof of it. One after another, by martial prowess, she has expelled from her domain every one of these powers, acquiring through this experience that mastery of the science and art of war which has made the French private a perfect soldier, and the French marshal a commander of a superior sort.

This France, until recently so unfamiliar to America, the peoples of Europe have always known. They have also learned from experience that military power is never satisfied with the security of a nation but seeks expression, that the French have been just as responsive through the ages to the glory and spoils of conquest as any other people on the continent. With the exception of Great Britain, separated by the Channel and guarded by her powerful fleet, there is hardly a country in all Europe that has not at one time or another been attacked and invaded by France. Visitors to the Colonial Exposition, had they cared to extend their travels to neighboring countries, Italy, Spain, Belgium, Holland, Germany, Austria, Poland, even far distant Russia, could have been shown, existing still, scars of old invasions, castles overthrown, galleries and churches where the French cavalry had stabled their horses, cities and towns plundered by passing armies, ruins that testify that in time of war peoples are all alike. And they need only to have gone to the Louvre to realize that the French too were not accustomed to come home empty-handed from their conquests in foreign lands. To imagine that all these wars were defensive wars in which France was always right and the rest of Europe always wrong or that these invasions were reprisals, whereas the invasions of France by other peoples were barbarous incursions wholly without justification, is to confess oneself either hopelessly ignorant or hopelessly prejudiced. For, indeed, no nation of Europe, whether ancient or modern, has held more tenaciously to the military ideal or carried conquest over wider areas of the earth's surface than has France.

Nor did this career of conquest come to an end with the establishment of the First Republic. The bells that rang all over the United States, heralding this new era, rang all too

soon. For though by this time, after centuries of aggressive warfare, France had lost one empire, in North America and in
India, she was girding herself for a second effort that was to
carry her first over Europe and then, more quietly, into every
corner of the earth.

There are those who think that Napoleon Bonaparte was
an intruder, that he came from outside French tradition and
broke the continuity of French evolution. But the opposite is
the truth. It was the Revolution that was the intruder. There
had been in France prior to that uprising nothing remotely
akin to a struggle for liberty. For one hundred and seventy-
five years no States-General had been convened. The divine
right was still accepted as a sacred thing. Absolutism held sway.
Across the Channel the modern world had begun. In the land
of the Bourbons the Middle Age still lingered, with concepts
and trappings of Imperial Rome. Into this ancient order of
things, kindled by a spark from the American conflagration,
the Revolution burst, interrupting the natural course of French
development. France, that had been thinking in terms of conquest, awoke to the Rights of Man. It was a sudden wakening,
as though the sleep were not yet over. Nor indeed was it over.
The Imperial Dream, broken for a moment as by a clap of
thunder, gathered itself together and flowed on.

Far more competent than his predecessors, the Bourbons,
had been, the young Cæsar who now took in hand the destiny
of France, caught up the emotion which Liberty had engendered and easily converted it into shouts for Empire. At once
it became clear why the Bourbons had been overthrown. Their
line had run out. The Grand Monarch had been strong. He
had given France glory and dominion. But these later Bourbons were weaklings, incapable even of holding what their
predecessors had won. The uprising of the French people that
put an end to this incompetence—effectively put an end to it
by the guillotine—was indeed an uprising for liberty. The
Grand Monarch had given them liberty and they had followed
him, into Prussia, into the Netherlands, into Austria, wherever
glory and dominion beckoned.

And here was another one! It mattered nothing that this
man was a commoner and a Corsican and had put down the
Revolution with an iron hand. For the Revolution had accomplished its purpose. It had brought forth not liberty, but liberty
of action—Napoleon Bonaparte. The hurrah with which this

young conqueror was greeted from the moment of his appearance on the ruins of the Revolution is sufficient proof that the Revolution was an intruder. The Republic was no more, but what of that? Here was a man of the imperial stamp, in all essentials a legitimate successor of the Grand Monarch, who, given time, would recover that lost empire and make the French name and the French nation known throughout the world.

Shall we say that all this came to an end with Waterloo, that at St. Helena died not only the French Emperor but the Imperial Dream? This might have been true had Napoleon Bonaparte been a man and nothing more. But he was the incarnate spirit of France, an integral part of her history, as indisputably a section of its evolution as any of the other great figures which that country has brought forth. The Napoleonic wars were an expression not of Napoleon Bonaparte but of France. And France did not die at St. Helena. Empires collapse but nations live on, and the character of nations. Individuals do not make that character. They only reveal it.

The years that followed Waterloo were years of confusion and hesitation, as though France had lost her way. Governments rose and fell. The weaklings had returned, first Bourbons out of the mold of the later Louis, followed by offspring of that other effete house—the House of Orleans.

Then another man appeared by the name of Bonaparte. Instantly the confusion vanished. France was united and herself again, fired once more to glory and dominion. First a *coup d'état* after the fashion of the First Napoleon. Then an election with a vote so overwhelming as to leave no doubt as to what lay deepest in the heart of France. No president of a French republic ever received such acclaim as this scion of the House of Conquerors. Wars followed, coming in quick succession, in China, in Mexico, in the Crimea, against Austria, and finally with Germany. But why a Bonaparte if peace were the aim? Could a Bonaparte be a Bonaparte and not add to the glory of France? And what glory if not the glory of arms? The Third Napoleon was carrying out the mandate of the French people.

Quebec, Waterloo, Sedan. Could any nation survive and still go on? Surely now the Imperial Dream is over. With the last of the Bonapartes goes the last of the conquerors. Henceforth France will be satisfied with France.

Nothing could be further from the truth. Indeed, it is republican France which has achieved where its imperial predecessors failed. Nor is this all. It has remained for republican France to distinguish between imperialism and conquest, to explain to a world which seems not to understand, why the former is odious and the latter of good repute. And this has been accomplished with all the casuistry of the schoolmen. Strangely enough, and particularly strange coming out of France so soon after the Great War, it recalls those famous German chauvinists, Treitschke and Bernhardi, whose appeals to the German nation were held up to execration because they justified war in the interest of Kultur.

"Imperialism?" asks René Pinon, Professor at the School of Political Science in Paris, in an article in Current History, May, 1929. "We must not confuse imperialism with the spirit of conquest. Alexander the Great was a conqueror, not an imperialist. Both the word and the thing represent a new phenomenon. * * * The first imperialism was that of Great Britain, and the word comes from the title Empress of India which Disraeli conferred on Queen Victoria." (An astonishing statement coming from a professor of political science.) "From this form of political expansion determined and made necessary by the need of securing outlets for raw material," France, he says, is wholly free. "She has extended her influence over North Africa. * * * She has marked out both in Europe and Asia, as befits a great civilized nation, the territory in which she claims the right to exercise her political, economic, and intellectual activity; . . . but her expansion does not have that characteristic of economic necessity which marks British imperial expansion. If there is a French imperialism, it is moderate and reasonable, and its chief object is to bring civilization to backward peoples." Conquest, therefore, is a glorious career for any nation. Only when it stoops to considerations of trade does it become reprehensible.

Sixty years had passed since the defeat of the last Napoleon when, in the summer of 1931, the Republic of France officially introduced to the world the French Empire.

Obviously then, through the rise and fall of governments in France, there is one thing that does not fall, but takes upon itself one after another of these governments like garments and casts them aside. One need only glance over history to realize that it is imperialism (or, if Professor Pinon prefers, the spirit of conquest) that in France ties the ages together, binding into one not only the Bourbons and the Bonapartes but the French Republic.

What does M. Maurois mean when he says, as he said in his address radioed from Paris to the American people on the 15th of last May, that "France has for a long time been a completed country and does not wish to acquire new territories"? Surely M. Maurois must know that within his own lifetime this "completed country" has gone out and acquired territories far more extensive than have been acquired by any other power in the world, Imperial Russia and Imperial Britain not excepted; that in fact within that short time it has not only doubled its territory but increased it tenfold, that had it not been for the intervention of President Wilson, Turkey too would have been dismembered and distributed by the secret Sykes-Picot agreement to which France was a party.

Let us glance at this empire of the French, enormous in extent, which despite vast losses in North America and Asia, still challenges Great Britain throughout the world. Indeed it would seem that these two great powers, despite all their antagonism, had divided the world between them. For looking out over their widely scattered dominions we see them in every continent and in every ocean. Only these two may fairly be called world powers.

Starting with the Pacific, that region farthest removed from Europe, we find under the French flag not continents—Great Britain has seen to that—but islands. In the Australian archipelago they lie, New Caledonia, Tahiti, and others. Passing to the Asiatic mainland, to China, we come upon an area larger than the state of Texas. Along the coast of India, there is Pondicherry, a remnant of her ancient Indian Empire. On into the Middle East, and we have Syria and Lebanon, spoils of the Great War, weighed out against those neighboring British acquisitions, Iraq and Palestine. Back in the North Atlantic there are diminutive St. Pierre and Miquelon, again fragments left over from her vast North American possessions. To the south, again in significant relation to the British Islands, Guadeloupe, Martinique, and others. Then on the mainland of South America, French Guiana, within a few hours' sail of the British possession of the same name.

But it is not in Asia or in the Americas we must look to find the empire of France. Her Atlantic and Pacific possessions represent not the living to-day but her yesterday that has gone down.

Future historians, looking back upon the centuries that lie behind us, will note with amazement the late arrival of Africa upon the horizon of Europe. How comes it, they will ask, that the powers of Europe, even Spain, should sail away across unknown waters to the far west, seeking shares in an unappropriated world, when right at their door lay another unclaimed continent, teeming with the possibilities of empire? How comes it that even Italy, descendant of Rome whose ruined cities still dot that northern coast, never woke to the lure of that neighboring land but sent her excess millions to find homes in the Americas? As a theater of imperial ambitions, Africa is the North America of to-day. And there again, come out of the ages and encamped for future conflict, we find these same old rivals building across its thousands of miles their rival empires.

That the hopes of France are centered in Africa, no one even casually interested in world politics can for a moment doubt. The frontiers of Europe are defined. The peoples of Asia are awake. The Americas are closed. Only Africa lies open. The far-sighted statesmen of England and France foresaw this situation a century ago. And they are there. Look out over this Dark Continent. Is it not to the twentieth century what North America was to the eighteenth? See how there too domain after domain is swallowed up, the holdings of other peoples passing under one or the other of those same two flags. Within a single generation, the Dutch, the German, the Spanish have disappeared. The old rivals are dividing the continent between them.

Take up the African possessions of France and lay them out over the continent of North America. They cover the United States from the Atlantic across the great plains and the Rocky Mountains to the Pacific. They reach down over the eight hundred thousand square miles of Mexico and on beyond the Panama Canal. Or, instead of spreading them beyond our borders to the south, turn round and lay them down toward the north. Canada, as we know, is larger than the United States, but the African possessions of France would almost cover both countries. Then add to these those scattered possessions in other continents and in other seas, and you have France.

If Napoleon Bonaparte could return and look abroad upon the French dominions, he would be astonished to find that the Republic of France has been more efficient in the building of an empire than the Empire itself.[1]

A proposal has recently been put forward in France by *Le Journal* to efface from the walls of France by official action the famous motto of the French Republic, *Liberté, Egalité, Fraternité*. This is one of the most astonishing and significant suggestions ever made. If it were a proposal to demolish the Louvre, Notre Dame, and the Arc de Triomphe, the whole world would justly be surprised. For these monuments are an integral part of the culture and civilization of France. Without them neither Paris nor France would be quite the same. But far more than the loss of the monuments themselves would be the profound change in the mind and spirit of France which even a proposal of this sort would indicate. What has come over this cultured people, we would ask, that art has ceased to appeal? Has industrialism, so long held at bay, captured this last stronghold of the classical age and driven from France that appreciation of beauty which was the outstanding quality of the French character?

Liberty, Equality, Fraternity. If the question were put, what are the most living words in all human speech, can there be any doubt that the final choice would rest upon these three? Throughout the ages and throughout all lands what hope have they inspired, what sacrifices have they called forth, what deeds of heroism have they kindled! And somehow it was France that made these words her own, caught them up and lifted them above the world. With no other nation do we so naturally associate them. In no other country do we find them so widely displayed, on palaces and prisons, on towers and archways, wherever the eye falls they are there, written all over the land. France may have her tricolor, but for more than a century these words have been the living symbol of the nation. Wherever France is known, these words are known.

The French Revolution it was that gave these words to France. Out of the agony and ecstasy of that revolt they came, cast up by its fury, to stand forever upon the walls of a new age. After centuries of oppression, the French people had spoken, and the words which they uttered kindled not only France but Europe. Something about them there was that

[1] This chapter is taken from the author's recent book entitled *Our Genial Enemy, France* (published by Ray Long & Richard R. Smith), a study of the militaristic and imperialistic aspects of French politics.

made these words stand out among words as Jeanne d'Arc among saints. Never had the Saxon brought forth words like these. England and America had had their revolutions and out of them had come charters of liberty and declarations of independence, but never out of those uprisings words comparable to these, Liberty, Equality, Fraternity. Here was the very poetry of revolt. Never before had three words transformed a continent as these three words were destined to transform Europe. In a single day France had leaped to the forefront of the new age, the accepted leader in the great struggle for human emancipation.

What has happened to this country of the ideal that a paper of standing and vast influence is willing to sponsor a suggestion that these words be effaced from the monuments of France? That a profound change has taken place since the Great War we have all of us been aware. But what enemy of France could have imagined this? What friend would have believed it possible? We can best realize the significance of this proposal if we imagine it made, let us say, in Germany or in Italy. How quickly from Paris would the news of it have been sent out over the world. We would have found it staring at us from the headlines of our morning papers. And the inevitable inference would have been there, that the spirit of the Hohenzollerns had reëstablished itself beyond the Rhine, that Fascist Italy was running true to form. "Let the act speak for itself," the French press would have said. "We told you so." Or if a year ago or even three months ago a rumor had come from Berlin or from Rome that France was contemplating this action, it would have met in Paris with high disdain or have been branded by the press of France as the propaganda of jealous neighbors. But it is from Paris the suggestion has come, from one of the leading papers of France, and we are informed that it has met with "vociferous approval." I repeat, nothing more astonishing has come out of France.

To those interested in the psychology of nations and in the making of history, here is something worthy of serious consideration. For it reveals a striking transformation in national character and shows the direction in which history is moving. That a new France has risen, there can be no doubt. The country is there, the monuments are intact, the course of daily life flows by unaltered, one can wander over the same pleasant landscape and meet the same charming people, but something is there that was not there yesterday. Or if there, not visibly there, not out in the open as it is out in the open to-day.

Is it that France has emerged victorious from the Great War, her lost provinces recovered, her empire enlarged, her coffers overflowing with gold, her army the greatest in Europe, her influence powerful in the Orient as in the Occident? There can be no question that the France we see to-day is not the France we saw yesterday. The psychology of defeat born of the disaster of '71 is gone. The confidence of the Napoleonic period has returned.

To understand the change which has come about, culminating in this astounding proposal to quench in France the last torch of the Revolution, we must go back beyond the Great War. The proposal itself may be new and startling, but that which it expresses is not new. The generation which in other countries grew up after 1871 and whose impression of France lasted on to the Great War was a generation that knew defeated France. There had been in the long ago, it is true, another France, but that France had passed into history. The third Napoleon who, following the dream of his illustrious uncle, had again launched the power of France throughout the world, into China, into Mexico, into the Crimea, into Austria, into Italy, and who, confident of his genius and of the conquering will of the French nation, saw himself master of the rising Germany, had suffered at Sedan an even more humiliating defeat than his ancestor had suffered at Waterloo. Out of that defeat France came chastened and sober, her sword laid aside, a peasant France, busy with her olives and her vines. With this France, from our school days, we had grown up, a thrifty, hardworking France, as different from the France that had followed the Bonapartes as the farmers of Rome were different from the legions of the Cæsars. Our sympathy went out to this invaded country that asked only peace and security. The lost provinces of France became the lost provinces of us all.

And this defeated France was a republic rearisen in a day when to be a republic was to be in the very vanguard of political and social enlightenment. For round the word republic still hung the glamour of its original meaning, the commonwealth. Under its beneficent reign inequality would disappear, opportunity would open to all, imperialism would end, and there would be peace between nations. It was the last word of human aspiration for freedom and justice, the goal of the collective dream through the ages. The sole remaining problem of the nations was to reproduce this new political form throughout the world.

It was natural, therefore, that the liberal peoples of the world should see in this second republic of France the pioneer of a new order in Europe, as the liberal peoples of the eighteenth century had seen in the first republic of France the pioneer of a new order. And this second republic was surrounded by monarchies just as that first republic had been. And these monarchies knew all too well what this new form of government meant. Europe might be large, but there was no room in Europe for these two, no room for the dynastic and the popular, no room for special privilege and equal rights. Sooner or later this new republic would be attacked precisely as that old republic had been. Around the borders of France, therefore, the liberal peoples of the world stood on guard. This new government was theirs. They would see to it that it was not destroyed.

And they stood on guard not alone because this new order of things was theirs, but because the people who had produced this new order had also brought forth the most perfect civilization of modern times, a cultural superstructure resting upon a foundation of small farms and small shops and small industries. As the first problem of the new world order was to reproduce this new political form, the republic, throughout the world, so the second problem was to spread throughout the world the freedom and grace of this perfect civilization. For here was a nation, the model of what all nations should become, self-contained and self-sufficient, with no imperialistic ambitions, a people without inhibitions, wise enough to allow the individual to come to flower. In summing up this civilization of the French nation, I can do no better than quote, incongruous though it may seem, from my recent book, "Our Genial Enemy, France." "For somehow in France, to a degree unequalled in any other country, the unity of life has been preserved. And this unity has been achieved with no loss of variety. It is not a unity brought about by conformity, but a unity of elements held together by the ideal. The colors are there, but there is also harmony. Nothing stands out to catch the eye and proclaim France as its especial representative. Religion does not obtrude itself. Work is not an obsession. Labor and leisure go hand in hand. Culture and trade and sport and politics interplay. Appreciation of art is a masculine as well as a feminine virtue. Beauty is not despised. Love is unashamed. Food and drink have their places in the economy of life. Sanity prevails." In no other country had Liberty, Equality and Fraternity found so complete an expression in the political and social life of the people.

Here we find the explanation of the fact that while, since the Great War, revolutions have swept over other nations, wrecking their political and social structure, France has remained what she was. Scarred from battle, her millions have returned to take up their accustomed tasks, content with life as it was and is, satisfied with the France of yesterday.

How then explain this amazing suggestion that comes from the upper regions of French politics?

I have said that this recent proposal to remove from the walls of France the last reminder of the Revolution represents the culmination of something, that while it seems startling and new, it is startling and new only in the form it has taken. It is startling and new only to those whose eyes before the Great War were fixed upon France in Europe. Unquestionably in Europe France was a republic; but outside of Europe there was another France. The France of Europe might be a republic, chastened and sober and mindful of the rights of nations, but the France of Asia and Africa was the France of the Bourbons and the Bonapartes, seizing wherever it was safe and profitable to seize. There the dynastic ideal survived and was having its way. To these outlying lands the sacred principles of the Revolution had never come. There the policy of the Republic was the policy of the Empire.

The truth of this statement is beyond controversy. For those who would challenge it we need only point to the fact that between the Franco-Prussian war and the Great War, the Republic of France acquired by force of arms territories larger than the whole of the United States, an achievement never approached by the Corsican himself, a record unequalled within the same period even by Imperial Russia or Imperial Britain. While we were bemoaning the provinces of France lost to Germany, in other continents primitive peoples were losing their lands to conquering France. And this France was a defeated France, a France that had herself suffered at the hands of the invader.

The France which emerged from the Great War was a victorious France. Let us consider the record of that France since the armistice of 1918.

It is interesting to recall, in this connection, the effect which victory had had upon the French nation following the establishment of the First Republic. The Revolution had brought forth, as we have seen, principles that kindled the hope of the world and won for France the leadership in the cause of human emancipation. Yet the same generation which produced that Revolution and set upon the walls of France those immortal words, with shouts of enthusiasm followed Napoleon to the Pyramids and to Moscow and reared over Europe one of the most colossal imperialisms of history.

Between the effect of that victory and the effect of the victory of the Great War we come upon an astonishing parallel. The leader is absent; the flying wedge of Bonaparte nowhere appears. But the imperial mind is there, functioning behind the mask of popular government, moving across the borders of Europe, consolidating the power of France throughout the world. Let us follow, step by step, the operations of that imperial mind and discover, if we can, in what respect republican France of the twentieth century differs from imperial France of the seventeeth and the eighteenth.

As out of the French Revolution rose for one moment a new order of things, so out of the Great War there emerged for one moment the hope and promise of everlasting peace. Suffering had brought, as prosperous days could never bring, the consciousness of the unity of humanity. Henceforth that unity was to be a living thing. The territories and rights of nations were to be respected. For the settlement of disputes, conference was to be substituted for war.

The ink was scarcely dry upon the Covenant of the League of Nations, under whose banner this new age had been set up, when France began hurriedly to rebuild the old order. It was a *volte-face* comparable to that which had taken place during the Revolution when the fervor for liberty was transmuted into a fervor for conquest. The spirit of Talleyrand was again abroad. Secret diplomacy moved once more through the chancelleries of Europe. The principle of the balance of power was restored. Allies were sought and found, Belgium, Poland, Czecho-Slovakia, Jugoslavia, and others. To these allies were distributed the war supplies left over from the American effort and purchased by France. To these allies also credits of hundreds of millions of dollars were extended. Within the League of Nations, created to protect the freedom and the rights of nations, France had organized a League of France to perpetuate her domination of the continent.

Outside of Europe, among races never quite adopted into the human family, this imperialism turned to arms. In the mandated territory of Syria an uprising of the native people for self-government was put down by force, and Damascus, its capital, was bombarded. War was carried into the Riff and its leader, Abd-el-Krim, was seized and banished, and the country incorporated into the French Empire. The old order was having its way, unconcerned with the new order at Geneva.

But it may be said a nation cannot be indicted for acts compelled by exceptional circumstances, acts not unlike those committed by other nations in other parts of the world. This is true. But if such acts are found to be not exceptions but parts of a consistent whole, if they are of the color and texture of a nation's policy, and if this policy shows itself one and the same wherever met with, then we are justified in taking these incidents into account.

We are inquiring into the change that has come about in France and are seeking to find out whether this change is an expression of French policy as it unfolds itself in French history. We have seen rise out of the French Revolution an age of reaction and that reaction carried by force of arms over Europe. We have seen between the Franco-Prussian war and the Great War a huge French Empire arise. We have seen that, following the Great War, the diplomacy of France was the diplomacy of the Empire. We have seen the sword of this Empire unsheathed in Syria and North Africa. Let us press this inquiry further to that central stronghold of imperialism, militarism. Is there any foundation for the charge, frequently made in recent years, that the Republic of France is to-day the outstanding representative of the old order of force?

That a nation is entitled to adequate protection has never been denied. Let us dismiss this, then, at the very outset as an accepted fact. If the menace in Europe since the armistice has been such as to necessitate the enormous increase in armament which France has made and if this armament measures up only to the needs of security, then no criticism can be made. A nation is entitled to its security.

When we examine the reasons put forward by French statesmen for this vast armament expenditure, we find them all facing across the Rhine. Across the Rhine it is that the menace lies. As before the Great War it was Germany, so to-day it is Germany. But the Germany of today is not the Germany of yesterday. Yesterday as the world watched on either side of the Rhine the rival growths of military power, criticism of France, if criticism there was, was tolerant in extreme. The friends of republican France understood. There could be no question that the menace was there. Imperial Germany was expanding. Her population was increasing rapidly. Her economic power was developing beyond that of any other nation of Europe. A mighty army was rising. Ships of war were multiplying upon the seas and under the seas. And crowning the German Imperial State was a figure that boded no good for the peace of Europe. Time and again from the Kaiser words had fallen that had alarmed the nations. Against this it was that France stood in arms.

What is Germany to-day? A nation dismembered, her empire gone, her fleet no more, her vast army of yesterday reduced to a police force of one hundred thousand men, bound by treaties and covenants which her conquerors have written into the laws of Europe, her economic life so prostrate that even her former foes have felt constrained to come to her aid.

And what of France? By the Treaty of Versailles the Allies, including France, bound themselves in solemn convenant to reduce their armaments to approximate the German reduction. In that clause of the great settlement lay the hope of the world. That kept, a new age was inevitable. To the fulfillment of that obligation humanity looked as it looked to no other provision of the treaties ending the war. Thirteen years have passed and so far from this agreement having been kept, it has been made a scrap of paper. Expenditures for armament in France have steadily risen since the armistice until to-day they have reached the colossal total of $600,000,000 a year, one-twelfth of the entire income of the French nation, the highest per capita expenditure in all the history of France. As a consequence we see, facing a disarmed and bound Germany, a France armed out of all proportion to any previous record, the most completely armed of any nation in the world to-day.

If we turn to the efforts which have been made since the armistice to bring the nations to an agreement to reduce military expenditures, we find France significantly in the forefront of opposition. No other country has resisted so desperately the forces of peace or shown itself more resourceful in scattering those forces and delaying their forward march. Other nations differed over this or that specific proposal. France alone showed hostility to the principle. The very discussion of disarmament was taken as an affront to France. The world has not forgotten the incident which occurred in Paris when, at a gathering of international peace leaders, eminent speakers from all over the world were shouted down and their deliberations brought to an end. Shall we say that this too, like the bombardment of Damascus and the seizure of the Riff, was an incident of no significance? Does it not rather fit into the whole tapestry of French policy since the armistice? In no other city of the world, with the possible exception of Tokyo, could this riotous demonstration have taken place.

But let us test the consistency of this policy in fields far removed from the security of France. Not along the Rhine but in those far regions we shall discover the sincerity or insincerity of the security defense.

In no part of the world as in the Far East to-day is the line so clearly drawn between the old order and the new. Out there, far more than in Europe, events are uncovering the essential policy and character of nations. Let us see if the France which we find out there is not the France of the balance of power in Europe, the France of Damascus and the Riff.

When the invasion of Manchuria occurred and the Council of the League of Nations was called to consider the situation, M. Briand was asked to preside. During those deliberations the reaction of the eminent Foreign Minister of France was identical with the reactions of the rest of the world. The sense of outrage which the nations felt at this assault not only upon China but upon the covenants of the world found in M. Briand instantaneous and passionate expression. A peremptory order went forth from Geneva that Japan withdraw from the invaded territory, and a time limit was set for that withdrawal. Then something happened which to this day has never been explained. The discussion in Geneva came suddenly to an end. The affair was transferred to Paris where in secret a small conference was held, and shortly afterward M. Briand disappeared not only from public office but from public life. Will it be said that this too was an incident, that the outspoken defense of Japan which from that day to this has filled the French press is the scattered expression of individuals and not the inspired utterance of French policy?

That France has made common cause with Japan in the Far East there can be no doubt whatsoever. Confronted with the choice of complying with the alliance concluded by these two powers in 1907 which provided for mutual assistance in that region, or of coöperating with the rest of the world in the enforcement of the Nine Power Treaty, the Pact of Paris, and the Covenant of the League of Nations, France chose the former. It was a consistent choice, in character precisely the same as that made immediately after the armistice between the old principle of the balance of power and the new principle of conference. Indeed, so far as the diplomacy of the great controversy is concerned, it is Paris, not Tokyo, that has shaped the strategy and directed the defense at Geneva. In the field of military operations, Japan had succeeded beyond all expectations; timing her assault to conditions throughout the world, she had seized and established her dominion in Manchuria with an ease that was amazing. Only in handling the reactions of the western world had she blundered, showing from the outset a total misunderstanding of the western mind. With the great trial approaching at Geneva where an accounting was to be made for the violation of treaties, something had to be done. Significantly enough, the conference which took this matter in hand assembled in Paris. To this conference, summoned in preparation for the approaching trial, came Yosuke Matsuoka, special representative of the Japanese Foreign Office, Haruichi Nagaoka, ambassador to France, Tsunuo Matsudaira, ambassador to England, and Japanese ministers from Poland, Switzerland, Belgium, and Holland. At that conference, held in secret, representatives of the French Government were present, including M. Herriot, then Premier of France. France was fulfilling the terms of her alliance which provided for mutual support in the Far East.[2]

I have said that French policy is a consistent whole, that whether we view it from the angle of France or the angle of the world, it is an imperial policy, shaped and determined not

[2] That world opinion finally forced France to cooperate with the other nations at Geneva does not alter the fact that throughout the whole controversy the Foreign Office and the press of France have gone as far as they dared in strengthening the hand of Japan.

from considerations of French security but for the maintenance by force of arms of the French Empire. Is it possible to challenge this conclusion written as it is all over the earth, or the logical corollary of this conclusion that the towering structure of French armament has arisen not for the purpose of national defense but to maintain and extend French Imperialism? For that policy and this imperialism are one and the same, whether we follow it along the Rhine, throughout Eastern Europe, along the Mediterranean, across the Sahara, or in the troubled region of the Far East.

And now, like a keystone in a great arch, capping its curve and completing the structure, comes the proposal to efface from the walls of France the last reminder of her Revolution, Liberty, Equality, Fraternity. The French mind, which is a logical mind, and which through all the vicissitudes of French politics, and all the revolutionary changes within the boundaries of France, has pursued throughout the world the same imperial policy, comes back to Paris to complete itself.

All this would be of little concern to the world if it concerned only France. But from this short study of French imperialism that has lasted on despite all changes, we come to a realization of the fact that somehow the forces of revolution never quite succeed in completely transforming a country. Bastilles of domestic abuses may go down, but the Foreign Offices remain what they were, and from these central strongholds of the old order the old diplomacy continues to function, the ancient game of conquest goes on, embroiling the nations. As though, driven from the lower plains of life, the forces of reaction had taken refuge in the upper, and there entrenched themselves beyond the reach of popular control, beyond even the desire to exercise that control. For the masses do not understand the great game that is going on, often thousands of miles distant from their own country. Provided revolution has bettered their own conditions and enlarged their own liberties, they are little concerned with what their governments do in other lands.

And yet, in the last analysis, it is the foreign policy of a nation that determines its ultimate destiny. If that policy be a predatory policy, militarism is inevitable. Conquest can be carried on only by force, and that force will mount and expand and eat away the vitals of a nation. Unlike evil growths in other fields, against which outside nations can easily protect themselves, militarism, rooted in one country, seeds itself in all the rest. From the operation of this inexorable law there is no possibility of escape. As water seeks its level, armament will rise to the level of its highest point, until somewhere in its weakest sector the great dam breaks and the innocent with the guilty are overwhelmed.

Recovery through revolution, shall we say? Is it not obvious that until revolution advances beyond the Bastilles of a country to the control of its foreign policy, there can be no permanent recovery? Here we are confronted with life's ultimate tragedy. Plan and build as we may within the boundaries of our national home, create if you please within these boundaries that utopia of which humanity has dreamed, the permanence of all this will depend not upon its worth but upon the fact that in some other nation the age of force is still enthroned.

THE CRUCIAL IMPORTANCE
OF POLAND

H ISTORY plays ironical pranks. All through the nineteenth century Russia was the symbol of oppression, the policeman of Europe so to speak, ready to throttle any revolution that would disturb the order and harmony established by the Holy Alliance. A century after the establishment of that League of Nations, Russia became for a while the prime mover of revolution all over the world.

Poland, all through the nineteenth century, played the very opposite part. Shorn of her independence, divided among Russia, Prussia and Austria, she had become the symbol of Europe's struggling democracy. Polish noblemen, in whose eyes the serf was not a human being—the killing of a peasant entailed a small fine in old Poland—once they themselves were pulled down from their high horse suddenly became champions of freedom all over the world. Ever since the American Revolution they supplied heroes and leaders of revolutionary uprisings in Austria, Hungary, Germany and France. They fought with George Washington and conspired with Karl Marx. They bled on the battlefields of revolutionary Hungary and on the barricades of the Paris Commune of 1871. Time and again they tried to rise against the powers that dismembered them and they always lost—in 1831, in 1846 and in 1863.

European radicals and Russian revolutionaries alike held the reëstablishment of Poland to be of paramount importance for the cause of European democracy. Ever since the rise of the Turkish menace, Poland repeatedly had been the shock-ab-

sorber of the well-nigh invincible conqueror. After their aid
had relieved the siege of Vienna, toward the end of the seventeenth century, the Poles began to call their country proudly
the "bulwark of Christianity." With Russia as the self-appointed
executor of the will of the Holy Alliance, oppressed Poland
assumed in the eyes of progressive Europe the part of a sleeping
giant-killer that had to be roused from its lethargy in order
to oppose the sinister liberty-destroying designs of the Colossus
of the North. Karl Marx called for revolutionary wars against
Russia, whose ultimate aim would have been the restoration
of Poland. Russia's greatest revolutionists of the middle of the
nineteenth century, Michael Bakunin and Alexander Herzen,
staked their popularity with their countrymen by openly
sympathizing with or supporting the Polish insurrection of
1863.

As time went by, with the consolidation of the great European powers in the latter part of the last century, the restoration of Poland became hardly more than a pious wish, a wish
that was taken as seriously as the constantly recurring yearnings
and protestations for disarmament and universal peace. The
three largest powers of the European continent had so thoroughly incorporated their Polish loot as an "organic" part of
their political and economic fabric that the mere thought of
reuniting Poland impressed the ordinary Russian, German or
Austrian citizen, even a Pole himself, as no less fantastic than
the idea of an independent Negro Republic in the Black Belt
would affect the average American not belonging to the Communist Party.

Germany, with her industries which attracted many workers
from the mainly agricultural Polish provinces, with her forcible
Germanization that forbade the teaching of the Polish language,
with her merciless policy of crowding out of the Polish farmers
and settling Germans in their stead, was inexorably pursuing
the aim of making good Prussians out of the few million reluctant Poles whose Catholic and nationalist politicians were
trying in vain to stop the Teutonic steam-roller. In a generation
or two the Junkers might have succeeded if it had not been
for the War.

The Hapsburg monarchy would cherish no policy copied
from its powerful neighbor and ally. With a German minority
facing the other nine nationalities of Austria-Hungary in a
numerical proportion of one to five, and with a backward

economic system at that, it was compelled to adopt another policy with regard to the Poles and other non-German nationalities. It was a policy of playing off one nationality against another, of stimulating their mutual jealousies and quenching their desire for independence by granting some of them the right to oppress their weaker neighbors—a thorough remedy against a national inferiority-complex and the rebellious leanings resulting therefrom. Thus, the ruling class of the Austrian Poles, chiefly the landed nobility and smaller gentry whose offspring would fill the ranks of the clergy and bureaucracy, were permitted to lord it over the Ukrainians of Eastern Galicia. Numerically the latter equalled the Poles, but being chiefly a nation of illiterate small peasants, with a very slight sprinkling of intellectuals, they were at the mercy of their Polish masters who owned the best lands in the Ukrainian section of Galicia as well.

Polish national sentiment in Galicia was not particularly aggressive. Whatever ugly mood it showed was not against the central government of Vienna, but against the occasionally obstreperous Ukrainian intellectuals and their peasant following. The latter kept wondering about, and sometimes even protesting, against that strange phenomenon of a territory, 80 per cent of whose inhabitants were Ukrainian peasants, being represented in Parliament mostly by Polish noblemen or their flunkeys. True, the latter claimed that what civilization there was in that God-forsaken corner of Austria was Polish—but this was rather an obscene joke. For the enormous majority of the "Poles" inhabiting the urban settlements, with the one exception of the Galician capital Lemberg, were small Jewish tradesmen, whose attachment to the Polish cause was—proverbial. They spoke Yiddish, and their only contact with the superior culture of the masters of the country was in the form of paying graft to the Polish bureaucrats. Their educated offspring—if they could afford to send their sons to college—were mostly Zionists, hated by, and returning the hate of, their Polish colleagues. For they were their future competitors in the liberal professions and in such public services as the railroad and post-office, which occasionally admitted Jews, while the judiciary and the political administration were reserved for "Christians only," of noble or at least well-connected families.

There was also a sprinkling of Socialists in this least civilized section of what once was a part of Poland. Their following was

small. Aside from the oil wells, there were practically no industries to speak of in Galicia. The Polish landed noblemen
thwarted any attempt at the development of manufacturing
industries on "their" territory, for these might attract the
landless or land-poor all but serfs, causing a scarcity of farm
hands and thus raising their wages. The Socialist leadership
consisted mostly of *déclassé* intellectuals and semi-intellectuals,
Poles and Jews. To the various malcontent elements of the
lower middle-class and to the working class of the country they
offered a grotesque combination of Marxian class struggle
terminology with the democratic and nationalist verbiage of
the romantic knight-errants of Polish freedom of the middle
of the nineteenth century. The "class war" talk was to get the
vote of the workers, scarce as they were, while "Polish independence" was to win over the growing ranks of the educated
or semi-educated lower middle-class elements. To them a liberated Poland meant prospects of steady jobs in the administration, the army, and all the other branches of public life.

There were Socialist students and workers among the
Ukrainians of Galicia to whom the protestations of international brotherhood sounded suspicious when coming from the
mouths of those Polish Socialists. Some of them had even the
courage occasionally to accuse the latter of being nationalists
pure and simple, and of dreaming of an imperialist Poland
"from sea to sea," that is, from the Baltic to the Black Sea—the
glorious old Poland that included Lithuania, White Russia [1] and
the Ukraine, as well as Eastern Prussia and the other Baltic
territories. This the Polish Socialists would indignantly deny,
attesting the Socialist legitimacy of their nationalist yearnings
with ample quotations from Marx and the decisions of International Socialist Congresses to which the Poles were always
admitted as a separate nationality though they had no independent country of their own.

The Polish Socialists of Austria took their inspiration from
Russian Poland. It was territorially and numerically the largest
section of the Poland that was partitioned in 1795, but it no
longer included non-Polish speaking lands such as the Ukraine,
which the old Kingdom had lost to Russia before. Russian
Poland had seen the tragic failures of the revolts of 1831 and

---

[1] The northwestern part of Russia, sometimes called "White Ruthenia."

1863, as the Austrian section had its own defeats in 1846, and the Prussian in 1848.

In counter-distinction to the other two sections, Russian Poland had highly developed industries with a growing working class. The economic development killed the nationalist aspirations of the Polish propertied classes. Russia became a good market for the manufactured products of the Polish industries. The landed nobility understood that any revolutionary uprising against Russia would lead to unpleasantness on the part of their own farm laborers. Thus, the only social group that refused to make peace with the Tsarist régime was the large group of impecunious, malcontent intellectuals and semi-intellectuals. Their advancement as the leaders and organizers of industrial and public life was blocked by the presence of the foreign invaders, who reserved all the privileged jobs for themselves. It was these malcontent intellectuals who undertook a heroic struggle for Poland's independence, a struggle which seemed hopeless, for they had to face the opposition not only of the Tsarist police, but of their own propertied classes as well. But they found other allies. They combined their nationalist vocabulary with Socialist slogans and persuaded large sections of the workers that Polish independence was the indispensable condition of their emancipation from capitalism. Joseph Pilsudski became the founder and leader of a powerful revolutionary organization called *P.P.S.* (Polish Socialist Party), whose heroic struggles against the Tsarist régime earned it the admiration of the whole Socialist world. That party attracted the best minds among the Polish intellectuals, for whom the cause of Polish emancipation, that is to say, their own rule over Poland, was identical with the cause of the Polish workers. They were, of course, not always conscious of the fact that they were using the workers as mere tools for their own interests, and that the "Socialism" they were preaching was only a cloak for nationalism.

They were, however, not so naïve as to expect to attain their aims through their own efforts, even though their desperate terrorist tactics directed against Tsarist bureaucrats, policemen and soldiers almost made it appear that this was their plan. Nor did they expect to win as the result of a victorious Russian revolution. In the first place, they were very skeptical about the prospects of a revolution in the empire of the Tsars. Moreover, such a revolution, even victorious, was not the solution of their problems. Such a revolution would, at best, grant them a broad autonomy within the Russian constitutional monarchy or democratic republic. It would not give them the full independence that alone could guarantee the control of the entire bureaucratic machine, the disposition of all the positions coveted by job-hungry intellectuals and semi-intellectuals of a country under foreign domination. They set their hopes on a much more "solid" basis. That basis was a European war, for whose outbreak they were praying as orthodox Jews pray for the coming of the Messiah. They had offered their alliance to Japan during the war with Russia in 1904–5, and since 1909, when increasing friction between Austria and Russia, caused by the conflict of Balkan ambitions, began to point more and more to an inevitable clash between the Central Powers and the Tsarist Empire, they openly collaborated with the Austrian General Staff. It was with the permission of the latter that they organized on Galician soil the nucleus of the future Polish insurgent army, which was to arouse the Poles of Russia as soon as the "Day" had come. Out of the turmoil of a victorious war they expected to obtain the independence, if not of all Poland, then at least of its most important part, which was under Russian rule. A queer "Socialism" one might say, but then the Socialism of the War and post-war period was to be even queerer than that.

The expectations of the Polish Socialists were fulfilled more than they anticipated in their wildest dreams. Not only were the Tsarist armies beaten by the Central Powers, which resulted in the separation of Poland from Russia, but the German and Austrian victors were beaten in turn by the Franco-British-American alliance. The result was a reunion of the three disjointed sections of the old kingdom, and the country got the benefit of a bureaucracy of its own which, to use a still valid *bonmot*, combined all the glorious qualities of Poland's former masters: the arrogance of the Prussian Junkers, the inefficiency of the happy-go-lucky Austrians, and the corruption and graft of the Tsarist "chinovniks." Without the victory of the Allies, Russian Poland would have been incorporated in either a "Greater Germany" or a "Greater Austria," or possibly reduced to the rank of a third-rate semi-independent principality *à la* Albania, with a scion of one of the many German dynasties as its king or duke. Poland's resurrection, yearned for by the best minds of democratic Europe, made its *début* with a symbolic gesture. The break-up of Austria encouraged the Ukrainians of Eastern Galicia to organize a little republic of their own. In doing so they acted as good Wilsonians, for the principle of "self-determination" was supposed to apply to all nations. But this was not to be. Claiming that the territory was Polish because its cities were Polish—they were in fact 80 per cent Yiddish—the knight-errants of yesterday put up a stiff fight against the Ukrainian usurpers. It has been until now one of the great grievances of Ignace Daszynski—with Pilsudski one of the founders of Polish Socialism and the country's greatest orator—that his son got no medal for his heroism in putting down the Ukrainian rebels. It was in this struggle that the Polish soldiers were permitted to have a little lark in the form of a pogrom, though the Jews had taken no sides in the fight. (There had never been any pogroms on Polish territory prior to its "liberation.") Moreover, claiming Eastern Galicia on the grounds that its *cities* were "Polish" did not prevent the Polish nationalists from claiming Upper Silesia from Germany on the ground that the *rural* regions were Polish when it turned out that the majority of the population, concentrated in the industrial centers, had voted for Germany.

Born at a moment when revolution was in full swing in Russia and Germany, Poland was in "danger" likewise of succumbing to the leftward swing of her eastern and western neighbors. But the group of radical officers and politicians in charge of the newborn republic decided that this was not to be. Whatever their delusions about the "proletarian" character of their "Socialism" might have been during the years of heroic struggle against the Tsarist régime, Pilsudski and his friends, now that they had achieved power at last, became fully conscious of what they really had been fighting for. They wanted no revolution that would disturb the property relations in their country and arouse the ire of their Allied liberators. A struggle of the workers against the well-to-do classes, once started, would eventually lead to a situation such as was created in Russia by the Bolshevist revolution. It might involve Poland in civil war. It might array her on the same front with Soviet Russia. For the Polish intellectuals, now at last at the helm of their country, it would mean a new subjection to Russia, though in another form. With the downfall of the Soviet régime, which they thought inevitable, it would mean perhaps a new subjection to, or incorporation in, the great Eastern Empire. This was not what they had suffered for. A capitalist Poland, in which the radical intelligentsia—with its working class following and the strategic points it occupied in the new Polish army—constituted an important political factor, was good enough for them. There were plenty of soft jobs for the asking, whether the radical intellectuals constituted part of the government or were heading the law-abiding opposition.

But how were the workers to be kept from thwarting these plans and rising in their own interests? That was comparatively easy. A cabinet was constituted, headed by an old-time Socialist, which convinced the workers that, at last, they had "their own government," an independent, Socialist Poland. What more did they want?

In the meantime the army, the police, the judiciary, the administration, in short all the instruments for the preservation of the "social order," were consolidated, and the ensuing elections put a damper upon the hopes of all those who had expected any radical changes in the country's economic structure. Representation in Parliament was divided between various reactionary and progressive parties, representing the interests of the landed nobility, the business spheres, the Catholic clergy, the richer and poorer farmers and various strata of the lower middle classes, including that section of the intelligentsia dabbling in labor politics. Over them all was hovering the heroic figure of Marshal Pilsudski, Chief of State and Commander of the country's army, who shortly after the beginning of the Great War, in his capacity of Commander of the Polish Legion, had ceased to call himself a Socialist, a term that was too narrow for his ambitions.

Having regained her independence, Poland had at the same time achieved the ambition of every oppressed nation yearning for "freedom." She extended her realm far beyond the mere ethnographic limits of a national state. But even the generous frontiers granted her by the Allies at the expense of millions of Germans, Ukrainians, White Ruthenians and Lithuanians were too narrow for her. With naïve cynicism a Polish Socialist paper in New York (*Robotnik Polski*) had advanced the idea, in 1917, that Poland should be reëstablished within her "ethnographical, historical, geographical and strategical frontiers," a formula which could be stretched to include not only the old historical Poland "from the Baltic to the Black Sea," with the non-Polish subjects constituting two-thirds or three-fourths of the population, but even from the Elbe to the Volga River.

A man of action, Pilsudski was waiting for the moment for carrying out this day-dream of the Polish romantics—radical and reactionary alike. But the time was not propitious while the Whites were still in the field. Assistance to the old Tsarist generals would have helped to bring back old Imperial Russia with all her disastrous possibilities for Poland. As soon as the Red Army had driven Kolchak to the wall and Denikin into the sea the Polish Garibaldi started his march upon the Ukraine. But the midsummer night's dream of Poland's past glory burst like a bubble. A counter-offensive brought the Red Armies close to the gates of the Polish capital and it was only French help that "saved" Poland from becoming a Soviet Republic.

The subsequent years saw a growing struggle between the reactionary block, originally centered around the person of Paderewski, and the Pilsudski coalition of lower middle class progressives, the peasant parties, the Socialist intellectuals and the national minorities which preferred the romantic Marshal to the much more jingoistic reactionaries. Due to the defection of the party of the more prosperous peasants, the reactionaries eventually gained the upper hand. The old national hero had to resign his military command.

Poland was thus on the road to becoming a country dominated by a set of reactionary landed noblemen, big manufacturers, Catholic clergymen, and sundry bureaucrats and army officers connected with these spheres. The educated lower middle classes and particularly the heroic radical patriots of the previous decades, whether they had already dropped their older proletarian vocabulary or still persisted, British Labor Party fashion, in "championing" the laboring masses, were to be left in the cold, or at best permitted to remain without any political influence whatsoever.

But the reactionaries had counted without Pilsudski, whose following in the army they had underestimated. The flower of the officers supported the old Marshal. He had been their undisputed leader in the days of their knight-errantry, as homeless exiles from a Tsar-ridden Poland. He had given them military training in the "Sharpshooters Corps" organized by him in Galicia with the permission of the Austrian General Staff. He had raised them to their army commissions in the

Polish Legion during the Great War. They felt that sooner or later they, too, were going to be removed from their positions. Were they to make room for the kinsmen of the cowardly nobility and the upper middle classes who had always ridiculed Pilsudski's heroic struggle against the country's historical fate? They revolted once more and joined the old Marshal in his *coup* of May, 1926.

It was an army revolt, pure and simple, with the civilian population only hazily realizing what its ultimate outcome would be in case of a victory of the rebels. The only changes effected, immediately after the victory, were new presidential elections and the assumption by Pilsudski of the post of Minister of War, the symbol of his at first disguised, and as time went by, undisguised, dictatorship.

Originally the *coup d'état* of 1926 was not meant as the starting point for the establishment of a purely military or a purely Fascist dictatorship. Whether Pilsudski was still unable to discard altogether his democratic prejudices, or whether France, his country's money-lender, frowned upon the introduction of methods which rendered any financial control impossible, the respectability of "continuity" was maintained and Parliament was permitted to proceed. But neither Parliament nor the electorate were impressed by his victory on the streets of Warsaw, nor by his attempts to form a political party of his own. That political party was a pathetic affair. It had no specific program to stand on and, though attacking the other parties for graft and corruption, it was chiefly engaged in winning over various groups from the other parties by the promise of governmental favors, the very method it pretended to fight. Industrial groups were promised contracts, and part of the landed nobility, particularly in the eastern districts of the country, were lured with the prospect of a renewed war with the Soviet Republic, which would return to them their Russian estates that had been seized by the peasants after the Bolshevik revolution. The educated lower middle classes saw the hope of new government jobs dangled before them, and large sections of the Socialist Party leadership were likewise won over by direct and indirect offers of subsidies, positions and the prospects of a dictatorship *à la* Mussolini.

The general situation in Poland was not propitious for the creation of a large party of personal followers of this would-be emulator of the Italian dictator. The specter of a working class revolution was not there to disturb the privileged classes. The Communists were an underground, illegal party, and the Socialists were a pink party of officeholders and tame labor leaders after the German model. They still persisted in using a "proletarian" vocabularly in order to hold their working class following against the encroachments of the Communists, —but they frightened nobody. The propertied classes had no need of "Italian" methods, nor of a purely military dictatorship based upon the Marshal's personal prestige, the new officers' caste which he had created, and ordinary careerists. Both Right and Left parties continuously withheld their support of the various cabinets which Pilsudski nominated since his *coup d'état.* Something had to be done at last to save the parliamentary régime whose outward trappings the Marshal was anxious to preserve. As a result he resorted to elections in 1930, at which Rumanian, Yugoslav and Hungarian methods were applied. They did not fail to give him a safe majority. Ever since that time Pilsudski has been dictator "by the will of the people," and all the medieval procedures of violence and torture applied to his more active opponents are being readily justified by a willing Parliament and by the still more willing courts.

During all these years, ever since the restoration of Poland, the economic situation of the country has been going from bad to worse. "Independence," while giving positions and power to a horde of job-hungry intellectuals and other members of the educated middle classes, had cut Poland off from the vast Russian "hinterland"—the best market for her industries. To regain that hinterland and to raise the country to the rank of a first-class power, Poland's ruling classes hope to recover the "lost provinces"—particularly the Ukraine—which centuries ago, at the time of Poland's greatest imperialist expansion, had been under the yoke of that easternmost champion of Catholic Christianity. This noble ambition has been diligently entertained by France, Poland's chief money-lender and military overlord. An annexation of Russia's western provinces would be a mortal blow to her industry and agriculture, and would make France, through its Polish and Rumanian vassals, the altogether undisputed overlord of Europe. Poland's military expenditures were mounting, constituting an ever-increasing burden upon the working population. Up to 40 per cent of the national income was used for that purpose. Soviet Russia's overtures toward the conclusion of a non-aggression pact were constantly meeting with subterfuges amounting to a refusal.

Strange as it may sound, it was the great world crisis that relieved somewhat the danger of a new Polish aggression against Russia, which could easily have become the starting point of a new world war. In such a world war, with continuously changing international relations, it would be as difficult to predict the alignment of the various powers as it is for a Chinese war-lord to count on the loyalty of his various allied generals. For while the "regular" constellation was France, with her Polish-Rumanian-Yugoslav-Czechoslovak vassals, plus England and Japan, as against Russia, Turkey, Italy, Germany and possibly the United States, the game assumed greater complications through the fact that the Germany of Bruening, as well as of Hitler or Schleicher, has been playing with the idea of an alliance with France and Poland, as against Russia. Poland and Rumania, which means chiefly France, were to get the Ukraine, in exchange for which Poland was to return to Germany the "Corridor" with Danzig, and possibly also Upper Silesia.

But these noble plans, envisaging an enormous Poland of perhaps sixty million inhabitants with hardly more than twenty million Poles among them, have been thwarted so far. Enormous sections of the Polish population have been literally pauperized. Poland being a grain-exporting country, the low grain prices have disastrously affected the 70 per cent of her population deriving their living from agriculture. They have also affected the industries. The peasants being unable to buy, and due to lack of foreign markets, about 75 per cent of the industrial workers are now unemployed. The large expenditures for the army, the police and the constabulary went on unabated until the hitherto always generous financial and military overlord refused to lend any further assistance. France has financial troubles of her own. Taxes were raised to ever mounting heights, without, however, being able to prevent a budget deficit. The situation was not improved by the fact that the country's industries are to a very large extent owned by foreign interests: from 15 to 23 per cent of the textile and metal industries, 65 per cent of the mining, 71 per cent of the oil and 76 per cent of the electric power industries, respectively.

Pilsudski's old enemies from the Right, the National Demo-

who have revived all the heroic traditions of the old-time underground revolutionary movement in Poland, with the provisions of the new Polish penal code against political dissenters incomparably harder than those of the old Tsarist laws.

A successful uprising headed by the Communists would automatically make Poland a part of the Soviet Union. This would shake to its very foundations the European equilibrium cherished by England and France. It would make Russia once more the greatest power on the old continent—a development that neither Paris nor London could permit, even though the older capitalist statesmen, in their cynicism, have long ago come to understand Russian Communism as merely a form of State Capitalism that otherwise can be permitted to exist alongside private Capitalism. The Soviet Government, in turn, is not eager to provoke international complications. It is more interested in building up the country's industries than in involving itself in a new war as a result of communist uprisings in the western countries. In this respect it is supported by the regular Communist parties the world over, though there are revolutionary dissenters who doubt whether such an attitude is defensible from the point of view of the working class interests in the rest of the world.

Thus, the Polish Revolution is, so to speak, suspended in the air as far as the "subjective" element is concerned. The utmost that the Polish Communists are now aspiring to is apparently not more than political liberty, of the French or British model, that will permit them to become a legal party, to publish newspapers, to hold meetings, and to engage in a less dangerous competition with the Polish Socialist Party for the control of the Polish working class. Should a new international war come, whether started over Danzig or over Manchuria, it may be safely conjectured that Poland will be one of the first revolutionary countries on the new calendar, and her example will find a repercussion in many European nations as well.

A war, if not successful from the start, might sweep away the militarist rule of the "Group of Colonels," giving power to the democratic, lower middle class and peasant parties, supported by the Socialists. A Polish Kerensky period of this kind might, however, set loose forces of which the various present-day brands of radicalism have no inkling as yet. The Polish workers have always had the reputation of great revolutionary vigor and combativity. They may not be satisfied with mere

Government ownership and a better administrative personnel, as supplied by the more radical leaders aspiring to power. They may raise the demand for an immediate large increase of their wages, for an immediate considerable improvement of their standard of living. Untrained in scientific thought, they may argue naïvely that they are as good as their swivel chair bosses, and that they conceive equality not merely in the sense of the equal right to a job, but of the equal enjoyment of the good things of life. A revolt of such a kind has all the chances of spreading to the neighboring lands—yes, even to the darkest corners of the world. For its slogans are very simple. Many benighted victims of the present social order are unable to rise to the understanding of the dialectical intricacies of the theoretical systems of modern socialism. The new "proletarian" version of the old, old, ultra-bourgeois "good-man" theory, according to which—taken as a whole—one set of politicians is better than another, leaves them baffled at times. After so many disappointments they are likely to adopt the attitude of that cynical or sophisticated indifference which in every struggle for power sees merely a contest of the "outs" against the "ins." But there could be no misunderstanding or hidden purpose in a direct struggle for a better deal waged against the employers and any government that happens to be in power. Such a bread-and-butter struggle for better wages, provision for the unemployed and the organization of public works on a large scale, would force the governments concerned to give the workers more than mere promissory notes redeemable in a distant future. It would force them to take over the industries and to use the incomes hitherto pocketed by the private capitalists and by the higher technical and administrative executives, for the immediate improvement of the lot of the workers.

Once started, such a struggle may mark the beginning of something more than an era of State Capitalism (or State Socialism which is only its euphemistic term), that is, of a new form of exploitation, with the office-holders and technicians enthroned in the place of the capitalists. It may sound the bugle call of a world-wide revolution for economic equality, that equality of incomes with the subsequent equalization of higher educational opportunities without which any social revolution amounts merely to a change of masters.

THE DANUBIAN TRAGEDY

IN a recent lecture delivered in Vienna, Mr. H. R. Knickerbocker, the able Berlin correspondent of the New York *Evening Post,* posed a compellingly interesting question. In a Europe and an America flattened by a disastrous crisis, blanched with economic misery, with seventy to eighty *million* people suffering by reason of unemployment, there has nevertheless been exceedingly little rioting, no mass violence, no revolution. Scarcely two *hundred* casualties throughout the whole world during the whole period of the crisis have been reported, as the direct victims of protest to utterly intolerable social-economic conditions. Why this astounding meekness? Are the hundreds of millions of suffering people in America and Europe merely damn fools?

Mr. Knickerbocker suggested two reasons for the apathy of the submerged sufferers. (1). Machine guns. It is indeed not easy for a mob to make a riot these days, when two or three soldiers can with comparative ease disperse a raging crowd of thousands. As Mr. Ernest Hemingway remarked in his "Death in the Afternoon," the tactics of revolution have had to enter a new phase now that streets in big cities are commonly paved with asphalt. Paving-blocks, the inevitable and very adequate first weapon of the Barricades, are no more. (2). Russian communism. You cannot drum up much interest in world revolution so long as the revolution in Russia holds up such slim rewards of victory. Later, maybe, after half a dozen more Five Year plans, it will be a different story, but to-day the workman outside Russia has little incentive to join his Soviet brethren. "An unemployed workman on the dole in Britain or Germany has a better living at the moment than an employed workman in Russia." Besides, the IIIrd International is a dead horse at the moment. Trotsky promised the fireworks of world revolution. But Trotsky is out. Under Stalin, the IIIrd International gets only a starvation wage, and all it tells the boys outside to do is cool their heels and wait, until things get better *in* Russia. Which is not exactly flaming doctrine. And which is scant encouragement to immediate revolution outside.

In Central Europe, by which I mean the Danubian or semi-Danubian states Czechoslovakia, Austria, Hungary, Rumania, Jugoslavia, Bulgaria, Greece, and Turkey, the extreme paradox of acute distress plus acute socio-political apathy reaches its most puzzling and pronounced expression. I do not name Albania among the countries under discussion because it is too small and unimportant, a little parody of a state. Greece and Turkey are off the direct Danube path, and have more localized problems. The other states form a solid block, roughly coterminous with the area of the old Hapsburg empire, which may be dealt with more or less as a whole.

Now, when the editor of this symposium asked me to contribute an article on "The Danubian Tragedy," I replied that I would like very much to do so, but that "The Danubian Comedy" might be a better title. Indeed, the chief point about the "tragedy" is that it is very nearly a farce. It is difficult, in the first place, to take altogether seriously these slightly shady pearls of countries strung along the Danube. To take them seriously *as* countries, I mean. Catch some peasant in the Banat, or the Ukraine, or the Polish marches, and ask him, despite fourteen years of earnest nationalist preaching, what country he belongs to, and the chances are one to five that he won't know. He will tell you the name of his home town. Or his religion. Or the patronymic of his grandfather. Or possibly if he lives in one of those areas directly bisected by the peace treaty frontiers, he will tell you he is a citizen of some country that does not exist, like "Macedonia." In Poland, one out of every three persons is not a Pole. In some of the towns of "Rumanian" Transylvania, the Rumanian language is even now virtually unknown.

Again, two paragraphs up I mentioned a "solid block" of Danubian countries. What holds this block together, if it exists at all, is the cement of hate. More deeply than he loves his own country (if he has learned what it is), does our Danubian friend hate his neighbor. The whole Balkan peninsula is an unstable pyramid of nationalist hates, and of minority hates within nations. You could make a pretty list of them. What is the worst hate in Central Europe? Does a Bulgar hate a Serb more than a Croat hates a Serb? Do the hates of both combined equal the hate of either for, say, an Italian or a Greek? Does a Hungarian hate a Rumanian more than a Rumanian hates a Bulgarian? Does a Galician from the Ukraine hate most his Polish or his Soviet Ukrainian neighbor? How about the internecine hates of Slovene, Slavone, Bosnian, Montenegrin, Voyvodenan, Croat, Dalmatian, Serb, and Macedonian, which together comprise the one so-called country of Jugoslavia? The idea of grave statesmen at Geneva setting out to control, canalize, modify, narcotize, nullify, cancel out, or lull to sleep these hates is one of the things that makes the League of Nations, to say nothing of Danubia itself, a little comical, if not ridiculous.

But people say, "Was not Vienna once a gay city, and is it not now terribly sad?" How reconcile this to a thesis of fundamental comedy? Well, the answer is that Vienna *is* terribly sad, but that it has never been gay, gay in the sense that Paris is gay. Vienna has always been a sad city. The enormous charm of Vienna is its sadness. You drink the heuriger in Grinzing, you go to the great Fasching balls in Lent, you laugh and smile and dance, and the peculiar Viennese quality to your enjoyment comes in the odd, easy-going, fatalistic acceptance of the idea of pleasure as only a fleeting interruption of an otherwise poignant, bitter-sweet routine of sadness. The great typical phenomenon of Viennese "gayety" is the waltz. But is not the waltz fundamentally a sad dance? Certainly it is not "gay" as a foxtrot or a rhumba is gay. There is a tear hidden in every swirl. This is a fancy way of saying that it is sentimental. Of course, and so in Vienna, and Viennese sadness.—Has no one ever thought of the political implications of the Vienna waltz? One might have a pleasant ten minutes developing the perhaps-fanciful argument that the decline of the waltz killed the empire. The waltz, a social soporific, soothed and tranquillized the contesting passions of Slav and Hungarian, Czech and Slovak. You really couldn't talk seriously of nationalism and secession when the whole empire was smoothly, loosely, sentimentally held together by the side whiskers of Francis Joseph and the strains of Johann Strauss. Even to-day, at provincial towns in minority districts, when the orchestra swings into "Wiener Blut" or "Blue Danube" the whole company rises, Hungarian officials ask the wives of Rumanian merchants for a turn, and Serb maidens swoon in the arms of Bulgar officers. But the waltz went out, jazz came in, and the Habsburg dynasty ended.

Now let us look for a moment at the present status of the Danube countries, comedy or tragedy aside.

1. *Austria.* Population about 6,500,000. Unemployment between 300,000 and 400,000. The country is 43% agricultural, 30% industrial. It consists of a large head, Vienna, which is Socialist and comparatively rich, and a clerical-conservative hinterland, shriveled, mountainous, and poor. Its trade balance deficit is about one billion schillings ($143,000,000) per year; i.e., it does not earn its keep. Its foreign debt is great for its size, about two billion schillings ($286,000,000); it has defaulted on transfer services abroad. The cost of living is very high. There are about 1100 suicides a year in Vienna alone, the highest rate in the world. Austria is generally considered to be in the most desperate plight of any country in Europe; its people, many of them, are near starvation; the fact that it lives at all is a miracle. The government is a weak, shifting coalition of conservative groups; the Socialists are the strongest party in the country, but are a minority in parliament, and will not accept the responsibility of power. Other items: the country spends $1,000,000 a year to support its opera. Arab horses still dance mazurkas in the state-supported Spanish riding school every Sunday morning. The children of the unemployed proletariat have virtually free access to the finest kindergartens, swimming pools, and gymnasiums in Europe, of a kind out of reach of any but the very rich in the United States.

2. *Hungary.* Population about 8,000,000. Unemployment comparatively slight, because the country is about 65% agrarian. Budapest has the most grisly slums and some of the swankiest nightclubs in Europe. The budget deficit is about 200,000,-000 pengoes ($35,000,000), almost one-quarter of the total budget. Foreign trade has shrunk almost 50%. Hungary is the most overborrowed state in Europe, with a total external debt of about four billion pengoes, almost $700,000,000. It is not transferring service abroad, i.e., is bankrupt. The organization of the land is feudal, the Government is based on the privileges

of landed gentry and petty nobility, and the prime minister is a military johnnie named Goemboes. His chief claim to fame: he hid the white terror murderers of Walter Rathenau, disguising them as gardeners on his estate.

3. *Czechoslovakia.* Population about 14,000,000. Unemployment about 900,000, perhaps more. 40% agrarian, 37% industrial. The most intelligent, stable, and democratic of the succession states, as well as the most prosperous, since it inherited most of the industry of the old empire. Trade balance unfavorable this year for the first time since the war. Has not defaulted on its foreign debts, because was shrewd enough to borrow only very little. An unsensational country, and sensible. It has come nearer to settlement of its minorities problem than any other Danubian country. Domestically, the big point of interest is what will happen when the aged President, Thomas Masaryk, dies.

4. *Rumania.* Population about 18,000,000. Unemployment almost impossible to ascertain, because the country lives on the land; it is 80% agricultural. Trapped by the paradox of plenty, it is poverty-stricken because it cannot sell the enormous glut of grain its fundamental richness produces. Trade balance is favorable, but the budget is out of balance by five billion lei (about $30,000,000), one-seventh of its total. Foreign debt, about $755,000,000; so far has not defaulted. Bucharest, a bright sub-Graustark, full of musical comedy tinsel, makes you forget the eleven million peasants strapped to the countryside with an internal agricultural debt variously estimated between $150,-000,000 and $250,000,000.

5. *Bulgaria.* Population about 5,600,000. A decent little country, terribly proud, terribly poor. 82% agrarian. Honest, thrifty, sturdy folk, the Bulgars are yet pugnacious people, and commonly pick the wrong side in wars; consequently they have hardly any country left. Trade has shrunk, and the budget deficit, about one billion leva, (or $7,250,000), is about one-eighth of the total budget. The honest Bulgars are paying 50% on their foreign loan service. There are more political murders in the streets of Sofia, the capital, than in any other city in the world, proportionate to population; this is because of the romantic Macedonians.

6. *Jugoslavia.* Population about 12,000,000. Unemployment about 300,000. The country is largely agrarian. The trade balance is slightly unfavorable; the budget deficit considerable.

Not much foreign debt, but transfers have been suspended, including service on the American Blair loan. Jugoslavia is the strongest, the most obstreperous, and the most dangerous of the Danubian states; a tough customer, and usually in trouble. The King, Alexander, tried to put the country in order through a personal dictatorship, but now has restored a limited constitutional government, which is shaky and weak. Chief external problem: fear of all its neighbors, especially Italy. Chief internal problem: to keep from splitting asunder under pressure of the Serb-Croat dispute.

In this group of countries we may ascertain several main situations, or movements.

The states which were in the enemy camp during the war, Austria, Hungary and Bulgaria, have, speaking generally, suffered most. This is partly because they borrowed more money from the victors than the others, and have been crushed ever since 1929 by the necessity of devising means of paying it back. Also, they lost territory. Austria, which has very little nationalism, has never made much fuss trying to reclaim its irridenta; it was quite glad, in fact, to get rid of the Czechs, and except for a tear or two has not done anything even about the forlorn cousins now being forced to eat spaghetti in the Italian Tyrol. Hungary is a different story. Austria lost comparatively few Austrians. But Hungary did lose pure Magyars, upward of a million of them distributed to Czechoslovakia, Rumania, and Jugoslavia, and ever since has waged an unremitting verbal war to get them and their territory back.

The natural result was a military alliance among the three gainer states, Czechoslovakia, Rumania, and Jugoslavia, under the benevolent patronage of France, called the Little Entente. The purpose of the Little Entente was, originally at least, to keep Hungary down. The members of the Little Entente did not flamingly love each other, but they did hate Hungary. Thus the six states became stratified into two groups, the winners, Czechoslovakia, Rumania, Jugoslavia, vis-à-vis the losers, Austria, Hungary, and Bulgaria. To keep the losers alive, the League of Nations, i.e., the great powers, gave them "reconstruction" loans. When a country, like Austria in the summer of 1932, comes to default on one of these loans, the powers immediately lend Austria more money, because they, the powers, have guaranteed the original loan, and would themselves have to pay the original investors if the default persisted. This is known as "saving" Austria.

Now, it is of the utmost importance to point out that this *political* cleavage of the Danubian powers, caused not only by the peace treaties but by the cumulative forces of many generations of history, does not correspond to the natural *economic* realities of the region. The political groupment is bad business, as business. Economically, Czechoslovakia and Austria should form one bloc, an industrial bloc, vis-à-vis an agrarian bloc of the great grain-producing agricultural countries, Hungary, Rumania, Jugoslavia, and Bulgaria.

One should not say "should" too lightly. Of course there are enormous difficulties. Purely from the point of view of economics, Austro-Czechoslovakia (if it existed) would not be big enough a market for all the grain of Hungaro-Rumano-Bulgoslavia. Germany would have to join the industrial brethren. France would object to this. So would Italy. And as well try to mix tea and ink and drink it as break the political Little Entente alliance with economic arrangements between such bitter enemies as Hungary and Rumania, or Jugoslavia and Bulgaria. All the recent attempts at Danubian salvage have broken on this issue, this fundamental and inescapable dichotomy between the political and economic interests of the region. The Tardieu plan sought to freeze Germany out. The German plan ignored the very legitimate French financial as well as political interests in the region. The Stresa conference sought to avoid politics and for this very reason its recommendations have so far come to nothing; politics must of necessity precede economics in Danubia; you may get an agreement among economic "experts" but it will never be applied until each Government with cold passion investigates its every political innuendo, implication, and possibility.

Still, beginnings have been made, and it would be disingenuous to scoff at them. An endemic series of agrarian conferences began in the summer of 1930 and has continued ever since, with Serbs, Bulgars, Poles, and so on sitting at a common table and not shooting each other. They have not accomplished much; still, they sat, which is something. And always they were frustrated and monkeyed with by the great powers. Again, a very sincere and able Greek politician named Papanastasiou overcame simply immense difficulties in staging a series of annual Balkan conferences, three so far, in which Greece and

Turkey have tried to whip their northern neighbors into conciliatory experiments in matters as varied as postal and railway communications, athletic meets, tobacco cartels, and even the problems of minorities. Politicians sneer; idealists hope. It is in the field of these Balkan conferences that Turkey, as a European power, has played its most considerable rôle; the Turks, miracle to relate, made up with the Greeks after 2500 years of fighting, and are now actually trying to be friends with Rumanians, Bulgars, Serbs, and Albanians, and common broker for them all. Having lost the Balkans by war, Turkey is trying to regain them by peace.

The Danube ripples; Europe rocks. Do not forget that the World War started in Danubia. Thus as soon as the new frontiers were drawn by the treaties (which, by the way, are not so heinous in toto as most present day revisionists make them out to be), the powers began to dabble for special privileges, alliances, coöperations, arrangements. Italy became the father of the "enemy" group, and by swallowing Albania whole and making deals with Bulgaria and Hungary, sought to encircle France's friend, Jugoslavia. The Little Entente had previously encircled Hungary in the same way. Thus two intersecting "iron rings" were driven into the Danube region. Later Germany, as if waking from slumber troubled by the old Mittel-Europa dream, dangled preferential tariffs for grain to Rumania and Jugoslavia, trying to seduce them from France. Germany offered Austria the abortive customs-union. And then came the world economic crisis.

Do not forget that this crisis, too, started in Danubia. Once the Credit Anstalt in Vienna was down, the German, British, and American banking structures followed like tin pans crashing down a concrete alley. Betrayed by the pound sterling, there was nothing left for modern man to believe in. Confidence left the earth. It has not yet returned.

The French, who may or may not have contributed to the fall of the Credit Anstalt by financial measures retaliatory to the German customs-union proposal, seized an opportunity which was indeed, and literally, golden. France started to rain "golden bullets" on Danubia. Now, France has not "bought" any country in Central Europe, and most of her loans were to her allies, but she did try to blackmail Austria into political submission, and she did try to make a sort of politico-financial deal with Hungary. The idea was to isolate Germany, to check

Mittel-Europa by nailing a French peg into the Danube at Budapest. And whereas there were once several camps in Central Europe, with the great powers competing for influence much as did Russia and Austro-Hungary in the Balkans before the war, there came to be, generally speaking, only one camp, and that was French. Everyone who was not in the French camp was out in the rain. Central Europe began to eat out of France's hand—when she stretched it out—which wasn't so darned often.

As to "Anschluss," the curious part of the whole business is that neither Austria nor Germany really pant for it. The customs-union proposal was not much more than a hand at political poker, a very unfortunate one for the world, as it turned out. Austria is not fond of Prussian kultur. Germany is not fond of the romantic and shiftless Austrians. Vienna is still incredibly the Vienna of Mozart, whereas Germany has gone from Goethe to Hitler-Schleicher. As for the "common" language, it is as hard for a Viennese to understand a Berliner as for a Bostonian to comprehend "erster" as "oyster" in the streets of New York.

The crisis came and conquered. And for once politics did give way to economics in the Danube basin. There has not been much talk of politics this last year, French or otherwise. It would be a brave soul to try to resurrect the hopeless project of a Danube Federation now. The people are sick of politics. They are hungry. And they see their countries throttled, stymied, hamstrung, spavined by the most outlandish set of economic nonsensities they can remember.

It is getting to be old, old stuff, of course, the pert remark that "people starve in the very shadow of grain elevators stuffed with rotting grain." But go to Rumania and see it happen. It sounds a little crazy to hear of thousands of pairs of boots stored in the Czech customs house with Hungarian peasants barefoot in the frozen mud just across the border. But it happens.

From Prague to Istanbul, the depression has become stagnation. I would give statistics, but they will be outmoded by new and lower ones by the time I can mail this to New York. The total foreign trade of Danubia has shrunk by more than 50%. Prices of agricultural goods have fallen to unheard of levels. Each country is walled off from the others by enormous tariffs, embargoes, and import restrictions. Currency regulations make travel reminiscent of the days just after the war. At the big

tourist bureaus in Vienna you could not for a time buy a ticket
to Paris or Madrid except in foreign currency—and you were
not allowed to buy foreign currency. Extraordinarily tedious
"clearing arrangements" have sought to revive trade by that
highly modern twentieth century process known as barter.
Austrian schillings and Hungarian pengoes are 25% to 30%
below par. To-day, a miracle, I saw an orange, an actual orange,
in a Vienna shop, the first one so seen in four or five months.
In Czechoslovakia you need a special license to import a thousand articles ranging from tennis rackets to dynamos to jam
to "keyboard instruments except organs" to artificial flowers.
In Bulgaria the volume of exports last year increased by 80%;
their *value* decreased by 3%. In Greece, automobiles may cir-
culate only on alternate days, according to odd or even num-
bered license plates, to save gasoline—with surplus gas inundat-
ing reserve tanks all over the world. The governments are
broke. The banks are broke. And the people are broke.

And what are they doing about it?

Nothing.

Which brings us back to the idea on which this article began.

Revolution, one may say, is founded on three things: Distress
plus Education plus Organization. Perhaps a war is also necessary. In Central Europe there is plenty of distress, there is
some education, and there is at least the alleged presence everywhere of the Communist Internationale, an organization.
But there has been no revolution. Nor is any social revolution
at all likely. Distress has produced, not violence, but apathy.
Why? Mr. Knickerbocker gave two excellent reasons. There are
many more, in so far as Central Europe is particularly concerned, and it may be well to outline them.

1. Nationalism. The basis of Balkan Nationalism is probably (language aside) poverty; each country is desperately
tenacious of its frontiers and jealous of its neighbors, because
the land, at least in the south, is poor and mountainous, and
every scrap is valuable. In Montenegro, for instance, soil is a
precious commodity, sold by itinerant vendors in carts as if it
were fish, bullets, or potatoes. As the state develops within
its carefully guarded frontiers, the basic passion of the citizen
becomes national, rather than social. Above all, he fears and
distrusts the neighboring state, not the social class or rulers
above him. His primitive energies are directed to the preservation of his own country, which, by Balkan tradition, is usually

in potential danger. Nationalism is the pipe through which his turbulent political passions are normally discharged; he has no energy left for social revolution, which, in fact, is a foreign and even obnoxious idea; his duty is to protect his own state, not try to overthrow it.

The hate-complex has its rewards. Jugoslavia might very well have fallen apart before this, except that the Croats and Slovenes know that they would be gobbled by someone else if they seceded from the Serbs. Now, a political revolution *is* possible some day in Jugoslavia, or even Rumania. But not a Communist-Social revolution. The people may be willing to change their rulers, in an extreme emergency; but their nationalism is almost sure to produce some sort of subsequent Government scarcely distinguishable except in the person of the ruler from the one before. The Balkans are adolescent, they are growing up. They still want a father, in the person of a nationalistic King.

2. *Social structure.* First of all, Danubia is at least three-fifths agrarian, and the majority of peasants own their own land. The industrial proletariat is weak, inconspicuous, and badly organized. You cannot get Soviets of workers in the Silesian mines to think in terms of potential coöperation with workers in Greek tobacco factories. There is no revolutionary ideology or tradition behind them. Again, the Balkans were Turkish within the memory of living men, and the organization of society is still basically that of individual peasant holdings. A middle class has grown up only in the last two generations, and is still very new and shaky; in Hungary, for instance, there is, practically speaking, no middle class at all. I do not mean to say that a middle class is necessary to revolution. I mean only to point out the extreme primitiveness of the Balkan social structure, which makes revolutionary propaganda difficult.

I found an admirable survey of this problem in the London *Times* recently, which added an interesting point, that of the sterilization from progress of the new Balkan intelligentsia. As independence was won, as the peasants were liberated, as their sons went to school, there came a great need for doctors, lawyers, teachers, high officials; and education became a fetish. For a generation there was room for these locally educated intellectuals. Now there is not. The lust for schooling knew no bounds. And thousands of university trained men jammed the very limited professional fields. To-day, for instance, in Bucharest, capital of an overwhelmingly agrarian country, there are 25,000 students at the university. The graduates may get jobs. More often "they turn political agitators for any organization which will pay them; the simplest way of paying a political agent is with a government post." Thus has grown the enormous bureaucracy of the Danubian states. The statistics are staggering. Austria, with 6,500,000 people, has more civil servants than England with 40,000,000. And are government job-holders likely to turn revolutionist? They are not. Instead, they train their own children to grow up in the same easy racket.

3. *Socialism.* Here, of course, Communism finds its truest enemy. The orthodox IInd Amsterdam International social-democrats, "Marxian" as they theoretically are, are a stiff bulwark throughout Central Europe against revolution.

Social-democrats are the biggest party in Austria, the third-biggest in Czechoslovakia, and of declining importance, numerically, throughout the rest of the Danube region. They have been powerful enough even in Hungary to have produced—indirectly to be sure—a considerable paternalism; there is a proverb in Hungary that the state takes care of you from birth till you are 15, and then from 60 till you die: the only trouble is that you have to shift for yourself in between. In such countries as even Greece, the state takes care of its citizens a great deal more handsomely than do we in our large, gaudy United States of America. Naturally, this oils the social wheels, it renders revolution unattractive. It costs money, to be sure. But until the crash there were always American bankers on the street corner pleading to be allowed to pay the bills, and after the crisis is over there they will be again giving their, i.e., our money, to Greek irrigation schemes, Czechoslovak kindergartens, and Austrian municipal breweries. Out of paternalism has come the dole, and as long as people get free living from the state, revolt is pretty unlikely.

It is in Vienna that European socialism has built its proudest monument, the magnificent modern tenements that now house over 60,000 families, at an average rental of $3.50 per month. These tenements were built out of taxes, not from loans; there is no capital charge whatever to be amortized. I find my socialist friends inclined to agree, a bit unwillingly, when you suggest that these buildings are almost fool-proof incubators of a new bourgeoisie. Put a workman and his family in a first-class modern flat, and imperceptibly but inevitably you will find his redness paling, you will find him, with his feet on the shiny new stove or dozing in summer on his private sun terrace, a little lazy about attending party meetings, and not at all eager to rush bomb in hand to barricades.

Another point is that in Vienna at least socialism is, despite its political straddling, red enough socially to have captured much communist thunder. I believe that in the city of Vienna there must be at least five Communists, but I have never seen one.

Social-democracy, you will say, is itself a force for revolution, it itself plans, when God and the capitalists are willing, to turn to Marx. This, of course, is to laugh. I refer you to Sidney Webb (Lord Passfield). Or to Braun and Severing, the noble heroes of the Prussian evacuation, when they let four miserable coppers pinch them without a struggle during the Papen episode last June. Stalwart revolutionists those!

4. Fascism. Here is another serious obstacle to an eventual Marxian upheaval, especially in Central Europe. It is quite obvious that Hitlerite propaganda has caught most of the overt forces of social unrest all the way from Berlin to Bagdad, and perhaps beyond. The swastikas are blooming like tulips in the spring. And it is the young, i.e., the valuable people whom the Nazis are bagging; I live next to a high school and I have fairly to fight my way through attentive young Nazi students to the street car every morning. The Nazis have captured no Government in Danubia as yet, and they are weak in inverse proportion to the agrarian strength of each country. Just the same, if there is to be any social revolution at all in Central Europe in the next few years I will wager it will be Nazi, not communist.

5. Capitalism. It is a sad mistake of most radicals to underestimate the capabilities of their opponents, and it is occasionally necessary to point out that not all capitalists are dumb. In Central Europe any threat of revolution is likely to be offstaved by the IVth Internationale, that of the bankers. If the bonus army had marched in Vienna instead of Washington, what a fright would have gone through the press of the world! And Austria would have been promptly "saved," and we would have paid for it. The Credit Anstalt crash in May, 1931, threatened mild trouble for the country. A gentleman went to the long distance phone, rang up Montague Norman, and there was 150,000,000 schillings ($20,000,000) on the books for Austria the next morning.

6. Communism itself. I have already mentioned the decay of the IIIrd Internationale. Stalin is starving it, although his eventual intentions are probably honorable. There is, practically speaking, no communist organization surviving throughout Central Europe, except in Czechoslovakia, where the communists are the No. 2 party, and in Bulgaria, where they control the Sofia town council. Trotskyism, but not Stalinism, has some local power in Greece. Elsewhere the movement is almost a blank.

There are many reasons for this, and one is that Central Europe has seen one genuine and one quasi-communist experiment, the only ones outside of Russia and China that have yet existed, and each miserably failed. Bela Kun was a flop in Hungary, and Stambolisky in Bulgaria was murdered just when his peasant internationale was getting into action. A white terror of unparalleled ferocity followed in each case. To justify their mass murders, the whites kept alive the legend of communist barbarity, elusiveness, and strength. Having tasted blood, the whites would not mind tasting more. Thus throughout Central Europe a certain propaganda has existed ever since, flaunting the communist bogey, keeping otherwise decent people alarmed and tense. Two young men, certainly communist, but guilty of no other crime save having been caught and arrested, were hanged in Hungary last summer with the most callous and perfunctory brutality. For these and other reasons, there is a more alert and forbidding anti-communist spirit in Danubia than anywhere else in Europe, I should imagine, except Italy. Hungary, Rumania, Jugoslavia, and Bulgaria have not even recognized the Soviet Government, and in three of these four countries communism, per se, is virtually a crime.

7. Psychological factors. Here I want to draw on a highly interesting report made jointly by the psychology department of the University of Vienna and the Oesterreichische Wirtschaftspsychologische Forschungstelle, following a recent investigation of unemployment in the hamlet of Marienthal, near Vienna. A textile factory in Marienthal closed down in 1929; as a result only 37 people out of Marienthal's total population of 1466 are to-day employed. Here, thus sharply demarcated, was ideal pasturage for a scientific check on the psychological effects of prolonged unemployment.

Misery and distress in the people of Marienthal did not, it

was revealed, produce violence; they produced the very opposite—torpor, mental and physical, and an almost pathological apathy. Is this not perhaps a hint of an answer to the question this whole article is asking? People cannot make revolutions when hungry for the simple reason that if the hunger is prolonged enough they become too weak.

In Marienthal, for instance, the gait of the unemployed men strolling around the village was timed. It was one and a half miles per hour. Only 6 out of 66 men checked did not stop for rest on the way to a given destination. Three things only exist: getting up, the noon meal, going to bed. Most of the day, indeed, is spent in bed, to save fuel, nor is there any light at night. "The inhabitants are literally drowned in time." By a system of controls too long to quote and explain, 19% of the inhabitants were adjudged "normal," 49% "resigned," and 32% "broken." This classification followed sharply the "income" (via the dole) of each group; those "normal" had to live on 34 schillings (about $5.00) per month, with their families; those "resigned" on 30 schillings ($4.30); those "broken" on 23 schillings ($3.30). In other words, starve a man sufficiently, and you break him.

Mentally the tests were even more striking. "The gift of leisure has been purely tragic." The number of books loaned from the free circulating library decreased by 49% in two years. The circulation of the *Arbeiter Zeitung,* the socialist organ, dropped by 60%, although copies of the paper cost the unemployed only 4 groschen (about half a cent). At the same time, a more amusing, semi-comic paper, the Kleinenblatt, dropped only 24%, although it cost 10 groschen (over one cent). The people simply did not have the steam to read about politics. The kindergarten is open, though without a teacher; but no children play there. At the last election, on April 24, 1932, the vote was very slim; and the socialists, the "revolutionary" party, lost one-third of their poll!

Now, one must not generalize too widely from one very isolated and possibly unique case; but Marienthal itself will tell you it is far, far beyond thinking of social violence.

So much then for prospects of revolution. They are certainly not bright. And for recovery without revolution? They do not seem very bright either. I rather think Trotsky's diagnosis of the crisis is in order. He expects capitalism to survive this crisis; he thinks that this crisis is a severe downward loop in a curve that has its next inevitable upturn. But the upturn will also be temporary, and meantime the general, basic slant is downward, pointing to an eventual cycle of depression far, far deeper than anything we have yet encountered. It may come in twenty years, thirty years, forty years. Then—goodbye, as they say, pointing to our present society, "to all that."

ITALY IN THE THROES
OF FASCISM

I

DURING the World War, and especially during the last year, the Italian politicians had made extravagant promises to the men in order to keep up their fighting spirit. A reform, root and branch, of the whole national life was to testify to the country's gratitude to those who had shed their blood for her; land was to be given to the peasants; youth was to replace age in public life. After the victory, the politicians found out that all those promises could not be kept, and promptly proceeded to forget them. The people remembered: the Capitalists—they said—had got the substance of war profits, and the soldiers, the shadows of false promises.

The promise which had been repeated most often during the war was, that this was to be the last war: peace was to be ensured for the children of soldiers and their children's children. The war was hardly over, when the military authorities organized a systematic propaganda campaign to convince the people that President Wilson and the Allied Governments of France and England were robbing Italy of the fruits of victory, since they prevented her from occupying Fiume, Dalmatia and Asia Minor. It was necessary to have revenge for this treason even at the cost of a new war. The result of this fury for revenge was D'Annunzio's raid on Fiume on September 12, 1919: a kind of "Private War," declared on the United States, France and on the British Empire by a writer devoid of moral sensibility and of common sense. After having been forced into an appalling war and disappointed in all the promises that had

been made them, the Italian people were told by the same
politicians, who had forced them into the war, that they had
shed their blood in vain and that a new war was necessary to
wipe out the failure of the last one.

At the same time a real economic earthquake was taking
place. The Italian lira had been kept up during the war by
loans from the allied governments. At the conclusion of peace,
the Italian Government had to fall back on its own resources
to meet 87 billion Italian lire (about 2 billion dollars) for
extraordinary expenses dependent on the war, which matured
from June 1918 to June 1920. Such a huge amount of money
could not be wholly derived from taxation; the treasury had
no other means than to increase the national debt by 26 billion lire and inflate the currency by 8 billion lire, from June
1918 to June 1920. As a result of inflation, the Italian lira fell
precipitously in 1919 and 1920. Prices rose accordingly. The
workers in town and country were no longer able to live on
their old wages, the purchasing power of which had been reduced to one-fifth. They asked for higher wages. When their
demands were refused or answered too slowly, they struck. The
public servants followed their example.

In the midst of this moral and economic upheaval, there
crept in the propagandists of anarchism and bolshevism, preaching strikes, local and general, hoping thus to pave the way for
social revolution. Not only economic, but also solidarity and
political, strikes were frequent. Many of them were exasperat-
ing, especially those on the railways.

During the two years of the most dangerous disturbances,
1919 and 1920, Mussolini made no attempt to lessen the danger
of the revolutionary crisis. At that time he was in the front line
of those who accused the Italian rulers of having been unfit
and cowardly because they had not resisted France, England
and the United States, when these countries were "mutilating
the victory" in the Peace Conference. The Italian people should
have proclaimed a republic and lent a helping hand to Russia,
Germany, Hungary and Bulgaria, which he called the "Proletarian Nations" in a new "revolutionary war" against the
"Capitalistic Nations." At the same time, Mussolini preached
that the workers' organizations should share in the management
of industries and of the public services. The land should be
given to the peasant veterans of the war. When, in March 1919,
in Dalmine, a town in northern Italy, 2,000 factory workers,

who were engaged in a wages dispute with their employers, occupied the workshops of Messrs. Franchi e Gregorini, this, the
first of such disorders, was itself promoted by Mussolini's followers, and Mussolini went himself to Dalmine, and addressed
the men, praising their interprise. He opposed the Socialists,
not because they were revolutionary, but because, as revolutionists, they were wholly incapable. When the Socialists demanded a 48 hour week, Mussolini's paper proclaimed that a
48 hour week was too much; anything more than a 44 hour
week was a betrayal of the proletariat.

By means of this chaotic mixture of nationalist and ultra-
revolutionary propaganda, Mussolini endeavoured to win over
the workers and peasants from the Socialist party. He succeeded
only in increasing the post-war restlessness and in gathering
around him the first groups of Fascists as his companions in
adventure.

This post-war restlessness was termed "Bolshevism" because
the Russian Revolution had made the term fashionable; and
because the politicians who had made war badly and peace
worse, the nouveaux riches, who aroused general indignation
by their insensate luxury, and respectable people who were in
a state of blue funk during those years, all found it convenient
to explain the universal restlessness by "Bolshevik" influence
and "Bolshevik" maneuvers. But if one classifies as "Bolshevism," only a social revolution which overthrows the well-to-do
classes, deprives them of power and destroys the economic and
political machinery of the country, then Italy was never in the
throes of "Bolshevism"! Italian "Bolshevism" was nothing but
an outbreak of incoherent unrest—the aftermath of the World
War.

Not only did this disorder never lead to a revolution, but it
also never hindered the economic and financial reconstruction
of the country.

The Italian economic system had been profoundly disorganized by the war. In 1913 Italy imported 11.8 million tons of
coal. By 1918 imports went down to 5.8 millions. In 1913–1914
Italian railways carried 42 million tons; by 1917–18 there was a
drop to 33.5 million tons. On the eve of the war, Italy's imports
totalled 1.8 billion dollars and her exports 1.6 billion dollars.
The difference was compensated by the invisible exports (re-
mittances from emigrants, tourist traffic, and freights of the
mercantile marine). During the war Italy's imports exceeded

exports by a yearly average of 1.1 billion dollars; and invisible exports almost completely ceased; the deficit in the balance of trade had to be met by foreign loans.

In 1922 coal imports reached 9.6 million tons. In 1921–1922 Italian railways carried 41 millions, despite the development of road transport. As regards the latter, we have the statistics of the number of motor trucks. They totalled 909 in 1914; 5,547 in 1918; 22,422 in 1921. In 1921 and 1922 Italy no longer needed to resort to foreign loans; the balance of trade had been restored by the resumption of invisible exports. All contemporary observers regarded 1922 as the moment when Italy made a definite recovery from the economic crisis produced by the war.[1]

Parallel with the economic convalescence, financial reorganization was carried on. After 1920 inflation was stopped; the circulation which had risen to 22.2 billion lire in December, 1920, never exceeded this amount again, and it fell by October 1922 to 20.7 billion lire. As a consequence, a slow process of revaluation of the lira took place. In December, 1920, one had to pay 28.57 Italian lire to buy a dollar; in 1922, one might have bought a dollar with 21.8 lire. In 1921 the rise in the public debt began to slow down. To meet 40 billion lire (about 2 billion dollars) of extraordinary expenses dependent on the war, maturing from June 1920 to June 1922, the government did not increase the national debt by more than 18 billion lire. Already in 1921 experts were predicting that the deficit would not exceed 150 to 200 million dollars in 1922-23, and that by 1923-24 the balance would be restored.[2]

It would be absurd to pretend that Italy enjoyed perfect happiness. She was a patient, recovering from a terrible illness—the war. She had passed through a severe crisis. But this was a crisis of readjustment and not one of disorganization.

[1] U. S. A. "Commerce Reports", Nov. 2, and 13, 1922; Jan. 1, 1923; BACHI L'Italia economica nel 1921, Citta' di Castello, Lapi, 1922, p. 7; MORTARA Prospettive economiche; 1923 pp. XVI; idem 1924, pp. XI, XIII; EINAUDI Italy in "Encyclopedia Britannica", 1926, p. 573.
[2] U. S. A. "Commerce Reports", Dec. 26, 1921; U. S. "Trade Information Bulletin", N. 67, p. 6; MORTARA, Prospettive economiche: 1923, p. XX.

II

THE RISE OF THE FASCIST DICTATORSHIP

Toward the end of 1920 the worst of the post-war crisis was over. After two years of ineffectual disorder, the idea spread among the people that social revolution had become impossible in Italy. As always happens in defeat, mutual recrimination grew bitter between the more moderate Socialists and Communists. The internal strife led, in January 1921, to a split between Socialists and Communists. The rank and file of the workers were bewildered by such division of opinion among their leaders.

Hardly had the fighting spirit among the working classes begun to show signs of flagging, than all the latent forces of reaction were unloosed, and the industrialists, the landowners and the bankers passed to counter-attack. From now Mussolini no longer attacked the Socialists from the left, charging them with being ineffectual revolutionaries. In 1921 he began to attack them from the right, calling them revolutionaries of a most dangerous kind. He had been *ultra*-revolutionary as long as social revolution seemed possible. He became *anti*-revolutionary as soon as the social revolution showed itself impossible. He continued, however, to make a great display of revolutionary fireworks and to call himself a revolutionary. In his mind, violence is revolution.

The industrialists, the landowners and the bankers had already, here and there, during the previous two years, subsidized some Fascist local branches. It is true that the Fascists proclaimed themselves ultra-revolutionists, but they fought the Socialists. It has always been the technique of the conservative parties to lend surreptitious help to the most extreme revolutionary groups, in order to have them weaken with their attacks the more moderate groups. As soon as they understood that Mussolini's verbal revolution was not directed against capitalist society but against the socialistic movement, the Italian capitalists in 1921 made general the scheme of subsidies and enrolled their own sons and followers in the Fascist bands. Thus the Fascist groups became the rallying points of all the conservative forces seeking to organize themselves.

The politicians who were in power at the end of 1920,

thought that it would be advisable to lend a hand to the conservative counter-attack by allowing the military authorities to equip the Fascists with rifles, machine-guns, bombs and trucks, and place in command of them retired officers and officers on leave. The police and judges received hints to take no notice of disturbances started by the Fascists, and to intervene only when it was a question of disarming, trying and sentencing those who attempted to resist.

Italy thus entered a new phase of political strife, which may be called one of "authorized lawlessness." Parties of Fascists, with free passes on the railways, swarmed into the towns, sacked houses, looted trade union quarters, beat and maltreated, banished and murdered the organizers. The country was terrorized by "punitive expeditions," which set out openly from Fascist offices in the towns. A terrible man hunt went on, organized by the military authorities with the connivance of the bench and of the police. Many who had been cowards in 1919 and 1920 became apostles of terrorism in 1921.

As early as the summer of 1921, not even a shadow remained of the "Bolshevist" peril in Italy. On July 2nd, 1921, Mussolini wrote: "To say that there still exists a Bolshevist peril in Italy, is, for interested motives, to substitute fears for reality. Bolshevism has been vanquished."

The politicians, who had given assistance to the Fascist movement in the beginning, believed that they could put a stop to it now it had ceased to serve their purposes. They soon found out that they had made a great mistake. The armed and organized Fascist bands were not disposed to allow themselves to be demobolized to suit the convenience of those gentlemen. Moreover, the high military authorities, who had acted on a hint from the government in arming and drilling the Fascists, realized in the course of 1921 that in their hands the new organization might become a formidable weapon for ensuring political power to the military caste. From that moment they ceased to obey the civil authorities.

The conspiracy of the high military authorities had a decisive effect on the subsequent development of the Fascist activities. The first Fascist groups, in 1919 and 1920, consisted of patriotic youths who thought that by their nationalistic exaltation and "anti-Bolshevist" activities they were serving their country. In 1921, Fascism became an anti-trade unionist movement in the interest of the "bourgeoisie." In 1922 it also became an anti-parliamentary movement in the service of a military "Black Hand."

The "March on Rome" could have been stopped easily enough, if the military staff had willed it. Not more than eight thousand Fascists surrounded Rome on October 28, 1922. Scattered up and down the country round Rome in localities unsuited and insufficient to house them, they were badly armed and as disorderly as carnival revelers. The forces of the regular army, concentrated in Rome, might easily have dispersed those loosely organized groups, one by one.

But as early as September 29th, the central executive of the Fascist party knew that, in the event of Fascist concentration on Rome, "the Army would observe an attitude of neutrality." A general was one of the committee directing the Fascist uprising. Another general had given military organization to the Black Shirts. Five generals commanded the groups which were moving toward Rome. The chief of the Navy, Thaon de Revel, and the chief of the army, Díaz, had a hand in the conspiracy.

The Fascists were allowed to enter Rome unresisted.

There was no revolution, as has been claimed, but a coup d'etat, staged as a spontaneous popular rising, but in reality carried out by a clique of high military authorities. This coup d'etat was directed not against Bolshevism, but against the Chamber of Deputies.

III

THE CONSTITUTION OF THE DICTATORSHIP

Until January 1923 the armed Fascist bands were private and illegal organizations. In January 1923 the new Government recognized them as the "Voluntary Militia for the National Safety," legally entrusted with police functions and paid with the taxpayer's money. The officers and soldiers of the militia swore a personal oath of fealty to Mussolini.

As soon as the Fascist party had made sure of possessing, in the Militia, the permanent intrument necessary to suffocate—with legal repression or with illegal violence—any attempt at opposition, it proceeded, between 1923 and 1929, to reform from top to bottom the entire old constitution of the realm.

In Italy, to-day, all periodical publications which do not submit to the control of the Fascist party are suppressed. All parties and associations whose activities may be regarded as hostile to the party in power, are dissolved. Anyone reorganizing the dissolved associations under new names, is imprisoned from three to five years. Any kind of anti-Fascist propaganda is severely punished. Any meeting in a private house may be declared illegal, whatever the number of those attending it be. Letters are opened by the police.

Public officials, judges and teachers are dismissed from their posts, and barristers, solicitors, chemists, engineers, and journalists are not allowed to carry on their professions, if they set themselves in opposition to the party in power. University professors must swear an oath of allegiance to the Fascist régime and pledge themselves to exercise the function of teaching with the purpose of forming citizens devoted to the Fascist régime.

Political crimes are tried, not by regular judges, but by a Special Tribunal, which is composed of a general and five officers of the Fascist militia, who as Fascists have sworn "to obey the orders of the Duce without discussing them."

The police are empowered to put under their surveillance, and even intern on small islands or secluded villages, those who have been tried and sentenced and already served their terms, and those "who have manifested the deliberate intention of committing acts subversive of the social, economic and national order, or capable of prejudicing national interests," even if they have never been tried or sentenced.

As regards the relations between capital and labor, a single organization may, in each district (provincia) enjoy legal recognition for each group of employers, employees and professional classes. Legally recognized organizations are grouped into thirteen national confederations: six for the employers, six for the employees and one for the professional classes. The officials of the organizations, in which the monopoly of legal representation is vested, must "give an undoubted guarantee of national loyalty," namely, enjoy the confidence of the Fascist party. They can be removed by the government, if they fail to manifest a sufficient dose of "undoubted national loyalty." The government may even withdraw legal recognition from the organization. In short, an organization cannot enjoy legal recognition and the privileges pertaining thereto, unless it consents to be controlled by men in the confidence of the party in power. The law admits the existence of de facto organizations; but no one has as yet dared to form one of these organizations independent of the party in power. Any such attempt would expose its founder to every penalty threatening those who "show the deliberate intention" of subverting the national order.

Nobody is obliged to become a member of the legally recognized organization of his group; but the labor exchanges which provide work to the unemployed must give precedence to members over non-members. On the other hand, everybody must contribute annual dues to the legally recognized organization of his group, whether belonging to it or not.

While in the associations of the employers, it is the members who elect their leaders, and the government confirms this election, in the unions of the employees and societies of the professional classes, it is Mussolini who appoints the national leader of each national confederation; the Fascist party appoints the secretaries in each district; and the secretary of the district appoints the secretary for each union or society in his district. The secretary may expel any members, who in his opinion, are "undesirable from a moral or political point of view."

Thus the leaders of the employers are elected representatives, whereas the leaders of the employees and professional classes are officials, appointed from on high and beyond any control on the part of their membership. The employer's class is an active factor and controls its own affairs; the classes comprising the workers and the professions are passive, subject to what their officials think fit.

All contracts concerning wages, hours of work, etc., are drawn up by the representatives of the employers and by the officials who run the employee's unions. And these contracts are binding on the whole of the employers and workers, whether they are members of the organization or not.

When the representatives of the employers and the officials who run the workers' unions do not agree, their dispute is to be decided by the court of labor, either regarding contracts in course of execution, or new ones. The court consists of a judge and two experts. All experts must be University graduates; thus the workers are automatically excluded from the court.

Strikes are forbidden and punished by a severe and progressive scale of penalties, the maximum being seven years' imprisonment. Lockouts are forbidden as well as strikes. But the law, while forcing workmen to labor under threat of imprisonment, cannot force an employer to give work if he declares that he can no longer maintain the old wages; the stoppage of work is then not a "lockout" but a "closing down" induced by a "justified" motive.

This is the so called "Corporative State": a bureaucratic machine by means of which the Fascist party controls labor.

Municipal elections are abolished. The municipalities are run by officials ("Podesta") appointed by the government. Elections for Parliament take place in the following way:— The officials, not the members of the legally recognized organizations, that is to say, the representatives of the employers and the men who control the employees and the professional classes, meet in Rome. The central executive of each national confederation announces the names of the candidates for their own organization. The audience applauds. Thus a list of one thousand candidates is drawn up. This list is "presented" to the Grand Council of Fascism, which is composed of about thirty members appointed by Mussolini. The Grand Council "designates" four hundred deputies, not only by selection from the "presented" list, but even by the addition of persons not included in it. This unlimited discretion makes a mere farce of the presentation of the preliminary list. When the Grand Council has "designated" the four hundred deputies, the list goes to the electorate for "ratification." The whole country forms a single electoral constituency. The voter is not allowed to choose between different lists of candidates: he is invited to declare whether he accepts, yes or no, the sole and whole list of four hundred candidates "designated" by the Grand Council. Thus there is no opposition press, no opposition party organizations, no possibility of propaganda against the party in power, and there are no opposing candidates. Whoever refuses to go to the polls reveals himself as an opponent of Fascist rule. The voter receives from the election inspector two different ballots. A tricolor ballot is given to answer yes, and a white ballot to answer no. They may be easily recognized. But the voter is allowed to retire into a secret closet where there is a polling box, and he is allowed secretly to put one of the two ballots into the box. Thus the vote is secret. When he gets out of the closet, he must hand over the other ballot to the election inspector. The "Corporative Chamber" is always unanimously in agreement with the government. The essential principle on which this constitution is based, is expressed in the sentence: "Mussolini is always right."

IV

THE ACHIEVEMENTS OF THE DICTATORSHIP

The economic recovery which already was on its way at the end of 1922, when Mussolini came to power, went on during the first three years of the dictatorship. The well-known old practitioner, Father Time, was doing his work. Moreover during those years the dictatorship had the good fortune to meet with a complex of favorable coincidences which strongly contributed to recovery. France, owing to her losses in manpower during the War, was obliged to seek foreign workers for agricultural labor and for the reconstruction of her devastated areas. It is estimated that in France, Belgium and Luxemburg there were, in 1925, 1,200,000 Italians. This is why unemployment was very low during those years. Then, in 1923 and 1925, Italy had two exceedingly good harvests. Lastly this was a period of prosperity in all the countries of the world, and these countries sent to Italy a large number of tourists who spent their money in Italy and thus helped to a great extent to balance the budget of international payments. The number of foreign tourists was exceptional in 1925, when the Holy Year brought into Italy nearly a million tourists, that is, half a million more than the yearly average, with an influx of money greatly superior to the normal amount.

At the same time the strain of the extraordinary expenses dependent on the war rapidly ceased. The pre-Fascist cabinets had to meet from June 1918 to June 1922 four billion dollars of war claims, i.e., an average of a billion each year. The Fascist dictatorship on the same account had only to meet $214,000,000 in 1922–23; $175,000,000 in 1923–24; $17,000,000 in 1925–26; and $8,000,000 in 1928–29. Also in this field, Father Time did his healing work conscientiously.

The dictatorship should have taken advantage of this favorable state of affairs to reduce the taxes and the public debt, to the extent that the extraordinary expenses caused by the war had ceased. It should have avoided every unnecessary increase of expenditures of a normal type. And really in the first two and a half years it succeeded in lowering the normal expenses from $840,000,000 to $700,000,000.

But the high military authorities who had armed the Fascists and had performed the coup d'etat in October 1922, demanded higher expenditures for the army, for the navy, for aviation and for the colonies. The capitalists who had subsidized the movement and who supported the party-controlled papers, wanted their concerns to be saved from bankruptcy at the taxpayer's expense. The Black Shirts, who formed the rank and file of the party, asked, as a premium for their labors, jobs in the government's bureaucracy or in public bodies controlled by the government. It was further necessary to increase the police budget in order to wrap the country in a mighty net of repression and espionage.

In 1925 the normal outlay began to swell replacing the extraordinary expenses from the war, which were ceasing. The normal expenditures which had been reduced to $700,000,000 in 1924–25, gradually increased to a billion in 1928–29.[3]

In order to pay a part of the 4 billion dollars of extraordinary expenses caused by the war and which fell due from June 1918 to June 1922, the pre-Fascist administration had increased the public debt by 2.3 billion dollars. The Fascist dictatorship, which had to pay 465 million dollars between 1923 and 1925, lowered the public debt by 150 million dollars. But in the fiscal year 1925–26 the public debt started to increase, in spite of the fact that the extraordinary expenses of the war had almost entirely disappeared. Between June 1925 and June 30, 1929 the public debt had increased by $370,000,-000.[4]

Also as far as the monetary policy is concerned, the dictatorship continued in 1923 and in the first months of 1924 the work of slow deflation and revaluation of the lira, which had been started by the pre-Fascist administration. But under the pressure of the industrialists who hoped to profit from a new inflation, and of the banks, who needed help to be saved from bankruptcy, the dictatorship embarked on a policy of fresh inflation in 1925 and in 1926. The Italian lira lost all the ground it had gained after 1920. In 1922 one might have bought a dollar with twenty-one lire; in August 1926 one had to pay thirty lire to buy a dollar.

To avoid a definite disaster, inflation had finally to be

3 *Relazione della Giunta Generale del Bilancio,* 29 aprile 1932, p. 37.
4 E. ROSSI, *I debiti pubblici dello Stato dal 30 giugno 1922 al 30 giugno 1929,* in "Riforma Sociale", sett-ott. 1930.

stopped and with the help of American loans the lira was again revaluated and stabilized in 1927 at nineteen to the dollar; that is to say at almost the same rate prevailing in 1922 before the "March on Rome."

But in order to prevent the fall of the lira below the level at which it had been stabilized in 1927, the Bank of Italy, which was entrusted with the monetary policy by the government, was compelled to buy systematically all the liras which were emigrating as far as the excess of the imports over the exports was to be paid for. The circulation, which amounted to 20.1 billion paper lire on December 31, 1926, was reduced to 16.9 billion paper lire in Autumn of 1929.

This violent reduction of the circulation caused a sudden fall of the wholesale prices on the internal market and a deep depression in industry and agriculture. The economic distress was further increased by the fact that the men who used to emigrate to the United States, were since 1924 refused entrance, and the effect of this real revolution in the flow of Italian emigration made itself more and more felt, as the enforcement of the American emigration laws was becoming stricter and stricter. And as if the American laws were not efficacious enough to block this safety valve of the Italian economic machine, the Italian government, starting in 1926, put many additional obstacles in the path of Italian emigration to all other countries. The crisis was most acute in 1927.

In a speech of November 9, 1927, Mussolini plainly admitted: "There has been a crisis and it has been a grave one. It was bound to come because of the monetary policy for which the régime accepts full responsibility. What stage has the crisis reached? I am convinced that the peak is already past." The peak was far from past. In another speech of June 22, 1928, Mussolini reiterated: "I believe that the end is in sight," and on December 9, 1928: "We are out of the dangerous waters; we are in full convalescence." But on October 2, 1929, he had to admit: "These very days have seen the culmination of the crisis. We have left the night behind and are marching toward the dawn." Three weeks later came the Wall Street crash. In a speech of December 18, 1930, the Duce explained: "Just as we were almost in sight of land, the American crisis of October 24, 1929, drove us back into the high seas."

To face this new disaster, it would have been necessary to reduce expenses, to put an end to any increase in the public debt and to stop the deflation process. Quite on the contrary, expenses mounted from 1 billion dollars in 1928–29 to 1.24 billions in 1931–32. The national debt increased by no less than $500,000,000 from June 1929 to June 1932.

The circulation continued to drop from 16.9 billion paper lire in the fall of 1929, to 13.5 billion paper lire in October 1932. The wholesale prices, which had already fallen 34% on account of the revaluation of 1927, lost 64% because of the depression which started in 1929.[5]

The seriousness of the crisis may be gauged by the unemployment statistics, though these are systematically falsified by the government in order to hide the reality of the situation. The highest figure of unemployment between the end of the war and the "March on Rome" was 606,000 in January 1922, i.e., half of that of February 1932, when unemployment rose to 1,147,000. Either the situation in 1922 was considerably less catastrophic, or that of 1932 is much more catastrophic than the Fascists would like to make us believe; or both statements are true.

The Parliamentary Committee on the budget of the fiscal year 1932–33, in their report of April 29, 1932, write as follows: "It is necessary to face the hard reality: also for Italy the crisis has become more serious, more widespread, more cruel" (p. 13); "it is estimated that in the United States of America the National income fell 33%; we assume that in Italy the total income was reduced in the same proportion" (p. 24); "in Italy the situation became much worse than the one we could observe twelve months ago" (p. 27).

Wages had risen from 100, in 1913–14, on the eve of the World War, to 505 in the second half of 1922, while the cost of living had risen from 100 to 498; that is to say, the Italian working classes not only were able to meet the rising cost of living by higher wages, they also gained a slight improvement. From 1922 to the second half of 1926, the cost of living rose to 653, and wages to 584: that is to say, the workers lost 15% on the advantage they had acquired by 1922.[6] In April 1927 the wages were reduced by 10%; this was followed by a further reduction of 10% in October 1927; in December 1930 another general wage cut took place, which amounted to 8%

5 *Relazione della Giunta General del Bilancio*, 21 aprile 1932, p. 36.
6 MORTARA, *Prospettive economiche:* 1927, p. 442.

in industry and from 15% to as much as 25% in agriculture; and on October 31, 1931, fresh reductions amounting in certain cases to 25%, were authorized by the government. The average wages of industrial workers are to-day one half of what they were in 1926. Those of agricultural laborers were reduced in many parts of Italy, particularly in southern Italy, much below one half. Meanwhile the cost of living did not change until the end of 1929, and only in the last two years it fell, but only by 25%. If one adds the losses caused by increased unemployment to the drop in real wages, one realizes the deterioration which has taken place in the standard of life of the Italian working classes since 1922.

To assert, that in these ten years of existence, the dictatorship has not accomplished any good, would certainly be unjust. There is no bad régime which does not introduce some improvement in some sphere of national life, while causing conditions to grow worse in other spheres. There is no good régime which does not commit mistakes. The Italian people has paid in taxation, during these last ten years, on an average, about 1 billion dollars yearly. It would have been impossible to throw away 10 billion dollars without producing any improvement at all.

On the main lines devoted to international traffic, the railroad service has been considerably improved. (On the secondary railroads one soon discovers that the trains run . . . . as well as they can). The most important highways in Northern Italy and in the neighborhood of large cities, have been rebuilt according to the most up to date standards. (The other roads are still in a terribly neglected condition). The public works, especially the more showy ones in the large cities, where many tourists can see them, have received a new impetus. The work of land reclamation, which was in progress for half a century all over Italy, has been intensified during the last years especially in the District of Rome: a foreigner, unless he be totally unknown, cannot remain a few days in Rome without being invited for a motor drive, to see some reclamation scheme in the vicinity.

But a régime should be judged as a whole, every way in which it has improved or made worse conditions being taken into account. The trains on the main lines run on time, but the letters are opened by the police. The center of Rome has been renovated, but for this purpose the municipality has borrowed 50 million dollars at 8% interest in the United States, while under the old régime any politician who would have incurred a foreign debt in order to beautify a city, would have been sent to jail like a criminal. To-day many roads are kept better than 10 years ago, but all Italy has become a prison. Strikes have disappeared, but industrial workers have lost at least 25% of their real wages, the day laborers have been treated still worse, and unemployment has reached dreadful proportions, etc., etc.

When the ground is cleared of all the lies with which Fascist "propaganda" has encumbered it, and, when one conscientiously strikes a balance of the advantages and damages, both economic and moral, which the Fascist régime has caused in Italy, the judgment of every honest person cannot be anything but highly unfavorable to the régime.

V

THE DICTATORSHIP AND THE ITALIAN PEOPLE

The ultimate test of all successes for a régime is to have its people satisfied and favorable.

Has Fascism achieved this success?

In an interview given to the *Daily Express* in January 1927, Mussolini asserted that no more than 2000 persons in Italy were hostile to Fascist rule. But in a speech on May 26, 1927, he assured his followers that he was in a position to stamp down any attempt at resistance:—"There are to-day in Italy"—he stated—"60,000 carabineers; 30,000 permanent militiamen; and 250,000 non-permanent militiamen. These forces are equipped with 774 cars, 290 trucks, 198 motorcycles, 48 motor boats, and 12 thousand bicycles." What a display of force to keep down no more than 2000 opponents!

From February 1927 to Autumn 1932, the Special Court for the Defense of the State has sentenced to death 9 persons, one person to life-imprisonment and 1902 persons to 10,157 years in prison. In the same period not less than 3000 persons have been interned on the penal islands; about 500 of whom have served a sentence of 5 or more years. It is impossible to ascertain how many people were interned in the small villages of Southern Italy and on the islands, and how many persons put under special police surveillance. It is evident, that, in January

1927, Mussolini underestimated a little too arbitrarily the number of his opponents. In his speech of May 1927 he himself had to admit that the present generation of the Italian working people is an unconquerable one, and that he expected that a new generation will come to the front more fitted to absorb Fascist ideals.

A Nation is not a homogeneous and compact mass. It is divided into classes. The interests, prejudices and feelings of one class differ from those of all the others, and often in the same social class the mood varies from year to year.

The workers in the city and the laborers on the land have always been and always remain, in their quasi-totality, opposed to the dictatorship. They allow themselves to be caught in the Fascist unions and, under the watchful eye of the union officials, they take part in Fascist parades, in order to keep their jobs and not to be reduced to hunger. But their hatred for the dictatorship remains deep and tenacious.

The middle and lower middle classes have never been compactly either for or against Fascism. Many were "Bolshevistic" i.e., dissatisfied with everything and everybody, in 1919; many became tired of the political disorder in 1920 and looked sympathetically toward Fascism in 1921 and 1922; but many became hostile to Fascism as it was gradually assuming the character of a dictatorship; since 1927, the economic crisis and the increase in taxation accomplished the rest.

In the ranks of Civil Service the higher-ups are Fascists, the middle categories are divided, the lower classes are anti-Fascists. In the Clergy, the Pope, the Cardinals and most of the Bishops are pro-Fascist, but the lower clergy in the cities is divided and in the country the parish priests are in great majority as anti-Fascist as the peasants amongst whom they live.

Among the intellectuals the older generations remain in the great majority opposed to Fascism: only a minority has "inserted" itself actively in the Fascist party and is exploiting its favors. The young people were, with more or less enthusiasm, Fascist, until 1926. In the schools they are forcibly fed with Fascist doctrine. But since 1927, the unemployment among intellectuals has been very serious. From year to year the newcomers find it increasingly difficult to obtain employment. As long as they are in school, the children and the adolescents sing Fascist hymns, take part in Fascist parades, repeat the Fascist catechism. But only few of them continue to be sincerely good

Fascists when, after leaving school, they must face the hardships of everyday life. In order not to be annoyed, most of them register with the Fascist organization without inner conviction, or they even profess the Fascist faith because this is necessary if one wants a job or desires a career in the dominant party; but they are really only thinking of their daily bread and butter. A minority revolts and devotes itself to anti-Fascist activities. It is remarkable that at the Universities the first symptoms of opposition against the dictatorship manifested themselves in 1930 and 1931, i.e., exactly when the generation which since 1923 had been incubated in the Fascist schools, started to reach the University.

In the upper classes only—the great landowners, the great industrialists and the important bankers—Mussolini and the régime have always found and still find full-hearted support. But not even in these circles is the mood to-day the same as it was six or seven years ago. The upper classes were enthusiastically in favor of Fascism until 1927, because the income from the land, the profit of industry and bank dividends were high, strikes were forbidden, and Mussolini "was keeping down" the lower classes which immediately after the war had become too insolent. But since the crisis of 1927 the enthusiasm of these gentlemen has cooled off considerably. The "Corporative State" has worked much to the satisfaction of the employers of labor. But, will it always be so? Could not Mussolini some fine day ask them to increase wages, instead of reducing them? Will he always trust the political loyalty of the employers? Will he never be tempted to unleash the unions against them? And would not the workers—in case of a collapse of Fascism—find in the Fascist unions a weapon with which they could legally perpetrate a real social revolution? All that the workers would have to do would be to assemble in the headquarters of the legally recognized unions, oust the present Fascist secretaries and elect secretaries of their own choice! Should the Communists prevail, they would declare the employers' associations illegal, and with the national confederation of the workers' unions, they would inaugurate a "Dictatorship of the proletariat." Should the Socialists win, the employers' associations would not be declared illegal; but in the relations between employers and employees the influence of the new Socialistic government would be brought to bear in favor of the employees. Instead of being grilled swiftly by the Communists, the employers would be cooked slowly by the Socialists. The Italian Capitalists are well aware of the fact that they themselves have spun the rope with which sooner or later they will be hanged. This fear of the future keeps them faithful to the dictatorship. Rather than face the certain dangers of an anti-Fascist revolution, they remain—though not enthusiastically—pro-Fascist.

If to-day a free plebiscite were to be held in Italy, one-tenth of the votes would be cast for the dictatorship and nine-tenths against it. In Italy, Mussolini's personal prestige has absolutely vanished except in the standardized and government-controlled press, and among those less intelligent Fascists who take the newspapers seriously. A saying goes the rounds in Italy: "One Italian curses Mussolini, two Italians do not dare to speak, and three Italians shout: Long live Mussolini." If the Fascists did not have the feeling of being permanently menaced, they would not gag the press, would not hinder the formation of free associations, would not evade municipal elections, would not make a farce out of the national elections, and would not have to keep the country under the terror of spies, of internment and of the penitentiary.

VI

THE ANTI-FASCIST CURRENTS

As the discontent cannot evolve into a legal, public opposition, it becomes illegal and secret.

The anti-Fascist groups are divided into three schools of thought: 1.) Monarchists; 2.) Republicans and Socialists, and 3.) Communists.

Those Monarchists who did not rally to the Fascist party, hope that the Italian people will find a way out with the help of the King and the army. In the army, the common soldiers, nearly all of whom are workers and peasants, are anti-Fascists. The junior officers actively in sympathy with Fascism from 1919 to 1922, became in the main anti-Fascist in the following years. They are indignant at the claims of the Fascist militia officers—adventurers whose records are often stained with crimes—that they be treated on the same footing as the regulars. If the King were to abandon his passive attitude, the situation would change forthwith. The King ought to make a coup d'etat against the Duce, just as the Fascists made in 1922 a coup d'etat against the Parliament. He should fire the Duce, order the arrest of the more turbulent Fascist chiefs and entrust the government to a Cabinet of generals. These generals should, with the assistance of the monarchical anti-Fascists and of the more reasonable or more versatile amongst the Fascists, reëstablish a little freedom of the press, a little self-government, a little electoral freedom. In reality these monarchical anti-Fascists are conservatives, who fear a revolution even more than they hate Fascism. They find that a certain amount of anti-Fascist movement is useful so far as it prevents the King from dozing quietly, and harasses them with the fear of a revolution, which would certainly occur, should not the dictatorship be substituted for by a less odious régime; but they hope that the movement may never degenerate into a revolution. Their hopes and expectations are devoid of any foundation. The King is incapable of any act of will. He is the "roi fainéant" par excellence. The Crown Prince is a low-witted, dissolute, bigoted man, imbued with absolutist and militarist prejudices. On the other hand, the army generals are nearly all pro-Fascist. They get from Mussolini all they want. Military and colonial expenditure increased from 120 million dollars in 1921–22 to 300 million dollars in 1932–33. What interest would the army generals have in taking the lead in order to change such an agreeable state of things? The anti-Fascist monarchists are carriages abandoned on a disused railway track. But if ever, by a miracle, the King or his son should assume an anti-Fascist attitude, the ranks of the anti-Fascists would swell to incredible proportions. To be freed from Mussolini, the vast majority of the Italians would gladly give credit even to the devil.

The Republican and Socialist current is composed of those groups which always have kept alive in Italy the tradition of anti-monarchical ideas, and of Socialists and Liberals who have lost all faith in the King and the heir-apparent. They predict that Italy can be freed from the Fascist dictatorship only by a revolution which overthrows at the same time the King and the Dictator. They recognize that a republican revolution could not occur and could not consolidate itself, except by the formation of a great coalition of all anti-Fascist groups: intellectuals, middle and lower middle classes, and the working classes in town and country. As the most powerful support of the republican movement must come from the working classes, the anti-Fascist revolution must be not only political, but also social. The cost of the revolution must be borne by the great landowners, by the great industrialists, the bankers and by those, from the King down, who are responsible for all the sufferings the Italian people are enduring under the yoke of the dictatorship.

Republicans and Socialists are very definite in rejecting the dictatorship of the proletariat. They aim to restore to the Italian people its political liberties and to reinstate representative institutions. Certainly, a revolution cannot be carried through with the methods of liberty and legality. The political groups staging a revolution cannot—before starting—ask the general electorate for regular authorization. After succeeding, they must for a certain length of time carry on a dictatorship in order to repel counter-attacks of the vanquished and in order to give the country a breathing spell in which to reorganize. But this period of provisional government must last only as long as it is strictly necessary. The temporary government must, as soon as it will have demolished the structure of Fascism, confiscated the property of all men responsible for the dictatorship, and reduced them to a condition which will prevent them from counter-attacking, summon a constituent assembly elected by general suffrage. This assembly will shape the organs of the new, regular government, granting to all citizens political freedom.

The Communists hope that the Fascist dictatorship will be succeeded by the "dictatorship of the proletariat," i.e. of the Communist party representing the proletariat. During the first years of the dictatorship the Communists were in a small minority, But, as the dictatorial character of Fascism was becoming more pronounced, and as the economic conditions were getting worse, there has been among the working classes and anti-Fascist intellectual youth a considerable swing to Communism. The suppression of all liberty and justice has exasperated them. People who claim that Mussolini has checked Communism in Italy, claim the reverse of the truth. The Fascist dictatorship has created a Communist danger which did not exist before its triumph.

The Republicans and Socialists have to face enormous difficulties: they must at one and the same time overcome the inertia of a terrorized people, escape the pressure of the Fascist government, and meet the challenge of Communist propaganda.

Moreover it should not be forgotten that, after all, the revolution is a "technical" problem, hard to be put across in a modern State.

Local revolt is of no avail against a dictatorship which can rapidly concentrate powerful military forces. When some desperate outburst occurs in a town, Fascists as a rule disappear for some hours, fearing a general uprising. But the militia is rapidly summoned by telephone from the neighboring cities, and reprisals reduce the place to a state of terror more suffocating than before. In purely local revolts the Fascists will always be victors. The dictatorship can be fought only by a general movement throughout the whole country, so that the Fascists, attacked everywhere at once, have no chance to concentrate their forces.

Revolution in a large country can only break out if two circumstances conjoin: unrest among large sections of the population, and some national event which stirs the people to its depths, sets the spur to its hatreds and hopes, and drives it everywhere to action, while, on the other hand, it disrupts and paralyzes the dominant party and makes it incapable of resisting.

Will such a moment occur? And when?

SACHIO OKA

THE SHADOW OF JAPAN

I

WAR IN MANCHURIA

WHEN General Honjo, the Commander of the Kwantung force of His Imperial Japanese Majesty's Army, gave the order to advance toward Mukden on that historic night of September 18, 1931, he was fully conscious of the significance of his action. As he had written six weeks previously in his secret memorandum to Army Minister Minami, he was closely following the plan of the late Premier Tanaka, whose "positive" policy declared Manchuria to be the first base of the Japanese military adventure toward the conquest of Asia. As is the case with every criminal action on the part of the ruling class, the course of this operation had been carefully planned, the methods fully prepared, and the pretexts skillfully fabricated.

(a) *Pretexts*

In July and August, 1931, Sze Yu-hsiang, one of Feng Yu-hsiang's former generals, organized an offensive with over 60,-000 men against the force of Chang Hsueh-liang. This seemed to be merely another one of a long series of local squabbles between ambitious warlords, but to the student of Far Eastern politics it was highly significant in that it was directly participated in by the Japanese General Staff. The real object of the offensive was to divert the force of Chang Hsueh-liang from South Manchuria and drive it into the northern part of China Proper, so that the ground would be fairly clear when the Japanese troops later intervened. This later invasion of China by Japanese troops would thus be fully justified in the name of the "protection of the lives and property of the Japanese residents." At the same time Japan was giving military as well as political and financial aid to the anti-Chiang Kai-shek groups of Kanton, in exchange for their assurance in regard to Manchuria. This strengthening of the opposition would so weaken Chiang Kai-shek's position that a new struggle among the generals would follow giving Japan due cause to intervene. Japan was also making secret agreements with Yen Hsi-shan and Feng Yu-hsiang for an attack against the anti-Japanese and pro-American bourgeois warlord Chang Hsueh-liang.

That, however, was not sufficient. The time has passed when the mere fact that warlords were engaged in military struggle within the "sphere of influence" was good and sufficient reason to warrant the sending of troops. In order to arouse mass support for a war, there must be a sensational incident involving the matter of peace, justice, and special rights acquired through the sacrifice of many thousands of lives. The first of those ingenious plots was the Wang-Pao-Shang Incident.

In May, the same year, nine Korean agriculturists backed by the Japanese Consulate of Changchung, "purchased," without the knowledge of the owners, some land near Mt. Wang-Pao located a few miles north of that city. They hired over two hundred Korean immigrant peasants and started irrigation projects. The landowners, stunned at the mysterious appropriation of their property, attacked and massacred a large number of the peasants with the help of Chinese troops and drove the Koreans out of the district. The Consulate at Changchung, which had been waiting for the result, immediately sent out an armed force and occupied the territory, at the same time spreading the news throughout Manchuria, Korea and Japan that Chinese were mercilessly destroying the lives and property of Korean immigrants.

The second plot was the Captain Nakamura Murder Case of June, in which a Japanese military officer and three other Japanese were murdered by unknown persons—Chang Hsueh-liang's officers, according to the Japanese claim. Japan took up this case and attacked the Chinese administration in Manchuria, "proving" that government was lax and discipline was almost non-existent.

These anti-Chinese agitations together with various political accusations, increased their intensity throughout Japan during the summer. Even supposedly "liberal" and "high-brow" magazines, not to mention the reactionary press, carried Sinophobiac propaganda. Schools were visited by lecturers subsidized by the army. Mass meetings were arranged in the cities and the villages sponsored by bourgeois organizations. Even labor unions were flooded with leaflets and pamphlets written by the "socialist" leaders who had apparently decided to replace their former internationalism by the fashionable social-fascism. The words "Chinese atrocity" were voiced everywhere. Class-conscious workers and intellectuals who dared to even hint the real intention of the imperialists were faced with whole-sale arrest, torture and imprisonment.

(b) *Japan Controls Manchuria*

In the middle of the night of September 18, when the skilled propagandists judged they had aroused mass sympathy for an armed intervention, a part of the South Manchuria Railway track near Tieling was blown up by "Chinese soldiers." Although the damage was rather too small to have been done by enemies, Major Kawashima's battalion, which conveniently happened to be maneuvering near the location, immediately opened fire. To the battalion were added other detachments from Mukden and Tieling. Before the dawn of September 19, Mukden was occupied without difficulty. More than one thousand Chinese troops and citizens were killed by the Japanese troops and no less than seven thousand troops and five thousand police were disarmed. Barracks were burned down and ammunition dumps were seized. When dawn came, over the city gates and garrison were fluttering flags with a scarlet ball in the center, the "Rising Sun" emblem of the Japanese Empire, declaring to the world the beginning of Japan's undeclared war against China.

By the middle of November Japanese troops practically controlled the whole of South Manchuria, and, moving northward, they crossed the Chinese Eastern Railway line, and captured the city of Tsitsihar. Other forces marched southward from Mukden and later seized the territory as far as the Great Wall. On January 3, 1932, the city of Chinchow, where Chang Hsueh-liang had established his headquarters, was taken. During the month the invaders renewed their attack upon North Manchuria, seized the Harbin-Changchung branch of the Chinese Eastern, and by February 5, Harbin, the most important center of North Manchuria, was under Japanese control.

(c) *Attempts to Smash the Anti-Imperialist Movement*

Japan's aggression in Manchuria was followed by a strong protest from the masses of the workers and peasants of China. Despite the mild attitude of the Kuomintang government, the people stood up in revolutionary defiance and answered the Japanese invasion with strikes and boycotts throughout the country. While in Manchuria the workers in the factories as well as on the railways and the docks carried out strikes in response to the Japanese invasion, in Shanghai the workers in more than twenty Japanese spinning mills went on strike along with other workers. The two thousand workers of the Shanghai Sen Chen Spinning Mill decided at their meeting on September 30, 1931, to arm themselves and organize a defense corps. In December, following the First Chinese Soviet Congress of November 7 at Shui-Kin in Kiangsi Province, thirty thousand cotton mill workers of Shanghai went on strike. The strike movement spread to workers of other factories and stores in Shanghai as well as in other cities. Many street demonstrations were held in denunciation of the Kuomintang and Japanese imperialism. Japanese-owned factories and stores were compelled to close their doors. Goods piled up in the warehouses. Imports from Japan declined. Thousands of workers and students occupied the government offices in Nanking and demanded that the Kuomintang cede to the masses' demand and take decisive measures for the defense of the nation.

The Japanese imperialists determined to crush the anti-Japanese agitation and boycotts, to fortify their military position in Central and South China, and to smash the soviet movement in those districts, by launching an attack along the valley of the Yangtse-kiang. The infamous Shanghai massacre and the attack against the Woosung forts and Nanking followed.

It was decidedly an imperialist war against the toiling masses of China. At the beginning of February near Shanghai there were more than fifty Japanese warships, fifty thousand marines, and nearly one hundred airplanes. British, American, French and Italian gunboats rushed up the river toward the soviet districts, while the Japanese completely devastated Chapei, the working class center of Shanghai, where a general strike had been declared. Tens of thousands of workers, men, women, and children, fell victims to the murder machine. The Kuomintang, the running dog of the imperialists, offered of course no defense. On the contrary, Chiang Kai-shek executed anti-imperialist elements in his army and ordered his troops to evacuate Shanghai. Helpless citizens fleeing into the International Settlement were brutally murdered not only by the Japanese but also by the American, British and French troops.

The expectations of the imperialists, however, were not fulfilled. Thousands of defenseless workers and their wives and children were murdered, but the will of the masses for freedom still existed. Rebellions occurred even in the imperial armies. Nearly one thousand Japanese soldiers had to be sent back home because they had become "homesick" and had revolted against their superior officers. Many were shot in Shanghai. Still more were thrown overboard on their way back to Japan. The soldiers of the well known 19th Army of China also rebelled. They discovered the real nature of their master, Kuomintang, and turned their arms against Chiang Kai-shek. Many of them united with rebellious Japanese soldiers and fired at their common enemy—the imperialists of foreign nations and their Chinese vassals.

The imperialists also failed in their attack against the Chinese Soviets. Their joint effort to smash the workers' and peasants' government of China merely showed the strength of the working class in its self-defense against imperialism. Foreign gunboats stationed in the soviet area were driven back without any measurable success.

(d) *The Establishment of the Manchu State*

While attempting to strike a death blow against the working class of South and Central China, jointly with other imperialist powers and the counter-revolutionary Kuomintang, Japan was preparing a military base in Manchuria—the result of many years of deliberation between the Japanese imperialists and their lackey warlords of China.

Immediately after the September incident, anti-Kuomintang governments under Japanese supervision were set up by Japan's Manchurian vassals. In February, while Chapei was on fire, the puppet State of Manchu (Manchukuo) was founded, including a vast area of Inner Mongolia as well as the whole of Manchuria. For the purpose of demagogy, the Child Emperor Pu-Yi of the former Chinese Empire was put in charge as the figurehead of this new republic. But the political machine was run entirely by Japanese advisers, office holders, and militarists.

Japan's partial victory in creating the puppet state did not, of course, satisfy the imperialists. Under the pretext of putting down the "bandits," they furthered their aims. Despite the misery of the Japanese masses at home under the heel of capitalist exploitation, despite the suffering of the peoples of Korea and Manchuria, Japan determined to push her arms toward the goal she had envisioned for herself.

The latest news tells us that Japan has taken the walled city of Shanhaikwan, and is attacking the Great Wall which divides Mongolia from China Proper. Japan is desperately trying to annex the Mongolian province of Jehol to the Manchu State, in order to complete her rule over the great area of North China.

And so General Honjo has followed to the minutest detail the instruction of his former chief who declared that Japan must pursue her "military aims and surround the heart of Manchuria and Mongolia with circular railways, in order, on the one hand, to smash the military, political, and economic development of China, and on the other, to hold back the penetration of Russian influence," for, with all the resources of China at her disposal, may it not become possible for Japan to conquer "India, the Archipelago, Asia Minor, Central Asia, and even Europe"?

II

JAPAN AND THE IMPERIALIST STRUGGLE FOR CHINA

For nearly half a century Manchuria has been a bone of contention among the imperialist powers of the world. The Balkan of the Orient, the Servia of the second world war, it is not only a rich land—vast, fertile, full of timber, grains, and mineral resources—but it is the key to China Proper. And in the present crisis, it is an important gateway to the Soviet Union.

The beginning of the imperialist struggle for the conquest of Manchuria dates back to 1894. Ever since then such empires as Czarist Russia, the United States, Great Britain, and Japan, have been scrambling to secure dominance over it.

(a) *Japan's Penetration of China*

Japan's ambition to annex China is traditional. Since time immemorial, there have been attempts on Japan's part to advance into the Asiatic continent through Korea and China, the first to appear in written history being that of Queen Jingu in the year 200 A. D. When in the middle of the thirteenth century Kubla Khan's Mongolian army became aggressive and made excursions into China Proper and Korea, and subsequently into Japan, the feudalists of Japan not only drove them out but actually planned to conquer their country. Korea had been looked upon as Japan's vassal state ever since the first century before Christ, and had been made to pay tribute to Japan. And the feudalists as well as the pre-feudal monarchists desired to extend their rule west of the Yalu. Their dreams went even so far as to sanction the myth that the great Genghis Khan was a brother of the first feudal Shogun Yoritomo. When in the middle of the sixteenth century Korea had become a protectorate of China and therefore refused to pay tribute to Japan, Hideyoshi, the chief councilor of the state, sent his army to Korea not only in order to drive the Chinese out of the peninsula but to pursue his military aims into China Proper. But Hideyoshi's death and Shogun Ieyasu's policy of closing the doors of the nation to foreign powers, shattered the advance. It was only after the bourgeois revolution of 1866, with the consequent downfall of the shogunate and its centralized feudalism, that the traditional dream was renewed.

(b) *The Japanese Bourgeois Revolution of 1866*

The bourgeois revolution of 1866 left Japan a nation of peculiar contradictions. The bourgeoisie failed to completely destroy feudalism: although the shogun's autocracy was abolished, a similar form of bureaucracy remained; modern industry sprang up, but as there was no agrarian revolution, the farms were merely transferred from the hands of the feudal lords into the hands of the big landowners, without being capitalistically reorganized. The result was increased impoverishment and consequent lack of purchasing power on the part of the peasantry over whom the bourgeoisie had practically no control. The peasantry, whose living conditions were no better than during the feudal times, carried out numerous rebellions together with the rising proletariat against the new absolutist government. When in addition to this the country met with increasing pressure from European imperialist nations, the bourgeoisie had to abandon its mission of completing the revolution. It rejected its liberalistic plan, and formed a bloc under its own hegemony with the feudal elements—monarchical, royal, military, and landowner—in order to defend the propertied class in general from its class enemy, the working class, and from foreign imperialists.

The compromise between capitalist and feudal elements resulted in a form of State capitalism and financial oligarchy such as is rarely seen in a typical capitalist nation. The constitution of the new Japan perpetuated the existence of various feudal remnants. Although economically under the hegemony of the bourgeoisie, the feudal elements, especially the landowner-military clique, soon began to play a leading part in the exploitation of the working class.

When external pressure became intensified and the lack of a home market and of raw material grew alarming, the ruling class of Japan began its penetration into China through Korea —the long dreamed-of conquest of the continent. But unlike the advance of other imperialist nations into China, it was a military advance rather than commercial and financial.

As Lenin said, imperialism wills to rule. Liberalism—the spirit of free competition—is pushed back stage by the oncoming imperialism, and the forcible seizure of markets becomes the main tactic of the capitalists. The military clique and the police, instead of the civilians, become the vanguard of the exploitation.

With the Sino-Japanese War of 1894, Japan, without completing her liberalism, entered the list of the imperialist nations of the world.

(c) Manchuria Merry-Go-Round Begins

Korea, then a protectorate of China, was on the verge of bourgeois revolution. Just as Great Britain had helped the anti-shogunate army of Japan in the hope of gaining control over the post-revolutionary Japan—tactics which European imperialists had exercised over many countries of Asia—so Japan encouraged the bourgeois liberals of Korea in their rebellion of 1884. Then under the pretext of "keeping the peace in the Orient," Japan put political pressure upon the turmoil. It was this action that developed into the antagonistic attitude of the

Chinese Empire against Japan and subsequently into the Sino-Japanese War of 1894–5.

Japan beat China without difficulty. She secured control over Korea, declared it independent of China, took control over Manchuria, and acquired the Liaotung Peninsula. At this juncture the Russian imperialists, eager to extend the Trans-Siberian Railway through Manchuria to an open port on the Pacific, became alarmed at Japan's victory, and together with France and Germany, interfered in Japan's taking of Manchuria, by means of diplomatic pressure. Japan, still a young imperialist nation, was compelled to cede to Russia; she returned the Liaotung Peninsula, withdrew from Manchuria, and contented herself with the annexation of Formosa, the independence of Korea, and an indemnity.

After Japan's diplomatic retreat, Russia secured the lease of Liaotung, acquired various rights in North China, and even attempted to extend her rule over Korea. By this time Manchuria was entirely under Russian control. The Russian bureaucrats built railroads, cities, forts; they stationed police and troops. Not only in economics, but in politics and even in the social life of the Manchurians Russian bureaucracy was dominant.

(d) The "Open Door" Policy

The Russian dominance over Manchuria and North China annoyed the imperialists of other nations who had interests in the Far East. First of all the United States promulgated in 1899 her "open door" policy as a threat aimed at the Russian imperialists. The content of the policy was the "internationalization" or the "neutralization" of exploitation rights in Manchuria. It was at first a declaration of equal commercial rights to all nations, but later it was enlarged into a protest against exclusive financial rights by any nation. Three years later the British imperialists, who also had interests in China, formed an alliance with Japan in order to drive the Russians out of North China. Various "bandit outrages," climaxed by the Boxer Rebellion, an uprising of the restless populace of North China, were utilized as a pretext by the imperialist nations, including Russia, to rush troops into Chinese territory as a preparation for an imperialist war.

After the Boxer Rebellion, the Russian imperialists completely ignored the warnings and demands of their rival imperialists. They put stronger pressure on North Manchuria, and extended their hands over Korea. Finally in 1904, Japan, assisted by the British and American imperialists, declared war.

The result of the Russo-Japanese War was a decisive victory on the part of Japan. But the imperialist nations that had used Japan as their spearhead against Russia, intervened through diplomatic pressure, and forced Japan to refrain from taking control over Manchuria. Japan had to content herself with the lease of Liaotung, succession to certain Russian rights in Manchuria, and the annexation of the southern half of Sakhalin.

The Japanese retreat was followed by the commercial and financial invasion of Manchuria and North China by the British and American imperialists, as well as the German and the French. They built railways, banks and various commercial firms. The noted affair between the Edward H. Harriman interests and the Japanese government concerning the operation of the South Manchuria Railway, and the four-power consortium of 1910, were the result of the "neutralization" policy of the British and American imperialists.

(e) The World War and Japanese Expansion

The "neutralization" policy was answered by the Japanese scheme of "localization." Japan refused the Harriman proposal regarding the purchase of the South Manchuria Railway, brazenly annexed Korea, and gradually established her commercial, industrial, and financial base in Manchuria. She strengthened her alliance with Great Britain in order to keep the hands of the American imperialists off China.

The year 1911 was marked by the upheaval of the Chinese bourgeois revolution. In that year Sun Yat-sen's revolutionary army seized Kanton and declared China a republic. At this time, however, the true nature of the revolution was not fully understood by the Japanese imperialists. To their mind, Sun Yat-sen's rebellion against the monarchical rule was merely another of the warlords' struggles. The semi feudalistic Japanese imperialists, who were concerned chiefly with the necessity for territorial expansion, thought it would be possible for them to annex China as they had annexed Korea, that is, by giving aid to the revolutionary army and thus acquiring prestige over the new government. They were totally unaware of the fact that a bourgeois revolution of a semi-colonial nation takes first of all the form of a chauvinistic nationalism to free it from foreign exploiters, unless suppressed in its early stage. Ignoring their own experience with the British and French imperialists at the time of the Japanese bourgeois revolution, they gave financial aid to the revolutionary force, with the hope of gaining at least Manchuria in exchange for the assistance. It was this attitude that was reflected in the Twenty-one Demands of 1915—the international document by means of which Japan sought to legalize her control over Manchuria while other imperialist nations were busy at the World War.

The war brought prosperity to Japan. While the European powers were unable to lay pressure on the Orient, she commercially and financially took their colonies and semi-colonies. In 1914 she occupied the German concession of Shangtung, and virtually became the dictator over North China, while by means of the Twenty-one Demands, she placed Manchuria under her complete control. During the period between 1915–19, Japan's exports totalled 5,400,000,000 yen—a sum more than ten times the amount of any pre-war year. Her commercial investment in Manchuria leaped from the 3,200,100 yen of 1913 to 96,392,350 yen in 1920, or from 40 commercial firms to 306. From a second-class capitalist nation, Japan elevated herself to the rank of one of the most important powers of the world. When the Japanese troops, under the command of the Army Minister Tanaka—the notorious author of the "secret memorandum"—together with those of other imperialist powers, invaded Siberia in 1918, Japanese capitalism was at its peak.

(f) *The Incompleteness of the Dominance*

The Japanese dominance over Manchuria, however, was not complete but merely "legal," contrary to the belief of the imperialists of Japan and despite their success in capitalist expansion. This was clearly demonstrated when the unsuccessful peace conferences between Sun Yat-sen's Kanton force and the Peking government were followed by the anti-imperialist and anti-Japanese movement of the Chinese masses in 1919. The failure on the part of the Japanese to dominate China was largely due to the already mentioned false perception concerning the nature of the Chinese revolution. The error was realized at this time by the Japanese capitalists, whose hegemony over the feudalistic elements suddenly grew, thanks to the

World War. The germs of the present situation in Manchuria—of the "positive" policy of Japanese imperialism—were beginning to show themselves. It was the turning point in the imperialist struggle for the conquest of China.

III

THE APPROACH OF THE SECOND IMPERIALIST WAR

If the foreign policy of a nation is a reflection of its internal policy, its internal policy is invariably very much influenced by its international relations. It was Japan's internal situation, under the influence of her position among the nations, that brought her foreign policy toward China to a turning point after the World War. Since 1866 the development of her policy has always accurately reflected the development of world politics—has followed the course of the intensification of mailed-fist government. The change in Japan's attitude toward China was an extension of the growing dictatorial power inside Japan caused by the several disturbing factors that accompanied the war prosperity: (1) The sharpening of the American-Japanese imperialist rivalry; (2) China's growth in the direction of capitalism—toward becoming a new competitor to Japan; (3) The strengthening of the revolutionary movement throughout the world; (4) The post-war economic crises.

(a) *The Sharpening of the American-Japanese Rivalry*

During the war Asia was virtually in the hands of Japanese imperialism. But American imperialism soon attempted to reestablish its former prestige in the Far East by denouncing and interfering with Japan's actions in the Orient and by spreading the "Yellow Peril" slogan through its jingo press. In 1919, the United States Senate voiced its absolute objection to the Japanese occupation of Shantung, which the Peace Conference had granted Japan as a right. Almost simultaneously the American imperialists opposed the Japanese occupation of northern Sakhalin—a strategic point on the Pacific—and a little later the anti-Japanese land law of California went into effect. In 1921, the United States signed an agreement with China to establish an American-Chinese wireless company, at the same time granting China a huge loan for the purpose of establishing an airplane service. The American-Japanese rivalry was so intense that it seemed as if the Pacific War were about to take place. Generals and politicians—not to mention the press— talked about it openly. The conflict which happened in August, 1921, between American and Japanese marines in Shanghai was a symbolic expression of the moment.

(b) *The Advance of the Chinese Revolution*

The second factor, the advance of China toward the rank of a capitalist nation, was observed clearly when in 1919 the Peking government made attempts to open a peace conference with the southern revolutionary force in order as a national unit jointly to face the foreign imperialist powers. In the same year, the commercial circles of Shanghai made a statement to foreign powers declaring the integrity of China. China's nationalism was now a force which all the armed might of Japanese imperialism could not stop. In order to retain her rights in Manchuria, Japan had to assist the bourgeoisie of China by granting loans through consortiums, but by doing so she was of course helping China's advance toward capitalism. The only solution of the dilemma was to enforce the Twenty-one Demands by stationing troops in Manchuria under the pretext of danger from Siberia, keeping her occupation of Shantung in the name of the "lives and property of Japanese residents," and by assisting the various warlords in order to prolong the course of the Chinese revolution. It was at this time that Japan's plan of founding a puppet state on the site of the present Manchu State was endorsed by Chang Tso-lin, the northern warlord whose ambition was to become the ruler of Manchuria and North China.

In 1921, China's menace became two-fold. While the Chinese Revolution was a movement toward bourgeois revolution, it was largely participated in by the radical liberals who were sympathetic to the working class. Sun Yat-sen's sympathy was distinctly directed toward the workers and the peasants of China, when he reorganized his party, the Kuomintang. He perceived in the bourgeois revolutionary movement a road to the proletarian revolution, and declared that the Kuomintang should coöperate with the Soviet Union, should permit the existence of communist "fractions" and should concentrate its effort upon drawing the support of the working class. The party was reorganized with a proclamation in this direction, despite the opposition of its gentry and business members. Under its leadership, the Chinese masses, influenced by the success of the working class dictatorship of the Soviet Union, and by the flourishing of the revolutionary tide in Europe as well as Asia, sprang up not as a nationalistic opposer of imperialism but as a class unit against capitalists, both foreign and Chinese. Beginning with the student movement of 1919, the workers and the peasants throughout China—in Shanghai, in Hankow, in Tientsin—stood up in armed revolt. The imperialists, including those of the United States, Great Britain, and Japan, brought their "gun-boat" diplomacy to bear on the situation. Japanese capitalism financed northern warlords, particularly Chang Tso-lin, in an attempt to distract the attention of the masses from the imperialists to the warlords, and at the same time to secure the right to send troops to Manchuria.

(c) *The Tide of Revolution*

The third disturbing factor which Japanese capitalism had to face was the upheaval of the proletariat in Japan Proper, as well as in the colonies and in foreign countries. The rise of Soviet Russia and the establishment of the Soviet Union were a deadly blow to the Japanese imperialists, not only because Japan was deprived of a market but because the October Revolution demonstrated the fact that it was possible for the working class to run its own government. Japan, as well as other imperialist nations, had attempted to shatter the course of the revolution by sending troops to Siberia on the frail pretext of coming to the rescue of some mysterious "Czechoslovakians," and of stopping "the wholesale murders and other sinister actions of the outlandish Bolsheviks," but the armed intervention had demonstrated not only the power of the Red Army and the will of the workers and peasants, but it had also revealed to the proletariat at home the truth about the capitalist system. In 1918 tens of thousands of Japanese workers and peasants, as well as intellectuals and middle-class citizens, suffering from the high commodity prices during the war prosperity, in revolutionary upsurge all over the country protested against capitalist exploitation and the imperialist actions in Siberia and North China. The colonial peoples also rose against the Japanese dictatorship, as for example the Banzai Affair, or the Incident of March 1st, 1919, in Korea.

The world-wide tide of revolution gave another blow to

Japan from outside. Great Britain, whose power was considerably weakened on account of the revolutionary events at home beginning with the railway strike of 1919 and the Irish rebellion of 1920, hastened to align herself with the United States, abandoning her alliance with Japan. This betrayal by British imperialism was demonstrated in its anti-Japanese policy at the Washington Conference and the new Four-Power Consortium. Japan's position was weakened tremendously.

(d) *The Post-War Crises*

Among the victorious nations of the World War, Japan was one of the first to be hit by the post-war crises. The fundamental features of Japanese economic and political make-up—semi-feudal capitalism, international relations, geographic situation—made it impossible for Japan to become a powerful nation of monopoly capital without colonial expansion. The war prosperity with its rise in commodity prices and high development of industry did not enrich the working class, but on the contrary impoverished the workers and particularly the peasants, as well as the small merchants and manufacturers. The decrease in purchasing power at home, competition with foreign capitalist nations, the refusal of the Chinese to use Japanese goods, and the rise of the colonial peoples against imperialism, compelled the bourgeoisie to further its monopolization process. The first post-war crisis of 1920, the subsequent panic of 1921, and the earthquake crisis of 1923 demonstrated this process. The economic life of Japan was constantly menaced by crises from that time until 1927, when the so-called "third period" of post-war capitalism, beginning with the Chinese Proletarian Revolution and the great general strike of Great Britain, arrived with another wave of panic.

(e) *The "Positive" Policy*

In August, 1926, Chiang Kai-shek started his northward advance. The masses, trusting him to be the leader of the revolution, followed his march and helped its advance. In December, Hankow was taken by his force and was declared the capital of Kuomintang China. By this time, however, Chiang's action had become definitely contrary to the principles laid down by Sun Yat-sen, and to the demands of the working class. He had driven communist elements out of the party, and had attacked the rebellious masses everywhere, as a service to the imperialist powers. The communist faction, in opposition to this, advanced toward the establishment of Soviet China with the full support of the workers, peasants, and students. When the red flag fluttered, for the first time in the history of China, in Soviet Kanton in 1927, the Chinese Revolution was entirely in the hands of the working class and the radical intellectuals.

This orientation of the revolution compelled the imperialists to change their tactics. The strength of the working class was so intense that the Kuomintang's suppression did not suffice to stop the anti-imperialist and anti-bourgeois movement spreading all over the country. "Gun-boat" diplomacy only aggravated the situation. The anti-British rebellion in Kanton and the Shanghai massacre were two of many similar struggles between the working class and the imperialists.

While the proletarian upheaval weakened the Kuomintang in the south, Japan's Manchurian vassal Chang Tso-lin took over political power in the north, established his own capital in Peking, and entitled himself the Generalissimo of the Chinese Army. Without the consent of Japan he had made plans for railroad building and had indeed some lines already in operation, thus threatening the Japanese interests in Manchuria.

Such was the situation outside Japan. Inside a great crisis was attacking her capitalist system. The failure of several large banks, including the state-owned Bank of Formosa, compelled the government to spend several billions of yens for the "relief" of the bankrupt capitalists. Due to this, factories were forced to stop their machines, and farms could not sell any of their produce. The price of silk became so low that valuable egg-cards became playthings for the farm children. Everywhere the arrival of the "third period," so exactly predicted by the Marxian economists, was apparent.

The government under Premier Tanaka planned the "rationalization of industry"—a project quite similar to that of the "Technocrats"—which they advertised would radically change the aspect of the farms by the process of mechanization, and which would spur the progress of industry. This, however, was a monopolization scheme followed of course by increased unemployment in the cities and intensified misery on the farms.

The Tanaka policy was answered by the working class with an organized revolutionary movement. The Communist Party of Japan, which in its embryo stage had been a party of intellectuals rather than workers and had been easily destroyed by the ruling class, now was reorganized on a sound mass basis and came out openly, though illegally, through the legal Worker-Peasant Party (Rodo-Nomin-To) and through the left-wing "Hyogi-Kai" (Japan Trade Union Council). The communists led strikes and revolts in various fields, menacing the bourgeoisie. The Tanaka cabinet put into force an amendment to the Peace Preservation Law of 1925, and arrested and imprisoned many thousands of class-conscious workers in an effort to kill the revolutionary movement. This effort, however, had precisely the contrary effect; the movement spread further and further throughout Japan and the colonies.

It was at this time that the "positive" policy toward China— an extension of Tanaka's internal policy—was born. As is shown in his "secret memorandum," it was from its very inception a program of imperialist expansion. In the name of this policy, the Tanaka cabinet sent troops to Shanghai and Shantung in 1927 in order to tighten its grip on the rebellious masses of China, and having, through its agents, murdered the betrayer Chang Tso-lin, thus showing its recognition of the corrupt Kuomintang, it demanded exclusive rights for Japan in Manchuria in exchange.

(f) *The War Begins*

The present Japanese policy in Manchuria is the logical following out of the "positive" policy. The Japanese imperialists had intended to start the campaign at an earlier date, but it had been impossible to do so owing to the following factors: the sharpening of the imperialist rivalry, as shown at the London and Geneva Conferences; the advance of the Chinese Revolution; the radicalization of the proletariat; and the advent of the deepening economic crisis.

The imperialists had to delay their plans, but while awaiting the right moment they prepared by making firmer the union of the capitalists with the military and fascist elements, by endeavoring to suppress the revolutionary movement, and by hastening monopolization through the "rationalization" scheme.

The moment for an active attitude on the part of the imperialists arrived with the outbreak of the world crisis in 1929. The crisis hit Japanese industry and agriculture like a tornado. Agriculture, in particular, was so seriously paralyzed that recovery—even by means of the ingenious "rationalization" plan —was despaired of. The workers and the peasants, comparing their misery with the achievements of the proletariat of the Soviet Union and the Chinese Soviets, arose in starving desperation against the imperialist policy.

The astonishing accomplishments of the Five-Year Plan of the Soviet Union further threatened the entire capitalist system of Japan. It was a death blow to the imperialists economically and politically. It showed definitely that the workers and peasants can better their situation by emancipating themselves from the capitalist yoke and that that is the only way out of the crisis. The success of the Plan was being closely followed by the masses of China and was an inspiration to the working class of Japan as well as of the colonies.

In order to smash the Soviet Union and to save themselves from the enveloping crisis, the Japanese imperialists were compelled to begin the military advance into Manchuria. In this campaign world capitalism found itself in the same boat with Japan. The imperialist powers, hit by the crisis, welcomed Japan's initiative. Even if it meant the possibility of Japan's dominance over China, it meant damage to the Soviet Union, and possibly the overthrow of Soviet China, with comparatively little cost to their account. The chance was worth taking.

For Japan, too, the chance was worth taking. If she acquired Manchuria, she might be able to invade the Soviet Union, and smash the communist movement in China. She might be able to acquire the great territory east of Baikal and the whole of North China, including Mongolia. After that, military power and prestige would be on Japan's side when the Pacific War should finally break out. Since she could acquire the powers' assistance in the "holy war" against communism for the asking, she would be foolish not to take it. And after all, it was impossible for her to wait longer. Thus on September 18, 1931, the war was non-documentally declared.

(g) *The Imperialists Assist Japan*

That the imperialist nations are in perfect accord with Japan's action toward the Soviet Union and the Chinese Revolution, cannot be denied. Although the jingo press of the United States, Great Britain, and other rivals of Japanese imperialism, has denounced the Japanese imperialist adventure on Chinese soil, this denunciation was not in accusation of

Japan's crimes but in preparation for a future world war. The American Secretary of State Stimson solemnly called to the attention of China and Japan the provisions of the Kellogg-Briand Pact, but one could read between the lines of his warning a secret approval of Japan's action. So long as Japan does not interfere with the interests of American imperialism, and so long as Japan is a partner with the United States in the imperialist offensive against the Soviet Union and Soviet China, the American imperialists are willing to send Japan ammunition for her Manchurian war. The accusation of the League of Nations Commission against Japan was only on the ground that without declaring war Japan had forcibly seized Manchuria, a Chinese territory, and had proclaimed it independent of China; in other words, Japan would be guiltless if a formal declaration of war had been made! And Lord Lytton, the head of the commission, suavely remarked to a journalist that the world should show "sympathy, tact and understanding" toward Japan. In the matter of the recent Shanhaikwan affair, the foreign imperialists are standing by and giving assistance to Japan, as is revealed in the Chicago *Tribune* cable from London of January 4, 1933, in which it was reported that diplomatic circles in the British capital had arrived at the conclusion that "nothing could be done but hope for the best." The fact that the gun-boats of the United States, Great Britain, France and Italy were sent, at the time of the Shanghai Incident of 1932, not to Shanghai itself but to the soviet districts along the Yangtse-kiang, and that all capitalist nations are engaged in a desperate attempt to discredit the achievement of the Five-Year Plan, while gathering their forces in their puppet states surrounding the Soviet Union, such as Poland, Czechoslovakia, and the Manchu State, further proves their intention without a shadow of doubt.

IV

JAPAN UNDER CAPITALIST EXPLOITATION

Despite the careful censorship of the Interior Ministry, news leaks out; despite the desperate effort of the government statisticians to understate the facts, truth cannot be totally hidden. The misery of the Japanese people to-day is too intense to be forever covered up. So in fear of the mass discontent which may explode if further attempts to conceal the facts are made, the bourgeois press and the government itself are publishing conservative estimates of the situation as a safety valve. Yet even the most conservative figures are terrible enough to indicate some radical change inside Japan in the very near future.

(a) *The Villages*

In June, 1932, in the midst of the agrarian crisis, a clever editor of the Tokio *Asahi*, a "liberal" newspaper financed by the great Mitsubishi Kingdom and protected by the "progressive" Minseito party, interviewed several Interior Ministry investigators on the farm situation. In one of those "slips that pass in the night," the faithful servants of the Mikado unanimously admitted the shocking state of things among the peasants.

"Do not ask the farmers about distress in the villages if you value your life," said one who had been to Nagano Prefecture. "Thousands of villages and small towns are already beyond the stage of ordinary misery. . . . Thievery in Nagano of rice, salt, and other food is common, and the police cannot stop it. In Ueda City—in that important center of the prefecture, people are actually reduced to primitive barter. To find a fifty-sen piece in a village is the hardest thing in the world. . . . Boiled wheat is a rich man's food; ordinary people eat wild fruits, but now even to find a fruit tree on the mountainside is difficult. . . ."

The following was the story of the official who had visited the neighboring Niigata Prefecture: "Niigata is supported by rice cultivation. But to-day, except on large estates, not a grain of rice can be found in the whole prefecture. The poor have to sell their daughters. As all the grown daughters have now disappeared, little school children are being sold. The prices vary from 100 to 400 yen, depending upon the age and the appearance of the girl. Prostitution and petty thievery are so frequent that they can be no longer considered crimes and there is no way of preventing them. . . . The food of a peasant is usually millet or wheat and dried sardines, which are at ordinary times used only as fertilizers."

On the situation in Iwate Prefecture an official narrates: "When I saw the miserable situation there, I felt as if my heart were being torn out. It really is beyond imagination. . . . A tenant farmer in a village showed me his budget for the year

1931, in which 130 yen had been put as the total income and 496 yen as the total expenditure. He was fortunately able to strike a balance with a loan, but such is an exceptional case. Ordinary peasants are barely able to exist even by selling their wives and daughters. Some of them had to sell their young girls for as low as 3 to 10 yen. . . . I visited an elementary school when meals were being served to starving children. They were fighting to get a little ball of rice, snatching it one from the other, and I saw some of them hurt. . . . The roots of brackens are now considered a luxury. Most people eat fertilizers—they boil the soy-bean cakes, give the juice to the horses and eat the boiled cakes themselves. . . ."

And so forth. Tragedies like these exist in the villages all over Japan. The situation is especially unbearable in the north-eastern parts of Honshu, and the north-western side facing the Japan Sea. These districts, where farming and sericulture are the chief means of support among the peasantry, have constantly been suffering from famines—ever since the bourgeois revolution of 1866—some of which were due to natural causes but most of which were on account of the exploitation of peasants on the part of the landowners and the financiers.

Japan as a whole primarily depends upon agriculture. But the geographical conditions and the backward system of agriculture have made it possible to cultivate only about one-sixth of the total area. Since the bourgeois revolution, the production from these arable lands has gradually dropped, due to the fact that Japanese industry has developed at the expense of the farms. Although attempts have been made since the time of the World War, and especially through the "rationalization" plan, to modernize the farms, the capitalists, who left agriculture in the hands of the feudal elements, have never been successful in their efforts. The result has been the hastening of the downfall of farm life.

In 1930 among the 5,599,670 farming households, the total for Japan Proper, only 3.6% owned more than 3 hectares of land, 27.6%, the "middle-class" farmers, owned 2 to 3 hectares, and the rest 68.8% had less than 1 hectare. The classification according to the form of ownership shows that 31.1% belonged to owner-farmers, including the big landowners, 26.5% belonged to tenant farmers, and 42.3% to tenant-owner-farmers—

tenant farmers who also possess a small field or two for their own use.

(b) *City Life*

The farm distress is closely related to the life in the cities. The agrarian crisis of 1930-2 is parallel to the industrial depression in the cities. There are at present approximately 7,500,000 jobless workers, who are compelled to wander from city to city, from agency to agency, looking for bread. The "lucky fellows" who are still holding jobs are constantly threatened by wage-cuts and unemployment.

Many concerns make attempts to hold back the pay. The Social Service Bureau of the Interior Ministry reports that the unpaid wages of factories alone in 1931 amounted to 2,095,723 yen, that of the textile industry being the largest due to the decrease in exports to the United States since the Wall Street panic of 1929. An investigator of the Bureau reports that a certain concern in Nagano Prefecture pays only 4 sen a day to its apprentice workers. And the employers preach, according to the report, at the "self-culture meetings" arranged for their employees: "Under the present depressed circumstances, nobody should expect to earn enough to live on. Employees should thankfully accept what is given and be cheerful about it."

(c) *In the Garrison*

The military system, a state organization consisting of at least 290,000 young workers at a time, is another of the means of monstrous exploitation. Through the "rationalization" scheme, the ruling class is making an attempt to mobilize and maintain the strongest possible army and navy with the least possible expense. The size of the standing force is being decreased by the abolition of two divisions and the reduction of man power in several other divisions, but it is being supplemented and enlarged by more machine and chemical equipment, and the increase and enlargement of civilians' military organizations.

A significant feature of the present military system, which has been worked out since 1920, when American-Japanese rivalry threatened the sovereignty of Japan, and which was finally perfected about the time of the London Conference of 1930, is that it is not only directed against foreign enemies but is specially equipped for civil war. The Imperial Guards

Division, for example, has been used since 1931 exclusively for counter-revolutionary purposes with special equipment for battles in the cities. The frequent air maneuvers in Tokio, Osaka and other large cities, and the recent establishment of strategic zones in Tokio, Osaka and the northern part of Kiushiu —the site of the governmental Yawata Iron Works and many mines and factories—also show this anti-mass campaign of the military authorities.

The life of the young workers in the army and the navy is hardly luxurious enough to keep them from becoming radicalized.

The class distinction in the army and the navy coincides with the social class distinction. Over 90% of the entire force— 50% farmers, 30% workers, and 10% small merchants, etc.— is occupied by the soldiers belonging to the working class, while the rest consists of officers belonging to the class of landowners, wealthy farmers, bourgeoisie and petty bourgeoisie. This is due to the fact that those who belong to the working class are forcibly conscripted, while those who belong to the middle and upper classes can, when they find they have to enlist, become cadets by paying a certain sum to the government, or else enter military academies before the conscription examination.

The number of privates taken every year is officially 120,000. After finishing the service of six months to three years, they enter the reserve service, during which they are called out at least five times. While they are in active service, they are completely deprived of their freedom and such elementary rights as the right to join a political organization, to vote or become a candidate, to join any labor union, to organize any group among soldiers, to sit in a jury, and to read any legal publications except certain reactionary books and newspapers chosen by the regiment. The enforcement of these rules is carried out by two thousand military police, including a large number of special "ideology squads," and by a reward system encouraging the privates to spy on each other.

The board that a private is given consists of 600 grams of rice, 186 grams of wheat, and a few simple dishes, the total cost per day being less than 20.1 sen. Many cases of malnutrition are reported by the military physicians.

The pay of a private is 5.5 yen a month, or 18 sen a day. This is barely sufficient for them to buy cigarettes and postal cards. Their families, put into a worse condition of impoverishment because of the forcible conscription of their work hands, have to manage to send their sons spending money during the service term. The minimum work day is usually ten hours. A work condition like this cannot be found even in the colonial factories, at least nominally.

Military duty not only deprives a youth of valuable time, freedom, health, and livelihood, but it also puts him into the army of the jobless. The employers take advantage of conscription, discharge the young workers with a promise of taking them back after they are through, but this promise is hardly ever kept. When the young ex-soldiers come out of the "prison," all they have is a humble title, membership in the fascistic Ex-Military Men's Association, a lost position, and in many cases a broken up family.

The ruling class, in view of the discontent among the soldiers and the masses confronting conscription, has attempted to draw support to the military system by announcing a shortening of the service term. According to the announcement the "rationalization" plan would better the living conditions of privates. But its real purpose in shortening the period was to enlarge the entire national military system by speedily creating retired servicemen, who will become the framework of a wartime organization. This plan will enable the ruling class to enlarge the force with a minimum cost, and less opposition from the people. The New York *Herald-Tribune* correspondent in Tokio reports on February 7, 1933, that the Japanese government is contemplating establishment of a council for national defense which would have the "effect of placing the nation's military organization on a wartime footing," and that although the hostilities with China are expected to be renewed in the spring with a drive against Jehol Province, it is not believed that even open warfare with China would necessitate preparations on such a scale as those now being carried out. Who would be the imaginary enemy of the Japanese Empire, with its huge war preparations, if it were not the Red Army of the Soviet Union? [1] The same correspondent further states that some

---

[1] The American historian, C. Hartley Grattan, has a significant comment on this Far Eastern tangle ("The Next War" in *Common Sense*, Feb. 16, 1933): "Even the openly confessed program for dominating Manchuria is sufficiently provocative and may very well lead to widespread disturbance. What are Japan's confessed aims and how they will affect world politics? Inazo Nitobe, leading Japanese liberal publicist, has stated frankly that the Japanese need a buffer state in Manchuria to

firms have sufficient orders to keep working full blast for two years, and that the present military supplies and munitions exceed by a great deal the stocks preceding the Russo-Japanese War.

The life in the garrison of Japan to-day is a whirlpool of two struggling forces, the intensifying wartime pressure from above and the increasing discontent of the masses of soldiers from below.

V

THE FORCE OF REACTION

The deepening of the economic crisis, the war, the intensification of the "rationalization" conspiracy—all these drive the masses into a deeper distress. The discontent of the masses and the radicalization of the working class grow accordingly. In order to halt this growth, the ruling class of Japan has equipped itself with a carefully laid out network of reactionary fascist forces.

(a) The Peace Preservation Law

The open fascistization of the ruling class coincides with the "positive" policy. Premier Tanaka, the originator of this policy, was one of the most reactionary politicians of Japan, though by no means the first. His entire career is smeared with the blood of workers and peasants of Japan and the colonies, as well as of Siberia and China. It is not extraordinary that it was his cabinet that made in 1927 the Peace Preservation Law of 1925 into a perfect murder machine, by means of an Emergency Imperial Ordinance, which can be proclaimed without the consent of the Diet.

According to the amended Peace Preservation Law, any person organizing a movement against the sovereignty of the

protect them against the Soviet Union; that they need access to the raw materials of Manchuria; and that they need an outlet there for surplus population (which we may translate as a need for markets). Kinosuke Adachi, described as a Japanese authority on international affairs, predicts that a war between Japan and the Soviet Union is absolutely unavoidable. In the light of this statement, we may interpret Japan's moves in Manchuria as simply preliminaries to a war on Russia and her refusal to sign a non-aggression pact with the Soviets as an effort to keep clear of embarrassing commitments."

present economic and political system—the system of private property and of constitutional monarchy—is punishable by death. Any person sympathetic to such a movement may be sentenced to a long term of imprisonment. Any person assisting such a movement without knowing its real nature may be arrested. It was under this law that in June, 1932, one leader of the Communist Party of Japan was sentenced to death, three to life imprisonment, and two-hundred-odd communists to the total of more than 1,030 years of prison terms.

This law is used by the ruling class not only for the purpose of exterminating the Communist Party, but the entire revolutionary movement. Under this law, such organizations as the Pan-Pacific Trade Union Secretariat, the International Labor Defense, and the Young Communist League, cannot legally exist in Japanese territory, and such organizations as the Proletarian Cultural Federation of Japan and the Industrial and Labor Research Institute are prevented from exercising normal activity. In 1932, even the League for the Struggle against Religion was ordered to dissolve. About twenty well known novelists, dramatists, and poets, including women, were arrested and prosecuted because of their sympathy toward communism.

(b) *The Police*

With this weapon at hand, the police terror against the radical elements is extremely vicious. Since the Tanaka administration of 1927–9 at least 100,000 workers and peasants have been arrested on the charge of revolutionary activities. Two leaders of the revolutionary movement, one a member of the Diet, and the other a well known organizer, were deliberately murdered by the police and its agents. Two large scale wholesale arrests each involving 5000 workers, were made in 1928–9. A number of similar arrests have occurred repeatedly since, and are going on daily in all parts of the country.

The Japanese police, created after the "Polizeistaat" of Prussia, is known for its well-organized system. It belongs to the Interior Ministry through prefectural governments, with the exception of the Metropolitan Police Bureau of Tokio which is directly under the Home Office. It is so organized that with the closing of a switch at the Ministry the police force of the entire nation can be mobilized without delay. The mass arrests of March, 1928, and those of April, 1929, were executed through this nation-wide system. Breaking up of strikes and peasant upheavals as well as mass meetings and demonstrations, interference at the time of national and local elections, censoring of publications, films, and theatrical performances, spying on workers, and various other forms of oppression are carried on by the police with the coöperation of the gendarmerie. The notorious massacre of 50,000 Korean workers, including women and children, by ignorant masses at the time of the great earthquake of 1923, was done by direct police instigation. The murders of twenty-odd revolutionaries, including a famous anarchist writer, his wife, and their six-year-old nephew, in the confusion of the earthquake were executed by the police and the gendarmerie themselves at the order of the Martial Law Headquarters.

Arrests of radical elements are so frequent that no complete record exists. Any person—a worker, a student, or a merchant—may be arrested because he happens to talk about communism on the street. Sometimes an entire mass meeting or demonstration is arrested.

Once arrested a worker meets with unimaginable tortures. Large police headquarters such as the Metropolitan Police Bureau employ a number of sadistic perverts as instructors of "tormentology." A radical may be hung up by his thumbs twisted behind his back; striped with a hot iron; beaten with wooden swords; his genital organs may be burned with lighted cigarettes; and his nails may be torn out. These tortures are done irrespective of sex or age.

An interesting instance of the reactionary rôle the police plays and of the fear of the bourgeoisie in regard to the working class is revealed by Musei Tokugawa, a famous humorist and film-interpreter. Once when the picture of the Five-Year Plan of the Soviet Union was being shown in a metropolitan theater, he was summoned to a local police station and was ordered to remain silent during that portion of film which shows the All-Soviet Communist Party Congress. When he asked why, the chief of police told him with an extremely dignified air: "Because when you say, 'There stands Stalin,' the entire audience clap and shout *banzai*, as if they were starting a riot. . . . I'll have to arrest you under the Peace Preservation Law if you don't watch your step. . . ."

(c) *The Fascist Mass Movement*

Lately the police brutality is increasing with geometric progression. Under the pretext of guarding His Majesty's City, the ruling class is enlarging the secret police force. Especially since the assassinations of three financial and political leaders including Premier Inukai in 1932, many detectives and stool pigeons of the secret service are stationed in railroad stations, harbors, factories, schools and even garrisons, with the excuse of "control of fascist and terrorist organizations." That this is an attempt of the ruling class to suppress the revolutionary movement cannot be doubted.

With this police mobilization on the one hand, the bourgeoisie is, on the other, preparing a nation-wide system of armed fascist force. Mobilizing all the reactionary mass organizations such as the Ex-Military Men's Association, the Young Men's Corps, the Patriotic Students' League, and reformist and social-fascist labor unions, it is persistently spreading its network over the cities and the villages. In Tokio a Metropolitan Guard was organized in 1932 with 600,000 members and held a "metropolis defense maneuver" in September in conjunction with the army. A number of "Patriotic Marches" of reactionary students were held in principal cities. Collection drives for the purchase of airplanes and comforts for soldiers were carried out several times on a national scale. Through the press, the radio, the film, and various other mouthpieces such as the churches, the temples, and the schools, fascism is propagated everywhere. Many street demonstrations and mass meetings are being arranged in order to draw the masses to the support of imperialism. As in the case of the armed clash between striking tenant farmers and a fascist party in Tochigi Prefecture of January, 1932, these reactionary organizations are working as the vanguard of the capitalist offensive against the working class. Their purposes are only too manifestly war propaganda and the counter-revolutionary drive against the masses.

(d) *Education and Fascism*

Fascism is the desperate effort of the bourgeoisie in its mortal agony to restore its former power by means of police-military dictatorship. The ruling class which has destroyed with its opiates of "sophistication" and "modernism" in corrupt arts

and journalism all the ethical and æsthetic ideals of liberalism,
is now engaged in an effort to complete its cultural dictatorship
by transforming the school from a place for education and research into a link in the chain of the nation-wide police system.
Science, except as a machine, can no longer find a place in the
school. Academic freedom, except as a mockery, can no longer
exist. School police chiefs and agent provocateurs camouflaged
as "superintendents of students' affairs," placed by the late
Premier Tanaka in all schools, are becoming more active than
ever in their campaign of suppressing students' organizations
and arresting progressive elements in the class room. The
"plan in regard to the left tendency of students" created by
the Inukai cabinet in May, 1932, just before the death of the
old Premier, attempts to justify the prosecution of radical
students by the school authorities, and includes the higher
politics of cleverly appeasing the arrested students for the purpose of using them as stool pigeons and spies.

The Saito cabinet established in September, 1932, at a cost
of 720,000 yen, an Institute for the Research of National
Spiritual Culture, where law, economics, literature, and other
subjects appertaining to the "nation's spiritual culture" are
studied by a staff of over one hundred "scholars", and where
one instructor from each of the 106 normal schools throughout
the country, and all the weak-minded student victims of the
anti-communist arrests are given training concerning the
"proper control of current thoughts." Under the direction of
President Yoshida, well known reactionary ex-professor of
Tokio Imperial University, these "educators" and "repenting
ex-communists" are trying to discover in the pages of worm-
eaten Machiavelli or Confucius the best methods of "ideology
guidance," so they will become efficient students' superintendents or heads of "red squads" of provincial police headquarters.
This Institute is an additional force to the forty-odd school
"thought-problem inspectors" now being trained by the Ministry of Education at an expense of 110,000 yen.

The "cultural" police rule in school is, however, but a part
of the stifling program of the ruling class. The Ministry of
Education, together with the Home Office, is carrying on various campaigns in the cultural field of reaction.

A Japan Labor Education Association has been established
by the Ministry for the purpose of teaching the workers, by
means of adult education courses, through military training,

and also by mass meetings, how to be obedient to their masters. The organization is run by a board of directors consisting of high officials of the two Ministries and university professors of the "Emperor Foremost" school.

The Education Ministry has also organized, in six of the larger cities, such activities as lecture courses on current thought problems and expositions of materials on the subject, in order to thoroughly acquaint educators with the problem of contemporary thought, present-day economics and politics, and to train in them the ability of "fair judgment and criticism" so that they will be able to "properly" guide their students.

These activities are supplemented by the governmental publication of books, pamphlets, and films on martial patriotism, and their distribution through various reactionary organizations.

The anxiety of the ruling class to utilize every possible occasion for the arousing of mass support for war and fascism is so intense that even the little marionette wagons of candy vendors in Tokio are made to propagate the justice of Japan's armed invasion of Manchuria!

VI

THE WORKING CLASS MOVEMENT AGAINST IMPERIALISM

The cogwheels of history cannot be turned backward by imperialism. The will of the proletariat cannot be forever suppressed by the bourgeoisie. Despite all the effort of the fascistizing ruling class of Japan, the revolutionary working class movement is moving forward with steady tread. The crisis and the war spur it on.

(a) Agrarian Uprisings

The miserable state of Japanese farms under the semi-feudal landowner rule is rapidly radicalizing the agrarian populace. The peasantry, which can find its road to life only in the agrarian revolution, has more than once sought to free itself from the clutches of the landowners. It was the left-wing peasant organization that took the initiative in the organization of the first mass party, Nomin-Rodo-To (Peasant-Worker

Party), in 1926, which the government suppressed three hours after its creation.

The peasants' struggle against oppression and exploitation usually takes the form of tenant-farmer strikes. Such strikes are caused by two factors: high rent, and the attempt on the part of the landowners to take the land from the tenants. In the semi-feudal Japanese farms, where the rent for a farm is usually paid in produce instead of in money, the tenants are made to pay 30% to 60% of the total produce to the landowners. When they cannot pay the rent, the landowners seize the crop or attempt to take the farm by preventing tenants from entering the fields. Invariably a fight ensues. It is not unusual for the landowner to receive armed assistance from the police and the reactionary Ex-Military Men's Association, the tenants being compelled to defend themselves against modern armament with bamboo spears!

One of the most remarkable happenings in the agrarian revolutionary movement in recent years is the "give us rice" campaign which was started in the famine areas in the early months of 1932 and spread over the entire country by summer of the same year. The campaign was caused by the intensification of the farm crisis since the embargo on gold shipment of 1931. The rise in the prices of commodities did not bring better times to the peasantry, because the rise in the prices of fertilizers much exceeded the rise in the rice prices. The peasants, who had already lost the greater part of the crop to the landowners and the financiers through mortgages, had to sell what was left for their own use in order to buy fertilizers. This led to the unusual accumulation of farm products in the cities and their practical non-existence on the farms. The peasantry now had to buy, if possible, high-priced farm products from the cities. This desperate situation, however, did not move the bourgeoisie to do any relief work. Instead the ruling class began the dumping of rice in foreign markets to rid the warehouses of 546,000 bushels. At this the agrarian masses, together with the workers of the cities, arose and organized the "give us rice" movement, demanding that the government give relief to the starving millions by distributing the rice in the Treasury warehouses. The government, in view of this discontent, disposed of a large amount of rice through profiteering merchants, who pocketed 20% to 60%. In June, 1932, the amount of rice disposed of was 2,500,000 bushels. But since the government at the same time purchased more than that amount in order to keep fresh products at hand for war preparation, the transaction only put the peasantry into a still worse situation. The furious agrarian populace advanced its struggle with the slogans: "Guarantee the farmers rice to eat," and "Open the rice warehouses for free distribution." The spreading of the "give us rice" movement may be seen in the following news clippings:

Karahuto (Sakhalin): The "give us rice" movement is spreading all over the southern half of the island. Cities such as Otonari, Esutori, Rutaka, Ochiai, etc., are seeing daily large masses of peasants and fishermen surrounding the municipal and prefectural offices demanding the right to live.

Hokkaido: In Otaru and Sapporo, nearly 10,000 signatures have been collected for the free distribution of rice by the government. Coöperative unions, peasant unions, and unemployed leagues are organizing marches to governmental offices for the purpose of demanding rice.

Honshu: In Tochigi Prefecture, the "give us rice" movement has become a riot. A number of women organizers of the National Peasant Union were arrested. An armed fight occurred between peasants and the members of the Seisan-To, an openly fascist party. In Ibaragi Prefecture, an entire village joined the movement. In Mie Prefecture five hundred peasants and jobless workers attacked the city office of Matsuzaka. In Tokio every day five to six peasants are being arrested in connection with the movement. From twelve prefectures of north-eastern and north-western parts were presented petition lists signed by 170,000 peasants in need of food. In Kiushiu and Shikoku, similar movements are taking place. Over one hundred representatives of farmers visited the Ministry of Agriculture and Forestry and were immediately arrested. The Diet, in view of the mass upheavals, armed its temporary session with 3,000 policemen. . . .

It must be noted that these upheavals in the villages occurred entirely "from below." It was not necessary for the communists to agitate the farmers; the starving people themselves stood up and organized their fight.

The leader of the general revolutionary struggle in the villages is the Zenkoku-Kaigi (National Conference) within the Zenkoku-Nomin-Kumiai (National Peasant Union), the "headquarters" group of which has turned so reactionary as to propose participation in the fascist *coup d'état* of the State-Socialist and Worker-Peasant-Mass Parties. The revolutionary opposition group at present constitutes the overwhelming majority of 2 to 1 within the union. Under its Marxist-Leninist doctrine it is leading tenant-farmer strikes, the "give us rice" movement, and various other campaigns.

(b) *The Industrial Workers*

Wage-cuts, speed-up and unemployment threaten the workers of industry just as the agrarian crisis is attacking the farm population. In addition to this the expression of the mass discontent is constantly battered down by the police-military oppression, and misled by the betraying reformist and social-fascist unions. Due to extreme censorship by the Interior Ministry and the post office, the exact figures showing the extent of recent clashes between the bourgeoisie and the working class cannot be obtained, but the increasing fierceness of the struggle can be seen by the reports in various revolutionary magazines.

Similarly sharp struggles are increasing day by day; the strikes of the Kitanaka Leather Factories, Tokio Celluloid Factories, Tokio, Municipal Railways, etc., are some of the major strikes in the past year. Many more strikes, such as that of the Singer Sewing Machine factories of Yokohama, in January, 1933, have been reported by the *Daily Worker,* of the Communist Party of U. S. A.

A significant characteristic of the recent Japanese strikes is that they are taking more and more the form of a political struggle, and armed clashes frequently accompany them. The masses refuse to remain passive under the fascistization of social-democratic and reformist unions, and the intensification of the police-military suppression.

The "Zen-Kyo", the left-wing organization, itself has still many weaknesses. At the end of 1931, the total number of workers organized under its banner was only 15,000—less than one three hundredth of the total 4,800,000 industrial workers, although it showed an increase of 500% as compared to the previous year. The women workers, who constitute 48% of the total number of factory workers, are practically outside the influence of the left-wing union. In the unemployment field, the Unemployed League consisted of only 3,000 members in 1931, while there were 2,500,000 workers out of jobs. These figures reveal considerable weakness on the part of the revolutionary organizations, most of which is due to suppression by the bourgeoisie and betrayal by reformists and social-democrats.

A similar situation is seen also in the political field of struggle. The illegality of the Communist Party and the demagogy of the pseudo-revolutionary parties hinder the mass growth of the revolutionary movement.

However, the economic struggle of the working class is rapidly merging with its political struggle. The frequent transformation of strikes and sabotage into riots during the recent months demonstrates that the present counter-offensive of the industrial workers against the bourgeoisie is but the prelude to the coming political crisis.

(c) *The Cultural Front*

A steady growth, though smeared with blood, is seen in the cultural movement of the proletariat. The proletarian culture of Japan first voiced by class-conscious workers and intellectuals in the beginning of the last decade has had its reverses and successes—had met with suppression and betrayal, but it is now spreading rapidly on a wide mass basis throughout the country. In literature, for example, the influence of Marxism is so intense that writing proletarian novels or essays is said to be one of the best ways to attain fame. Social-democratic and "liberal" writers are using revolutionary phraseology to acquire mass support. "High-brow" magazines invariably buy stories or articles on workers' life and struggles. Popular magazines demagogically give space to pseudo-revolutionary works of self-styled Marxists. Books on Marxian economics and culture flood the book-stores. In the schools those instructors who cannot discuss Leninism are called subnormal by the students.

As a movement revolutionary culture is propagated by the Proletarian Cultural Federation of Japan (KOPF), which consists of twelve organizations representing science, education, literature, music, theater arts, fine arts, cinematography, photography, Esperanto, atheism, birth control and workers' libraries. Beside publishing its monthly or weekly organs, each of these organizations is carrying on the agit-prop and organization work of its chosen field in shops, farms, schools, reactionary organizations and garrisons. Through its anti-war and anti-imperialist campaigns, its educational campaigns in the shops and on the farms, and its relief work in coöperation with the MOPR, the Unemployed League, and the unions, the KOPF is receiving a wide mass support. It is reported that each organ of the various KOPF organizations has a circulation of from 2,000 to 50,000. The ruling class has arrested and imprisoned nearly one hundred leading members of the KOPF—many of them famous authors, dramatists, musicians, and educators— during the past year on the charge of sympathy with the communist movement, but suppression clarifies the issues and spurs on the work. All the constituent organizations of the KOPF, most of which were more or less societies of professional artists at first, are now on a mass basis. "The atmosphere is so refreshing," an English journalist writes about a revolutionary play presented by the little theater Left Wing, a member of the Pro-T (Proletarian Theater League). "The atmosphere is not unlike that of a field theater where everybody—the actors and the audience—takes part in the play. The technique is entirely modern with a lot of German and Soviet influence, coupled with the picturesqueness of the old *kabuki*. But this technique is improved by the super-technique called 'masses' . . . It was this super-technique that impressed one deeply in Tokio at the time of the anti-war week of last summer, when a series of revolutionary plays was presented at a theater not only by professional actors but by a large number of men and women workers as a part of their street demonstration . . ."

The masses, though constantly distracted and deceived by the demagogic culture of the fascists and the social-democrats, cannot find in it any way of life, any road to recovery. The economic and political situation inevitably radicalizes them. Marxism gives them a new perspective. Day by day more of them join in the cultural movement of their own class, and contribute their share in the fight against imperialism, against fascism, for the defense of the Soviet Union and Chinese Soviets, and for the overthrow of the bourgeois-landowner-monarchical dictatorship of the Japanese Empire.

CHI-CHEN WANG

COMMUNISM TAKES ROOT
IN CHINA[1]

THE destiny of China is the most important problem in the world to-day. Nowhere else have there occurred so many changes and upheavals during the last decade; nowhere else are further changes and upheavals so imminent. One can easily see how the destiny of any one considerable portion of the world will profoundly affect the rest. If the United States should turn Communist, revolutionary socialism would be materially advanced; conversely, the overthrow of the Soviet Union would set back the revolutionary movement at least one generation. But as far as we can see there is no immediate prospect of a revolution in the United States, nor any immediate likelihood of the downfall of the Soviet system.

China, however, is in a state of flux. Her traditional civilization and institutions have broken down. Intellectually she is in a state of ferment, her intellectuals not *playing* with ideas but clutching at them with desperate earnestness. Materially her plight is the most appalling of all—millions dead, millions dying of famine, disease, banditry, of murderous wars inflicted upon them from within and without . . . Under such intolerable conditions, things are bound to happen, and so they do in China, with astonishing rapidity.

Let us take some of the more spectacular events. Within the last year she has lost, for the time being at least, Manchuria

---

[1] This article is primarily concerned with the psychological and human aspects of the topic. For more detailed factual material the reader is referred to a short bibliography at the end of the article.

in the northeast, thus confirming the worst fears of her friends as to her helplessness, while a few months later she demonstrated her mettle at Shanghai against great odds, thus upsetting all predictions that her ill-equipped troops would be as helpless against the modern army of Japan as a jellyfish against a steam roller.

In 1926 the cause of the Chinese revolution seemed invincible, but a few months later the revolutionary party machinery fell into the hands of reactionary forces and the system of bargaining, compromises and wars between the military adventurers was again renewed. For a while the prospects of the Communist Party, which assumed the leadership of the revolution in place of the Kuomintang, seemed quite hopeless, but again surmises were mistaken, for as Communism went underground in the cities, the remnants of the red armies out-maneuvered the forces of reaction in the provinces, consolidated and established sound Soviet centers in south-central China. To-day it is estimated that one-sixth of China proper is under Soviet rule with a population of 90,000,000.

Three things might conceivably happen in China. First, China may be subjugated and converted into an amenable market, and thus provide temporary relief for the ills of undernourished capitalist imperialism, thereby furnishing a new and rich prowling ground for its continued existence. There is little likelihood of this eventuality, both because of the proverbial jealousy among thieves and the all-powerful fetish of nationalism which still sways foreign offices and popular sentiments. Second, China may somehow manage to establish an independent industrialized state, either through the leadership of the present Nanking régime or through some new alignment of the conservative forces. This is the hope and aspiration of a large portion of the articulate Chinese, for just as the average worker or peasant aspires to the position occupied by the bourgeoisie, so an exploited nation has usually no higher aspirations than to achieve the position of an imperialist power. In this case China will simply aggravate the ills of the capitalist system and hasten its collapse. There remains the possibility that the Chinese Soviet will grow in power and prestige until all China becomes united under its leadership. In this article we shall try to indicate the forces that tend to make a Communist revolution possible, if not inevitable.

I

USUAL ARGUMENTS AGAINST THE POSSIBILITY
OF COMMUNISM IN CHINA

One of the most often encountered arguments against the possibility of Communism in China is that China is too poor and its masses too ignorant to make Communism practicable. Thus Chang Tung-sun, a Chinese student of western philosophy, observed, after touring the "interior" and witnessing the harrowing sights of poverty and suffering, that China was not ready for "isms" and that her first task was to relieve distress by industrialization and to stamp out ignorance through education. The late Liang Ch'-i-ch'ao had in mind about the same thing when he wrote that "in Europe and America the most urgent problem is how to improve the position of the working-men; in China the most urgent problem is how to transform the majority of the population into working men."

Amongst the foreign journalists, especially the more reactionary veterans, this argument is often reiterated. But in these writers one detects a note of snobbishness. Mr. J. O. P. Bland, writing in the *English Review* in 1930, tells us with an air of final authority that:

"The two Chinese hieroglyphics which figure on the Red Armies' flags, to express the idea of Communism, simply mean "Divide Property." ["Share" would be a better and more accurate translation than "divide."] In a country where three quarters of the population live habitually on the verge of the hunger line, and where, for the past ten years, the peasantry have been driven desperate by the grafts of officialdom and the assaults of bandits, a slogan of this kind could hardly fail to attract large numbers of the countless victims of misrule. . . . The benefits which they seek to derive from the redistribution of wealth are not, like those envisaged by Mr. Snowden, social conceptions; they begin and end, quite frankly, with the individual and his family. There is, in fact, no place for Communism in the Chinese social system, nor any likelihood that the economic doctrines of Karl Marx will become popular there, for many generations to come."

In other words, it is all right for Occidentals to talk of Communism and Socialism, but not for the illiterate starving Chinese. But Mr. Bland forgets the fact that the population of England has too few Mr. Snowdens (whatever he is worth in a really well balanced system of values) and altogether too many Mr. Blands. Besides, how can it be otherwise but that the benefits sought by the habitually starving masses should "begin and end, quite frankly, with the individual and his family"? For them such "individualism" is quite understandable and excusable, for anyone from the propertied leisure class to be any less than Mr. Snowden would be the most brazen insensibility.

A second argument is that China is not sufficiently industrialized, that it does not have a large enough proletariat that can be aroused to class consciousness and made to serve as the vanguard of the revolution. The answer to this is that since the revolution is dedicated to the abolition of classes it must abandon all scientific prejudices and utilize whatever happens to be the most numerous group of oppressed masses; it matters not whether this group happens to be industrial workers as in the west or agrarian workers as in China. Lenin must have recognized this when he declared in 1920 before the second Congress of the Communist Internationale that "one must abandon the scientific prejudice that each country must pass through capitalist exploitation" and that "the power of Soviets . . . can be established in those countries in which capitalist development has not attained any serious proportions."

This raises the question whether there is in China an oppressed peasantry. Opponents of Communism hold, of course, that there is not, some estimating that 90% of the Chinese peasants own their land. This estimate is true, however, of only certain parts of China, notably Shantung and Chihli. An American writer (W. Hunter, *China Weekly Review*, Jan. 31, 1931) estimates that in Kiangsi and Hunan 75% of the peasants were tenants of absentee landlords and that in the eastern-central provinces less than 50% own their lands. The data collected by the National Christian Council in 1928 regarding land ownership in Kuangtung is illuminating. According to this survey about 40% of the cultivable land comes under the classification of public land, which includes "ancestor's" land owned by the "clan," the rents of which are used to maintain ancestral worship, village land, property of the village temple; and school land. After this there is the Government land, then private land. Needless to say public land is entirely controlled and managed by the "gentry," and Government land by the officials from whom the gentry naturally receive preferential treatment in renting and sub-renting. The result is that no less than 70% of the peasants in Kuangtung were tenant farmers. In these provinces, which are the richest and most thickly populated, the peasants' grievances and plights can be objectified in the persons of the landlords and they are therefore good material for communist indoctrination. And in fact this has been the case; it is precisely in these districts that the Chinese Soviets have taken hold and flourished.

II

CLASS CONSCIOUSNESS ONLY PREREQUISITE

All these arguments are based upon two fundamental fallacies. The first is that masses "make" revolutions and the second that the masses must have reached a certain predetermined stage of development before they are capable of participating and bringing about a revolution. Nothing is further from the truth. The real motivating force of all revolutions is a sound idea, with its small group of devoted exponents. An oppressed and disgruntled mass is necessary only as an instrument.

The ideal of a classless society is as old as the institution of private property itself, for no sooner did it emerge than its evils and injustices became obvious even to the most callous, in their reflective moments, while to the spiritually sensitive they constituted a continual source of torment. Whether they manifested their outraged sensibilities by renouncing this life altogether or by devoting themselves to social reform, there is no question that in our religious men and reformers we find unmistakable evidences of the ancient dissatisfaction with a system which makes possible such contrasting spectacles as habitual hunger and pain on one hand, and ease and luxury on the other.

Obvious as its evils are, yet not until the 19th century did it dawn upon us to criticize the system itself, not until then were we irrefutably convinced of the futility of religion and reforms, not until then did we, in other words, become class-conscious. The reasons for this are not far to seek; first, it was not until the beginning of the 19th century that we finally and completely realized that the system was not decreed by the caprice of an omnipotent god but developed out of the cupidity of men; second, contemporaneous with this realization, the evils of the system became aggravated and made more glaring by the industrial revolution.

It was with this realization that Karl Marx began his study of the capitalist system and through these studies developed his theory of the class struggle as a means of effecting fundamental changes in the system; it was this realization that made the acceptance of his theory and the organization of the Communist Party possible; it was this realization on the part of the Bolsheviks that brought about the October Revolution in Russia. In other words, a sound idea, if it grips the imagination of the intellectual world strongly enough, is paramount in accelerating revolutionary progress. Conversely, the mere existence of classes in a given society does not necessarily bring about a revolution. And so because of the determination of a small but compact group of men, Russia became the first, and so far only, Communist society in the world, though it is of the western powers the least industrialized; and similarly Great Britain and the United States, because of the apathy of its intellectual world, have proved the most complacent and reactionary of capitalist countries, though they are in the world the most industrially advanced. As far as the success of a revolution is concerned it matters not whether the masses be heavily afflicted and illiterate, as in China, or comparatively well-fed and respectable as in the United States. If anything, the more terrible the conditions of the masses, the more ready are they for change. Now there is no question as to the misery of the Chinese masses unless one goes about with blinders or shuts one's self up in one's house. Harrowing sights greet one everywhere in "normal times"—sweating and panting coolies, sore-ridden beggars, undernourished children and sallow, lean men—it is not necessary to go to the famine districts. China may not be as rich in resources as some other countries, but side by side with these monstrous spectacles of human misery one sees such sharp contrasts of abundance and luxury as to make anyone but the insensate wonder if there is not something seriously distorted with the system, if something cannot be done to change it. One does not have to understand the theory of the class struggle to want to protest, for one's self or for one's fellow sufferers.

Added to these "normal" sufferings there is the oppression

of the war-lords and corrupt government officials. One observer (J. Jarvis) reports after touring Szechwan in 1931 that taxes had been collected from thirty to forty years in advance, in some districts 99 years! Opium-growing, on which a high tax was collected, was forced upon the peasants. If they do not grow it, they are taxed anyway for "laziness." There are besides these the outright looting by troops, extortions, forced labor, requisitions, etc., to say nothing of the bandits. If the "so-called" Chinese Red Armies of Mr. Bland are recruited from no more respectable material than such human "trash," literally stinking, so much the worse for the ruling classes and the imperialist powers.

III

THE TRADITION OF AN INTELLECTUAL
ARISTOCRACY

The real obstacle to the cause of Communism in China is the tradition of an intellectual aristocracy. Title of nobility was usually granted for life only, or hereditary in a decending scale so that it disappeared a few generations after the granting of the title. Moreover, the mere inheritance of title did not necessarily mean privilege; it was necessary to show one's merit first through the literary examinations. The bulk of the Mandarinate, the ruling class in China, was recruited, then, through the examination system. The preparatory education required was within the means of humble peasants with only a few acres of land. Every village had its school or schools, each presided over by one tutor, under whom one learned the classics by heart and how to write the stereotyped essays required. Not every one got to the preliminary examinations, but every one who showed an aptitude for such exercises of skill was encouraged and despatched to the examinations. As soon as he passed his first examination and obtained his degree, assistance for further training under more competent tutors was assured to him by friends and relatives eager to help, for his degree automatically raised him to a respected position.

The efficacy of the system may be dubious; it may be questioned whether proficiency in the highly artificial compositions necessarily implied administrative ability or a superior intellect. It is common knowledge that some of our best writers and poets failed at these examinations and many of the successful candidates manifested no more exceptional talent than the average mediocre but persevering Ph.D. But nevertheless the system gave a verisimilitude of privilege by merit and held out the alluring promise to all of achieving the Mandarinate. The Chinese word for mandarin (*kuan*) simply means a Government official, yet to the Chinese masses it connotes something vastly more, more even than titles convey in European countries, such as a lord in England, because a mandarin was synonymous with a scholar, an aristocrat of the intellect.

We may say that because of the dynastic system every Chinese was an aspirant (openly if he had sufficient power, secretly if not) to the Throne just as every American can entertain aspirations toward the Presidency, and that because of the examination system every Chinese was an aspirant for the Mandarinate. In either case success (whether through the electorate or the examination) did not necessarily mean real merit, intellectual or otherwise; in either case chance (the whim, caprice, and prejudice of the voters or the examiners, amongst other things) and the knack for vulgar oratory and publicity or for literary acrobatics must play a large part. In the Chinese system the element of chance was especially obvious, for in the first stages of the examinations real merit must, thanks to the tremendous number of candidates, be as difficult to determine as the entries in a $50,000 slogan contest. But the masses cannot make such distinctions; to it the pseudo-merit system might as well be real.

Furthermore the Chinese, like the English and the Americans, are primarily a race or nation of individualists, in the malodorous sense of the word, in the sense that an individualist is concerned in maintaining his personal identity—his life—at all cost, in the sense that he would never go to the extent of championing his ideals in face of danger, as he is only interested in his skin and all that makes his skin safe and respectable; he is conservative, calculating, compromising, is willing to bargain for life and security at the cost of all spiritual values, of passion, of courage, of intellectual honesty. It was not for nothing that Confucius had been for over two thousand years their prophet!

Now in this portrait of the individualist we should have no difficulty in recognizing the typical bourgeois, the average Chinese, Englishman or American. Perhaps we recognize in this portrait the average man everywhere, but unless we cease generalizing altogether about peoples, I think it is not too far wrong to suggest that in this we do not find the typical Russian temperament. It is difficult to conceive, for instance, a Chinese, an American or an Englishman tortured by the terrible problems which beset Dmitri Karamazov or a Raskolnikov. And it was perhaps this typical Russian trait more than anything else that made the Russian revolution possible, whereas the antithesis of this trait makes revolutionary changes slow and difficult at best.

To individualists of this common variety the examination system must be a boon, just as the election system is gratifying to individualists in pseudo-democracies. Both systems give him a chance to achieve privilege and distinction over his fellows without danger, without undue intellectual effort. In the Chinese system the emphasis upon pseudo-intellectual merit further makes it difficult to see class forces. The merchant used to occupy next to the last rung in the Chinese social scale, being only above the soldiery. To achieve wealth might mean to achieve a certain degree of power, but it was not achieving privilege or prestige, which literary attainments alone could give. The Chinese merchant was properly humble, and because of his humble position his wealth was overlooked or disdained. The intellectual or scholar class, which ought to have been the leaders of social change, was thus flattered into accepting and making the system as just as was possible. In the meantime the other classes prepared their children for the examinations, hoping thus to lift themselves up into the ruling class.

This pseudo-merit system through the literary examinations has, then, given rise to a false tradition of intellectual aristocracy. This tradition represented the real obstacle to the development of revolutionary socialism, because it obscured the real issues and corrupted the more enterprising members amongst the masses, just as the pseudo-democracy through the voting system has tended to obscure the class issues in the United States. In the latter country it was the depression and the exposures of voting frauds and other political corruptions during the last few years that have gradually awakened the intellectual world to their false position; in China it was contact with the West that destroyed the last illusions of an intellectual aristocracy and thus prepared the way for Communism.

IV

THE INTRODUCTION OF CAPITALIST VALUES

We have thus far described the situation in China before she came into active contact with the West, the dominant civilization of our time. It is a historical truth that when two civilizations meet, the culture and institutions of the "dominant" civilization must prevail. In the present instance, as in all instances, the changes were at first confined to the physical plane, such as in the introduction of the art of modern warfare, her defeat in the Opium War by Great Britain having made her realize the necessity of learning from her victors; of science and scientific methods; of engineering and technology; and toward the end of the last century, the introduction of the science of Government. In 1907 the examination system was abolished. The Modern school system was introduced and students were sent to study abroad in increasing numbers. But the tradition of an intellectual aristocracy was not at once affected; the traditional reverence for the literary class under the old system was simply transferred to the graduates of the modern schools.

However, the new literati did not at first have quite the influence and prestige of the old, for although China became a republic in 1912, the old mandarinate continued to rule under new names for at least another decade. Moreover, psychologically the new literati belonged to the old tradition. The first recruits of the higher government institutions and the first students sent abroad were as a rule men in their late twenties, many with degrees from the old examinations. Those who went abroad were put under the charge of commissioners whose duty it was to see to it that they learned only what was needed and did not get into their heads the perverted moral notions of the "barbarians." They led an isolated and segregated life and remained, for all their residence amongst foreigners, unmistakably Chinese.

But a change gradually took place. Younger and younger men went abroad to study. In most cases they had already had training in missionary and Government institutions. They not only readily adapted themselves to western ways, but even eagerly adopted them. Where before a young man brought up under the old tradition took up "practical" studies reluctantly from a sense of duty—a feeling that such were the country's needs—most of them since the 1910's have begun to take up not only science and technology but even banking and business, with more and more alacrity. Surveys conducted during the last decade showed that of the students in this country those studying business subjects out-numbered those engaged in any other branch of learning. It is scarcely necessary to remark that no lofty motives and patriotic ideals were back of this utilitarian choice.

This second generation of "returned students" are often the sons or younger brothers of the first generation of returned students, who have gradually assumed power and influence and who have come to constitute the only recognizable privileged class in China. Often they would go to the same school as their fathers or brothers and study the same subjects, so that they might carry on "the tradition," that is, *business,* of the family, be it banking, soliciting, or department store merchandising. In them we witness the total breakdown of the Chinese intellectual tradition and the triumph of the code of the American Babbitt, the adoption of money as a standard of all values, the enthronement of Banking and Big Business. This change is not only observable in the students of banking and business but also in the professions, such as law. Formerly a Chinese student studied law because he felt the need of legal reform in China and the urge to help make its laws; but now he takes it up with the idea of practicing it as a lucrative profession. Education is thus no longer looked upon as a training for intellectual leadership but a means to privilege. Where before a student took up trade and business as a patriotic duty, now he takes it up with the idea of profiteering; where formerly a merchant was a pariah for all his wealth, now he considers himself a Brahmin because he too has had an "education."

This portrait is not meant to be true of the average "returned student;" it is not even meant to be true of the average student of law or business, but it is true of the typical "returned students" who now rule China, who have introduced into China the obnoxious bourgeois ideas of the West! Moreover, under the new educational system it is practically impossible for the poorer classes to rise to privilege, for the long years of preparation required for a higher education obviously put it out of reach of any but the well-to-do. As to studying abroad, it is the privilege of only the wealthy and rich, unless one should happen to win a scholarship, which still does not alter the situation any, since in order to be eligible to such scholarships one must first have graduated from some higher educational institution. Thus the moneyed class becomes also the privileged class and a closed privileged class.

The composition of the revolutionary leadership in China will perhaps indicate the alignment of the class forces. In all stages of the Chinese revolutionary movements the "returned students" have played an important rôle, but the importance of the rôles of the various national groups is roughly in the following descending order; first students returned from Japan, then those from Germany and France, and lastly those who have studied in Great Britain and the United States. Many reasons may be advanced for this particular grouping, amongst which the prevailing ideology of the intellectual class in the various nations named may be mentioned, but the most significant reason lies in the cost of living in various countries. The crossing of the China sea costs no more than the trip between Peking and Shanghai, and tuition and living expenses in Japan are not more than twice as much as a year's outlay in some large university at home, probably not appreciably more if a student has to economize and knows how. But a year in the United States or Great Britain requires, let us say $1500, which at the pre-war rate of exchange was equivalent to the entire annual income of the better paid university professors holding advanced degrees from foreign universities, about five times the annual income of the average high school teacher, ten to twenty times that of primary school teachers, fifty to a hundred times the annual wage of the average domestic servant! At the low rate of silver during the past few years, the equivalents mentioned above are just about doubled. The implications are obvious.

As the course of the revolutionary movements grew more radical in nature, the rôle of the returned students became less and less important and the various national groups dropped out in a reversed order from the above. When the revolution finally came to mean a Communist revolution, the returned students from the United States and Great Britain practically dropped out of the picture altogether. At present the leaders of the Communist Party are mostly men who have never studied abroad at all, except those who were sent to Moscow in the early twenties to be trained for revolutionary work.

The most subtle change that has come over China is perhaps in the importation of the bourgeois expression "good family." We hear this word used as yet largely amongst returned students from Europe and America. There is nothing in the Chinese idiom which quite conveys the insinuations and prejudices of the expression "good family." The literal equivalent is *liang shan jên chia,* but it is used in the sense of a family of good, honest and law-abiding people. Other epithets are occupational or traditional designations. Of these are *kêng tu jên chia* ("family of plowers and scholars,") *shu hsiang jên chia* ("family full of the fragrance of books") *shih chia* ("a mandarin family"), and *shang chia* ("merchant family"). None of these terms implies any social discrimination. If anything, they are held in popular esteem in the order given; if there is any odium attached, it is to the last category. The merit tradition was deeply ingrained in the Chinese consciousness. Pride in birth was practically unknown. The sons of high officials were sometimes made eligible for public office without their passing the examinations, by special imperial favor, but to such privilege there is always attached the odium of not having arrived at distinction by the "open road," and such privilege was not therefore sought with particular eagerness. The only social disadvantage that one could acquire by birth is confined to such cases as when one's parent should be a professional pimp or prostitute, actor or actress, petty thief, or engaged in such occupations as that of barber, manicurist, or domestic servant, to which Chinese tradition has attached a profound prejudice.

The class forces and class alignments sketched so far have been observable during the last two decades, becoming more and more apparent as time went on. But these changes were too gradual, too insidious, too subtle to objectify the growing sense of disgust and despair of the intellectuals and the discontent of the masses. It was not until the coming into power of the Nanking Government that class issues became clear, for more than any of the previous factional Governments Nanking stood for the bourgeoisie, championed the cause of the bankers and capitalists, suppressed all movements of the poor and oppressed.

V

THE BOURGEOIS REVOLUTION OF THE KUOMINTANG

The revolution of 1911 was primarily a revolt against the Manchu Dynasty in which the masses took no part. The republican government set up at Peking was headed by men of the old school. The country fared no better and conditions became very much worse after Yüan Shih-k'ai, a Chinese mandarin who betrayed the Manchu court for the promise of the revolutionaries that he would be made the first president of the republic, died in the midst of his monarchical schemes, leaving his generals fighting for control of the Government. The optimistic attitude of the intellectuals during the first two years of the republic gave way to a deeper and deeper pessimism and despair. But out of this despair was born a new consciousness, a realization that a mere change in the form of government was not enough, that a fundamental intellectual revolution was necessary.

This new consciousness found expression in *La Jeunesse* (better known to English-speaking writers as *The New Youth* though the magazine itself carries the French title) edited by Ch'ên Tu-hsiu (Cheng Du Shu) a professor of the Peking National University with radical leanings, who later became the chairman of the Chinese Communist Party. Traditional Chinese notions were vigorously and effectively attacked; revolutionary ideas, ranging from conservative socialism to communism and anarchism were introduced and passionately discussed. One of the things attacked was the stilted and lifeless formalism of the Chinese literary tradition. It was realized that in order to bring the masses into participation in the political life of the country it was necessary to reform the written language, to discard the antiquated and difficult "literary style" for the vernacular of the people. This movement soon overshadowed all other problems and with the entrance of Hu Shih and the adoption of the vernacular style *La Jeunesse* became identified with the Literary Revolution movement.

In the meantime China was becoming more and more nationally conscious because of foreign aggression. There were first the Twenty-one Demands of Japan; then the betrayal of

China and the ratification of those demands by the Peace Conference. What happened immediately after this is familiar history—the uprisings of the students in May and June, 1919, followed by the refusal of the Chinese delegates to sign the Peace Treaty. Interest in the literary revolution became intensified, for it was reasoned that more than ever it was necessary to arouse the masses and that the written language must coincide with the spoken language of the people. New magazines sprang up by the hundreds in the new style; free schools were established by the students, using the facilities of their school buildings.

But this student movement was nationalistic rather than revolutionary; its political ideal was that of the leading powers—bourgeois democracy—though the more radical elements under the leadership of Ch'ên Tu-hsiu realized the eventual mission of the revolution. Now, precisely because of the Chinese tradition of an intellectual aristocracy, the students were naturally looked upon as the leaders of any movement. Their attitudes and beliefs were reliable indicators of the attitudes and beliefs of the articulate public. And so the revolutionary army set out from Canton in 1926 not under Communist but under Nationalist banners, though the directing genius behind it was Communist. Communist tacticians were evidently aware that the general Chinese intellectual world was not sufficiently conscious of class forces to accept the theory of the class struggle.

The triumphal progress of the Northern Expedition, the growing divergence between right-wing Kuomintang aims and true revolutionary aims, the capitulation to the imperialist powers after the Nanking incident of March 24, 1927, and the expulsion and suppression of the Communists,—with these we need not concern ourselves here. For an understanding of the course of the true revolutionary movement it is more important to study the character of the Nanking Government set up by the reaction and to point out why under its régime class forces came to a focus and thus gave birth to class consciousness in the intellectual world.

Whatever the faults of the Peking Government, it did not openly and flagrantly champion the cause of the moneyed classes. The Peking warlords may have been illiterate men, ignorant of the modern economic structure, but they were not, whatever misery they brought to the masses through their misrule, without their human and admirable qualities. When Chang Tso-lin found his *fêng-p'iào* falling, he had some of the bankers and money changers in Mukden arrested and summarily shot, because he thought that their manipulations must be responsible for the fall of his notes. He may have been wrong and high-handed, but he was wrong in a very human way, for surely it could be reasoned that the bankers and money changers must be responsible since they usually profited by fluctuations of the currency while the people in general suffered by them. Imagine the Nanking Government committing such an admirable crime. Instead it works closely with the bankers and capitalists, for its leaders, most of whom are returned students, know who are the real masters in the modern industrial world.

Peking was afraid of public opinion. It was frightened by the students' and merchants' strikes and yielded to their demands though it could have suppressed them with brutal force if it had wished to. The members of the Nanking Government knew, on the other hand, how to deal with public opposition, having recently taken part in the student uprisings against Peking. Like Chang Tso-lin, the Nanking military dealt summarily and barbarously with those opposed to it but whereas Chang Tso-lin shot bankers and money-changers, the Nanking military murdered idealistic youths in order to uphold the bankers and money-changers.

The relationship between the Nanking Government and the imperialist powers has also tended to discredit it and to show the alignment of class forces. It is true that the various powers used to side with one or the other of the old war-lords, playing the one against the other, but there was no united front amongst them. In the past the powers had in general sided with the revolutionaries and gave asylum to them in their concessions and settlements. Without these asylums on Chinese territory the republican revolution against the Manchus would probably not have been won with so little cost. During the period of the Nationalist revolution, the powers were uneasy because of the radical manifestations of the revolutionaries and only grudgingly gave asylum to them. But during the last few years the settlement authorities have not only refused asylum to Communists and Communist suspects, but have actually arrested them and handed them over to the Nanking authorities for execution. Not only this, but they have given active gunboat support to Nanking whenever they had an excuse. It has been claimed that in 1930 the Communist army had to retreat from Changsha after taking it and holding it for five days largely because of the bombardment of the city by British and American gunboats as a "retaliation," claiming to have been fired upon by the Communists while evacuating their nationals.

Finally there is the reign of terror conducted under the pretext of Communist suppression. "This task was entrusted to two minor men in the Kuomintang party who, utilizing the Chinese detectives in one of the foreign police organizations and a large number of persons connected with the Blue Society, one of the two principal secret societies [*i.e.*, gangs] operating here, made such a cleanup of Communists as no northern general would have dared to do even in his own territory." This is from Mr. George Sokolsky, an American journalist in China, who certainly cannot be suspected of being more partial to the Communists than to Nanking.

VI

THE AWAKENING OF THE INTELLECTUALS

This "White" terror was the last straw so far as the intellectuals were concerned, and equally so with the students. One by one they turned left, to the support of the radical cause. The most important of these "conversions" is perhaps that of Kuo Mo-jo, the leader of the Creative Society group, for he has probably the largest following amongst the younger generation. His conversion, followed by others of the Creative Society, is all the more remarkable because he and his colleagues started out shortly before 1920 under the banner of individualism and art for art's sake. In "Below the Water Level," a group of miscellanies written during the winter of 1924–5, he pictured the harrowing experiences he had as an investigator of the recently devastated regions of the Kiangsu-Chekiang war and his growing consciousness of class inequality. It is "a naked record of one man's new orientation," from which one can see the new social orientation, "for the change of one individual is but the reflection of the direction of the whole."

In "Appendicitis," the title essay of another group of miscellanies written after May 30, 1925, on which day the massacre of Chinese demonstrators by the British settlement police at

Shanghai took place, the capitalist is described as the appendix of society, a parasite who feeds on surplus values and who always threatens the existence of human society, just as the appendix threatens the existence of the individual organism. Elsewhere he declared that after coming into contact with those living below the water level he no longer could live and work under the illusion of an individual freedom without reference to society, that "I have come to realize that if we want to develop the individual, we must *all* have a chance to develop the individual; that if we want freedom, we must all have a chance at freedom," and that before the ideal stage is reached, the intellectual leader must sacrifice his own individual happiness and freedom, and fight for the general cause. True to his convictions, he joined the Nationalist revolution of 1925–7, but since the triumph of the reaction he has allied himself with the opposition, and later became a member of the Left Writers' League.

Another "conversion" probably just as important is that of Chou Shu-jên, better known by his pen name Lusin. He embodies the best qualities of the genuine intellectual, and at the same time his weakness. Although about ten years older than Hu Shih (who became an institution, "the Father of the Literary Revolution" by the time he was forty) he has always been identified with the younger generation. He never allowed his position and reputation to corrupt his intellectual honesty and his personal integrity, but is always fighting feudalistic ideas and conventions, national and cultural chauvinism, respectability, and all forms of muddle-headed notions, however fashionable and hallowed they might be at the time. He criticized the Peking régime when it was in power, but when the general fashion veered toward Canton and revolution became a shibboleth, he wrote:

Revolutionaries, counter-revolutionaries, non-revolutionaries.
Revolutionaries killed by counter-revolutionaries; counter-revolutionaries killed by revolutionaries.
Of the non-revolutionaries some are taken for revolutionaries and killed by the counter-revolutionaries; others are taken for counter-revolutionaries and killed by the revolutionaries; still others are taken for nothing at all and killed indiscriminately by revolutionaries or counter-revolutionaries.
Revolution, revolutionary-revolution, revolutionary-revolutionary-revolution . . .

In this thrust, as in all his writings, Lusin conceals his profound sympathy for the suffering masses under a most effective cloak of cold, relentless, "objective" satire. But intellectual honesty often paralyzes action, and this has been largely true of Lusin. His first volume of short stories, which together with his essays and miscellanies constitute probably the only documentary testimonial to the validity of the "literary revolution," was significantly entitled "Nê Han" or "Cheering at the Sidelines," for he frankly admitted that he was temperamentally disqualified for action but that he was willing to cheer or even follow the leaders in their fight for worthy causes.

Again by his own admission, he was afraid to lead (for again and again he is heralded as the leader of various literary movements), especially inexperienced youths who read him for spiritual guidance. Such hesitation may seem inglorious, but it is certainly more honest than the false leaders who lead by standing still, by advising youth to attend to their studies and let the warlords and politicians fight it out among themselves. Once when pressed by a correspondent for his views on the immediate objectives that youth should follow, he answered that they were first to maintain existence, second to secure warmth and food, and third to develop human possibilities. These objectives may seem obvious at the first glance, but if consistently pursued they imply an uncompromising and incessant struggle against the forces of oppression and its allies such as conservatism, cultural chauvinism, religion (be it Christianity or Confucianism), and all forms of escape. This answer shows how sensitive Lusin is fundamentally and how he is preoccupied with the sufferings of the helpless masses. It was this moral and spiritual sensitiveness which finally enabled Lusin to orient himself. In an article that appeared in the *Herald Tribune* book section, May 25, 1930, Agnes Smedley described him as standing at the crossroads like many other Chinese intellectuals, identifying him with a group of writers that "beats back and forth, confused, chaotic, yet sincere"; but he has since turned left and become identified with the Left Writers' League.

The Left Writers' League was formed in 1930 and its membership includes practically every author of any importance, particularly young writers or writers with a large following among the young. In their manifesto, as reported in the *China Forum* (special number, May, 1932), it was declared "that the duty of the new proletarian literary movement in China is to raise the political, educational, and cultural level of the masses . . . and to fight for the existence of Chinese Soviet power."

Similar organizations of artists, playwrights, social scientists and other groups have been formed.

That this awakening of the intellectuals is based upon a deep conviction of the justness of the Communist cause, the soundness of its theoretical assumptions and its practical program needs no elaboration if we bear in mind what it means to oppose the ruling power in China. No accurate figures are available, but one can safely say that at least hundreds (thousands, according to Communist figures) of civilians have been executed for no other crime than professing or being suspected of Communist sympathies. Early in 1931, a group of twenty-four youthful political prisoners, students and writers for the most part, were executed. Amongst these, five were members of the League of Left Writers, one a young man of only twenty-two, one a young woman of twenty-four; the oldest was only 30.

VII

THE PROSPECTS OF THE CHINESE SOVIETS

We have so far dealt only with the psychological background of the Communist movement in China; we have dealt with this phase of the problem at such length because it is of more fundamental importance than the spectacular and surface manifestations. Let us now ascertain the reasons for the failure of the Communist movement of 1926–7 and point out what important lessons have been learned.

The fundamental mistake of the Communists was, I think, their coöperation with the Kuomintang. It has been repeatedly pointed out that the Communist-Kuomintang alliance was one of expediency: the Communists sought to utilize the Nationalistic aspirations of the Kuomintang, and of the Chinese people in general to weaken the position of the imperialistic powers in China, thus preparing the way for an uprising of the masses; the Kuomintang accepted the aid of the Communists because of the revolutionary technique and the material aids that the latter would bring to them. Each was biding its time to eliminate the other as soon as mutual usefulness was ended and their aims and interests began to conflict. Tactically this might have been sound, but psychologically the position of the Communists was weak, for under the arrangement the Communists were placed in such a position that they could not escape the charge of "duplicity and treachery" once they began to assert their aims, and tried to eliminate the nationalists—an untenable position because of the deep-rooted ethical prejudice against duplicity and treachery.

We have pointed out that the northern expedition started out from Canton under Nationalist colors. Even before the alliance, representatives of Soviet Russia had publicly stated that their aim was not to bring about a Communist revolution in China but to help China to achieve national independence. In a joint statement issued by A. Joffe, the Soviet ambassador to China, and Sun Yat-sen on January 1, 1924, it was declared that

> Dr. Sun Yat-sen holds that the Communist order or even the Soviet system cannot actually be introduced into China, because there do not exist here the conditions for the successful establishment of either Communism or Sovietism. This view is *entirely shared by Mr. Joffe,* who is further of the opinion that China's paramount and most pressing problem is to achieve national unification and attain full national independence, and as regards this great task, he has assured Dr. Sun Yat-sen that China has the warmest sympathy of the Russian people and can count on the support of Russia. (ital. mine)

With this understanding Chinese Communists were admitted into the Kuomintang and Russian advisors began to take an active and directing rôle in the revolutionary activities. Being experts in organization, the Russian and Chinese Communists were able to control the party machinery. Tactically it was a great victory for the Communists, but psychologically it was a defeat, for by mutual understanding and by public utterances it was made clear that it was the Communist who had embraced Kuomintang principles and not the Kuomintang that had accepted Communism.

For a while the alliance was successful, for in the initial stages the interests of the two elements did not clash. The conservative elements in the Kuomintang did not like the rising power of the peasant and labor unions, organized under Communist leadership, but they did not protest very vigorously because in the initial stages the peasant and labor uprisings were essential in bringing about the disintegration of the enemy, thus assuring the success of the Nationalist armies. By the time the expedition reached the Yangtze, however, the peasant and labor uprisings became less and less useful and more and more embarrassing to the conservative Kuomintang leaders. After the Nanking incident of March 24, the suppression of the Shanghai labor unions and the general massacre of radical workers, and the setting up of a reactionary Government in Nanking by Chiang Kai-shek, the differences in aims and in interests diverged to an intolerable degree. A break became inevitable. The time came when one must "eliminate" the other in order to survive.

The immediate occasions for the break are well known: the "exposure" of Russian participation in the revolution as a result of the Soviet Embassy raid and the exposure of the instructions of the Communist International to the Chinese Communist Party to strike and to seize control of the Hankow Government, which was then looked upon as the legitimate Kuomintang Government in China. The former exposure greatly enhanced the cause of Nanking, which had become by that time frankly anti-Communist; the latter alienated the left-wing Kuomintang elements at Hankow. It would be idle to speculate as to what might have happened if the Chinese Communists, carrying out the instructions of the International, had struck before it was too late; the point is that the enemy struck first and eliminated the Communists.

Under the circumstances it was impossible for the Communists to escape the charge of duplicity and treachery. There was an immediate revulsion of feeling generally against them, which has been only gradually counter-acted by the reign of terror and of reaction introduced by Nanking. This lesson is as important as it is costly in blood. Tactically, expediency may be justified, but it is necessary to make sure first that the expediency will not compromise the fundamental issues involved and damage one's own position. Revolutions must be carried on underground at first, but once a revolution has come out into the open, it must fly its own colors and not borrow those of a potential enemy.

But it must not be understood by this criticism that the alliance between the Communist Party and the Kuomintang was without its practical benefits for the former. For besides giving Communist commanders several regiments in the Kuomintang army which later served as the nucleus of Red Armies, which in turn made the Soviet centers possible, the alliance and the subsequent split also served to focus and clarify the class issues for the general public. It is easy for us to point out the psychological error after the fact, but we must also realize that without the alliance, not only would there probably be no Nanking Government but there would also probably be no Chinese Soviets either!

The anti-Communist campaign of 1927 also found the Communists without a base to retire to, where they could recuperate and consolidate their forces. The Communist commanders led their armies through the mountainous regions of Kiangsi, Fukien and Kwangtung, dodging and attacking, generally gaining and increasing in numbers though suffering occasional reverses. Were it not for the fact that the attention of the Nanking Government had been centered elsewhere, because of threatened or actual revolts of Kuomintang generals and political squabbles, the Communists would probably have been eliminated. But because of these favoring conditions and the peasant uprisings, the Red forces were able to establish themselves in large areas in Hupeh, Kiangsi, Hunan, Fukien, and elsewhere.

The treaty ports on the Yangtze, such as Hankow, Shasi and Kiukiang, and elsewhere, such as Changsha, have thus far proved serious obstacles to the Communists. Several times they could have taken Hankow, for instance, but as this would inevitably bring military intervention of the imperialist powers they withheld the attack, for under present conditions Chinese Soviet forces are not ready for armed conflict with the foreign powers. It was because of this consideration that the original plan for the Northern Expedition was to leave Shanghai alone until Peking had been reached and most of China unified under the revolutionary party, when Shanghai could be "starved out." This obstacle is a very unfortunate one for the Communists, for these foreign spheres of interest prevent them from uniting certain Soviet centers: a unification might have otherwise been effected.

In spite of all the disadvantages, however, the Communists have been able to establish numerous Soviet centers, notably in Kiangsi, where the Kuomintang forces have not only been eliminated, but a Soviet Government has been entrenched long enough to establish tax agencies, work out agrarian programs, establish banks, open schools and carry out other constructive measures. If we compare the relation of the Chinese Soviets to the rest of China with that of Soviet Russia to the rest of the world, we may say that the Chinese Soviets have now entered upon the Stalin period of stabilization, upon some sort of Five-Year Plan. And just as the Chinese Soviets are more subject to armed invasions from without than is Russia, so there is more likelihood of a general Chinese Communist revolution in the near future than there is of a general world revolution.

As to what the Chinese Soviets have been able to do for the Chinese peasants and how the peasants themselves react to the Soviet system, let us quote from the recent Japanese White Book, which contains an extensive appendix on Communism in China:

> In a locality, once raided by a Red army, the people, having had a taste of Communist rule, are not liable to forget, even after its fall, the apparent benefit it has conferred upon them through land distribution, lowered prices, and people's participation in government, but are likely to retain permanent interest in and attachment to Communism.

Whether the benefits enumerated are real or "apparent," the Chinese peasants themselves are perhaps better judges than the Japanese foreign office! Or take the following report, from non-Communist sources, to the *New York Times,* of January 31, 1932:

> Foreign missionaries writing from the zones recently overrun by the Reds report that the peasants and common people are giving a hearty welcome to the returning Communists. They said that after comparing their status under previous Communist rule with the bad government and confiscatory taxation enforced upon them after the arrival of the Nanking troops last summer, they enjoyed greater liberty and a greater degree of prosperity under the Reds than under Nanking.

VIII

THE FUTURE OF COMMUNISM IN CHINA

What is going to happen in China depends a great deal upon what may happen in other great cultural and economic centers, as suggested at the beginning of the article. Assuming that the alignment elsewhere in the world will remain what it is for some time, then the Chinese Soviet must bide its time as Russia has been doing. It is even conceivable that a temporary truce might be arranged between the conservative elements (Nanking) and the Communists, especially during such times of national danger as caused by the aggressions of Japan. But it will be only a truce, and not a compromise of principles, for they are irreconcilable.

A more pertinent line of questioning is the future relation between the Communist elements in China and the Communist International. In other words, assuming the success of the genuine revolutionary elements, would we have a *Chinese* Communism or would we have a Communist China? Orthodox Communists will denounce this suggestion as a contradiction in terms, for according to them there is no Communism outside of the Comintern. Then let me put the question thus: will revolutionary Socialism remain, under the leadership of the Communist Party of China, as a section of the Communist International, or is it going to take on a national complexion? This is a baffling problem to those of us who are sympathetic toward all movements aiming at a classless society, but it is one that cannot be escaped. Mere silence will not make the possible impossible.

And Chinese Communism, that is, a Chinese revolutionary Socialist movement friendly or coöperating with but independent of the Comintern, is a possibility because Nationalism is still a living force and will be for at least another generation. Patriotism is the one loyalty-commanding ideal; especially is this so of the weaker nations with a remote past of "glory" and an immediate past of shame and humiliation, such as China. Distrust of the foreigners who have dominated China for the last hundred years is deeply ingrained in the masses. Even Soviet Russia has not been above suspicion. There was the case of Soviet-instigated independence of Outer Mongolia and the case of Soviet neutrality in the present Sino-Japanese conflict in Manchuria. So anxious were the Soviet authorities to avoid complications with Japan, that when a group of Chinese students arrived at Vladivostok on their way to Manchuria for volunteer propaganda work in the spring of 1932, they were arrested and detained, and finally deported back to Shanghai on the plea that since the Soviet was neutral it could not allow them to travel through its territory to Manchuria. For the average person it is difficult to see the difference between safeguarding the Soviet Union for Communism and safeguarding it for the Russians.

This "Chinese Communism" need not be, should not be nationalistic; it can perhaps be better described as the regional development of Communism. This, in fact, is what the immediate aim of Soviet Russia comes to. In the present stage of human development, with national prejudices still so strong, such regional development is perhaps not without advantages. "Socialism in one country" may not be practicable if one defines "country" strictly according to the present national boundaries, which are often artificial, but that Socialism in a large geographical region which has been unified by a common political or cultural tradition, as in the case of Russia, China, and the United States, is practicable is demonstrated by the continued existence of the Soviet Union in spite of great difficulties. It is certainly more realistic to struggle for such a regional development of socialism than to refuse to coöperate with such a regional Soviet régime while awaiting a non-existent and remote world revolution.

Another question is that of the united front of the Chinese Communists. "Individualist" China is favorable to the rise of factional strife. Admitted that there is but one ideal: but who is to dictate policies and propose means for achieving that ideal? how are differences to be reconciled? This problem faces all social groups, but with the Chinese it has proved to be a much more basic difficulty. The same critical and individualistic qualities in the Chinese that make such an absurd phenomenon as the adulation of Lindbergh impossible also make coöperation difficult. We may sum it up by saying that the Chinese will make excellent members of a communist society but they do not as yet make very good organizers of one.

BIBLIOGRAPHY

"Ten Years of the Kuomintang: Revolution vs. Reaction". T. A. Bisson, FOR-EIGN POLICITY ASSOCIATION REPORT, Feb. 15, 1933. Contains in the appendices material not generally available. As this book is going to press a report devoted to Communism in China is scheduled for publication in April.

"Communist Policy and the Chinese Nationalist Revolution". Maurice T. Price, THE ANNALS OF THE AM. ACADEMY OF POLITICAL AND SOCIAL SCIENCE, November, 1930.

"The Communist Situation in China", Yang Chien. Semi-official pamphlet, Nanking, 1931. Gives summaries of Communist policies, including that of the Left Opposition.

"The Tinder Box of Asia", George E. Sokolsky, Chapter 12. 1932.

"Soviet China". By M. James and R. Doonping. International Pamphlets, 1932.

THE CHINA FORUM, special number on "Five Years of Kuomintang Reaction", May, 1932. A spirited and vivid presentation of the case against Nanking, with photographs.

PART THREE

WHITHER THESE STATES?

I

THE Great War, the Russian Revolution, the Economic Crisis—these master events of our time dominate our thought and are shaping the course of history.

The War shook Europe to her foundations. It put an end to the political and social equilibrium, however precarious and unstable, that gave a sense of security to the reigning houses and ruling classes. It destroyed the Habsburg, Hohenzollern, Romanov, Ottoman empires. It raised a multitude of new States, and transformed old ones. It destroyed lives innumerable, wealth untold, and put upon nations a load of debt under which they are still groaning; but it also demonstrated the immeasurable productivity of labor in modern industry under collective stimulation. In several countries it ruined, or greatly weakened, the middle classes, sharpened the antagonism between the polar extremes of society—capitalists and wage-workers, and prepared the ground for Fascism—that twentieth-century Bonapartism, which is to save capitalist society by forcing it into a straitjacket, and infuse new vigor into its decaying body by multiplying the parasites that feed on its life-blood. It strained severely the British Empire, that stupendous world-wide organization of exploitation, and it is by no means certain that even the surrender of sovereignty to the Dominions can save the Empire from dissolution; the oppressed and exploited subject countries, notably India and Egypt, are not likely to be pacified thereby. Asia, which contains more than one-half of the total population of the globe, was roused from her age-old slumbers; European prestige received a shock from which it has not yet recovered. China, rocked with internal convulsions, nevertheless dares now and then to present a defiant front to the imperialists of Europe and America; but for Japanese aggressive violence, and the fear of their own peasant Communists, even her incompetent and corrupt rulers might have been more successful. India is in turmoil; divided into hostile castes and religions, her physically and morally enfeebled peoples are nevertheless giving the British imperialists a fearful headache. The Turk, retiring within himself, presents an impenetrable wall to European influence, financial and political; balancing force against force, he seems on the whole to incline toward the Soviet Union and away from European finance and diplomacy, toward the world that is being born and away from the world that is visibly dying. Persia ventures to demand an accounting of the British oil monopoly. The Arabian-speaking world of Western Asia and Northern Africa is cowed, but profoundly disturbed. The Dutch, French, American possessions in Southeastern Asia are also stirring.

II

The War annihilated, dissolved, or enfeebled the ruling elements of Europe; it also destroyed the prestige of the Social Democracy, that pre-War political organization of the ruled classes, and set in motion forces that are bound to destroy it utterly. The War demonstrated that the Social Democracy was a broken reed, that the hope it raised in the workers of the world was a delusion, that its Marxian phraseology was a sham and a snare, that the social revolution which it promised was a Pickwickian expression, a figure of speech, an esoteric doctrine not meant to be taken in any practical sense. And of all Social Democratic parties, the most powerful—the German— proved the feeblest. Confronted with a revolutionary situation of utmost pregnancy, it weakly surrendered without striking a blow, transformed itself into a willing tool of the old order, and robbed the workers of hope, confidence and energy. If it took Ludendorff to order the establishment in Germany of a parliamentary government, it took the Social Democrat Scheidemann to proclaim a bourgeois republic in order to save Germany from Bolshevism, and it took a Social Democratic government to stifle in bloody treason every effort to establish in

Germany the rule of the proletariat. In conjunction with its Liberal and Catholic allies, the Social Democracy founded a republic that has retained the imperial bureaucracy, judges and generals, that has turned over as outright gifts to the former reigning houses Crown property worth hundreds of millions of dollars, that has not dared to break up the landed estates of the junkers, that has not abolished titles of nobility, and even permits members of the former ruling houses to be elected to the highest offices, including the Presidency of the Reich. The Social Democracy put its own Ebert into the Presidency, in order to save capitalism in Germany; it voted for the Centrist (Catholic) Marx, in order to save Germany from the junker Hindenburg; it voted for Hindenburg, in order to save Germany from the Fascist Hitler. By every act it proclaimed its own shame and utter worthlessness. It received its reward in the form of dictatorial government at the hands of Papen, Schleicher, and Hitler.[1]

The course of the German Social Democracy is typical of the course of Social Democratic parties everywhere. The War enfeebled the ruling classes of Great Britain and gave the British Labor party its great opportunity; that opportunity was utilized by Ramsay MacDonald, Philip (now Viscount) Snowden, and J. H. Thomas to serve capitalism and imperialism, while the remaining leaders, thoroughly demoralized themselves, lack the understanding, energy, and capacity for leadership. Everywhere—in France or in Poland, in Italy or in Spain—the Social Democrats have become an appendage to the bourgeoisie, and partake of its moral and intellectual decadence. Give them a parliament to talk in, and they are happy; but if a Mussolini or a Pilsudski takes their pretty toy away from them, they whine in utter helplessness. Did not their great theoretician, Karl Kautsky, state at the outbreak of the War, in excuse of their surrender to the war makers, that the Social Democracy can function only in time of peace, and not of war?

III

On reading Thierry's "History of the Third Estate," Karl Marx made the observation that while the parties of the third estate were rising and falling, the class—the bourgeoisie in embryo, in process of development—was steadily rising and gaining in power. Thus it goes also with the proletariat, the

class that is destined to displace the bourgeoisie as the determining force in society. Even while the Social Democracy was
betraying its own past and proclaiming its own bankruptcy,
the Russian Revolution came to revive the hopes of the exploited, oppressed, disinherited throughout the world. The
greatest event since the great French Revolution, the most revolutionary event since the beginnings of recorded history, the
Russian Revolution is to us of the Western world the most
astounding event that possibly could have happened. Is there
one, even one, among the Western socialists of our time who
foresaw the coming proletarian revolution in Russia? Because
Marx deduced the coming of socialism from the life-processes
themselves of capitalism, because he proved that capitalism itself generates the forces—mighty collective industry and the
proletariat—that are destined to destroy it, therefore no Marxist (of the Western world, that is to say) could imagine that
socialism was to take its triumphant start in the most backward
of the capitalist countries of Europe. Yet Marx himself foresaw, as early as 1870, that a "terrible social revolution" was
impending in Russia, and again in 1882 he laughed at the
German socialist leaders of his day who regarded as phantas-
tical the idea that the next impulse to social revolution in
Europe was to come from Russia. And even if we could not
see with the eyes of a Marx, the revolution of 1905, defeated
though it was, might have taught us to look to Russia if we
had had the eyes to see. But Lenin and Trotsky saw, and the
proletariat of Russia saw the unparalleled opportunity, made
the mighty attempt, won out in the face of a hostile and deri-
sive world, amid perils and hardships unexcelled if ever
equalled, and thereby inaugurated a new era in the history of
humanity. And now a vast realm—one sixth of the globe—is
being ruled by and for the workers, hand workers and brain
workers, workers in the factories and on the great collective
farms, while an astounded world, sunk in lethargy and misery,
unemployment and chaos, looks on in bewilderment, half-
incredulous, amazed that the impossible has happened, that
not only the dreaded Tsarism has been overthrown, but even
capitalism itself, the very foundation, as has been commonly
and stupidly believed, of all human association. Freed of Tsar,
landlord, and capitalist, backward and poverty-stricken Russia
is rebuilding herself on new and broad foundations, finds work
and bread for every living soul, finds abundant means for

spreading education and knowledge to remotest North and East, among unlettered, barbarous populations for whom even an alphabet has to be adapted, while the leading countries of civilization, in possession of wealth and knowledge and skill and the stupendous modern forces of production, are perishing in misery. Never before did the world witness a contrast so striking and spectacular, so calculated to arrest the minds of men and impress their imagination. And most certainly, no one could possibly have foreseen or imagined that the contrast between capitalist chaos and proletarian order would be presented so soon, so forcefully, and on so vast a scale.

IV

The world-wide Economic Crisis is the third great event of our time. Just as there never was a war so destructive as the Great War, just as there never was a revolution so extreme and thoroughgoing as the Russian Revolution, so there never was an economic crisis like the crisis of 1929–1932. Modern capitalism has known economic crises—financial, industrial, agricultural, commercial—ever since the end of the Napoleonic wars. Their causes have been analyzed, their course has been described, their effects have been noted. Not only Marx and the economists of his school have studied them, even the academic bourgeois economists could not close their eyes to them. Latterly even the businessman of no more than average intelligence had heard something concerning a "business cycle," though its causes remained to him as much of a mystery as ever, and whenever it came, it broke like a bolt from the blue. But our late and comparatively long-lasting prosperity—it lasted, with one break, from 1915 to 1929—had completely intoxicated not only the average citizen, but even his most distinguished prophets, the professors of political economy with the widest reputations for knowledge and prognosticating ability. America, we were assured, had entered on a New Economic Era of everlasting prosperity. And when the crisis came, it struck with all the more devastating force, like a veritable Great War or an irresistible force of nature. It ruined countless prosperous bourgeois, drove unnumbered people to suicide, and left in its wake millions upon millions of unemployed workers who became dependent on public and private charity. Above all its predecessors, the present crisis is distinguished by "the universality of its theater and the intensity of its action," to use an expression which Marx applied to the crisis of 1873 *before* it happened, when he saw its coming and was predicting it.

The excessive force of the present crisis may be attributed to the destruction wrought by the War, the load of debt and taxes with which it has burdened mankind, the dislocation of trade that has resulted from the creation of new States and new customs frontiers—the Balkanizing of Europe, the Nationalist agitation in India, the civil wars in China, the partial exclusion of Russia from the world-market because of financial blockade, consequent upon her total exclusion because of military and naval blockade (Clemenceau's malicious *cordon sanitaire*), foreign intervention, civil war, and famine. With all these additional causes to account for the excessive intensity, extent and duration of the present crisis, we may feel reasonably certain that the crisis *as such* would have been accounted for in the popular mind by one or more of these factors, that is to say, as due to some special cause or causes, which had nothing to do with the inherent nature of the economic system of capitalism; just as the crisis of 1907 was ascribed to Roosevelt's anti-trust pronouncements, or the crisis of 1893 to the fear that the United States would go off the gold standard. The press, the politicians, and the more or less official economists would certainly have done their very best to create this impression in the minds of the masses, partly, no doubt, because they themselves would largely have been victims of the same delusion. And the masses, we may be certain, would have believed them, and would meekly and humbly have accepted the crisis and all its attendant suffering, just as they had accepted all the preceding crises—as an act of God, or unavoidable fate. But now, after the Russian Revolution—with a Soviet Union in existence —with the first Five-Year Plan completed and a second being inaugurated—with mass unemployment abolished—now it is becoming increasingly difficult to make any thinking person believe that these periodically recurring world-devastating crises are due to God, or chance, or the folly of individual financiers and statesmen. Now every intelligent, thinking person cannot help seeing that the economic crisis is a scourge not of God, but of Capital, that it is a necessary and unavoidable phase in the life-process of society only so long as the capitalist system of anarchy and chaos endures, and that it lies in our power to bring order and plan and foresight into the economic life of society. With the Soviet example before us, even non-Marxist economists and publicists who have the welfare of the working masses at heart have begun clamoring for some sort of a planned society. They forget or ignore the fundamental fact that, in order to formulate a plan of production, there must be a purpose, an aim, a goal; that in the Soviet Union the aim of the Plan is the satisfaction of the wants of every worker living within its borders, the raising of his economic and intellectual level, the development of his physical and mental faculties, the invigorating of the entire social organism, while everywhere else—in Europe and America and wherever capitalism prevails—the primary and determining aim of production is the multiplication of profits. And this difference in purpose and aim is again determined by the masters and directors of the social-economic process—there workers, here capitalitsts. The moral is inescapable.[2]

I am not of those who feel certain that this is the last crisis of capitalism, that capitalism has here and now reached its ultimate phase. To me it is quite conceivable that capitalism may recover from, and survive, this crisis, just as it had recovered from precedent crises. Precisely because the economic crisis is an inevitable phase of the modern-capitalistic life-cycle, and not a mere chance occurrence, it is quite possible, and even probable, that the present crisis will be followed, after a shorter or longer period of depression and stagnation, by a period of recuperation and comparative prosperity—to be followed in its turn by another crisis. Many factors may contribute to this recovery. The practical abolition of German reparation payments at Lausanne is one of them. Cancellation of their indebtedness to Washington would help in balancing the budgets of several European countries and lifting their economy out of the slough of despond. A possible relaxation of tension among the States of Europe, with a consequent reduction in armaments, would certainly help the recuperative process. It cannot fail to have been noticed that, as the crisis increased in severity and American loans ceased flowing to Europe, Mussolini ceased making speeches threatening war on France; latterly Italian diplomacy has even inclined toward armament reduction. Another disturbing element in Europe, the Polish dictator Pilsudski, has assumed a more amicable, or less hostile, attitude toward the Soviet Union; the crisis is laying a paralyzing hand on one saber-rattling dictator after another. The process of recovery might also be helped by the cessation of chronic warfare in China, or by the suspension on the part of Japan of her aggressive policy in Manchuria and China, or by the quieting of the Nationalist agitation in India. At present there is no sign of any of these things coming to pass, yet they may come to pass, at least temporarily, out of sheer exhaustion; and if and when they do, they will undoubtedly have a restorative effect on the capitalist system of Europe and America by reopening old markets, stimulating international trade, and providing work for many of the unemployed. A similar effect would be produced by American recognition of the Soviet Government and the granting by American capitalists of long-term credits, or even loans, to that government; according to competent American authorities, Russia can for years to come absorb billions of dollars worth of imports annually. Indeed, the mere destruction of capital as a consequence of the crisis, the prolonged stagnation of production, the exhaustion of existing supplies and the necessity for replenishing them, may produce a revival of industry, however temporary or feeble. An established social system does not die automatically, like an individual organism; it does not perish unless it is destroyed. Certainly, capitalism contains within itself the seed of its own destruction: on the one hand, the contradictions inherent in great industry and its complement—the world market, the problems that are beyond solution and explode in a Great War, an economic crisis that embraces the whole world, a bankruptcy and overturn of governments; on the other hand, the proletariat, itself a creation of the great industry. But unless the proletariat is resolved upon its destruction and proceeds to act in accordance with that resolution, capitalism will surely survive.

V

But whatever possibilities lie in the womb of the future, it is certain that we are living in a revolutionary age, that normal times are a thing of the past. The golden era of British capitalism passed away with the Victorian age; the rise of America and Germany to the position of first-rate economic powers did away with the virtual British monopoly of the world-market and her primacy among the Great Powers. The War, which ruined Germany, also dealt Britain stunning blows. Germany, the keystone of capitalism on the European continent, is now in a chronic state of social and political turmoil, confusion, chaos; in the island kingdom the process of social and political disintegration has not yet proceeded quite so far, but it is proceeding at a rate quite unimaginable before the War. The most striking evidence of this is the fact that, in order to reëstablish their power, the British Conservatives were obliged to call in the aid of the renegade labor leaders, just as in France at an earlier date the bourgeois availed themselves of the services of the renegade socialists—Millerand, Viviani, Briand, or as in post-War Germany capitalism had to be saved by the Social Democracy.

Compared with the major capitalist powers of Europe, America still presents an aspect of firm, immutable social stability, and political power is still a monopoly of the Republican-Democratic twins. Nevertheless if we look beneath the surface of appearances, we cannot help seeing that even America is grievously sick of a slow and wasting disease. The late lamented prosperity, with the universal speculative fever that accompanied it, was due to quite exceptional causes—the developments of the War and after, that is to say, the economic ruin of Europe. Such a series of events cannot possibly repeat itself. The present crisis not only puts an end to the artificially induced era of prosperity; it does much more than that. *It resumes the process of evolution that was interrupted by the War and post-War developments.* Before the War, conditions in these States were by no means entirely healthy. Industry was in an almost chronic state of depression; buoyancy was the exception. The farmers never ceased complaining, notwithstanding the persistent rise in the price of foodstuffs that began in the last years of the nineteenth century; apparently, the benefits of higher prices were absorbed by interest, rent, taxes, middlemen, and higher prices for industrial products. Labor was restless, and strikes were common, particularly in the steel, coal, and textile industries. The I.W.W. were gaining adherents. The concentration and centralization of capital were proceeding apace; small capitalists—mere millionaires—felt uneasy. Repeated outbreaks of "insurgency" in the Republican party testified to the deep discontent of the agricultural West, Roosevelt's progressivism and Wilson's "new freedom" to the complaints of small capital, while the male vote of nearly a

million cast for Debs in the Presidential election of 1912
seemed to announce the political awakening of the American
wage-earners. The War and its sequences changed that situation, but only temporarily; the crisis is bringing it back to
us in an intensified form. The unparalleled rise of American
capitalism, due to an exceptional set of circumstances, is now
definitely terminated. Henceforth the American standard of
living, for every class in the community, is bound to decline.
The poorer farmers are facing ruin. The wage-workers, of
whom more than two million were unemployed even at the
height of prosperity in the early months of 1929, are now confronted with mass unemployment on an unheard-of scale, while
the more fortunate ones are glad to obtain partial employment.
Wage reduction has become general and drastic; the total
wages paid to the working class are estimated to have been cut
in half during the depression.[3] Even the Railway Brotherhoods,
hitherto the most privileged group of labor, are not exempt.
The restriction or annulment of the purchasing power of millions of farmers and wage-workers is bound to have a permanently constricting effect on the internal market and on industry; the cost of production will rise, profits and dividends will
shrink, the employers will strive to recoup themselves by means
of further wage reductions, and when these become impossible,
by means of improved processes and machinery which dispense
with labor. Unemployment will, of course, contract as well as
expand, in accordance with the alternate expansion and contraction of capital in the cause of its periodic cycle, as well as
its more limited and partial oscillations in the various industries; but mass unemployment, "the reserve army of the unemployed," will be ever with us, whether because of the never-
ceasing technological revolution, or because of the formation
of national and international trusts, cartels, etc., and the consequent limitation of output. With the contraction of American
loans abroad, because of past losses, the export of commodities
will correspondingly contract, and therewith the opportunities
for employment. In these circumstances, the American wage-
worker will cease to regard Al Smith as the perfect ideal in
whom he sees the realization of his own hopes and ambitions;
on the contrary, he will become as chronically discontented as
his European brother. He will demand unemployment insurance, and most likely he will get it; in European countries,
particularly in Germany and Great Britain, unemployment

insurance has come to be regarded by the more discerning politicians and economists as insurance against social revolution. If he is a member of a union, he will be demanding a more aggressive leadership, one that is less pliant to the employer; the labor organizations will be forced by the employers themselves into a more militant attitude. He will vote for his own Labor Party, whether it call itself Socialist or by some other name, and the leaders will desert him and betray him as regularly as the Labor and Socialist Party leaders have done in Europe. Then will the failure of parliamentarian, or bourgeois, democracy become as palpable here as in the countries of Europe. The workers will turn to Communism, while the capitalists and their satellites will seek safety in Fascism. But it may be noted, *en passant,* that in the United States Fascism need not at all assume the aspect of an extra-constitutional dictatorship. The President possesses, and on past occasions has exercised, all the constitutional powers that may be required to "save society" from rebellious elements in the community. The Constitution of the United States has never yet failed its devout worshipers. Moreover, vigilance committees and lynching bees were known in this country before Mussolini.

The failure of capitalist democracy—call it parliamentarism, call it constitutional government—has a twofold aspect. To the bourgeois this failure presents itself primarily as the inability of regular government to curb the workers and hold them down to their tasks. That this government has during the past several decades been unable to cope with the grave problems pressing for solution in every sphere of social interest—economics, law and justice, education, international relations—he hardly notices. But when the regularly constituted authorities hesitate to suppress rebellious workers with sufficient promptness and ruthlessness, then the bourgeoisie—and particularly its upper, plutocratic layer—calls in the "strong man" to reëstablish the disturbed social equilibrium. There ensues a personal dictatorship, which is but the concentrated expression of the dictatorship of capital. The liberal State reverts to the police-State. The petty bourgeois and the bulk of the intellectuals invariably accept the decision of the leading stratum. To the worker, on the other hand, the failure of democracy means that he cannot realize his modest aim—a decent, secure human existence—under the established social order; he is therefore impelled to seek to overthrow it and to establish his own order, which is based, not on property, but on labor. This entails a more or less violent, more or less protracted period of revolutionary transition, depending, on the one hand, upon the strength of the workers' organization, their resoluteness, their intelligence, and the skill and insight of their leaders; on the other hand, upon the strength of capitalist resistance encountered, nationally and internationally. The immediate aim of the proletariat is to overthrow the dictatorship of the bourgeoisie and to establish its own class dictatorship, which may or may not assume temporarily the form of a personal dictatorship, or even of a mere personal ascendancy (due to exceptional genius for leadership) that is regarded by the uninitiated as a dictatorship. In either case, the essential aims of the revolution would not be affected thereby. The personal dictatorship of the first Napoleon did not defeat, but on the contrary secured, the essential aims of the French Revolution, so that even the Bourbon Restoration produced no more than a surface ripple. But it must be obvious that a personal dictatorship in the service of a revolutionary class requires a quite exceptional degree of ability on the part of the dictator, for his task is the creation of new forms of work and life, not the conservation of existing ones.

Such, then, is the prospect before us here in America: a declining standard of living for practically all classes of the population; chronic mass unemployment; the spread of discontent to practically all classes, but particularly to the wage-laborers and poor farmers; widespread demand for governmental relief, which government has neither the means nor the will to grant (what means the government has are absorbed by the debt service, the army and navy, etc., and in time of extraordinary distress by the banks, railroads, and other corporations on the verge of bankruptcy); the rise of impotent and treacherous Labor parties; and ultimately, the choice between the brute force of conservatism turning into reaction, and that of revolution.

VI

At the present time it is altogether impossible to predict the form that the final fight between reaction and revolution in America will assume; nor need we at present speculate upon it. Even the occasion that will precipitate it cannot be guessed at.

It will certainly not be a trivial occasion; great masses of people do not lightly break with the past; a powerful impulse is needed to shake them out of their everyday routine, to inspire them with a death-defying idea. Conditions must have become practically unendurable for large sections of the population, and must have continued for a considerable length of time, in order that the social atmosphere might become generally charged with revolutionary electricity; and even then a powerful impulse is needed to release the charge and convert it into an active force of destruction and construction. We know that in Russia a revolutionary atmosphere prevailed during several decades, even generations; Marx's prophetic foresight would have convinced us of this, even if we did not know the facts. Yet it required no less a force than the Great War, with its accompaniments of gross governmental incompetence, treasonable actions, a succession of defeats, economic disorganization and lack of bread, to release the revolutionary energy of the nation. In Germany, notwithstanding military defeat, economic disorganization, State bankruptcy, widespread suffering, and general conditions infinitely more favorable for a communist revolution than in Tsarist Russia (because of the immensely superior economic and general cultural development), there has nevertheless been no such revolution, largely because of the absence of a revolutionary tradition, and of a revolutionary mood that involves even the ruling classes. Present and prospective conditions in the United States are bound to create a general discontent, and a feeling of uneasiness even among the capitalists; but between that and a revolutionary atmosphere in which all classes are immersed, there is a long, long step. On the other hand, it is quite possible that we may need no Great War, nor any powerful impulse comparable to it, to shake America out of her immobility. We must never forget that the mere existence of the Soviet Union and her continued progress in well-being and prosperity, constitutes of itself a powerful lever of revolution throughout the world. The peoples of Russia are rendering a vicarious service to all mankind, just as in its day the great French Revolution made their work easier for bourgeois reformers and revolutionaries throughout Europe.

There is another factor forcing us to the conclusion that in the United States the communist revolution—whatever its form —is as yet only a distant prospect, namely, the all but complete absence of the necessary intellectual preparation. A thoroughgoing social revolution must be preceded by an intellectual revolution equally thoroughgoing, breaking with the ideas of the past and creating a new set of ideas in their place; there must be wide acceptance of a new conception of human life, a new *Weltanschauung*. It is well known that in eighteenth-century France the bourgeois intellectual revolution penetrated into the *salons* of the aristocrats. It is not so generally known that the intellectual revolution initiated by Marx and carried on more or less effectually by Marxists of every shade—from the most timid Mensheviks to the boldest Bolsheviks—had penetrated into every nook and cranny, as it were, of the Tsarist empire. Russian was the first language into which "Das Kapital" was translated. Russian economists, sociologists, historians, publicists of every party, even the more intelligent government officials, were more or less familiar with Marxian theories, and accepted or rejected them. Wide-awake working-men had listened to lectures on Marxian sociology and economics, which often had to be given in secret hiding places to small circles, even in the depths of the forests. Revolutionary literature circulated everywhere "underground." In Germany, and more or less in every country throughout Europe, the ideas of Marxism are undermining the existing social order. It is unnecessary to say that such is not yet the case in America. Here all this work of intellectual preparation is yet to be done. Here even non-Marxian radicalism—the habit of a critical evaluation of existing institutions—can hardly be said as yet to have gained a foothold among broad strata of the population; one only has to consider that the *New Republic* and the *Nation,* until recently the only journals of this type in the country, have a comparatively small circulation in this vast nation, though their influence, to be sure, may exceed their circulation. Not only the average citizen, even the intellectuals have yet to acquire the habit of critical thought; the vogue of religion and church among our men of science, even the foremost, bears undeniable testimony to this state of affairs. Anti-evolution laws are the appropriate reward of this scientific timidity.

The immediate prospect is by no means exhilarating. Confident as we may be of the ultimate outcome, a realistic appraisal of existing conditions and of such as may in all probability be expected to develop in the immediate future, compels us to take a sober view of near-term revolutionary possibilities. To be sure, there may be surprises in store for us. A triumphant proletarian revolution in Germany, which in all likelihood would bring on an explosion in Poland and Central Europe generally, might have powerful repercussions on this Continent. But we cannot calculate with these uncertain potentialities. We can only proceed from the certain present and the probable immediate future. Assuming that the course of events will be, in a general way, as outlined above, how may we expect the active, forward-looking elements of the population to react to them?

Naturally, this question concerns only those who are not affiliated with the Communist party. The members of that party never entertain any doubt as to their course of action. Their work is laid out for them. They are the nucleus of active militants. They obey the word of command, without asking questions. This perfect discipline is admirable, even indispensable, in time of revolution. It is because of this discipline that the party has been able, in spite of its small numbers, to play so conspicuous a part ever since the crisis broke upon us. While the acknowledged leaders of organized labor, loath to break away from their subserviency to capital, have fed their following on empty words, the communists have led the unemployed demonstrations, have borne the brunt of police brutality, and here and there have even succeeded in forcing municipal governments to hand out doles to the hungry. But excellent as this discipline is in time of action, its utility in dull times, in an era of social stagnation, like the one from which we are only now beginning to emerge, is in some respects open to question. It certainly does not tend to encourage the active exercise of the intelligence, and critical intelligence is precisely what we most stand in need of at the present juncture. But in any case, the question we are now considering is not the attitude of the convinced and organized enemies of the existing order, but the probable reaction of the more advanced elements of the various classes to present any prospective developments.

VII

The great class of manual wage-workers presents the least difficulty in answering this question. They are the essential product of capitalism, its creation and inevitable accompaniment. Capital can exist without wage-workers no more than a monarch without subjects. It multiplies their numbers, brings them together in large masses, forces them to resistance even while it facilitates their organization. The opposition of labor to capital is natural and inevitable. It is latent even when it subsides into inactivity. Ignorant and corrupt leaders may imagine themselves to have entered into a permanent partnership with capital, but times like the present soon dispel such vain imaginings. Labor unionism, which has sunk so low during the era of prosperity, is sure to be revived and reinvigorated. The petty craft unions, with their parochial spirit, will be displaced by unions embracing entire industries, and these again will federate among themselves. More and more the workers will come to understand that every question which touches their entire class, or large sections of it, is a political question, and can be dealt with effectively only through an organization embracing their entire class, namely, a political party. They will come to understand that foreign policy—the question of peace and war—is as much their concern as domestic policy. They will fight policies that lead to war—imperialism in every shape—with all the power at their disposal. They will sternly insist on a policy of friendship and coöperation with the Soviet Union, the only Workers' State now in existence, the only State that stands for peace and universal disarmament. To the disastrous policies of capital, at home and abroad, labor will surely oppose a decisive answer, however long delayed that answer may be in coming. Whatever else we may doubt, this we cannot doubt. It is dictated by the inner logic of events.

The question is not so easily answered for the farmers, who do not constitute one homogeneous class, as do the manual wage-workers notwithstanding the diversity of their earnings. There are large capitalist farmers (only recently has it become generally known that insurance companies own vast numbers of farms), well-to-do middle-class farmers who regularly employ wage-laborers, and poor farmers who have hardly more security in life than wage-workers, work as hard or even harder (for there is no union and no law to limit the length of their working-day), and whose standard of living is no higher, or even lower. The farmers as a whole cannot possibly be persuaded to join the industrial workers in a revolutionary transformation of society, though individual intelligent farmers can certainly

be won over, just as individuals from other classes who are
able to rise above their narrow class interests. But the vast
mass of poor farmers, tenants, share-croppers, etc., many of
whom do not own the land they till or other means of production, and even when they do own them in whole or in part,
do so under a precarious tenure, subject to a mortgage payments on which must be promptly met—these farmers are the
natural allies of the city workers. The small farmer used to be
a business man and land speculator on a small scale; he is that
no longer. His income is steadily declining, likewise the cash
value of his holding. Sooner or later the poor small farmer is
bound to come to the conclusion that the day of the small
farm is past and gone, that he cannot possibly compete with
the large capitalistic farms, which are cultivated with power-
driven machines—are in fact industrialized plants—employ expert specialists, and can turn out wheat or any other crop that
enters the world-market at much lower cost and at correspondingly lower prices. If present tendencies are allowed to continue, the poor American farmer is bound to sink to the level
of the European peasant. The only salvation for the poor
farmer is large-scale socialized farming, conducted according
to plan under a Workers' State. That the revolutionary workers need the farmers as allies in their common struggle against
capitalism, was recognized by socialists long ago, even as far
back as 1848 and earlier; but the genius of Lenin and the
experiences of the Russian Revolution have made the alliance
of the workers and poor farmers into an axiom of revolutionary
strategy.

The brain workers of every description—intellectuals, as they
are now commonly called—present a complex problem. The
intellectuals do not constitute a distinct social class. Throughout history they have been the servants and organs of other
classes, usually of the ruling classes; for excepting the medieval
priesthood in Europe, they have had no material interests of
their own to champion. Under capitalism the number, as well
as the importance, of the intellectuals has greatly increased,
and their functions have been greatly diversified. Vast numbers of them are in the service of the government, or of corporations engaged in agriculture, industry, mining, transportation, banking, etc., while others, like doctors, lawyers, etc., are
still working largely on their own account. Their incomes and
mode of living show a maximum of variation, from capitalist

to near-proletarian. Their attitude to the workers' revolutionary movement shows a corresponding degree of variation. Superficially it might be assumed that, being accustomed to exercise their mental faculties, the vast majority of them would rise above the vulgar prejudices of the bourgeois, who know neither the past history of mankind nor can they imagine a future that knows no exploitation, no poverty, no chaos. But in actual fact, most intellectual workers are familiar only with the more or less narrow specialty in which they are engaged, and after their day's work have neither the strength nor the elasticity of mind to become deeply engaged in the study of social and political problems. As a result, their social and political views are usually colored by their environment and associations. There are, of course, numerous exceptions. There are technologists who are disgusted with the fact that their knowledge and skill serve no other purpose than the multiplication of their employers' profits. There are lawyers who revolt against the injustices of the law, doctors who are aware of how noble their profession might be if they didn't have to work for money, teachers who resent the inadequacy of existing educational methods and facilities, writers who long for freedom of thought. But on the whole, the intellectuals are not in revolt against the existing state of things. They are now serving capitalism; when the revolution is victorious, they will serve socialism.

Of late, there has arisen among American literary men a strong trend toward Marxism; strong, that is to say, by comparison with the total absence of such a trend in the recent past, for of the few pre-War Marxists in the Socialist party, some were reduced to silence by the socialist leaders, while others welcomed the opportunity which the War gave them to correct the errors of their youth, break completely with their past, and go over bag and baggage to the enemy. The new and still very young group of Marxists have before them the glorious task and opportunity of bringing about the intellectual revolution of which America stands in such need, and without which no social and political revolution is even thinkable.

VIII

Technology—control over the forces of nature in the service of production—determines economic relations; these in turn determine politics and law, literature and art, religion and philosophy. But "the tradition of all dead generations weighs like a nightmare on the brain of the living," and retards the adaptation of economy to technology, of institutions and ideas to economy. Man's own handiwork stands in the way of his further advance. The burghers of medieval towns looked upon the residents of the nearest town as foreigners; they were parish patriots. But as the burghers evolved into capitalists, they created the nation—the highest political achievement of bourgeois society. Nowadays industry and the market transcend the borders of the nation; their ramifications are world-wide. Hence arose colonialism and imperialism, breeders of endless war. But war, too, has been transformed by industry into a universal destroying force. Europe is bleeding from the strife of nations and imperialist ambitions. War menaces her civilization, her rich heritage of culture, her very existence. Her salvation lies in a union of her nations and States, which would do away with wars and the causes of wars, abolish customs barriers, create a rational division of labor among her people, and give her peace, security, and a great area for the free exchange of the products of her industry. But the intense, narrow passions of an anachronistic nationalism, derived from and fostered by the entrenched private interests of capitalists, large and small, stand in the way of such a consummation. A United States of Europe can come into existence only through a victorious revolution of the proletariat.

The United States of America has had from the very beginning of her existence this incalculable advantage over Europe: peace and free trade within her vast area. Hence her rapid progress and great prosperity. But the Great War has shown that America is now involved in the fate of Europe, of the entire globe. The economic crisis confirms this interconnection of the Continents. The wars, revolutions, crises of distant nations affect us profoundly. German reparation payments to England and France concern us. Japan's aggressions in China and Manchuria are our affair. We cannot oppose, nor can we pretend to ignore, the great Russian Revolution without paying for it heavily in loss of trade and increased unemployment, as well as in an access of power to the conservative and reactionary elements among our own people. We cannot stand out against a world. We cannot cut loose from Europe. Russia is in the van, but Europe, the whole earth is in motion. We must follow, even if we do not lead. The old order is dying. It cannot be saved in America. No Hoover, no Mussolini, no Hitler can save it, not even a temporary restoration of Hohenzollern or Wittelsbach. Of the ultimate outcome there is not the least doubt. But in the great war for human freedom and happiness there are bound to be defeats and retreats as well as victories and advances. Much depends on the attitude of the American proletariat. Its weight thrown on the side of the revolution would be tremendous. The American proletariat has not yet declared itself. It was deluded by prosperity, it is now stunned by adversity. Sooner or later it will declare itself, range itself with the communistic workers of Europe. The day of that declaration will be the last day of the reign of capital on this goodly earth.

NOTES TO WHITHER THESE STATES

1. At the annual convention of the German National Industrial Association at Dresden, Sept. 4, 1926, Paul Silverberg, director general of the Rhenish Brown Coal Syndicate, the principal speaker, declared that "credit must be given to the German Social Democracy and its leader, Friedrich Ebert, the first President of the German Republic, for having curbed the wave of revolution after the war in time to save the Fatherland from complete destruction. Amid the cheers of this big gathering of diehard industrialists, Herr Silverberg declared that the Socialist party, representing as it does the overwhelming bulk of German labor, could not be left out of the government of the German nation."—*New York Times,* Sept. 5, 1926.

In the *New Republic,* Nov. 30, 1932, appeared an article by R. R. Kuczynski, of Berlin, Germany, in which he quoted at considerable length "from two letters recently sent through a service sponsored by the National Association of Manufacturers to a selected number of captains of industry." These quotations reveal a completely elaborated theory and policy for maintaining capitalist power in Germany with the aid of the social Democracy. The capitalists are aware that they "have become too small a class to maintain their dominating power without assistance." To trust to military force alone they regard as "a most dangerous procedure." They must therefore "ally themselves with classes belonging to a different social level." During the first period of post-war consolidation, the Social Democrats, "thanks to their social character as an original workers' party . . . chained organized labor to the bourgeois State machinery and by doing so paralyzed the revolutionary energy of the rank and file. . . . Ever since the end of the World War, the one condition on which hinges the social reconsolidation of bourgeois supremacy in Germany is the splitting of the proletariat. Any firmly aligned labor movement born out of the masses is bound to be revolutionary, and against such a movement a bourgeois government cannot be maintained in the long run, even with the help of military force." During the first post-war period of reconsolidating the bourgeois regime (1923-30), the tide of revolutionary energy was stopped by increasing the wages and standard of living of the organized and skilled workers, thus separating them from the unemployed and the fluctuating masses of the unskilled. This economic separation corresponds to the political division into

Social Democrats and Communists. "The possibility of a Liberal (non-Fascist) social constitution of trust capitalism depends on the existence of an automatic dividing mechanism among the workers. A bourgeois regime interested in a Liberal social constitution must not only be parliamentary, it must have the support of the Social Democratic party, and it must leave that party a sufficient number of the improvements they have gained for the workers."

It would therefore appear that in the appointment of Papen, Schleicher, and Hitler to the Chancellorship, the Fascist wing of the German capitalists gained a victory over the Liberal wing. In passing, it may be noted that American capitalists have been following the policy prescribed by their Liberal German *confreres* in their attitude toward certain favored groups of workers, for instance, the Railway Brotherhoods.

2. In his remarkable book, "The Coming Struggle for Power," John Strachey says that in England the "national planners" are the monopolistic capitalists who would be greatly aided by the "national plan" in absorbing the smaller independent capitalists. As regards the proposal in general, Mr. Strachey rightly says that "a non-competitive organized capitalism is a contradiction in terms." The only "regulator" of capitalism is competition, the market, that is, a succession of slumps and booms. Do away with the regulator, and you do away with capitalism.

3. More than that, according to Miss Frances Perkins, industrial commissioner of New York State. For the two months Dec. 1932-Jan. 1933, the index of factory payrolls was down to 40 per cent, or two-fifths, of the 1925-27 figure, and 26.7 per cent less than in the preceding year. Employment, too, was still falling. For January the index of State factory employment was 14.8 below that of the preceding year.—*New York Times*, Feb. 11, 1933. It will be noticed that total wages were falling nearly twice as fast as employment, due to wage reductions and part-time employment.

V. F. CALVERTON

AMERICA'S REVOLUTIONARY
HISTORY

IN the nineteenth century, when America was in its great expanding stage, and the country stretched its arms out from ocean to ocean like a vast colossus, promising territory and protection to nameless millions, optimism was abroad in the land. The frontier lent life the thrill of a melodrama, which captured the minds of the masses in Europe as well as America. Industry and invention colored the movement of the country as a whole, transforming intractable forests into arable farm-lands, changing trading forts and scattered settlements into populous cities, lacing them together by a network of tracks and canals, and converting the nation itself into a dynamic organism in which everyone felt himself a part of its pulsation.

Such was America during the first two thirds of the nine-teenth century—a nation created by small men, men without social station or distinction, men without means but with pluck and courage and determination, men who were individualistic-minded, democratic-spirited, and patriotic to the core. That America was animate with aspiration, impregnated with a be-lief in itself and its future. When Mrs. Trollope traveled through the America of that day she was constantly annoyed by the bombardment of patriotism which greeted her on every side, in villages, towns, and cities, as also was de Tocqueville who found the Americans the most obstreperous chauvinists he had ever encountered. That patriotism, born on the rising tide of expansion of that day, penetrated throughout the length and breadth of our life. It was shared by the politicians, the literati, the well-to-do, and the populace on the street. It was in American history, symbolized in the work of Bancroft, that that spirit became most unrestrained and vociferous. In the eyes of Bancroft, for example, everything American was sacred; everything this country ever attempted was right; from the founders of the country to the leaders of that day no blemish was to be noted, so noble had been their intentions and so fruitfully had they been fulfilled. Like the cherry tree Washington of Weems' biography, the country and its leaders were sheathed in a mist of fabled rectitude and virtue.

As long as the country remained in its expanding stage, that tendency of interpretation continued to dominate the spirit of American history. When the twentieth century arrived, however, and the days of expansion were over, and the small man found himself being beaten over the head by the big man in the field of business as well as agriculture, that tendency ceased. Since that time the halo which once enshrouded American institutions and leaders has disappeared. Beginning with the era of the muckrakers things American have been made to look exceedingly sick and shoddy. With the advance of liberal scholarship, an outgrowth of the muckraking decade and of the spirit of despair which had come upon the land with the defeat of the small man on the economic field, the American scene was subjected to a new interpretation. Exposing as it did the monetary machinations behind many of our most lauded achievements, the liberal tradition encouraged the tendency to scoff and sneer at American traditions. It was out of that tendency that the "debunkers" of American history sprang. The achievements of the Revolutionary War were debunked; the importance of the Civil War was debunked; the pertinence and place of various individuals in the historical process were debunked—in fact, everything was debunked with an indiscriminate enthusiasm which betrayed the lack of historical insight involved in the whole approach. Instead of seeing the development of America as part of its progressive advance as a historic whole, and evaluating its phenomena and its leaders in relationship with that development, the debunkers adjudge everything and everybody in reference to the immediate criteria of today, stressing with a narrow-mindedness culpably characteristic of defeatist historians the corruption involved in the *means* but neglecting entirely the significance involved in the *ends.* It is easy to attack the motivations behind many of the

leaders in the Revolutionary War or the Civil War or the
Reconstruction period, but it is a much more difficult and
valuable task to determine the significance of those events in
relationship to the historic advance of the country as a unit.

The great problem confronting and challenging us to-day,
therefore, is not that of debunking our past but of revaluating
it in terms of our revolutionary tradition. In a word, we must
learn not to scoff at our revolutionary past but to build upon
it.

What we must see is that in every phase of our development
there have been progressive as well as reactionary forces at
work, and if the progressive forces of one day lose their pro-
gressiveness in the next that is no reason why we should disregard the important influence which they exerted at the time
they were progressive. What we must do is to evaluate every
period in terms of the forces active at the time, differentiating
those that were progressive from those that were retrogressive,
showing in just what ways those that were progressive tended
to shape those developments in our society which are important
to understanding its character to-day and its possibilities of
change to-morrow.

By employing that approach, it can be seen at once that
things American must be adjudged by different standards than
things European, since American social and economic conditions have been so different from those present in Europe.
American history is usually misjudged because of the neglect
of that difference. In discussing the theme of this article, for
example, it can be said at once that if we mean by a revolution
what the French Revolution of 1789 signifies or the Bolshevik
Revolution of 1917, then America has had no revolutionary
history at all. What is necessary to stress at this point, in keeping with our previous observations, is that America has evolved
differently from European countries, creating a different cultural pattern in the process, and developing a different series
of social struggles with different revolutionary implications.
It is those differences which must be understood first if there
is to be any appreciation of the significance and challenge of
our revolutionary history.

In Europe the great social struggles of the seventeenth, and
early nineteenth centuries were those fought between the
landed aristocracies and the commercial and industrial bourgeoisie. In America those struggles took on an entirely different

character. The earliest approach to a landed aristocracy that America ever had was in the patroon system and the vast landed estates which had been dealt out by English kings as special grants to various individuals who stood high in royal favor. But that landed aristocracy, largely Tory in extraction, which, due to the rapid rise in power of the merchant class, had never been able to function effectively, disappeared with the close of the Revolutionary War. Its representatives or defendants, Tories in the main, were driven out by force by the bourgeoisie who were the patriots of the period. The Revolutionary War, then, was a progressive war in that it dealt the first death-blow to American feudalism. After the Revolutionary War, the only remnant of feudalism which persisted was the presence of the plantation aristocracy in the South. The struggle between the North and the South which raged during the first half of the nineteenth century, reaching its climax in the Civil War, marked the last conflict between the landed aristocracy and the bourgeoisie in the nation. The Civil War meted out the final death blow to feudal institutions in this country. After the Civil War, the class struggle in America changed character and became a conflict between the upper bourgeoisie and the petty bourgeoisie, big business and small business, with the growing proletariat of the time allying itself politically with the cause of the latter. The landed class disappeared as a separate social force and became absorbed into the maw of the commercial and industrial structure. Big business in the form of the banks, the loan associations, and the railroads, sunk its tentacles into the land, mortgaging it beyond redemption. The small farmer and the small business man found themselves face to face with the same foe, big business in the guise of the financier and the industrialist. The struggle between those two forces absorbed the *revolutionary* energy of the American people throughout the nineteenth century and in decreasing degree continues to do so even to-day.

Now the very fact that the struggle against feudalism in America assumed in the Civil War the form of a sectional conflict instead of a national conflict of classes, thwarted the development of a revolutionary ideology on the part of the bourgeois forces which were bent upon the destruction of the feudal way of life. In all European countries, for example, the battle which the bourgeoisie carried on against feudalism led to the creation of a revolutionary ideology which found dynamic expression in economics, politics, religion, and ethics. Freedom of speech, press, religion, became the great rallying cries of the revolutionary bourgeoisie. The struggle for the right to economic freedom, that is freedom for the middle class from the restrictions of the aristocracy, and the struggle for the right to political representation, lent the cause of the European bourgeoisie a fierce fighting character which found its summation in the liberal idealism of the eighteenth and nineteenth centuries. The fact that that conflict followed sectional instead of national class lines in this country robbed us of that heritage of progressive liberal idealism, and twisted and distorted our whole political outlook in such ways that class interests became blurred by sectional prejudices, with antagonistic classes resolving their conflicts with each other (which under different conditions would have led them to open strife) into a mutual alliance against their accepted sectional foe. Even to-day the South provides a clear-cut example of the confusing consequences of that alliance. Active as various aspects of the class struggle are in the South to-day, the South as a whole, proletarians as well as sharecroppers, poor whites as well as successful bourgeoisie, stand politically as one in their uncompromising support of the Democratic party. (Only the religious issue in the election of 1928 could in any way shake the strength and solidity of that union.) In short, their sectional hostility to the North, derivative from the struggle between the two sections in the Civil War, is still greater than their class hostility to each other. This sectional fact has definitely held back the development of a nation-wide revolutionary outlook along class lines in this country.

Paradoxically enough, because of the factors we have stressed, liberalism in America has been forced to play an economically retrogressive instead of progressive rôle. The progressive liberal tradition developed by the bourgeoisie in England, for example, sprang out of its fight against the aristocracy and the need for destroying the feudal way of life. The so-called liberal tradition in America, on the other hand, developed as a definite defense against the advancing bourgeois way of life. Its energies were wasted, however, in a futile attempt to hold back the progressive development of capitalist enterprise. Beginning with Jefferson, it favored agrarianism as opposed to industrialism and fought the introduction of manufactures into American life; it advocated decentralization instead of centralization of

government and enterprise, with the result that it defended
competition as the basis of progress and attacked all forms of
corporate organization and control. It gave its energies to re-
tarding the progressive rôle that big business, by the very nature
of its objectives, was scheduled to perform, namely, to eliminate competition within the respective industries by the organization of corporations, trusts, and monopolies to take the
place of the myriad-fold competing enterprises and proprietors.[1]

In brief, American liberalism from the very start was reactionary in that it defended competition instead of opposing it,
thereby helping to hold back the progressive advance of our
economic life. Sentimentally, to be sure, it stood up for the
cause of the individual, defending his rights against big business
and the centralized state; politically it was progressive in its
fight for the right of franchise; realistically, however, it fought
to preserve a way of life which from the very beginning
of the nineteenth century had begun to become retrogressive. It defended the interests of the small farmer and the
small business man against those of the large capitalist and
financier, although it was the large capitalist and financier, the
Rockefellers, the Carnegies, and the Morgans, who were to make
possible the reorganization of our economic life in such ways
as to prepare the ground work for a more coöperative world
wherein competition would not exist and individualism would
disappear. It was in this sense that American liberalism was
retrogressive instead of progressive in its outlook. It was as
capitalistic in its logic as big business, save that it wanted capitalism to proceed on a small scale instead of on a vast, concentrated one. It wanted a world which was filled with predatory
wolves and foxes but in which there were no all-powerful lions.
What it did not see was that it was the lions, though at the
cost of life of the smaller animals, who brought order out of

[1] It is important here to observe that while big business tended to engulf the small
proprietor, and thus destroy competition within the individual industry, it did not
tend of itself to destroy competition between the large industries, corporations, or
trusts. Nor did it tend to destroy competition on the international field; in fact, in
many ways it tended to accentuate it there. John D. Rockefeller, for instance, practically eliminated all competition from the oil field in this country, but that did not
mean that he eliminated competition on the international field. On the contrary,
it made international competition, as between Standard Oil and Royal Dutch Shell,
a matter of much graver import, with warlike implications writ large in its structure.

chaos, lifting the world in which they lived from a lower to a potentially higher stage of existence.

Indeed, we can say at this point that the whole development of revolutionary thought in this country has been impeded and distorted by the retrogressive character of American liberalism. In the early conflict between Jefferson and Hamilton, for instance, it was the conservative Hamilton who was right in his emphasis upon the importance of encouraging industries and in his advocacy of a sound national finance, while it was the liberal Jefferson who was wrong in his hostility to industries and in his opposition to every form of national control. A century later, American liberalism was guilty of the same fallacy. Bryan had not advanced a step beyond Jefferson in his economic philosophy, except that he did not attack the development of industries,—industries having grown by that time to so large a stature that the only thing possible to attack were their tendencies toward expansion.

In fact the whole history of American liberalism stretching from Jefferson to Bryan, and then down to Wilson and Lafollette, did nothing more than comprise new and ever more pathetic testimonies of the futile, regressive character of the liberal cause. Industrialism having planted itself ineradicably in our soil, Jefferson's stand on the question could no longer be defended. But the attempt of the later liberals to restrain the development of industry was essentially no less reactionary an influence. Woodrow Wilson's platitudes about the "new freedom" were no more sound or progressive than Theodore Roosevelt's promises to fight the trusts, or Lafollette's proposals that we return to the days of 1776. Franklin D. Roosevelt's pleas in favor of the "forgotten man" retain the same retrogressive echo. Without exception then American liberalism has continued throughout our history to play a fundamentally unprogressive rôle.

It is only by appreciating that most significant fact that we can understand the peculiar character of America's revolutionary history.

But it is necessary for us here to analyze those forces in the life of this country which made liberalism function as such a retrogressive force. In the first place it must be realized that America during the overwhelmingly greater part of its history has been an agricultural country. Indeed, it was not until the close of the nineteenth century, when America went on the

gold standard, that the nation became predominantly industrial. But the agrarian fact in America was more than a quantitative reality. The American farmer, as Brackenridge described him and as his history affirms, was extremely unlike
the European peasant. If in the East for a time, because of the
indenture system, he was forced to accept certain of the limitations of the old order of static economic relationships, circum-
scribing his opportunities as an individual agent, he swiftly
freed himself of those restrictions once he migrated to the
West where the frontier conditions that prevailed were totally
unwedded to the past. There in that West as farmer, towns-
man, or city-founder, he worked out a philosophy of life which
was born of the individualistic independence of the environment. It was a philosophy which was overwhelmingly agrarian
in character, because it was the farmer's interest which gave it
substance. When we remember that as late as 1840 the United
States Census figures recorded 25% of the population as landowners, we can more easily realize why that philosophy became
so deep-rooted a part of our cultural life. Since the soil was
there to be exploited, and since it promised him livelihood
as an individual, he was inclined at the least instigation to
assert his independence of the organized state whenever or
wherever it tended to impinge upon what he considered his
natural rights and privileges. It was that fact which bred in
him what has been characteristically known as the American
spirit of independence. The European peasant, derived from
a different economic and cultural milieu, possessed no such
spirit. He was too enslaved both by the cultural incubus of the
past and the physical limitations of his environment. In consequence of that contrast, the European peasant, save in the
early peasant wars, has seldom tended to initiate revolts on his
own part but in general has been preceded in that rôle by the
workers, while the American farmer, on the other hand, has
tended, in the past at least, to take the lead in revolts and
rebellions against the status quo.

It was this very independence of the American farmer, and
the fact that for the larger part of the nineteenth century he
constituted the major part of the populace, that made American
radicalism take on an agrarian cast. It was into the field of
agrarian radicalism that the revolutionary energies of the
American people were poured in unstinting stream throughout
most of the nineteenth century. While in Europe, as I indi-

RECOVERY THROUGH REVOLUTION

cated above, it was the workers who took the lead in radical protest with the peasantry relegated to the background, in this country it was the farmers who became the leaders with the workers reduced to second rank in the intransigeant process. In fact, for a considerable period, workers' movements became nothing more than the tail-kite of frontier movements. Such a development was inevitable in America of the nineteenth century, for the individualistic ideology of the frontier swept over the country, influencing the whole political and cultural life of the nation. More than that, it was precisely this dominance of agrarian radicalism that prevented proletarian radicalism from becoming a dynamic, growing force in the life of the nation.

The farmer, fortified by the obvious virtues of the environment, and the advantage of isolation from the power of the national state, became a fighter from the start. Beginning with Bacon's rebellion against Governor Berkeley, the farmers never hesitated to battle for their rights or to carry their fight against the state if necessary. The environment, which made them expert at the handling of arms and equipped them with a knowledge of the country which made it possible for them to give strong battle to adversaries, whether Indians or State troopers, endowed them with an independence of outlook that never failed to flare up whenever occasion demanded. From the time of Bacon's memorable rebellion down to the recent Sioux City riots, the farmer, haloed as "the embattled hero" in our poetry, has continued to represent the spirit of recalcitrance in our political and economic life. Since the beginning of the twentieth century, however, or more precisely since the failure of the Granger and Populist movements toward the end of the nineteenth century which signified the definite decline of his power, his recalcitrance has lost much of its old intensity. The Non-Partisan League gave a last flare-up to his protest, but even that, despite its progressive influence in such a state as North Dakota, died out before its flame could be felt over the country as a whole.

But the fact that the influence of the farmer has lost its vigor to-day should not lead us to underestimate the significance of his rôle in America in the past.[1] It was because the farmer in

[1] It should be noted, however, that even today, despite the loss of his old influence and his waning power as a class, it is the farmer who is more active in protest and revolt than the worker.

the eighteenth and nineteenth centuries was more resistant to the state than the worker, that the latter tended to adopt the petty bourgeois ideology of agrarianism. The radical agrarians at that time had both the advantages of environment and numbers. In Shay's Rebellion it was the farmers who were foremost; in the Whisky Insurrection, it was the farmers again who led in the combat; in electing Jackson and breaking down the dictatorship of the Atlantic Seaboard, it was the farmers once more who supplied the decisive force. It was only after the Civil War, when the North started to industrialize rapidly and industry proceeded to spread out over the country as a whole, that the workers began to play a more aggressive rôle in the development of American life. But even then, the political ideology that the workers adopted, and which constituted the essence of their political demands, was in large part a product of, and to a considerable extent identical with, the radicalism of the agrarians. Even to-day despite the enormous changes which have been consummated in our economic life that influence has not disappeared.

Before dealing further with the ideology of agrarianism, however, I should like to devote a few paragraphs to showing its spirit in action. Almost any of the agrarian rebellions would suffice in this connection, but the one which, in my opinion, represents it better than any other is the Whisky Rebellion of 1791. In 1791 Congress passed an excise law, laying a special tax on all spirits distilled from grain. Since most of the farmers in the north-western regions made the better part of their livelihood from the manufacture of such spirits, they were naturally opposed to the government's interfering with the profits which they derived from such traffic. When government agents tried to collect the taxes, the farmers attacked them, drove them out of the territory on rails, sacked the houses in which they lived, and made it desperately clear that if any further interference were set up by the State they were prepared to fight it to the last degree. Most historians, including Charles Beard, have failed to stress the significance of the Whisky Rebellion at the time. When the farmers said they would fight the State they meant it.

But rather than describe what happened in my own words, I shall quote a few descriptions of the Rebellion from the words of Hugh Henry Brackenridge who lived through it and participated in it in a suspiciously dubious way from the very

beginning. Here we are face to face with the rebellious spirit
of the American farmers in active form:

> "I am decisive in opinion that the United States
> cannot effect the operation of the law (the excise law)
> in this country. It is universally odious in the neigh-
> boring parts of all the neighboring states, and the
> militia under the law, in the hands of the President
> cannot be called out to reduce an opposition. The
> midland counties, I am persuaded, will not even suffer
> the militia of more distant parts of the union, to pass
> through them. . . .
>
> "Should an attempt be made to suppress these
> people, I am afraid the question will not be whether
> you (The Government) will march to Pittsburgh, but
> whether they will march to Philadelphia (then the
> capital of the country), accumulating in their course,
> and swelling over the banks of the Susquehanna like
> a torrent, irresistible, and devouring in its progress.
> There can be no equality between the rage of a forest,
> and the abundance, indolence, and opulence of a city."

In another place, Brackenridge described the spirit of the
people in these words:

> "I saw before me the anarchy of the period; a shock
> to the government; and possibly a revolution—a revo-
> lution impregnated with the Jacobin principles of
> France, and which might become equally bloody to
> the principal actors."

In still other sections of *Incidents of the Western Insurrection*, which was his account of what happened during the
Whisky Rebellion, Brackenridge describes in exciting detail
the warlike spirit which dwelt among the farmers in the western territories. In twenty-three townships, there was "what
amounted to a declaration of war." When the national government threatened to send an army to quell the insurgents, the
Pittsburgh Gazette replied:

> "Brothers, you must not think to frighten us with
> fine arranged lists of infantry, cavalry, and artillery,
> composed of your watermelon armies from the Jersey
> shore; they could cut a much better figure, in warring

with the crabs and oysters about the capes of Dela-
ware."

These were the words of men who were willing to fight for
their rights and knew how to fight for them when occasion
demanded. That the rebellion was finally defeated by a national
expedition in which Alexander Hamilton participated is of
less importance than the fact that even that national expedition
might have been unsuccessful if it had not been for the treachery of certain of the leaders of the insurgents, in particular
Brackenridge himself.

The spirit displayed by the farmers in the Whisky Rebellion
was not singular. The same spirit had been manifest before in
Bacon's Rebellion, and was to repeat itself in other revolts on
the part of the agrarians.

I described the character of the Whisky Insurrection in such
detail because it illustrates so well the spirit of the American
farmer in rebellious mood. It was the nature of the country
which created this farmer and inspired his rebelliousness. At
the same time it was the nature of the country which shaped
the interests of that same farmer and determined the direction
of his rebellion.

What were the interests of the American farmer?

The American farmer was anti-Wall Street, if you will, but
pro-Main Street. He was opposed to the East because it represented commercial and financial oppression, operating through
the political agency of the national government which taxed
him, and, as time progressed, through the tangible economic
agencies of the railroads and the banks which exploited him.
In short, he was capitalistic-minded in the small sense instead
of the large. He wished to protect, as an individual capitalist,
his own interests against those of industry and finance which
represented large capitalism. A pygmy in the capitalist sense
instead of a titan, he fought for the perpetuation of a nation
of pygmy capitalists. Because he represented during the
major part of the nineteenth century a larger percentage of the
population than the working class, he was able to make
his impression felt upon the history of the nation in a way
that was impossible for the working class at that time. In fact,
as indicated above, it was because of that numerical advantage
that the working class followed his lead in the political arena.
It was that alliance unfortunately which prevented the Ameri-

can working class from apprehending the real direction of its interests—a direction which was definitely opposed to that of the individualistically minded farmer. The farmer wished to perpetuate an individualistic world; the working class needed an anti-individualistic, that is, socialized world to insure its emancipation.

But the farmer for a period was powerful enough to enforce his interests upon the nation. He succeeded in literally plunging Andrew Jackson into the White House; he was instrumental in electing Van Buren; he converted Tippecanoe Harrison, with his inevitable barrel of cider, from an Indian fighter to a national president; he was even decisive in placing the log cabin hero, Abraham Lincoln, upon the presidential pedestal. Even after the Civil War his force was felt in national politics although with diminishing intensity. In the Granger and Populist revolts he made his last stand. To-day his cause is bankrupt. Nevertheless, he still fights, as we have seen, and at the present time, by virtue of his belligerent refusal to surrender his mortgage-ridden land to the mortgage holders, he has violated the theory of the sanctity of contract upon which capitalism is built and threatened to upset our whole system of finance in consequence.

But why is his cause bankrupt? Because political influence is expressive of economic power, and the economic power of the farmer has been destroyed in the twentieth century by the depredations of industry and finance. A small capitalist still, petty-bourgeois minded to the core, he has not yet come to realize that the cause of the small capitalist is irretrievably lost and that the only way out of his economic dilemma is a socialized system of society in which all capitalists will disappear.

The American working class was unable to make headway in the nation because of the agrarian dominancy just described. It was numerically smaller than the peasantry and, handicapped by the segmentary character of American industry and the influx of immigrants speaking different languages and imbued with conflicting convictions, it was impossible for it to organize itself with any continuity along national class lines.

Then, too, there was until very near the close of the nineteenth century always the West, which, promising escape as it did to oppressed workers, discouraged proletarian solidarity over extended periods. The movement of industry itself, spreading from one section of the country to another, creating new industrial centers constantly as it expanded, proffered new and ever more enticing opportunities for individual workers, particularly in skilled lines, all of which tended to thwart the development of class-consciousness on the part of the proletariat as a whole. The proletariat became wage-conscious instead of class-conscious. Moreover the fluidity of class lines which made it possible within the span of a decade or a generation for many of the oppressed to become the oppressors, and many of the humble to become the haughty, militated against the development of a class-conscious philosophy on the part of the American proletariat. It is not at all surprising, therefore, that the American proletariat in the nineteenth century tended to follow the petty bourgeois leadership of the agrarian radicals instead of creating a proletarian radicalism expressive of its own interests.

II

Nevertheless, despite its adoption of a petty bourgeois outlook, which resulted in its failure to build up a political party of its own, the American proletariat was no less vigorous or violent in defense of its economic rights than the American farmer. In fact, it imbibed the same spirit of independence that dominated the outlook of the farmer in this country, and it was that independence that inspired it to such ready expression of violence whenever its rights were threatened. Beginning with the riots in the second quarter of the nineteenth century, riots which occurred in New York City, Allegheny City, Philadelphia and elsewhere, the American workers built up a tradition of violence which found its earliest, most concentrated and melodramatic expression in the activities of the secret order of the Molly Maguires. The order of the Molly Maguires, which grew up in the anthracite mines of Pennsylvania, openly adopted terrorism as its method of fighting the employers. It unhesitatingly murdered mine-operators and bosses and even labor-leaders who opposed its fight for higher wages and better living conditions. Its tactics were no less ruthless than those employed by the Russian terrorists of the nineteenth century. The order ultimately entered politics and in various mining communities practically dominated the political scene. The Mollies did not believe in compromise with the mine-owners;

when the latter would not give them what they demanded, they promptly killed them off and threatened to kill off any subsequent owners who continued to refuse their demands. By this method, dubious at best and yet inevitable in such a milieu, they raised the living conditions of the miners as a whole, and certainly instilled fear of the workers in the minds of the bosses. But the Mollies only marked the beginning of a tradition. In the riots of 1877, beginning with the B & O strike in July, resulting in open warfare between the railroad men and the militia and breaking out into bloody riots in Martinsburg, Baltimore, and Cumberland, the belligerent spirit of the American working class displayed itself again with challenging clarity. Within a very short time other railroads joined in the strike, and as the wave of opposition spread, riots developed in city after city extending from coast to coast.

The fight for the eight-hour day which was waged by the anarchists in Chicago in the eighties terminating in the Haymarket riot of 1886, carried on the same tradition. The use of dynamite by the various unions, in particular the Iron Workers, which became a matter of public news with the arrest of the McNamara brothers in 1911 and the notoriety won by the case, was in perfect keeping with the tradition of violence developed by the American working class. Although beaten down time and again the American workers, with courage characteristic of their history, were ever ready to meet violence with violence, unafraid to defy the employers to the point of bloodshed. The courage they displayed in the Homestead strike in 1892 was not less inspiring than that shown at Ludlow in 1914 or in Pittsburgh in 1918 or Centralia in 1919. It was the I. W. W., the most indigenous of American labor organizations, that did more to perpetuate that tradition in the first quarter of the twentieth century than any other group. To-day it is the Communists who have undertaken the task of preserving that tradition and of giving it more revolutionary form.

The American workers thus as well as the American farmers have constituted an army of fighters. They have not surrendered to necessity without a struggle. They have fought for whatever they got, and, despite the fact that the prosperity period of the twenties threatened for a time to undermine their morale, they are ready to fight again. The trouble in the past has not been with their fighting—but with the inadequacy of what they fought for. The American workers are swift to resort to force and quick to turn it into violence. What is necessary, therefore, is not to educate the American workers to be willing to use force in a social emergency—they need little education in the advantage and wisdom of force—but to teach them to use force in the right direction, namely, to destroy the present capitalist order of society and replace it by a collectivist one in which economic life can be socialized and classes abolished.

In the nineteenth century America was still predominantly an agricultural country, and with the proletariat numerically inferior to the peasantry, it was impossible for the working class to develop a radical class consciousness along national lines. In the twentieth century, however, with the positions of the peasantry and proletariat reversed, the country is prepared for the development of radical class consciousness along national lines. In the past, strikes were for the most part sporadic occurrences, developing in specific localities and ending there. This was particularly true in the craft-union phase of American labor history. To-day, with the industrial union facing us as the new labor necessity, that condition no longer prevails. In the future strikes will begin to take on national instead of local proportions, which is the necessary next step in our revolutionary history if the workers are to be able to create a new society instead of merely fighting against isolated bulwarks of the old.

Already signs of change are in the air. In Sioux City, the farmers have taken to action again, and if the American workers have not yet begun to stir, their leaders, even in the reactionary unions, have already given utterance to sentiments that foreshadow the change that is bound to follow. The lull in the workers' psychology in the last twelve years is past. Signs of return to action are everywhere manifest. Even so reactionary a figure as William Green, the President of the American Federation of Labor, has declared that the workers must begin to fight the wage cutting policy of the bosses. In various labor magazines, as J. B. S. Hardman has shown, protest has already become vociferous. In an editorial in a labor magazine, *The Hosiery Worker*, it was declared that "a militant and radical labor movement is unevitable in the United States and probably a no less militant agricultural movement. War cannot be declared against a nation without that nation accepting the challenge." In *Labor*, the well-known railroad publication, there appears the definite assertion that "this is not a passing depres-

sion. It is the stormy dawn of a new age. It is high time for our
political doctors to stop dawdling with opiates and palliatives for
our economic ills, and root out the cause." *The Railway Clerk*,
another labor periodical, is equally emphatic in its stand:

> "The most hopeful sign of the times is that organ-
> ized labor here and there is beginning to resist wage
> cuts. A nationwide wave of first-rate strikes would, we
> believe, be the best stimulant to business; because it
> would serve notice on employers that labor had de-
> manded an end of wage cutting."

When such a nationwide wave of first-rate strikes hits the
country a new page in American labor history will have begun,
for out of those strikes will spring a class consciousness that
has been all too sadly lacking in the American labor movement
in the past.

Within the last few years, however, America has entered a
new and more critical stage in its history. In the past, whenever
the workers and farmers began to shed their lower middle class
ideology, a return of comparative prosperity would rob their
rising class consciousness of conviction, and turn the majority
of them into self-deluded petty bourgeoisie again in their
psychology. That past, however, is gone. The prosperity rise
between 1922 and 1929 will never again be repeated. Not that
there will not be a recovery from the present depression. There
will. But it will not be a recovery to prosperity, but merely to
less depression. The economic set-up of our society is so constituted to-day that, regardless of whatever recovery we ever
make, we shall never be able to restore the vigor to the lower
middle class psychology which it possessed in the past.

While the struggle between the big bourgeoisie (big business) and the petty bourgeoisie had been settled in so far as
fighting was concerned even before the decade of the twenties,
it was the developments of industrial enterprise in the twenties
which put the final quietus on the struggle, leaving the petty
bourgeoisie in a state of blind and helpless retreat. The Democratic party, which in 1912 still represented the interests of
big business by the turn of the twenties was spokesman for the
smaller vested interests. The twenties furthered that alliance.
A number of the small industries, headed by individuals who
were members of the Democratic party, were transformed into
large industries during that decade, and it was those individuals

whose interests had become identified with those of big business who secured control of the party. At the present time, for instance, the dominant controls in the Democratic party, represented by such big business men as Raskob, DuPont, Young, and others, are more definitely allied to big business than to small business. This change, reflecting the surrender of the lower middle class on the political field as well as on the economic, predicates the beginning of a new epoch in the political as well as economic life of the nation. The lower middle class, becoming more and more absorbed into the maw of the industrial structure and shot off into the proletariat, can no longer function as a decisive force in the country. Even in 1924, when Lafollette arose as the political and economic defender of the lower middle class, declaring himself in favor of a return to the days of 1776 and an opponent of all forms of trusts and monopolies, the lower middle class challenge had lost its sting. If the boom years which preceded the crash of 1929 saved the lower middle class for a time from appreciating the real nature of its status, the panic years which followed taught it the truth about its situation. At this very moment the remaining strength of the lower middle class is being sapped at the root by the economic crisis which is upon us. Although when this panic is over and the wheels of industry begin to move once more, the lower middle class will not vanish as a class, it will never be able to regain even the waning vigor which it possessed before the crisis. The entire direction of our economic life will prevent it.

It is the collapse of the lower middle class which is helping to prepare the way for the rise of the proletariat. Along with the breakdown of the petty bourgeois ideology will disappear, slowly perhaps but steadily, the petty-bourgeois-minded outlook of the American proletariat. As the conditions of economic life make it impossible for the philosophy of the lower middle class to inspire the masses any longer with its promise of individual opportunity and advance, the American working class, in consonance with the European working classes, will adopt a proletarian ideology in keeping with the realization of its new status. The very structure of industrial enterprise in America at the present time is inevitably bound to increase the strength of the proletariat at the same time that it weakens the position of the lower middle class.

In the light of these facts, we can look forward in the next decade to a greater harmony between the objective situation and the psychological forces in our civilization. Big business will undoubtedly develop dictatorial tendencies in its control of the state,[2] and the working class will become ideologically conscious of its class rôle, and thus learn to prepare itself for the revolutionary action which in America to-day it is so unfit to undertake.

III

In conclusion, it must not be forgotten that the revolutionary struggles of the workers and farmers have not been in vain. As a result of them, the record of the American political and cultural tradition has taken on a different cast. The American tradition, expressed in records, speeches, statements, and documents, is rich with revolutionary inspiration. Few more revolutionary documents have ever been composed than the American Declaration of Independence. "Whenever any form of government becomes destructive of these ends" (life, liberty and the pursuit of happiness), the Declaration reads, "it is the right of the people to alter or abolish it, and to institute a new Government, laying its foundation on such principles, and organizing its powers in such form, as to them shall seem most likely to effect their safety and happiness." In a later sentence, the Declaration explicitly states that whenever a government tends to disregard the people's rights, it is not only their right, but "it is their duty to throw off such government, and to provide new guards for their future security." The Declaration of Independence was a revolutionary document; it was the Constitution which was a reactionary document. It is the Declaration of Independence, therefore, which should be cherished as part of our indefeasible revolutionary tradition—and not the Constitution. (The only part of the Constitution which retains any revolutionary significance is the Bill of Rights.) Thomas Paine and Thomas Jefferson were the men who did more than any others to carry on that revolutionary tradition. It was

[2] What we are moving toward at the present time is a modified form of state capitalism, what with the state practically supporting and subsidizing the industrial and financial set-up of the nation by means of the monies afforded by the Reconstruction Finance Corporation. In time, if such subsidies continue, and the railroads and industries which have accepted them cannot meet the obligations that they necessitate, there will be no other recourse than for the State to take them over.

Jefferson in fact who, suspicious of the Constitution, endeavored to keep alive the revolutionary state of mind out of which the Declaration of Independence had been born. Shay's Rebellion, which so frightened the bourgeoisie of the time, was welcomed by him in words which have gained rather than lost their challenge in recent days:

> "Can history produce an instance of rebellion so honorably conducted? . . . God forbid that we should ever be twenty years without such a rebellion. . . . What signify a few lives lost in a century or two? What country can preserve its liberties if its rulers are not warned from time to time that the people preserve the spirit of resistance. Let them take arms. The tree of liberty must be refreshed from time to time with the blood of tyrants. It is its natural manure."

As Jefferson's words definitely stated, he was always ready for the oppressed to use arms to overthrow their oppressors. But not only did Jefferson's words vibrate with the spirit of revolutionary challenge. Even the state constitutions of the time carried over something of their challenge. The constitution of Florida, for instance, stated that the people "have at all times an inalienable and indefeasible right to alter or abolish their form of government in such a manner as they may deem expedient." A similar statement can be found in most of the state constitutions of the period, including those of Alabama, Arkansas, Kentucky and Connecticut, and later on in those of Kansas, Oregon, and many others. There is nothing equivocal in themselves about the words "alter" or "abolish," except in the way they may be interpreted by those in power. It was no less a leader than Abraham Lincoln who, in time of crisis, gave their meaning explicit form when he avowed that whenever the people of this country "grow weary of the existing government, they can exercise their constitutional right of amending it, *or their revolutionary right to dismember or overthrow it.*" (Italics mine)

The first part of the problem that confronts us, then, is how to get the American workers and farmers to think in class-conscious terms. In the past, as we have seen, they have thought largely in terms of lower middle-class aspirations. To-day, as we have shown, with the loss of economic stability on the part of the lower middle class, the appeal of the lower middle-class ideology has begun to lose its vigor. Within the near future the American working class will undoubtedly begin to disembarrass itself rapidly of its former lower middle-class psychology and develop a radical outlook comparable to that of the European working classes. The task which must be undertaken is that of accelerating the development of that class consciousness, and directing it into revolutionary instead of reformistic or reactionary channels. To undertake that task with success it is necessary to keep in mind the American masses which have to be dealt with, so as to learn to speak to them in terms of the American tradition which they know. In the effort to radicalize those masses, the revolutionary traditions upon which this country was founded must not be neglected, but utilized in order to give unified and coherent meaning to the struggle that is to be undertaken. Jefferson and William Lloyd Garrison and the importance of what they stood for in their day must not be forgotten; they must be used as symbols of challenge and advance. The American masses must be addressed in terms of that challenge and advance, for it is in such terms that they can understand best the radical rights which are theirs by virtue of their own revolutionary tradition. Revolutionaries must not isolate themselves from the American tradition, but use it to their best advantage, so significant is it in meaning and inspiration. It was no less a revolutionist than Lenin who appreciated the significance of the American revolutionary tradition. Lenin recognized the importance of building upon that tradition. "The best representatives of the American proletariat are those expressing the revolutionary tradition in the life of the American people," he wrote. "This tradition originated in the war of liberation against the English in the eighteenth century and in the Civil War in the nineteenth century. . . . Where can you find an American so pedantic, so absolutely idiotic as to deny the revolutionary and progressive significance of the American Civil War of 1860–1865?" The American revolutionary tradition is a tradition which the American masses will quickest understand, and which to neglect, as has been done in the past, is to hinder rather than help the cause of the second American revolution.

While the conditions of the country have changed vastly since the days of Jefferson and Lincoln, and the particular social philosophies which they advocated have been outmoded in terms of their economic applicability, the revolutionary spirit embodied in the challenge which those men addressed to the American people, and which the American masses responded to, constitutes part of the progressive development of the American revolutionary tradition. The objective should be to advance that tradition and not let it rest where it began. In other words, it should be directed into channels which are revolutionary to-day. Its spirit should be utilized in terms of to-day and not of yesterday. Few things are more absurd in these days of finance-capitalism, when individualism has been crushed at the root, than to listen to a defense of Jeffersonian individualism and liberalism as applied to the contemporary scene. It is not Jeffersonian individualism and liberalism that must be preserved. They belong to the past; they constitute dead doctrine to-day. It is the progressive spirit of revolt in the Jeffersonian philosophy which must be salvaged and used. It is not the Lincoln who was the politician who should be defended, but the Lincoln who defended the revolutionary right of the masses; it is not the William Lloyd Garrison who was an enemy of labor who should be extolled, but the Garrison who as a heroic Abolitionist played such a progressive rôle in the historical advance of this country.

In brief, what must be learnt is not to scoff at the American revolutionary heritage but *to build upon it*. If the American workers can be taught to be proud of the revolutionary development of their tradition, they can be inspired with renewed faith in the revolutionary possibilities of the future. There is no reason for Americans to be ashamed of the revolutionary aspects of their past. Parsons, Engel, Frank Little, Bill Haywood, Eugene Debs, Sacco and Vanzetti, and a score of other workers have laid the proletarian groundwork for the past. There need be no fear of nationalistic dangers in building upon such a basis. "Are we enlightened Great Russian proletarians impervious to the feeling of national pride?" wrote Lenin in his essay, "The National Pride of the Great Russians." "Certainly not! We love our language and our motherland; we, more than any other group, are working to raise its laboring masses (i.e., nine tenths of its population) to the level of intelligent Democrats and Socialists. We, more than anybody, are grieved to see and feel to what violence, oppression, and mockery our beautiful motherland is being subjected by the tsarist hangmen, the nobles, and the capitalists. . . . We, Great

Russian workers, filled with national pride, wish by all means
to have a free and independent, sovereign, democratic, republican, proud Great Russia, which is to maintain in relation to
her neighbors the humane principle of equality, and not the
serf principles of privileges that humiliate a great nation."

It is such "national pride," if you will, that must be stirred
up in the American workers and farmers—a pride in their revolutionary traditions. Such pride can help inspire them with the
fight necessary to overthrow the present ruling class of financiers and industrialists. The American workers must learn to
hate the "violence, oppression and mockery (which their)
beautiful motherland is being subjected to" by those financiers
and industrialists. Hate and not love is the emotion which
they must nurture. The gospel of love belongs to the ruling
class; it is its best protection, for by its very preachment it tends
to prevent the misery it spreads from volatilizing into violence.
The gospel of hate belongs to the proletariat, for it is only
by such hate that the energy necessary for its struggle can be engendered. More, it is only by virtue of that hate that a new
social world can be created in which the gospel of love can
have either place or meaning.

"Between communism with all its chances, and the present
state of society with all its sufferings and injustices," John
Stuart Mill wrote, "all the difficulties great and small of communism would be but as dust in the balance." It is that realization which many American intellectuals have already reached;
it is that realization which many American workers will reach
within this decade if their growing spirit of protest and revolt
is not channeled off into futile directions.

It is only by revolution that that realization can be translated into action. Society can be saved in no other way. Our
task is to create that revolution, to cultivate the forces that
are necessary to its success. It is no little task that confronts us,
and it behooves us to gather up all our energies and dedicate
all our strength to its achievement. To do less is but to fail.
And to fail in that task is to betray the cause of human progress, to sacrifice the future freedom of the human race.

REVOLUTIONS: OLD AND NEW

I

THE DECLINE OF CAPITALISM

REVOLUTIONS are inevitable. That was the conclusion of a bourgeois scholar whose study of the "natural history" of revolution was issued in 1927. The development of social-economic and class forces reaches a point where revolutionary change becomes inescapable. The conclusion was thus amplified:

"This country, in common with all others in which the industrial revolution has developed, is destined to evolve through capitalism into some sort of social control of industry.

"A laboring man of to-day—except, perhaps, in Russia—is a person still insignificant compared with the capitalist. But through the agency of his organization he is superior to the farmer. The laboring man seems destined to be the ruler of the future.

"We may take it for granted that revolutions, even violent revolutions, will occur periodically for a long time to come. We hear some talk about substituting peaceable evolution for violent revolution, but such talk is only what the theologians call 'pious opinion'—laudable, but imaginative. No technology is being developed for the purpose of translating this talk into action."[1]

These words were written during the "new era" of American prosperity everlasting and were, except to the communist, of only academic interest. Essentially and vulgarly pragmatic, the

[1] L. P. Edwards, *The Natural History of Revolution*, pp. 6, 211, 218.

American bourgeois considered revolution "washed up." The revolutionary upsurge in Europe had been beaten down, capitalism was temporarily stabilized, and the Soviet Union (according to bourgeois opinion!) was restoring capitalism instead of building socialism. Revolutionary struggle prevailed in China and was being prepared elsewhere, but that was considered exceptional. In any event revolution was the resort of inferior peoples, not of the American. "We" were realizing the "new order" by means other than revolution—by increasingly higher wages, control of cyclical fluctuations (no more depressions and hard times!), the abolition of poverty. The scholarly student of revolution himself insisted that revolution was not an American issue:

"It is certain, almost to the point of mathematical demonstration, that there is no possibility of a violent revolution within any future that need cause concern to persons now alive. The immediate symptoms of revolution are entirely absent from our society. The remote symptoms, if they exist at all, are so slight as to be unrecognizable."

The scholarly student of revolution echoed the vulgarly pragmatic businessmen inflated by the pretensions of the "new era." But the scholar as prophet was a washout; he said, for example, of the Soviet Union:

"The state capitalism established by Lenin . . . exists to this day and in all probability will continue to exist for generations."

Within one year the Soviet Union reversed the retreat toward capitalism, the capitalist elements which sprang up like weeds in the soil of the New Economic Policy have been wiped out, and the Union is now engaged irresistibly in socialist construction.

The scholarly prophet was also a washout in his appraisal of the American scene. Within three years of his "mathematical demonstration" that there is "no possibility" of revolution in the United States, the elements of potential revolution multiplied. Unprecedented prosperity crashed into an unprecedented depression, the world's mightiest industrial mechanism was afflicted with creeping paralysis, unemployment rose to over 15,000,000 men and women deprived of work and forced to depend upon their meager savings or charity for a "livelihood." Breakdowns of this magnitude are latent with the threat of revolution. The idea of an American revolution evoked only bourgeois belly laughs in the great days before the great depression; now the fear of revolution sends shivers up and down the bourgeois spine. There is, of course, no immediate threat of revolution; but the bourgeoisie and its hirelings, partly out of fear and partly out of low cunning, interpret as revolutionary the most elementary struggles of the workers (strikes, hunger demonstrations, resisting evictions) justifying the resort to bullets and gas. But while the situation is not yet revolutionary it reveals many immediate and remote symptoms of revolution.

The economics of this depression indicate that American prosperity can never revive on the old scale, that chronic crisis will prevail in the United States as it has prevailed in Europe for fifteen years, that revival will be accompanied by an enormous number of unemployed and unemployable workers and by declining standards of living, and that American capitalism is definitely in the stage of decline. The depression set in motion the social-economic forces making for revolution and thus constitutes the prologue to the American revolution, *the* problem of *our* generation.

II

THE CHARACTERISTICS OF REVOLUTION

The scholarly student of revolutions portrayed their characteristics in meaningless social-psychological terms—the Puritan revolution was "pious," the American "mild," the French "ferocious." But all three were manifestations of the onward sweep of bourgeois revolution and all three resorted to violence and dictatorship—the piety of the Puritans did not prevent the execution of a king nor the use of violence and dictatorship to crush the opposition, while the American revolution was far from mild in the suppression and expropriation of the loyalists and in the crushing of Shay's Rebellion.[2]

Historically and sociologically the characterization of revolutions must include:

(1) The general character of revolutions, the aspects which

---

[2] The Civil War was measurably the completion of the American bourgeois revolution; the war was waged ruthlessly, even ferociously, the Lincoln government functioned as a dictatorship, and violence and dictatorship characterized the measures of Reconstruction.

determine their *unity* in cause and effect, as a method of social action.

(2) The specific character of revolutions, the aspects which determine their *differences* in purposes and action, as a completion of one revolution by another.

The general unity of revolutions indicates that they constitute an historical series, in which one revolution flows from another as an inescapable determinant of social progress. The specific differences in revolutions express the changes in purposes, class make-up and operating conditions which distinguish one revolution from another—and which incidentally explains the puzzlement of the learned owls who prophesied that the proletarian revolution in Russia would devour itself in the fashion of the bourgeois revolution in France. . . .

The general unity of revolutions appears in their being the completion of fundamental social-economic changes. These changes are conditioned primarily by technical-economic forces, by changes in the mode of production. The technology and economics of production inseparably condition one another (as well as the social relations of production), but their relative importance may vary. Feudalism was the result of social-economic, not technological, changes. The commercial revolution of the sixteenth and seventeenth centuries was accompanied by important but not decisive technological changes—improvements in tools, construction of more complex machines; its essential features were social-economic, including the rise of a trading class, increasing production for markets, breakdown of the handicrafts and the division and specialization of labor in the early factory system—changes preparing the technical-economic (and social) basis for the industrial revolution of the eighteenth century, in which *technology* was relatively the most important factor.

At the basis of revolution is the conflict between old and new modes of production, not merely in their technical-economic aspects but, more important, in their social-class aspects. The conflict might be resolved in terms of necessity and efficiency *if* technology and economics were the *only* conditioning factors and not themselves conditioned by a series of other historical factors. The technical-economic foundations of the prevailing mode of production are interwoven with definite social relations of production and their corresponding class, cultural and political relations and institutions.

Consequently the conflict between old and new modes of

production is resolved socially, by means of the class struggle
and its economic, cultural and political impacts. *Economic,* as
two modes of production are in conflict, the development of
which sets in motion a conflict of class interests; *cultural,* as the
prevailing culture and ideology represent mainly the older
social relations of production, class interests and class domination, against which there arises the cultural and ideological
revolt of the class representing the new social relations of production; *political,* as the class struggle, the purposive or "subjective" factor in social change and revolution, is directed toward the retention or conquest of political power.

A revolutionary class consequently wages war on all fronts
against the entrenched ruling class. The class struggle is marked
by advances, retreats and compromises, but its end is the revolutionary overthrow of the old order and the establishment of
a new order with its own economic, cultural and political relations and institutions.

The long-time causes of revolution lie in the accumulation of
economic, cultural and political developments which sap the
foundations of the old order and prepare the objective (or
social-economic) and subjective (or class-ideological) conditions for a revolutionary overthrow; the immediate causes of
revolution lie in the accumulation of economic, ideological
and political strains and stresses, the aggravation of contradictions and antagonisms which prevent the old order from "de-
livering the goods," the maturing of a favorable combination of
forces providing the revolutionary class with the opportunity
to strike for the conquest of political power.

But within the essential unity of revolutions there is a diversity which does not contradict the unity but dialectically
complements it. The diversity shapes the problems involved
in revolutions, old and new. Unity is in the *objective,* the conquest of political power; diversity is in the *means* adopted to
accomplish the objective (and in the way the newly conquered
political power is used). Means change because of changes in
the technical-economic foundations of production and its social
relations, in class alignments and political forms, in the character of the revolutionary class; the two constants in the means,
force and dictatorship, also change in their bases, application
and purposes.

While the most important aspects of diversity are determined
by differences in the successive revolutionary classes and the

technical-economic and ideological conditions under which they operate, there is also diversity in the revolutions of a particular class. The classical bourgeois revolutions were marked by substantial diversity within the limits of their essential unity; the belated bourgeois democratic revolution in Russia was succeeded almost immediately by the proletarian revolution, while bourgeois democratic revolutions in colonial or semi-colonial countries are now bound up with the anti-imperialist struggle for national independence and the revolutionary upsurge of the proletariat. National differences in economic development, historical traditions and ideology impart to the proletarian revolution itself a considerable diversity, although infinitely more unified than any previous revolution.

The diversity of revolutions and the problems involved in revolutions, old and new, are profoundly influenced by two increasingly important developments:

(1) An acceleration of the revolutionary process, which progressively shortens the intervals between one revolution and another.

(2) An increasingly purposive character in revolution, the result of a larger awareness of purposes and means.[3]

The revolutionary process was extremely slow, if not nonexistent, in antiquity. Civilization after civilization collapsed or stagnated because of the slow growth of new social-economic forces. There were many insurrections but scarcely any revolutions. A new ruling class usually arose out of conquest and not out of internal social changes. Technology measurably conditioned social life, but the natural environment dwarfed technology and its development was hampered by the social-economic relations of primitive agriculture and slavery. There was only a slight accelerating impact of technology upon social change.

The commercial bourgeoisie which arose in antiquity was unable to break the barriers of the old order. The class struggles which rent the Roman Empire for 500 years resulted in "the common ruin of the contending classes," despite the beginnings of serfdom which anticipated feudalism: the Empire collapsed under the weight of its own decomposition and

---

3 Cultural diffusion and borrowing are important factors in the diversity and increasingly purposive character of revolutions. While these factors were present in the bourgeois revolutions, they appear most clearly and dynamically in the Russian Revolution. The problem is worthy of serious Marxist analysis.

the barbarian invasions. Although feudalism had a shorter span of life than antiquity, it endured 900 years before a revolutionary process began with the rise of the bourgeoisie in Italy and the coming of the Renaissance.

Within 300 years the bourgeois revolution was triumphant in England and France; 150 years later capitalism dominated the world. Acceleration was marked in the bourgeois revolution and in the social changes involved. But acceleration is still more marked in the development of the proletarian revolution. Seventy years after capitalism itself was definitely challenged by communism, by the *Communist Manifesto* in 1848, the proletarian revolution was triumphant in Russia, the Soviet republic celebrates its sixteenth anniversary fifty years after the death of Karl Marx, and capitalism is everywhere being challenged by an aggressive, unified international revolutionary movement. Acceleration is cumulative.

Objectively the speeding-up of the proletarian revolution is determined by the acceleration of technological change and its impact on social-economic relations. Technological change was slow in antiquity and only tardily acquired greater momentum. But the technology of capitalism, primarily because of the increasing technological application of science, is a demon force which perpetually revolutionizes technical-economic relations,[4] multiplying and aggravating the contradictions and antagonisms of capitalist production; the result appears in the increasingly disastrous cyclical breakdowns, economic decline and imperialist wars which throw the proletariat into revolutionary struggle for the conquest of power.

The acceleration of technological change accelerates changes in social-economic and class relations and hastens the coming of proletarian revolution, the final victory of which on a world scale will be the accomplishment of our generation.

Subjectively the speeding-up of the proletarian revolution is determined by the maturity of the purposive and conscious factors in revolution. There was no awareness of the purposes

---

[4] The bourgeoisie cannot exist without constantly revolutionizing the instruments of production, and thereby the relations of production, and with them the whole relations of society. Conservation of the old modes of production in unaltered form was, on the contrary, the first condition of existence for all earlier industrial classes. Constant revolutionizing of production, uninterrupted disturbance of all social conditions, everlasting uncertainty and agitation distinguish the bourgeois epoch from all earlier ones.—Karl Marx and Friedrich Engels, *The Communist Manifesto.*

and means of revolution in antiquity: the awareness appears in the bourgeois revolution, if only in its later phases. Although the awareness was incomplete, there was in some of the leaders of the bourgeois revolution a measurably conscious understanding of purposes and means, of the direction and problems of their struggle. But the conscious and purposive factors in revolution appear completely only in the proletarian revolution, which is scientifically aware of the laws of social development underlying its program and action.

Marxism-Leninism, which is communism, clearly understands its purposes, immediate and final, and consciously and creatively acts upon class forces to accomplish the purposes. It is no longer largely a case of the impact of social forces upon revolutionary purposes and means, but of the impact of purposes and means upon social forces—*awareness becomes itself a social force.*

Man, the worker, dominates *this* revolution, within the limits of appropriate objective conditions. The revolutionary process is accelerated. This appears clearly in the proletarian revolution in Russia: Bolshevik awareness of purposes and means creatively manipulated the prevailing combination of circumstances toward a Socialist conclusion while Menshevik "Marxists" insisted that only a capitalist conclusion was possible and advisable.

Awareness, as well as conscious purpose, distinguishes the proletarian revolution from its predecessors and constitutes a vital difference in revolutions, old and new.

III

REVOLUTIONARY CONTRASTS

The fundamental contrast is this: the bourgeois revolution meant the rise to power of another propertied, exploiting class and a new system of class rule and exploitation; the proletarian revolution means the rise to power of a non-propertied, non-exploiting class and hence the abolition of class rule and exploitation. This is bound up with other contrasts which profoundly influence the strategy and tactics of the revolutionary proletariat.

Strength and independence were imparted to the bourgeoisie

by its possession of property.[5] The bourgeoisie owned the new means of production, which piled up wealth and power for the new class. Even while it still maintained its political power, the feudal class came to depend upon the economic power of the bourgeoisie, forced to recognize and make concessions to the new economic forces and their class representative. In the sense that it "balanced" the conflicting interests of aristocracy and bourgeoisie the absolute monarchy itself represented an increasingly ascendant bourgeois power. The rising bourgeoisie might compromise with the aristocracy and the monarchy and yet accomplish its essential purpose because possession of the new form of property (which irresistibly became the dominant form) strengthened the bourgeoisie and weakened the feudal class. Compromise was not fatal to the bourgeois revolution.

The bourgeoisie, moreover, possessed its own culture and its own intellectuals. This culture was neither potential nor subsidiary: it was actual and pervasive. The university, science, improved technology and learning in general were manifestations of bourgeois development, under bourgeois domination, and waged the bourgeois cultural struggle against the feudal order.

Intellectuals (and professional workers, *e.g.* technicians, lawyers) were also a product of bourgeois development, thrust forth by the new social forces and the new social needs which, under the prevailing historical conditions, promoted bourgeois class interests and ideology. Some intellectuals might depend upon feudal lords for patronage, but they were bourgeois to their marrow; they were negated by the older and developed by the newer social relations of production, which bound the intellectuals to bourgeois interests and purposes with coils of steel. The very existence of the intellectuals undermined the old order, against which they fought many epic struggles in religion, science, politics. In waging war on the cultural front the bourgeoisie had the overwhelming support of the intellectuals (except the clergy, who were really feudal intellectuals).

Another advantage of the bourgeoisie was its appearing as the revolutionary representative of all the exploited classes—peasants, artisans, wage-workers—and in having only one class to fight, the feudal aristocracy. The bourgeois revolution called

[5] The implications of this bourgeois possession of property and of the proletarian contrast are discussed in Daniel De Leon's *Two Pages from Roman History*.

the masses to struggle and the masses responded; it then betrayed the masses, imposed upon them new forms of exploitation and permitted older forms to persist where they did not
interfere with bourgeois ascendancy, but meanwhile the revolution had been accomplished. (This betrayal caused the up-
thrust of a proletarian left wing in all bourgeois revolutions
except the American.) The existence of only one class to fight
delimited the bourgeois struggle, lessened its complications and
clarified issues and objectives, strategy and tactics. The prevailing class alignments measurably simplified the bourgeois
revolution.

None of the bourgeois advantages is possessed by the proletariat. Fundamental features of the bourgeois revolution
appear in the proletarian revolution—force, mass struggle, expropriation and suppression of the opposition, new forms of
legality and revolutionary dictatorship—but they are influenced by the very different character and purposes of the new
revolutionary class as well as by the disadvantages that historical development has imposed upon the proletariat.

The proletariat is a non-propertied class. The objective basis
of the proletarian revolution, of socialism, is the increasingly
social character of production (and its influence on class alignments and class power). But the means of production are in
the ownership of the capitalist class; where, under conditions
of monopolist capitalism, ownership is separated from management, the managerial employees and petty stockholders are
overwhelmingly bound up, economically and ideologically,
with the dominant financial capitalists. The proletariat is in
physical *possession* of the means of production (the basis of
its revolutionary significance, vigor and power), but the assertion of this possession is possible only by means of organization,
an ideological transformation and a revolutionary act; while
ownership of itself almost automatically made the bourgeoisie
the ruling class.

Where technical-economic developments worked directly for
the bourgeois revolution, they work only indirectly for the proletarian revolution (undermining capitalism by multiplying
and aggravating the contradictions and antagonisms of capitalist
production, and making the proletariat the indispensable class).

The proletariat is also the representative of all the exploited
—whether the proletariat is the majority as in highly industrialized countries or the minority as in economically backward

countries. But the proletariat has more than one class to fight. Although elements of the lower middle class, professional groups and intellectuals will swing over to the proletariat, the middle class as a whole will oppose the proletarian revolution, and must be fought to a standstill or neutralized. The new middle class, composed essentially of petty stockholders and managerial and supervisory employees in corporate enterprises, is economically, *and ideologically,* bound up with monopolist capitalism and imperialism, and will provide the sinews of Fascism, the final resort of capitalism to maintain its ascendancy.

Being itself also a sort of petty bourgeoisie and necessarily opposing prevailing feudal forms of property, the peasantry almost automatically accepted the hegemony of the revolutionary bourgeoisie, a hegemony for which the revolutionary proletariat must maneuver and fight. Even where the agrarian classes offer no problem, as in Great Britain, the problem reappears in the form of the peasant masses who are indispensable in the colonial revolutions which are a crucial phase of the British (and world) revolution.

Revolutionary movements must wage war on the cultural front. But unlike bourgeois culture, proletarian culture is primarily potential and only partly actual; it is, moreover, always in danger of being repressed and distorted by the weight of the pervasive institutional culture of capitalism. The university, science, technology, the means of molding opinion and learning in general are under bourgeois control and bourgeois in spirit. Against the class nature and reactionary aspects of this culture the proletariat wages war; but the revolutionary culture of the proletariat under capitalism, while it includes many of concrete cultural achievements (*e.g.* creative literature and art), is necessarily and mainly a culture of revolutionary *criticism* and ideological struggle, projecting the spirit of socialist culture, interpreting and clarifying the tendencies and changes in existing culture which may become contributing factors in the socialist culture after the overthrow of capitalism.

The cultural struggle (and theory, which is the inescapable condition of the practice of the proletarian revolution) requires intellectuals. But while the bourgeois revolution depended upon its own intellectuals, who were created and invigorated by bourgeois emergence and power, the proletarian revolution draws many, if not most, of its intellectuals from petty bourgeois circles. The intellectuals are nourished by bourgeois and not proletarian conditions of living, they are usually the repository of petty bourgeois modes of thinking, prejudices *and instability,* all of which they bring, consciously or unconsciously, into the proletarian movement. Glorious have been the revolutionary services of the intellectuals (Marx, Lenin, Trotsky, Luxemburg, De Leon), but the danger and treason of the intellectuals have also materialized repeatedly. The danger was insignificant in the bourgeois revolution!

The proletarian revolution, finally, is much more fundamental than the bourgeois revolution. No bourgeois revolution was as thorough and complete as the proletarian revolution in Russia. Where the bourgeois revolution replaced older forms of private property and exploitation with newer forms, the proletarian revolution annihilates all forms of private property and exploitation. There can be no compromise between socialism and capitalism; compromise between feudalism and capitalism revealed their exploiting identity. Capitalism developed inexorably in England despite the restoration of monarchy after the Puritan revolution. Aristocracy was enriched, particularly in England and Germany, by industrial exploitation of the mineral resources on the great landed estates. An older system of class rule adapted itself to the newer. The bourgeoisie might compromise with the aristocracy and still accomplish its essential purposes. The proletarian revolution cannot compromise with the capitalists and still accomplish its purposes, since the capitalists cannot be absorbed into a socialist order—which has no new ruling and exploiting class.

Thus the proletarian struggle is enormously complicated. But the complications are offset by acceleration of the revolutionary process, and they are dangerous only if they are not properly understood and evaluated. These complexities are fatal to socialism and laborism, because these movements neither understand nor evaluate the complications, are dominated by (instead of dominating) the complex class relations, and reject the necessity of creative revolutionary action in favor of the reformism which inevitably merges into capitalism because of the economic, cultural and political weight of the capitalist class.

Compromise with the class enemy is fatal to the proletariat, which must strike ruthlessly when the moment is favorable; otherwise its forces may break apart, temporarily but still disastrously, as capitalism is favored by its class, economic, cul-

tural and political domination, and also because the allies of
the proletariat are characterized by instability. The German
socialists rejected the dictatorship of the proletariat, and the
result was that capitalism consolidated its power anew; the
Italian Socialists rejected the dictatorship of the proletariat,
and permitted the ascendancy of Fascism; the Spanish Socialists
reject the dictatorship of the proletariat, allowing Capitalism
to develop its own institutions and supremacy.

Where the proletariat, if the conditions are favorable, does
not seize power there is an inevitable, if temporary, renewal
of capitalist ascendancy. But the awareness of purposes and
means which is implicit in revolutionary Marxism may creatively manipulate the complications to *hasten* the proletarian
revolution—as the Bolsheviks did in Russia. Creative initiative
and inflexibility are not only necessary in the revolution but
also in all the preceding stages of the proletarian class struggle. The proletariat is under the economic, cultural and political domination of the capitalist class, susceptible to the lures
and wiles of reformism, prone to half-measures and weaknesses,[6]
hampered by the conservatism of its organizations and by the
bureaucracy, as well as by the intellectuals who avoid and betray revolutionary struggle.

Hence the communist policy of inflexibility and no compromise with the class enemy, of balancing ultimates and imme-
diates, of an indissoluble unity of theory and practice:—revolutionary ideology becomes itself an objective force. But
simultaneously the utmost flexibility is necessary in approaching
the workers, of moving with them even when their actions are
characterized by half-measures and weaknesses, of maneuvering
in the midst of the complex conditions of the proletarian class
struggle, of combining the immediate needs and struggles of
the workers with their larger interests and purposes.

These apparently contradictory but dialectically complemen-

[6] Proletarian revolutions . . . criticize themselves constantly; constantly interrupt
themselves in their own course; come back to what seems to have been accomplished
in order to start anew; scorn with cruel thoroughness the half-measures, weaknesses
and meannesses of their first attempts; seem to throw down their adversary only to
enable him to draw fresh strength from the earth and again to rise up against them
in more gigantic stature; constantly recoil in fear before the undefined monster
magnitude of their own objects—until finally that situation is created which renders
all retreat impossible, and conditions themselves cry out: "Hic Rhodus, hic salta!"
—Karl Marx, *The Eighteenth Brumaire of Louis Bonaparte.*

tary factors impose the necessity of an inflexibly revolutionary and disciplined communist party of the most conscious and advanced workers, a party which, precisely because it is inflexibly agreed on final purposes and means, can flexibly approach the complex social and class conditions under which the proletariat operates, be both participant in, and vanguard of, the struggle of the masses until they rally to the party's revolutionary leadership, and quantity is transformed into quality.

The proletarian revolution is distinguished by its scientific awareness of purposes and means, its emphasis on a disciplined revolutionary party, and its creative manipulation of class forces to accomplish its purposes. In one of its dynamic aspects Marxism-Leninism is essentially revolutionary engineering.[7]

IV

THE PROLETARIAN REVOLUTION

The proletarian revolution is the final one in the series of revolutions which have marked the upward movement of society.

It was the creative act of genius when Karl Marx saw in the proletariat the class destined to overthrow capitalism, end all forms of class rule and exploitation, and transform the world. This was sheer madness to the vulgarly comfortable bourgeois and the humanitarian reformers. The proletariat was a small class, isolated, exploited, brutalized, despised. Yet Marx saw it

[7] But in only *one* of its aspects. The engineering aspect of Marxism, which is simply the practical application of its scientific awareness, has been vulgarized by Max Eastman, who insists on making it the *whole* of Marxism. According to Eastman, whose approach is pragmatic and not Marxist, Marxism must discard philosophy because "science in its mature forms casts loose from philosophy, just as earlier it cast loose from religion and magic." (Introduction, Karl Marx, *Capital, The Communist Manifesto and Other Writings*, p. vii.) Engineering is merely the technological application of science; it does not set goals but realizes goals set for it and with the means science provides. As science expands, the necessity of a philosophical synthesis becomes increasingly apparent, and it is only the reactionary scientist who casts loose from philosophy (or seeks to restore Deity in the universe under new forms). The engineering aspect of Marxism is the concrete expression of the unity of theory and practice, based upon a conception of history, economics and society, and a method of revolution, all of which are implemented in the philosophy of dialectic materialism. The economic reorganization proposed by Marxism involves a whole cultural revolution, the essential oneness of which appears in the unity of Marxist philosophy.

as the essential class in capitalist society, growing in numbers, organized by the mechanism of capitalist production itself, becoming increasingly aware of its revolutionary tasks.

It is sometimes argued that the Marx of 1848 was simply a petty bourgeois revolutionist, as distinguished from the "later" Marx. This is a complete distortion. Proletarian revolution first manifests itself as the left wing of bourgeois revolution. Moreover, the essence of the Marxist approach is that the revolutionary movement must base its immediate strategy and tactics upon the objective reality of prevailing social and class forces, upon which it creatively acts to further the proletarian revolution. In 1848 there was a bourgeois revolution in Germany and France; Marx urged participation, an independent class participation, to accomplish larger objectives and transform the bourgeois revolution into a proletarian revolution. In 1850, in an address of the Communist League, Marx wrote:

"During the struggle and after the struggle the workers must at every opportunity put forth their own demands alongside those of the bourgeois democrats. They must demand guarantees for the workers the moment the democratic citizens set about taking over the government. They must if necessary extort these guarantees, and in general see to it that the new rulers pledge themselves to every conceivable concession and promise—the surest way to compromise them. In general they must restrain in every way to the extent of their power the jubilation and enthusiasm for the new order which follows every victorious street battle, by a calm and cold-blooded conception of the situation and by an open distrust of the new Government. Side by side with the new official Governments they must simultaneously set up their own revolutionary workers' Governments, whether in the form of municipal committees, municipal councils or workers' clubs or workers' committees, so that the bourgeois democratic Governments not only immediately lose the support of the workers, but find themselves from the very beginning supervised and threatened by authorities behind which stand the whole mass of the workers. In a word: from the first moment of victory our distrust must no longer be directed against the vanquished reactionary party, but against our previous allies, against the party which seeks to exploit the common victory for itself alone. . . . While the democratic petty bourgeois wants to bring the revolution to an end as quickly as possible, it is our interest and our task

to make the revolution permanent, until all the more or less
possessing classes are driven from power, until the proletariat
has conquered the state power and the association of proletarians, not only in one country but in all dominant countries
of the world, has advanced so far that competition with the
proletariat in these countries has ceased, and at least the decisive
productive forces are concentrated in the hands of the proletarians. For us it cannot be a question of changing private property but only of its destruction, not of glossing over class antagonisms but of abolishing classes, not of bettering the existing
society but of founding a new one."

And the Marx who wrote these words is considered a petty
bourgeois democrat! In all important respects the analysis and
directives of the Marx of 1850 were incorporated in the strategy and tactics of the Bolsheviks in 1917, which transformed the
Russian bourgeois revolution into a proletarian revolution.
But that is precisely the point, argue those who want to discredit Bolshevism in its applicability to countries more highly
developed economically than Russia was, the Bolshevik tactics
are in the spirit of the Marx of 1848 but *not* of the later Marx
who emphasized peaceful trade union and political organization and struggle. This is another distortion. The *fundamentals* of Bolshevik strategy and tactics were not determined
by peculiar Russian conditions but by the theory and practice
of the proletarian revolution, including the all-important dictatorship of the proletariat. Both the "earlier" and the "later"
Marx insisted on the dictatorship of the proletariat. Marx
wrote in the 1850's: "The class struggle leads necessarily to the
dictatorship of the proletariat, and this dictatorship is the
transition to abolition of all classes and to the creation of a
society of the free and equal." And Marx wrote in the 1870's:
"Between the capitalist and the communist society lies the
period of the revolutionary transformation of the one into the
other. To this corresponds a political transition period in which
the state can be nothing else but *the revolutionary dictatorship
of the proletariat.*" There is no break between the "earlier"
and the "later" Marx.

The revolutionary upsurge of the European proletariat from
1830 to 1870, which shaped Marxist theory and practice, was
determined by the development of industrialism and belated
bourgeois revolutions. After 1870 the labor movement was
dominantly moderate. An economic upswing of capitalism was

initiated by great technological changes which multiplied the chances of profitably investing capital and, primarily, by the development of imperialism: export of capital, exploitation of agrarian countries, new markets which temporarily eased the strains and stresses, the contradictions and antagonisms of capitalist production.

The economic upswing permitted concessions to labor, particularly the upper layers of better-paid workers. Trade unions, under domination of the conservative aristocracy of labor, which ideologically merged with the lower middle class, developed as organs of peaceful struggle for limited purposes, the political movement itself assumed overwhelmingly democratic parliamentary forms, and the labor bureaucracy acquired vested interests and an ideology which instinctively rejected revolutionary purposes and means.

Ascendant reformism revised Marxism in theory and practice. The "theoretical" revisionism of the petty bourgeois intellectual Eduard Bernstein was reinforced by the "practical" revisionism of the trade unionist Karl Legien. Revisionism argued that the economic upswing would proceed smoothly and forever, that capitalism was being transformed by modification and potential elimination of its contradictions and antagonisms, including crises and the class struggle, and that the "catastrophic" proposals of Marx were inapplicable as capitalism was gradually, peacefully, and inevitably "growing into" socialism by means of successive reforms on the basis of democracy and the capitalist state.

The revisionists emphasized Marxism as a science of social development, repudiated and suppressed Marxism as a philosophy of revolution, and transformed the inevitability of socialism, as an inherent necessity of capitalism as such, into the misleading doctrine of "gradualism." But there was no "growing into" socialism, only a growing into state Capitalism and imperialism! Compromise was not disastrous to the bourgeoisie in its struggle against feudalism; compromise delivered the proletariat to the mercies of the imperialist World War.

The increasingly social character of production strengthens the proletariat and constitutes the objective basis of socialism. But there is another and contradictory aspect: the socialization of production, under capitalist relations, results in monopolist Capitalism and imperialism which strengthen Capitalist reaction and power. Monopolist capitalism and imperialism, moreover, despite their initial "easing" effects, aggravate and multiply all the contradictions and antagonisms of capitalist production, increasing the instability of Capitalism. Instead of the "modification" and "transformation" of Capitalism, of the "growing into" socialism—intensified exploitation of the proletariat and colonial peoples, and the catastrophe of the imperialist World War.

In a sense the development of proletarian organization corresponds to the bourgeois ownership of property. The proletariat, organized by the mechanism of capitalist production itself, imposes, by means of its organizations, limitations upon the absolute sway of capital. But these very organizations turn into fetters upon action for larger purposes. Labor organization becomes entangled with the limited aims of the aristocracy of labor, is influenced by the economic, cultural and political domination of the ruling class, develops the vested interests of a bureaucracy frightened at "disturbing" actions, assumes the protective coloration of adjustment to the capitalist environment. The imperialist war, which introduced an objectively revolutionary situation, revealed clearly, tragically that labor unionism and the dominant opportunist socialism had become bulwarks of capitalism, rejecting the proletarian revolution.

But out of the contradictions arises a dialectic synthesis. Imperialism undermines itself by multiplying the parasitic aspects of capitalism, thereby inaugurating its decline, and by plunging the world into catastrophic wars which provoke proletarian revolution and its unity with the revolt of colonial peoples. Already before the World War it was apparent (even to Karl Kautsky!) that a revolutionary epoch was approaching.

Stationary or declining standards of living, an ultimate result of imperialism, aroused revolutionary opposition in the conservative labor organizations, creating left wings in the Socialist parties which upheld Marxism against revisionist and Centrist .opportunist distortions. These developments were augmented by the World War. The final synthesis was in the proletarian revolution in Russia—the imperialist war undermined Russian Capitalism, the Bolshevik conquest of power, despite Menshevik opportunist opposition, was a triumph of unfalsified Marxism, and the Communist International emerged as the expression of the new revolutionary epoch and as the international organ of struggle against Capitalism and its opportunist labor-socialist allies.

The dialectics of the proletarian revolution indicate that an inescapable phase of the revolution is the struggle against the older organizations and their limited aims, which is a struggle to transform quantity into quality. "Proletarian revolutions criticize themselves constantly; constantly interrupt themselves in their course; come back to what seems to have been accomplished in order to start anew; scorn with cruel thoroughness the half-measures, weaknesses and meannesses of their first attempts."

Capitalism was seriously shaken by the war and the proletarian revolution in Russia, threatened by the revolutionary resentment of the masses. But its apparent enemies rallied to the support of Capitalism and permitted a reconsolidation of its power. The proletariat was baffled by the opposition to revolutionary action of its own labor and Socialist organizations, which, particularly in Germany, rejected force in *favor* of a proletarian revolution but used force to the utmost *against* the proletarian revolution. Under the weight of this opposition, and the economic, cultural and political domination of Capitalism, the proletariat broke apart, resulting in a temporary reconsolidation and stabilization of Capitalism. But only temporarily; the multiplying contradictions and antagonisms of monopolist Capitalism and imperialism inexorably worked their will and produced another disastrous breakdown of Capitalism, the most disastrous economic crisis in history. These developments are accompanied by a resurgence of revolutionary struggle, in which three major factors are involved:

(1) The highly developed capitalist countries are in the midst of a general crisis and decline, aggravated by an unprecedented depression; markets, national and international, are restricted while technological improvements increase the productivity of labor and industry's capacity to produce goods, resulting in a *permanent* army of unemployed and *unemployable* workers and declining standards of living which move the proletariat to revolt.

(2) Capitalist growth in the colonial and semi-colonial countries is hampered by the general crisis of world Capitalism, upon which they are dependent and whose crisis is aggravated by their industrial development and competition; imperialism is shaken by the crisis and colonial liberation movements (in which the revolutionary proletariat strives for hegemony).

(3) The Soviet Union, under the planful direction of its proletarian dictatorship, is actively moving toward socialism,

inspiring the workers of the world, a revolutionary symbol and force.

Capitalism is in crisis. But, in the words of Lenin, there is "no absolutely hopeless crisis of Capitalism." The crisis becomes hopeless for Capitalism *only* if the proletariat consciously and purposively moves toward the conquest of power! All the forces and stages of revolt are unified in the strategy and tactics of the Communist International, which is scientifically aware of the social-economic conditions of revolution and the necessity of manipulating them for revolutionary purposes.

V

THE AMERICAN REVOLUTION

The apologists of Capitalism insist that revolution is alien to the American scene. What that means is simply this: revolution is now alien to the exploiting and decaying class whose interests the apologists rationalize.

Revolution has played a decisive part in American developments. Colonial migrations were thrust forth by the developing bourgeois revolution in Europe and its transformation of the feudal order. Puritan settlers represented some of the most fundamental and uncompromising aspects of the revolution. Colonial class struggles often produced revolts. The American bourgeoisie secured its independence of Britain by means of revolution, which organized itself as a practical dictatorship, violently coerced the majority where necessary, and expropriated the Loyalists. Samuel Adams deliberately planned and organized the revolution through years of agitation and organization, the Committees of Correspondence being essentially a revolutionary party which was measurably aware of purposes and means. Shay's Rebellion, an agrarian revolt against the revolutionary reaction, led Thomas Jefferson to say there should be such a rebellion every twenty years, because "the tree of liberty must be refreshed from time to time with the blood of tyrants." After independence was secured the French Revolution became a rallying force in the struggle between "the masses" and "the classes." The new republic encouraged revolutions in Latin America, declared that it would resist European attempts to restore or extend colonial rule, and was the haven of revolutionary exiles.

All through the nineteenth century the agrarian radicals led movements which might have become revolutionary under other social-economic and class relations. In the essentially revolutionary struggle of the Civil War the bourgeoisie completed its revolution by destroying slavocracy, the industrial capitalists acquired control of the government (subordinating the northern petty bourgeoisie), and the victory was implemented by the ruthless dictatorship and expropriation of Reconstruction. Then the dominant bourgeoisie set itself as flint against revolutionary ideas (which, in the case of the Civil War, had been forced to break the barriers of a cowardly policy of compromise and ineptitude), it increasingly rejected the older ideals of liberty and democracy, of encouraging revolutions and acting as the haven of revolutionary exiles; imperialism made the United States an international reactionary force instead of a progressive one, and American history (particularly the Civil War and Reconstruction) was rewritten to deprive it of its revolutionary "sting." Yet the indisputable historical fact is: the American bourgeoisie rose to power by means of one revolution and consolidated its power by means of another.

The peculiarities of American development prevented revolutions leaving their imprint on labor's mind. In every European bourgeois revolution the workers developed a definite left wing, the action and experience of which not only built up a proletarian revolutionary tradition but also shaped the development of Marxist theory and practice. No such left wings appeared in the American revolutions. Where the French Revolution produced Babeuf's communist revolt, the American revolution produced Shay's agrarian rebellion against the creditor merchant class. Agrarian radicalism profoundly influenced the character of the American labor movement.

In Europe agriculture supplied workers to industry; in the United States an agriculture renewed and vitalized by an expanding frontier attracted discontented industrial workers (who were replaced by immigrants). As a result of these and other factors, class relations were of a decidedly shifting character (where they were relatively stratified in Europe), farmers outnumbered the workers and were, moreover, frequently in revolt against capitalist political domination, the speed and continental scope of economic expansion practically justified the individualism of self-help and rising, and created a middle class which after the 1870's organized "popular" revolts against trustified Capitalism. The result was that the immature and shifting proletariat came under the influence of agrarian and petty bourgeois radical demands and ideology. Repeatedly a proletarian political consciousness emerged only to be submerged again by agrarian and petty bourgeois radicalism and the social-economic instability of the working class.

Marxism appeared in the United States in the 1850's and considerably influenced the labor movement of the 1870's, but the movement in general developed on a non-Marxist basis. This is usually explained as the result of an antipathy between Marxism and the American mind. There is no such antipathy in any real or permanent sense. While Marxism envisages all stages of the labor movement, its emphasis is revolutionary, the synthesis of the larger and final class interests of the proletariat. Marxism was accepted by the European labor movement in its earlier revolutionary phases; when the movement later became reformist it retained the Marxist tradition *pro forma* but rejected or modified it in practice.

The American labor movement emerged under the influence of agrarian and petty bourgeois radicalism, because of national peculiarities in social-economic and class relations; such a movement, particularly after it came under the almost complete domination of the better-paid skilled workers, the aristocracy of labor, would necessarily reject Marxism. But the social or national "mind" changes in accordance with changes in social-economic relations and class needs, which condition the various forms of social consciousness. An ideology may linger beyond its social-economic basis, but only precariously and under sentence of death. The "American mind" has accepted ideas and institutions which it subsequently rejected, and this process has not come to a standstill (except in the minds of the reactionary ruling class and its apologists). When the American proletariat lets loose its offensive against Capitalism—an offensive now being prepared—it will accept Marxism because Marxism is the theory and practice of the revolutionary class struggle of the proletariat, expressing the needs and experience of that struggle. Significantly, nearly every revolutionary opposition in the American labor movement has been inspired by Marxism; and communism, which alone challenges Capitalism, is based four-square upon Marxism.

The American proletariat, moreover, *has* traditions of militant organization and struggle, and in many fundamental as-

pects it has paralleled the development of the European proletariat. The American proletariat has, through its unions, imposed limitations upon the despotic power of the employers
in industry, in which is latent the final struggle for political
power. Its militancy was incomparable in the great economic
struggles of the 1870's and 1880's, in the great Pullman strike
of 1894, in the great strikes of the 1900's and in 1919–22. The
militancy was deflected from becoming politically class conscious, it broke apart because of peculiar American conditions.
But the tradition of militancy is there to build upon.

Revolutions do not arise because of revolutionary traditions,
however, and they may arise without any traditions. If the
social-economic and class relations are appropriate, revolutionary struggle arises and creates its own traditions, under pressure
of the needs and action of the workers. What are the character
and prospects of any oncoming American revolution?

The revolution against Britain expressed the same class forces
as the European bourgeois revolutions (despite differences in
the agrarian aspects); it enthroned the bourgeoisie politically,
accompanied by ruthless measures against the urban and agrarian masses. The Civil War was the political revolutionary
expression of the conflict between two modes of production,
that based upon slavery and that based upon capitalist wage-
labor; it enthroned the industrial bourgeoisie politically, accompanied by ruthless measures not only against the slavocracy
but against the workers, middle class and farmers (marking the
definite subordination of agriculture to capitalist industry). The
proletarian revolution will enthrone the workers politically, accompanied by the socialist reconstruction of society and the
abolition of classes and class exploitation. In the older revolutions the workers played the part of "supers," the victory they
helped to gain was subsequently turned against them; in the
oncoming proletarian revolution the workers will march upon
the stage of history as a conscious and independent class purposively shaping events to its needs and aspirations, which are
the needs and aspirations of humanity.

This revolution will be the work of the proletarian masses,
rallying and leading other discontented elements of the people.
It depends upon the development of appropriate social-economic and class relations, of proletarian struggle, organization
and consciousness, the communist party being the spearhead of
the process. Neither insurrections nor revolts constitute a revo-

lution; only the proletarian conquest of political power constitutes the revolution, and this is necessarily preceded by a process of social and class change which throws the proletariat into action against Capitalism and the capitalist state. No revolution is independent of social-economic and class relations, as seems to be the theory of the Fascist Malaparte, who makes revolution the conspiracy of a determined group which seizes the strategic points of industry and Government.[8] An American revolution is dependent upon the appropriate objective conditions, which includes the preparedness of the proletariat to act.

At the basis of the oncoming revolution is the transformation of American economic life. Capitalist domination is based upon the industrialization of production and the increasing concentration of industry, which involves an objective socialization of production. This socialization provides the basis of socialism, since the social organization of labor and the integration of industry project the possibility and necessity of the social ownership and planful control of industry.

The transformation of American economic life has been accompanied by a profound change in class relations. A century ago farmers constituted over 70% of the population and 50% fifty years ago; in 1929 they constituted only 13% of the gainfully occupied. Where a century ago the working class was a relatively unimportant minority, wage labor in 1929 constituted 58.5% and clerical labor 10.1% of the gainfully occupied. The working class, of which the industrial proletariat is the spearhead, is objectively the dominant class, its existence and interests bound up with that socialization of production which is the characteristic of Capitalism and the potentialities of which can be released only by the planful social regulation and control of socialism.

Not only are the farmers now a minority, they are no longer an independent propertied class, are doomed by the mechanization of agriculture and the agricultural crisis, and can no longer dominate the political demands and ideology of the workers. The upper bourgeoisie, essentially a class of financial capitalists, is a parasitic class separated from production, the management of which is in the hands of hired managerial employees.

8 Curzio Malaparte, *Coup d'Etat: The Technique of Revolution*. Malaparte consistently confuses the coup d'etat, which is the seizure of power by a group within the ruling class, with a revolution which means the seizure of power by a new class which recasts social-economic relations in its own image.

Finally, *class relations are relatively stratified;* the older ideology of individualism, of self-help and rising, may linger, but it no longer corresponds to reality, and the fluidity of class relations, which was so important in the past, is no more. Objective social-economic and class relations favor the emergence of the proletariat as an independent class whose action will become increasingly conscious and revolutionary under the impact of events.

American Capitalism, moreover, has entered an epoch of economic crisis and decline. Monopolist Capitalism and imperialism, which now dominate the American economy, multiply and aggravate all the contradictions and antagonisms of capitalist production. The scope and intensity of the depression express not merely a cyclical breakdown but a general crisis and decline of Capitalism. An increasingly social form of production clashes with the social relations of private property and individual appropriation. Productive capacity increases beyond the capacity of markets to absorb the output. There is a desperate struggle for foreign markets to absorb surplus capital and surplus goods, but other imperialist nations are engaged in the same struggle, while the economically backward countries further limit foreign markets by developing their own industries; these countries, moreover, are also thrown into the crisis by dependence upon their highly industrialized competitors. Imperialist antagonisms are aggravated, driving directly toward war. Meanwhile a large army of unemployed and unemployable workers develops, which must result in declining standards of living and the revolt of the workers. The breakdown of Capitalism sets the revolutionary process in motion.

These developments are profoundly influenced by the acceleration of technological change. Improved technology increases the productivity of labor and the output of industry, while the social relations of capitalist production limit mass purchasing power and markets, thus aggravating the contradictions and instability of Capitalism. *The acceleration of technological change accelerates the breakdown of Capitalism.* But the solution is not technological, it is social; it lies in the overthrow of Capitalism and the resultant Socialist reconstruction of society, which is the task of the revolutionary proletariat, rallying to itself all exploited elements.

Apologists of Capitalism argue that the high development

of technology in the United States is a factor against revolution. On the contrary: technology not only facilitates revolution by hastening the breakdown of Capitalism, it also strengthens the proletariat by making its control of industry all the greater. Who will run industry, and will it not collapse? The organized workers aided by the necessary engineers will run industry. Increasing unemployment among engineers will drive many of them to become allies of the workers, while there are groups of highly skilled workers who could temporarily replace engineers. The idea of an engineers' revolution is sociological nonsense where it is not disguised Fascism. Technological and economic complexity and domination project the necessity of a "government of the industrially and integrally organized producers (including engineers and other professional workers), whose function Engels designated "the administration of things" and the creation of which is a task of the dictatorship of the proletariat.

American economics poses the problem of social revolution. The unfolding of the problem will be accompanied by:

(1) A chronic economic crisis and capitalist decline which will torment and set in motion the various classes.

(2) The upper bourgeoisie, the financial capitalists and their underlings, will cling to power and thrust all the burdens of crisis and decline upon the backs of the other classes, particularly the workers and farmers; it will multiply repressive measures and intensify its imperialist adventures as a way out of the crisis.

(3) The farmers will be increasingly enmeshed in the agricultural crisis, increasingly deprived of their propertied independence, and pauperized; they cannot escape under capitalism and by their own efforts but will ally themselves with other classes, including the revolutionary workers.

(4) The middle class, tormented by instability, will initiate reform movements, including proposals for national economic planning, which, as it consists merely of partial controls and not planned economy, must necessarily aggravate the very conditions it aims to reform. (Partial controls in the form of trusts, cartels, public regulation and other departures from free competition constitute one of the aggravating factors in the present depression; these controls interfere with the free play of economic forces, which is the only method Capitalism knows of restoring and maintaining the economic equilibrium,

but they are too limited in their "planning" to restore and maintain prosperity.) The reforms will not work; and as the crisis and decline of Capitalism are intensified and the proletariat's militancy increases, the middle class will rally to Fascism, the last desperate resort of Capitalism to maintain its ascendancy.

(5) The proletariat will organize and struggle, emerge as an independent class waging war upon Capitalism, its purposes and means increasingly revolutionized until it engages in the struggle for the conquest of power. In these developments the Communist Party acts as the organizational and ideological spearhead of the proletariat, rallying and combining the struggle of the workers with the struggle of the pauperized farmers and of the more radical middle class elements accepting the hegemony of the revolutionary proletariat.

These developments will influence the intellectuals. The intellectuals are not an independent class; they are bound up with the bourgeoisie, are revolutionary or reactionary in accordance with the stages of bourgeois development. But the overproduction of intellectuals, and capitalist decline, will create discontent and unrest among the intellectuals. Some will rally to monopolist Capitalism and rationalize imperialism. Others will rationalize laborism, or Socialism or, particularly, Fascism. The minority will rally to communism; but these intellectuals are apt to retain their petty bourgeois mentality and prejudices,[9] resent the theoretical and organizational discipline of communism, considering unimportant the every-day struggles over the workers' elementary needs. One of the most important communist tasks is a merciless struggle against the intellectuals who spread illusions among the workers. Communism creates its own intellectuals, who are intimately identified with the revolutionary struggle.

The development of an American revolutionary movement is a supreme task in that engineering which is the concrete application of the theory and practice of Marxism-Leninism.

Class relations are complicated, the middle class is powerful, making potential Fascism all the more menacing, there is considerable cultural lag, and American Capitalism and imperialism are the mightiest in the world. But the dialectical move-

[9] Communism has both a theory and a history, the mastering of which should be the first task of an intellectual moving toward communism. Yet all too frequently the intellectual ignores or just dabbles in communist history and theory: he wants to be a "communist" and retain all his old intellectual lumber.

ment of these forces will itself provide the opportunity for revolution, for communism, with its scientific awareness of underlying social forces, of purposes and means.

And while it must first settle scores with its own bourgeoisie, the proletarian revolution is international. The bourgeois revolution also had an international character, but this character is much more marked in the proletarian revolution. Imperialism converts the world into one revolutionary arena. The American revolution is linked up with the revolutionary struggle in Latin America, with the Soviet Union, with the whole international struggle against Capitalism and imperialism. The final victory of socialism is realizable only on a world scale.

THE ENGINEER SURVEYS
REVOLUTION

I

SCARCITY AND THE MACHINE AGE

THE Machine Age is a thing of the past. We live in a new Power Age. The distinction is all important—it emphasizes what is peculiarly the essence of our time, distinct from any other period in human history. Power—and electrical power in particular—is the thing without which our civilization would lose its identity. It is the major disrupting force within our antiquated economic system.

The Power Age as distinct from the Machine Age, therefore, is more than a verbal nicety. The latter designates adequately the hundred years that followed the first Industrial Revolution of the late 18th Century. The Power Age on the other hand is hardly 40 years young—it is a product of the second Industrial Revolution—a momentous development in human history which passed practically unnoticed.

Up to the time of the first Industrial Revolution, all progress and culture were conditioned by one constant factor. The production of wealth was limited strictly to the muscle power and handicraft skill of the individual worker. Nations were richer or poorer only according to their natural resources, and the degree to which they had developed science and technique —always limited as stated—and according to their success in war, and hence their success in appropriating to themselves what belonged to somebody else.

The defining fact in an agrarian and handicraft age was scarcity. There simply wasn't enough to go around, a condition on which Malthus based his famous theory. If anyone was to be

rich it meant that someone had to be so much the poorer.
The age-old relationships of oppressor and oppressed and the
recurring revolts of the downtrodden against the specially
privileged have persisted since the beginning of time for the
same reason.

The first Industrial Revolution and its Machine Age aftermath, profoundly affected but did not alter the fundamental,
underlying fact of scarcity.

The revolution began with the invention of machines, glorified tools which permitted a more effective utilization of the
existing power resources—i.e. man power, beasts of burden,
water wheels and windmills. Thus, for example, the inventions
of Arkwright and others transformed the English textile industry and greatly increased output.

But while the steam engine was developed almost at the
same time, its application in industry proceeded more slowly
than the introduction of new machinery. The fact is significant
as will be seen later.

During the 19th Century, inventions multiplied and the
steam engine, later to be supplemented by various internal
cumbustion engines, furnished the motive power for industry
and transportation. Man, at last, after thousands of years had
begun to control natural energy and to utilize it for doing his
work. He skillfully devised new tools, which he called machines,
through which this new power was made effective. He was
ceasing to be dependent on the vagaries of weather, on fickle
winds, on streams that ran dry or flooded, on his own feeble
muscles. Nevertheless, though industrialization proceeded rapidly and with far-reaching consequences shaping and coloring
the history of the time, there remained certain serious limitations in steam power and Machine Age production. These
limitations, in fact, were so great that the change which was
to lift civilization to an altogether new level, to start history
off again at an altogether new pace with Plenty and not Scarcity
the dominating economic fact—this great change was yet to
come.

II

THE SECOND INDUSTRIAL REVOLUTION

The limitations of steam powered production are best seen in contrast with the practically unlimited possibilities of electrified production. At the same time it becomes clear that the distinction between the Machine Age and this Power Era is very real —and that the difference is not only quantitative but qualitative as well.

Curiously enough the first use to which electricity was put, after a practical generator had been devised, was for illumination. The possibilities of its application as power remained for years only a dream of a few forward-looking engineers. Once the initial problems were solved, however, the electrification of industry went forward at an astounding rate. Fifty years ago the total output of electrical generating stations was 175,000,000 kilowatt hours, used almost exclusively for lighting. In 1929 the total central station output of the public utilities alone was 92,350,000,000 kilowatt hours, of which only 10 per cent was sold for domestic use, of which approximately half went for industrial requirements—about an equal amount being generated by factory power plants!

What is it about electrical power which has enabled it to play its stupendous rôle in human affairs? Briefly, it *is power devoid of bulk—energy available any place at any time in any quantity—without storage—*energy, furthermore, which is applicable in many forms. This flexibility and ease of control are the qualities which have made electricity the vitalizing, all-pervading force which has revolutionized not only industry but all our living.

Electric motors were first installed in industry to operate overhead traveling cranes. Here the advantages of electrical power as against the cumbersome, slow and unreliable steam engine were most obvious.

Other applications followed. Electric motors were soon used to run mine elevators for example, replacing the old-fashioned steam hoists, and affording greater safety, more speed and better control.

A really significant step was taken, however, when motors were hooked up to drive shafts in factories and mills. At one stroke the long steam pipes that had been necessary to connect the old engines to the distant boiler house disappeared—while substantial savings were effected by the elimination of engine attendance, wear and tear on bearings and main pulley belts and increased efficiency in utilizing the power.

Another forward step was taken when long shafts were split

and "group drive" introduced—with separate motors for groups of machines. Next, motors were hooked up to individual machines, with resulting great economies, particularly in plants with a variety of machines, some of which were used only part of the time. Thus the machine, formerly shackled to belts and pulleys, was set free and the way cleared for profound changes in shop arrangement and production methods.

The old layout, machines standing in rows under the transmission shafts, with aisles between, became pointless—as did the traditional organization of shops according to trades and crafts and type of machines.

Machines, capable of doing work wherever placed, were combined into new groupings according to the consecutive operations in the production process. New methods were devised for internal transportation and material handling. Machines were set up in the path of travel of the worked material, each receiving its work from the adjoining machine, adding its touch to it and passing the material on to the next machine. Several machines were grouped under one operator, and chutes and conveyors devised for passing the material from machine to machine.

Thus in a few easy stages production was revolutionized—and the conveyor type of mass production with its enormous possibilities of volume output at low cost became a reality. Making it all possible is the compact little electric motor—and the invisible driving force of electricity,—doing the work of thousands of men.

But so far, the electrification of industry had really just begun. It continued rapidly in two directions—the adaptation of specially designed, electrically-actuated machinery, and the development of electrical control of quality and precision in manufacturing processes.

The modern rayon factory furnishes an excellent example of the high development which electrical machinery has reached. Individual motors drive thousands of spindles on the spinning frames at a high rate of speed. The whole complicated process by which the viscose is transformed into thread, twisted into yarn, wound into skeins and warped, is carried on by electrical processes—even to automatic devices for tying the ends of the yarn together—or for stopping the machinery in case a thread breaks.

But whether the material is soft as silk or hard as steel, electric power does the job.

In modern steel plate mills, for example, the plates are handled entirely by mechanical means in one continuous process—from white hot ingot to final inspection. A single man on the control bridge handles the whole process by pushing buttons, watching indicators and pulling levers!

We begin to see how far behind we have left the Machine Age, for increasingly in modern industry, not only has the physical strength of the worker ceased to be of importance, but his skill as a craftsman as well. Power not only drives the machine, each separate part of it, starts it, stops it, loads and unloads, but power also furnishes the skill. Electrical controlling devices such as the "electric eye" of a photo-electric cell, the sense of touch or temperature of a pyrometer are unerring—and independent of the trained instincts of the old craftsman.

The examples of modern power production mentioned are of course only two out of any number which might be cited. In every case, "remote control" of the manufacturing processes gives modern production its distinctive color and drama. Picture for example, a solitary operator in the control room at the Massena plant of the Aluminum Company of America. He has charge of the temperatures in 14 electrically heated "soaking pits," controlling their operating cycle by means of electric signals. He also directs the mill crane operator and the gantry crane in the charging and discharging pits. Then again visualize the Volkhov aluminum plant in Russia where 60 men by means of electrical equipment convert crude bauxite ore into 36 tons of aluminum daily!

Printing is another industry which has been revolutionized by electricity. Since the days of Gutenberg presses were built on the principle of a mechanical impact between type and paper. Electricity, however, needs no mechanical contact; it works at a distance. The modern press has an electrically charged roll, inked with a colloidal metallic ink. As the paper unwinds with synchronized speed opposite the printing roll, the ink jumps on the paper, drawn by a rapid succession of electrical discharges. There is no pull, no strain on the paper stock, no pressure, no blurs, no dents, no breakage—none of the aggravations of old time printing—and a greatly increased speed limited only to the rate at which centrifugal force would burst the fast-revolving roll.

When power machinery reaches a stage of development such as this, we find ourselves with a mechanism which we can only describe as a new kind of machine. It is so thoroughly permeated with electrical forces that it is no longer a machine with electrical attachments, nor an electrical apparatus with mechanical details. It is a unique and integrated whole, a producing unit which in appearance, function, force and principle is totally dissimilar to anything heretofore known—and as we must already have suspected and shall soon consider, the worker stands in a unique relation to it—a relationship which is distinctly "something new under the sun."

The process of the electrification of industry, which we have so sketchily considered, is perhaps even more significant in respect to the development of thermo-electric and electro-chemical products. Electrolytic processes, in refining metals and minerals, have revolutionized not only metallurgy but the construction of machinery, and made aviation, high speed cutting of metals, etc., possible. Electro-thermic processes of treating numerous metals and alloys have offered unexpected possibilities in the development of new products by the aid of electricity.

We use daily all kinds of products such as carborundum, ferronickel, ferro-tungsten, graphite, phosphorus, etc.—all produced electrically and contributing each in their own way to the progress of industry.

While the instances given could be extended almost indefinitely to show how electrical power has altered production processes, it is not being suggested that electrification has proceeded at an equal rate in all industries. Some industries are backward—some materials are less tractable than others to modern processes. But the same development does go on—*the trend is toward increasing automaticity in production, with man power and trade skill of less and less importance.*

Even in mining and quarrying, between 1919–1929 the use of electricity increased from 2,789,383 horsepower to 6,124,799 horsepower—only 18 per cent remaining unelectrified.

The total increase of horsepower available to American industry since 1919 is estimated at 50,000,000 horsepower, which translated into human terms or manpower is equal to one billion electrical "robots."

III

THE NATURE OF THE TECHNOLOGICAL
REVOLUTION

We have been largely concerned up to this point with drawing a distinction between the Machine Age and the Power Age—
and thereby determining precisely the nature of the technical
revolution ushered into industry by the application of electrical
power. We have seen specifically the stages by which the permeation of industry by invisible forces has made mass production possible on a scale undreamed of 30 years ago. We have
seen how modern production is essentially independent of both
muscle power and trade skill; we have in fact reached the point
where we recognize that the all-important fact of our new
Power Age is that *man hours have ceased to be an index of
output*—and that increasingly in all industry the number of
workers bears no relation to the amount of goods that are
produced.

The revolutionary implications of this fact, of course, transcend factory walls. The impact of this change on our economic
social and political structure is the accepted cause of the world's
major disturbances to-day. First, however, let us examine some
of the more direct results of power production on labor itself,
on management, on the consumer and finally on the financing
of production. They all have a definite bearing on our ultimate
question.

Modern power production has completely altered labor
qualifications. As we have already seen, strength and old time
trade knowledge are no longer of much importance. What is
required is a new set of qualities which may best be characterized as (1) *sustained attention* to all instrument indications,
signals, etc. (2) *correct perception* and interpretation of these
signals and (3) *prompt reaction,* so that the right levers are
pulled and the proper buttons pushed to avoid damage or interruption of work. In other words, the worker is becoming more
and more a *supervisor* of processes. Intelligence is coming into
the factory; trade lines are vanishing, together with the old
distinction between the "white collar man" and the "man in
overalls." Training for this kind of work may be given in a
few weeks time, contrasted to the years formerly spent in ap-

prenticeship! The logic of the trend is the emancipation of the worker from the machine, rather than his enslavement by it. The worker of the future will have time to devote leisurely to his own self-development, and to the enjoyment of life rather than to spending years "learning a trade."

The technicians and engineers, on the other hand, are finding that the demands of their profession exact more and more of their time. Long years of training in technical schools are necessary to prepare them for places in modern industry—and then fast-changing technology, new inventions, new methods necessitate constant reading and study if they are to keep up with the procession. The burden of production, then, has shifted from man power to brain power.

This becomes all the clearer when we consider the all-important function of scientific management in modern production. Where the aim of management in the Machine Age was to make the worker *personally more efficient,* to-day the emphasis has shifted to *maintaining an uninterrupted flow of production.* The modern power machine will do work well or not at all; its speed, accuracy, etc. are no longer dependent on the worker who runs it. With the rate of production of each machine determined, the problem is to group and operate the machines in such a way that there will be a steady supply of work for each succeeding stage in production.

The *product* is the center of attention, and electrified machines, readily moved about, are grouped and regrouped as a changed product or improved process may require. Current technical literature, not to mention advertising, is full of references to modern plants where "no human hand touches the product."

The main task of modern plant management, therefore, is *planning* production to take full advantage of all technologic possibilities.

Now the principle and technique of planned production is being extended beyond factory walls; and the application of these methods to the solution of larger problems within industries, between industries and even among nations is one of the pressing necessities of the immediate future.

It is worth noting at this point that when we talk of the vast increase of energy placed at man's disposal in the last several decades, we miss half the point if we overlook the "mental energy" without which this Power Age would be an impossibility. Increased output is not a function merely of physical power, be it supplied by man, steam engine or dynamos. The sudden spurt in productivity in the textile industry at the beginning of the First Industrial Revolution was accomplished without added physical energy, as we have already seen. It was "mental energy"—*invention*—that made the increase possible. To-day we are earning further dividends on dead men's labor— the accumulated heritage of scientific knowledge; technology and invention must share with power itself the credit for our vast productive resources.

Scientific management, as one of the forms of "mental energy," continues daily to speed up our industrial tempo. The accomplishments of management in increasing output and reducing the amount of labor and time required, without increasing appreciably either power or equipment, are accepted commonplaces in modern industry. These contributions of management raise important problems, as we shall see later.

While modern power production has altered the status of labor, opening new vistas to the workers, placing at the same time new burdens and responsibilities on technicians, engineers and management, its effect on the financing of production— and ultimately on the consumer—is even more profound. It is at this point that we first encounter one underlying cause of the disjointedness in our present economic system and financial practices created by our new productive means.

Modern factory equipment is naturally much more expensive than the old time, simpler machinery. Thus the structure of our industrial capital has changed radically.

The constant portion of it, representing the value of plant, has been greatly increased, while the variable portion of capital—representing payroll,—has relatively diminished. Consequently items of depreciation, obsolescence, interest, taxes, insurance and interest on investment have risen very rapidly. Every hour of idleness in a modern plant means thousands of dollars of accumulated "unabsorbed overhead."

Consider now, what happens to prices—and real wages—when idle plants continue to draw its pay in the form of interest on the money invested in it.

Overhead charges are usually distributed over the total volume of output, regardless of how short of possible output the actual production may be. Consequently the prices of goods are high in order to pay for the idle equipment.

The fallacy of such practices has been denounced long and persistently by engineers. They have maintained that the cost of product should not contain any other charges than those actually incurred in its manufacture; that the cost of an idle plant is a *loss* of an enterprise due to the poor judgment of the owners who invested in excess capacity. Why, they ask, should the consumer be made to pay for these mistakes? No landlord has ever dared demand that a tenant pay the rent of a vacant apartment in the same house!

The extent of the idleness in our industrial plants, and the resulting heavy burden on the purchasing capacity of the population is seldom realized. Take the woolen industry for example—even during the peak war-time demand its output was less than 70 per cent of capacity. Our coal industry can produce over twice the tonnage actually needed; our shoe and boot industry has a capacity for 600,000,000 pairs of shoes a year—but production amounts to only half that figure. Our clothing factories are about 45 per cent larger than necessary; printing plants are from 50 to 150 per cent over-equipped; the window glass industry has a capacity of 15,000,000 boxes but consumption is only 5,000,000 boxes. And so it goes; the list could be extended to cover dozens of instances.[1]

The destructive consequences of this trend were clearly foreseen a dozen years ago by Gantt, Knoeppel, the writer and other engineers, but their warnings fell on deaf ears. Recently an increasing number of engineers and accountants have been insistently urging the scrapping of excess plant capacity as an inevitable step if we are to forestall the collapse of our economic structure.

Without a doubt any program for restoring the balance between production and consumption must provide for the elimination of these heavy burdens of idle capital which crush purchasing power, and in time of depression and falling production speed the process of disemployment, thereby only making matters worse. It is an ironical commentary on the insanity of our times that idle machinery should draw its pay while idle workers starve.

---

[1] Figures given refer to the period of 'prosperity', not to the present crisis.

IV

CAPITALISM'S DILEMMA: PRODUCTIVITY VS. PURCHASING POWER

The utter inadequacy of an economic system rooted in the feudalism of the Middle Ages, and of financial practices developed during the Machine Age, to meet the needs of our new Power Era, becomes more and more glaringly apparent as we survey the developments of the past ten years.

The most conspicuous fact that confronts us is the collapse of purchasing power that climaxed the ten years preceding 1929—a period in which the insatiate quest for profits, spurred on by the "new economic era" religion of "rugged individualism," finally out-ran itself and plunged to disaster.

Despite the tremendous increase in productivity per man-hour, total wages paid remained practically constant throughout the period up to 1929 while the amount of profits and invested capital soared to dizzy heights and kept soaring even after the crash, while wages fell off to less than half.

This same increase in productivity, we find, was not accompanied by a decrease in working hours, but by a decrease in number of workers to the extent of some 12,000,000 unemployed, to say nothing of the millions on a part-time basis, when production started falling off in 1930 to pre-war levels.

Great as is the tragedy and waste of present unemployment, it appears merely a stupendous folly when we consider what would be the consequences if our present policies were pursued to their logical conclusion! If our present productive equipment were brought up to its possible efficiency, we should then be compelled to reduce our working population to the mere 375,000 which could produce all that we needed for subsistence!

Let us look into these matters more closely.

During this period the increase in productivity per man-hour was accompanied by an increase in the use of electrical power, as well as an increase in employment and total wages.

These particular figures cover the increase in productivity per man-hour in the early stages of the Power Revolution, from 1914–1925:

Rubber Tires	211 per cent	Pulp and paper	34
Automobiles	172	Cane and sugar ref.	28
Petroleum Products	83	Meat packing	27
Cement	61	Leather	26
Steel	59	Boots and shoes	6

The per cent of change in the amount of electrical energy used, employment and total wages in the same industries during the period 1919–1929 was as follows, 1919 taken as 100:

	COST OF POWER	NO. OF EMPLOYEES	TOTAL WAGES
Rubber	+32.9	− 5.9	+ 6.9
Automobiles	+69.9	+70.3	+17.4
Cement	+69.5	+30.8	+47.1
Steel Roll Mills	+32.7	+ 5.3	+ 8.1
Pulp and paper	+36.8	+12.57	+27.5
Sugar	−23.5	−30.5	−27.8
Meat Packing	−11.8	−23.9	−28.1
Leather	−31.4	−31.2	−28.1
Boots and shoes	−20.2	− 2.5	+ 5.5

Interpreting the figures given above, we see clearly illustrated the fact that productivity per man-hour generally corresponded with technologic improvements as reflected by the increased use of power.

Furthermore, *as long as a market existed,* the technologic advance was pretty generally followed by an increase both in number employed and in total wages paid. On the other hand, the last four industries which showed but a slight increase in productivity per man-hour, reduced their power consumption, and decreased the number of workers and the wages paid.

The same trend is indicated in an analysis of 40 groups of manufacturing industries as follows:

Increase in power account	16.35 per cent
Increase of number employed	6.03 per cent
Increase of total wages	20.6 per cent
Increase in average earning	13.9 per cent

So much for the charge that technological advance was responsible for unemployment. The opposite is true and we must look elsewhere for the causes of the displacement of workers.

The increase in productivity during the past decade has been otherwise expressed as follows: "if the working force of 1923 had remained unchanged, the amount of product turned out in a 35 hour week in 1931 would have been the same as was produced in a 51 hour week in 1923."

No such reduction in working time took place—but the proportion of unemployed is about that of the increased productivity. When the index of production fell after 1929 men were thrown out of work rather than the working time cut, until the army of unemployed now numbers over 12,000,000.

Considering the common belief that an eight hour day commonly prevails in American industry it is rather surprising to note figures like these: that in 1929 men employed in blast furnace operations were working from a minimum of 33.8 hours per week to 83.4 hours; in machine tool building from 37.3 to 57.0 hours per week; in petroleum refining from 31.7 to 66.5 hours per week; in lumber manufacturing from 27.9 to 57.6 hours per week, etc.

Great as the increase in productivity has been in the past ten years, it represents only a fraction of the potential increase. The variation in efficiency between the best and worst managed plants in industry is amazing. In the most efficient blast furnaces, for example, 1313 tons of iron are produced per thousand man-hours; in the poorer group only 145 tons are produced—i.e. nine times less. Again in the group of 305 lumber manufacturing establishments the productivity per man-hour ranges from 13 board measures to 173 board measures per man-hour—one group of plants being 13 times more efficient than another. A still more astonishing difference exists in the petroleum industry. Here we see a group of refineries processing 635 barrels of crude petroleum with the same expenditure of man-hours of work as another group processing 141,829 barrels—a difference of 224 times greater output per man-hour!

What would be the effect on unemployment and incomes if the efficiency of our industries were raised to the uniform high level which is already in evidence in the more progressive plants? Simple arithmetic applied to the problem discloses that the average physical output could be increased 80 times.

Assuming that this were done should we then maintain a 44 hour week—and discharge every worker except the necessary 375,000 who could maintain the 1929 output? Or should we reduce the working time from the prevailing 2400 hours per man per year to 30 hours per man per year? Or shall we set 600 hours per year per worker as the maximum, and increase production and consumption from the average $900 a year budget to a level of $18,000 a year?

Obviously such speculation is nothing but a pipe dream as far as social realities are concerned. From the engineering point of view it is perfectly possible. The other side of the equation, however, is in the province of economic readjustment and politics.

These figures, however, do possess certain real implications of immediate importance. This very process of increasing efficiency does go on. Not only is technology constantly advancing —but in a time of depression the trend is steadily toward a higher level of efficiency within industries, as the less efficient producers go out of business, and surviving competitors speed up the improvement of their plants in the fierce struggle for existence.

If the present low level of production and the present working hours are maintained, therefore, it is obvious that the number of disemployed will steadily increase.

The real nature of our dilemma is now clear. If technological advance has actually been accompanied by increased employment as long as a market existed for the products of industry,— what has happened to the market?

Cold statistics give the answer. While wages in manufacturing industries remained practically constant during the decade 1919–1929, the value of product and profits increased by five and a half billion dollars. In other words, while the cost of labor, material, supplies, fuel and power remained nearly constant, the capital charges on new equipment and the profits derived therefrom rose rapidly.

Taking the year 1926 as 100, the new capital issues increased by the first half of 1929 to over 200 per cent. At the same time dividend and interest payments continued to climb while wages declined, thus:

Indices: 1926 as 100 per cent

YEAR	DIVIDENDS & INTERESTS	PAYROLL AVERAGE
1923	81.6	104.3
1924	87.4	94.6
1925	93.0	97.7
1926	100.0	100.0
1927	126.8	96.5
1928	137.2	94.5

Indices: 1926 as 100 per cent

YEAR	DIVIDENDS & INTERESTS	PAYROLL AVERAGE
1929	172.8	100.6
1930	188.0	81.3
1931	187.3	61.5
1932*	171.6	45.5

* First half of the year. (Data from Bulletin Taylor Society, Oct. 1932.)

The story behind the figures is clear enough. The great increase in productivity per man-hour led to tremendous profits. Of necessity these were invested in further means of production. Wages continued to be paid according to old standards which no longer hold. Idle capital, invested in surplus plant, continued to draw its pay, further increasing the burden on purchasing power.

Necessarily, in a profit system there is bound to be a gap between the total price of all goods offered for sale and the purchasing power—since price includes profits which are not spent for these goods. For a time this discrepancy did not make itself felt; foreign markets helped absorb the surplus, and installment buying, which undermined future purchasing power, delayed the inevitable day of reckoning. In the meantime the debt load on production grew heavier and heavier.

When the crash finally came it was followed by frantic attempts to maintain the very condition which had caused the débâcle. To maintain the integrity of the existing debt structure, workers were discharged by the thousands and then by the millions; wages and salaries were slashed again and again. With every cut in workers and wages, conditions only became worse, production fell off still further and the descending spiral of depression continued with all its attendant distress. Finally, these methods having failed, a final attempt was made to maintain the crumbling debt colossus by pumping millions of dollars of credit into its veins under government supervision. Thus complete chaos was deferred. The disturbing question is, for how long?

It begins to look as though the predictions of Veblen, Gantt, and other economists and engineers, made a decade ago, were coming dangerously near true. It was Gantt who said—"any scheme for the utilization of the energies of the community for the benefit of one class of people only would soon destroy democracy and develop an oligarchy which would be ultimately overturned by revolution." . . . He warned us that unless the existing régime was altered "there is apparently nothing to prevent our following Europe into an economic confusion and welter which seem to threaten the very existence of civilization."

There are several points at which our present dilemma differs from previous ones, and the distinction is not merely one of severity or duration.

In the past, confronted with an economic crisis, it was possible to reinvest the accumulated profits in new plants, to enlarge the existing ones, build railroads, open up mines, drill oil wells, etc. This activity provided employment in the "producer goods" industries, earnings were spent in "consumer goods" and the wheels started humming again.

To-day we have too much plant and equipment; too much, that is, to operate profitably under existing conditions. We have too many railroads and too much rolling stock. There is no West to open; no new resources to tap. As far as the export trade is concerned—long a convenient safety valve—we are balked by tariff walls; Europe is pauperized, the Soviets are feared, colonies and remote markets are monopolized by other nations. Our farmers are crushed under a debt load of their own, and are reverting to horse plowing, having no cash to buy gasoline or to repair their tractors.

Hope for recovery through further exploitation of foreign markets persists as one of the fondest delusions of all the hard-pressed nations. The very necessity for exporting surpluses of manufactured goods, because they cannot be consumed at home, requires that capital must take its payment for these goods in the form of foreign investments. This process has led to the industrialization of the world's major markets which are now producing surpluses of their own, for which they in turn seek foreign outlets.

In the final analysis the dilemma in which our profit system finds itself to-day is generally this: Power production, as we have seen, has swept away the relation which formerly existed between the number of workers employed and the quantity of product manufactured. Again it has eliminated the relation which once existed between the value of a plant and its productivity and hence profit ability. To-day it is possible to multiply the productivity of a plant—and the profit derived therefrom without investing additional capital. Change of procedure,

slight rearrangements, a few controlling devices under a
different technique of management, time and again have cut
manufacturing costs, sometimes in two, at trifling expense.
These advantages are not distributed either to the wage earn-
ers or consumers. The paper value of the plants, and the corporations owning them, soars in the effort to catch up with this
non-existing relation between productivity and value, profits
increase and another burden is added to purchasing power.
This is typical of *the inherent conflict between our modern
productive machine and our ancient profit system.*

Where, in an age of scarcity, ownership readily collected its
tribute and consumed its earnings, in an age of plenty ownership cannot possibly consume its share of the flow of goods. It
has no recourse but to extend its ownership and tribute-collect-
ing rights by reinvesting its earnings in further means of production. Yet, as we have seen, if we continue to limit the wages
of labor to subsistence levels, the available purchasing power
cannot possibly absorb what is produced. And yet such mass
consumption is necessary if there is to be mass production, and
mass production is necessary if ownership is to collect its profits.
On top of all this, in a profit system, wages are commonly considered "costs" of production and are therefore to be kept as
low as possible—while rapid technological advance continues
to make the total number of workers required less and less.
Capital ultimately finds itself in the ironical predicament where
it is attempting to do "business without a buyer" and where it
chokes on its own surfeit for which there is no profitable outlet.
The profit system, in short, ceases to be profitable!

Power production within a profit system presents a contradiction which cannot be resolved—and since we cannot abolish
power production it is apparent that we sooner or later must
abolish the profit system.

In the face of this dilemma our government so far remains
impotent. Necessarily it seeks to maintain the very contradictions which have created the dilemma. Furthermore, its policies,
dictated by conflicting selfish interests, are in themselves inconsistent. Thus, for example, we erect tariff barriers on the one
hand, and as a result are forced to extend moratoriums, which
in turn leads to a simultaneous outcry that the debts must be
paid—and the tariff walls raised still higher! It must be admitted
that the prospects of securing the adoption of a unified policy

that bears any relation to the realities of the situation are at the present very dark indeed.

V

THE FUTURE OF THE PROFIT SYSTEM

America to-day is at the crossroads. One way ahead is to follow the road along which we have been traveling, to muddle along, to make disjointed attempts to resuscitate a dying order by powerful stimulants such as further credit extensions, moratoriums, and currency inflation. Such a road leads but one way —to complete collapse, with consequences which we cannot yet fully envisage.

Another road is the one toward which we appear to be turning. It is likely that the profit system will make its last stand, with government taking an increasingly greater hand in industry and business, under some form of economic planning on a national scale.

Most of the signs point in this direction. Revision of the anti-trust laws to permit larger scale combinations and the planning of production probably lies in the near future. This will eventually mean an elimination of much competition, production at a higher efficiency, and a scaling down of the top-heavy debt burdens which are strangling us. Production will in a measure, at least, be stabilized and employment will be more regular. It is, however, a question how far this planning will be carried to its logical conclusion. To the degree in which it is done, profits will be reduced, wages will rise and working hours will be shortened. Means will be found to control investments and to eliminate many of the abuses of speculation, financing and present banking methods which have contributed to our troubles.

It is likewise probable that various schemes for unemployment insurance will be put into operation, and yet we must recognize that such measures are only palliatives that have no bearing on the root causes of our dilemma.

As a matter of fact this is true of economic planning as a whole under a profit system. Carried to its logical conclusion, the profit system would be "planned" out of existence. In other words, when we try to iron out those factors in the system which lead to depressions like the present one, we find ourselves eliminating those features which make it what it is. We cannot, for example, raise purchasing power to a point where it will absorb all the goods we produce, without wiping out profits altogether—and hence confiscating, as it were, all private ownership rights in production.

For this reason, attempts to establish a planned society, even though this course seems to be the only way to give private ownership a longer lease on life, will encounter all manner of opposition from conservatives who can't see the necessity of the step, but who in their blundering nevertheless express the underlying incompatibility of economic planning and a profit system.

Just what form such a "planned society" may take remains to be seen. It will at any rate represent an oligarchy in which vested interests, entrenched with government authority, will be able to prolong their régime for a while, conceding to the laboring and consuming masses as little as possible, but which necessarily will have to be a lot more than at present.

What lies beyond? So far, the one nation that has gone the farthest in planning its political, social and economic system in terms of the new productive forces of our century is Russia. But if Communism is the answer, the form it will take will have to be vastly modified to conform to our economic background. Therefore, to the question—what lies beyond?—we can find no specific answer at this time, nor indeed is it necessary that we should find one.

We must accept, therefore, the necessity for planning, as other countries have been forced to accept it because it is clear beyond dispute that no further progress can be made under laissez-faire policies. We recognize, furthermore, that Fascism is that kind of planning that attempts to reconcile the contradictions of technical progress and the profit system—whereas Communism eliminates them. The aim of Fascism is the maintenance of special privileges with the necessary concessions to the masses; while Communism seeks the creation of the highest possible standard of living for all without the opportunity for the reestablishment of special privileges. (Since the name "fascism" and the word "dictatorship" are more or less offensive to most Americans, we shall probably have to find ourselves a new label—as well as a new color for our shirts).

There is still one other road we might take in the immediate future: the road of consciously planned, armed revolution. The possibilities of this occurring appear to be remote, at least at present. There is, in the first place, no well-organized revolutionary group and no competent leadership. In the second place, social consciousness has not been fused and probably will not be fused into active hatred of any one class or group sufficiently to make for concerted action. Neither is there any definite program to which the masses might be rallied. Add to this the fact of our ingrained tradition of individualism and the popular faith in the unlimited opportunity to become rich, and it would appear that the chief requirements for successful revolutionary action are lacking. Interestingly enough the Third Internationale has no hope that a revolution is at hand.

It is more to the point, then, to consider what will be done to speed the essential changes which the times demand, seeking to provide for an "orderly transition" through our established form of government.

VI

THE ENGINEER AS A REVOLUTIONIST

Amid the welter of our confusions stands the engineer. Avowed revolutionist in the field of production, creator of new forces which have precipitated the necessity for fundamental changes in the organization of society, what is to be his rôle in this revolution? What help can we expect from him in seeking means to enjoy the abundance and the leisure his work has made possible; in devising new economic policies, in setting up new functions of government to lead us to a new order?

The engineer occupies a unique position. He is, indeed, essentially a revolutionist. There is but one tradition in the engineering profession, and that is, to have no traditions! Science, as well as its technologic application, in the endless striving for perfection, never ceasing in the quest for a better way, with its tireless research into new as yet unknown forces, untried methods, unsuspected means, is no respector of any established form or proven procedure. On the contrary, the spirit of engineering is to reject any established routine on the general principle that it may be improved.

Not even the "natural" precedents and examples can halt the engineer's search for new forms and revolutionary departures. Indeed, only insofar as the engineer disregarded *nature's way,* did he get anywhere. Man observes in nature only a lever with force applied and work done on one side of the fixed point, (as in the bone and muscle of our limbs) but Archimedes's fame is associated with a lever where the pivot is in the middle and force applied on one side of it while the work is done on the other. Likewise, there is no organism based on the principle of a wheel but, where would we be without the cart, the fly wheel and our numerous spinning and revolving mechanisms?

In the past man knew in nature only the direct connection of moving parts—yet the engineer has devised the electric generator or motor revolving freely within a magnetic field. Such examples may be multiplied endlessly.

But, having discovered a new principle, an engineer does not stop. He applies it to his problem. He criticizes its functions, improves upon it and continues the search for ever better technique. And when this is found he casts away the old and devotes his efforts to the perfection of the new.

As soon as the steam engine was invented, its shortcomings were criticized and improved upon; when it seemed that the limit of excellence was reached, the very principle of reciprocating movements was questioned and a steam turbine came into being in its turn at once subjected to searching analysis and criticism that brought about further improvements. Hardly was the first electric dynamo built when a new search was begun to increase the radius of electric distribution. To meet this need alternating current was discovered and its uses perfected.

In the technology of textiles, of steel and other metals, in every field and zone of engineering endeavors, we see the same attitude, the same ruthless dissatisfaction with "what is" and the indefatigable search for "what is not yet."

Romantic and ruthless as the engineering profession is, searching, experimenting, destructive of the past, revolutionary, engineering aims and engineering achievements are affecting the social economic structure of society *despite the will* or *conscious purpose* of the individual engineers.

An engineer creates or perfects a new technique. This new technique changes the mode of production. New production processes change economic relations and economic transformations in turn, bring about social readjustments. Thus, new social forces and relations no longer fit the political pattern worked out in the past to regulate traditional social and economic relations. This ensuing *maladjustment of realities* of life to political dogmas fosters discontent, and life grapples with dogma. Thus the engineer and his work is at the bottom of any social revolution.

Yet the engineer as an individual is not a political revolutionist. Quite the contrary is generally true.

An engineer strives for technical perfection. He applies the latest scientific discoveries to the life-sustaining process. He aims to do bigger and better things. He strives to reduce drudgery and lighten toil. He aims to conserve energy and natural resources. He creates facilities to make life fuller, working hours shorter, leisure hours more enjoyable. He conquers space, time and energy—welds communities together, facilitates communications, increases the interdependence of men, communities and nations.

To do all this, to accomplish any part of his task he needs a well-regulated social environment, assuring his undisturbed work and the application of his attainments. Thus he grows politically conservative or mildly liberal. He fears any external disturbances not only because they upset or retard the progress of his work but because they jeopardize his very livelihood. He becomes a supporter of the political "status quo" which insures the security of his income and the pursuit of his chosen profession.

And so the engineer of to-day is a tragic figure. A ruthless revolutionist in the field of technology, he undermines by his own work the very foundation of a society which he seeks to support! He works himself out of a job and the economic advantages connected with it, yet he dares not apply his radicalism to the rebuilding of society so that his services may be used on a broader scale.

Nevertheless, the engineer cannot help seeing more clearly than many other trained observers the inevitability of sweeping social changes.

Technology, through his labors, has altered the mode of production to the point where the old curse that man must "eat his bread in the sweat of his brow" has been redeemed, but only at the cost of hunger amidst plenty. Leisure, long sought and long dreamed of by generations of men has been created but it is the enforced leisure of unemployment—the product of an old system of wealth distribution based on scarcity and private ownership of the means of living.

Science adds its own query as to the validity of such a system when Professor Frederick Soddy asks why, since all invention and all technological progress is the product of accumulated *collective* contributions, should it be individually owned? We are charged no premiums on the accumulated medical knowledge of the past century. Why then should the labors of the countless dead line the pockets of a few financiers, denying to the masses their share in a common heritage?

We may take it for granted that the masses will not so be denied. When the working classes become conscious of what they are deprived, they rebel, as they have always rebelled throughout history—and these revolutions are provoked not by those who suffer but by those who suppress them!

The revolutionary ferment is perhaps strongest within the intellectual classes, not only because their intelligence, education and reading gives them a clearer insight into the essential problems of our time, but because they see wider opportunities for service and a greater freedom of expression under a different order. Teachers, doctors, artists and writers, for example, are usually motivated by broader social aims than mere money-making. To-day, furthermore, their economic position in common with the "white collar" class as a whole is becoming more and more straitened. They have everything to gain and little or nothing to lose.

Greatest of all compulsions to change, however, is possibly the growing consciousness on all sides of the epic "release of cultural and humanistic values" which will attend man's entry into a new era of mass leisure. In this there is no doubt something of the old enchantment and delusion exercised by all visions of El Dorado—and yet this time the attainable reality would indeed be something of a Utopia in comparison with what man has known before. What new problems mass leisure will bring, is beside the point. A happier world is in sight—it does lie beyond the seas—even though the crossing will be a stormy one and many will perish on the way! We may take it for granted that in this age where knowledge is disseminated so rapidly—and discontent has so many mediums of expression —that we will not passively endure for long the monumental folly of our "paradox of plenty."

VII

TOWARD ENGINEERING STATESMANSHIP

While it is true that engineers are generally conservatives in their economic and political views, it is likewise true that in the past few years they have become more conscious of their social obligations and opportunities.

Technocracy is a case in point, and that its "findings" represent merely a spicy salad of facts already long familiar to economists and engineers, is of secondary importance. A catchy name and good publicity succeeded in drawing public attention to our essential problems. That the process of reëducation, once begun, should be continued, and that misinterpretations should be ironed out is a responsibility which other engineering groups must not overlook.

Discussion and clarification of these issues is going on to-day in committee meetings, open forums, conventions of major engineering societies as well as in such societies as the League of Professional Groups, the Taylor Society, The Technical Branch of F. S. U. and other organizations.

Certainly engineers will be prepared to place in the hands of our politicians "blue prints" and "specifications" for reconstruction if asked for them. To create conditions under which these plans can be utilized is, of course, a job for our law-making bodies.

If we concede the point that these legislative measures in the near future will be designed to permit a degree of economic planning, on the fascist order, we may expect to see engineers taking an important part, both in making those plans and executing them. It is here that engineering technique and method, developed within factory walls, will find their wider application. Inadequate and piece-meal though this planning will necessarily be, within a profit system, it will be a training period for the day when the engineer is entrusted with the larger job of the full direction of our society.

Then the revolution, which is only now beginning, will have been completed. The technical forces which are now beginning to be understood, the economic suffering which is still being endured, will have finally created that *social conscious-*

ness without which no revolution is possible, by its impact forcing political realignments.

Whether such a revolution be violent or a gradual readjustment, it is essentially a part of the *evolutionary* process by which society grows. If pent up social forces are finally released in an explosion, the difference is primarily one of degree. The causes and consequences of the change are eventually the same.

The engineer is not primarily the wrecker, but the builder. His job begins when the smoke has cleared away. Some engineers may think, as they did in Russia, that they will lose their economic and social standing in the event of revolution. But even though the upheaval should be as violent and complete as was the Russian revolution, the contrary is the case. The engineer is indispensable in the up-building process, in which he finds new opportunities to build for mankind's benefit.

When the viewpoint is finally accepted that in this Power Age we can no longer entrust the management of human and non-human forces to those who know nothing of science, or of the physico-mathematical factors that shape our existence, nor of the engineering technique necessary to control a high speed civilization grown too complex for rule-of-thumb methods, then society will force the emergence of engineering statesmanship.

This obviously means engineering in a broader sense than mere bridge building or factory management, just as it means statesmanship in terms of the widest human objectives.

The planning of production, consumption, and distribution obviously will be the engineer's job, as will the execution of those plans since the engineer alone knows how to produce, when and how to transport and distribute goods.

Engineers will manage the economics of the system, because exchange will be based on real physical values and not on metaphysical units with no relation to production or human needs.

A certain amount of engineering "polytechnic" knowledge will be a part of every one's education since without it no one will be fitted to live a useful and intelligent life in the new world.

Engineers will play an important rôle in the direction of the new mass leisure, for it is they who have so far produced those two great civilizing agencies: the cinema and the radio—and who will produce others yet to come.

Engineers will manage exports and imports, as they now handle store room service and internal transport within factories.

Together with the nation's doctors they will coördinate and provide for national sanitation and health.

Above all, however, the statesmen-engineers of to-morrow will direct and carry on the scientific and social research by which the progressive betterment of society will be assured. Thus the critical spirit, the engineering tradition which is to have no traditions, will find its full expression in a dynamic society, fulfilling its destiny under the guidance of man's intelligence, forever seeking new levels of attainment, new experiences, greater richness of life.

SAMUEL D. SCHMALHAUSEN

COMMUNISM VERSUS FASCISM

> "If we are to have a dictator, our peo-
> ple and institutions of wealth would
> like him to be of the Mussolini type.
> However, he is more likely to be of the
> type of Lenin. That, for obvious rea-
> sons, would not suit them at all."
>
> COL. E. M. HOUSE [1]

THE mind undergoes its disillusionment far too slowly and reluctantly. Illusions—myths, fictions, rationalizations, the ritual of make-believe—stir the imagination, imparting to one's beliefs a false and beguiling dignity. But facts delimit and outrage the mind's infinite capacity for self-delusion. Man clings to his illusions like a child to its mother's breast with a sucking tenacity, half bite and half caress. The process of weaning begins in infancy and outlasts senility. Man cannot easily be weaned from his illusions. Nor do I foolishly imagine that a mind, however realistic and critical, can completely empty itself of infantile attitudes, if these be vitalizing and consolatory.

The essential difference between minds is not determined by the absence or presence of illusions but rather by the amount of critical insight into this inherent process of self-delusion that runs its curve of growth—as experience and new knowledge mature and reëducate the mind—from beliefs factually outmoded (I should prefer to call this psychological rather than cultural lag) to beliefs more in tune with facts newly emerging. I suppose one might say, without being too cynical, that the success of a system depends upon making fictions look like

[1] Quoted from his article entitled "Does America Need A Dictator?" (in *Liberty Magazine,* Jan. 7, 1933). A sub-title, no doubt editorially inspired, wistfully reads: "A Warning to Selfish Wealth and Narrow-Minded Politicians to Uplift Our Capitalistic Civilization."

facts. Hence the illimitable importance of illusion in the scheme
of things. If illusion departs too widely from actuality, the
system is on the defensive, doomed. Private capitalism is caught
in such a catastrophic crisis now. The ugly underlying realities
make its democratic illusions (ideals!) all the more contempt-
ible.

America is a democracy. That's a fiction. America is a capitalistic democracy. That's a fact. What a devastating difference.
We can look back now with disillusioned wise eyes and perceive
that the success of the bourgeois scheme of government depended almost wholly upon confusing the public mind concerning the nature of its democracy. For it is difficult to
imagine two more contradictory concepts than democracy and
capitalism. Democracy is a social concept and involves the welfare of the underlying population; if it isn't that, it isn't anything. Capitalism is by its very nature anti-democratic, feudalistic, its mechanisms and motivations utterly dissociated from
the social well being of the masses. We know this to be exactly
true from that long bitter and murderous history of Capitalism
that resulted, under the most desperate conditions only, in
making piecemeal concessions to the disinherited groups (the
so-called citizens of a democracy). I do not wish to be guilty of
a frivolous use of words, but I think the point will be driven
home a little more incisively if I speak of this brazen camouflage as demockracy. The point is that Capitalism has never
liquidated its heritage of feudalism: its institutions are saturated
—honeycombed—with pyramidal practices; serfs at the base,
lords and barons (landlords, coal barons, Governmental potentates) at the apex, stratified servitors and sycophants of high
and low degree cooped up between apex and base.

One can as sensibly speak of chaste prostitution as talk of
capitalist *democracy*. Capitalism is capitalistic precisely to the
extent that it prevents democracy from being democratic,[2] hence,

[2] The tendency, recently so conspicuous both in England and in this country to
cut down on educational and social service, functions deemed by the ruling class
not wholly necessary, certainly not in time of capitalistic crisis, illustrates emphat-
ically enough the irrelevant nature of democracy within the present system. Here
is an illuminating paragraph on that point: "Finally, the tax reductionists attack
first of all those services which are the best proof of civilized existence. Their practical offensive involves the 'abolition of school gardens and teacher training schools;
elimination of medical inspection in schoolrooms; eliminating adult educating
classes, vocational guidance work, summer schools and fire prevention departments;
cutting into appropriations of museums, libraries, hospitals, homes for the aged and

the ease of transition from Capitalism to fascism, the one im-
plicitly and the other explicitly rejecting the social logic resident in the democratic ideal. The historical significance of both
Capitalism and fascism is the attempt by force and fraud to
prevent the masses from coming to power.

The great illusion of the 19th Century—in post-war retrospect it looks suspiciously like the great collusion—whereby
Illiberalism in industry was camouflaged by Liberalism in
politics remains something of a puzzle still. The palpable breakdown of the liberal "philosophy" both in England and America, leaving a trail of homeless pseudo-radicals in its somewhat
ludicrous wake, is a graphic culmination of a process of intellectual corruption (self-delusion?) that traces its unclean source
to the illusory belief in the democratic possibilities of Capitalism (predatory and anti-democratic in every known item of
its theory of business enterprise).

If you look at the predicament of the nice people under
Capitalism, whose income and prestige accrued from capitalistic
institutions and contacts but whose scientific or philosophic
training permitted a more humane insight into the possibilities of the underlying realities, it is not difficult to understand
their psychoanalytic dilemma. They were primarily with the
system but incidentally against it (its more flagrant "abuses").
This ambivalence is the psychologic key to the duplicitous
and eventually rather feeble philosophy of liberalism. The
liberals were never sincerely, and certainly not courageously,
interested in challenging the very basis of the status quo; they
were happy enough, in alliance with one of the major capitalistic parties, if they could stir up some enthusiasm for reform
from within. The shallowness of this point of view is now pretty
clear to all of us and may be likened to the attempt of a professor of ethics, drawing his splendid stipend from the vested
interests who sit as boards of trustees in his institution of "hire"
learning, to lecture his feudal overlords—the coal barons, the
oil barons, the steel magnates, the power potentates—on the
sublimities of the Sermon on the Mount. It is difficult to decide
whether this duplicity of the liberals [3] was more knavery or

---

handicapped. . . .'" This is cited by Harry Elmer Barnes (who quotes from an
important "statesmanlike" article from the *Virginia Quarterly Review* by Henry
Pratt Fairchild and William L. Nunn) *World-Telegram*, Feb. 2, 1933.

[3] See C. Hartley Grattan's fine article "The Treason of the Intellectuals" in *Behold
America!*

innocence (i.e. ignorance of the desperate underlying realities in the lives of the masses). Scratch a liberal and you'll find a capitalist.[4]

Socialism, particularly in its so-called Marxian dress, seemed so alien from Capitalism and from liberalism that it took the lightning clarity released by the Great War to split in half that historic philosophy of socialism which the world mistakenly conceived to be genuinely, because realistically, opposed to the postulates and practices of Capitalism. The great disillusionment precipitated by the War was this bitter realization of the liberal-capitalistic nature of Socialism, in actuality. It was the incorruptible sincerity of Lenin's mind that hammered into our contemporary consciousness this deeper insight into the essentially bourgeois nature of socialism. If we have not as yet learned that the historic function of what calls itself Socialism has been to *prevent* the proletariat from coming into power, we have missed the most salient lesson of almost one hundred years of "radicalism." The very need which arose of qualifying adjectives, to make necessary distinctions between honest and dishonest uses of the various brands of radicalism, as for example in categories like radical socialists, revolutionary socialists, is significant evidence of how conservative and anti-prole-

[4] Gilbert Seldes, a scatter-brained commentator on the American Scene, quite unwittingly hits the nail on the head when he says: "To me the significant thing is that we are losing a lot of our blind faith in our economic institutions. Given changes in the economic structure we could without changing the form of government have anything from dictatorship to democracy in America. I think we are going to have a modified capitalism if we are lucky and intelligent enough." There are two keen little errors in this sage utterance. If Mr. Seldes will place before the word dictatorship the accurate adjective *fascist,* and before democracy the illuminating modifier *capitalistic,* his insight will not only gain in profundity but most precisely reveal the basic truth about "our" economic institutions. This capitalistic democracy can indeed be quite easily transformed into a fascist dictatorship; for the very good reason that the democracy part is a fiction and the capitalistic part a reality. And it will indeed require a genuine revolution of a communistic complexion to undo once for all this evil and disastrous alliance between the social logic of democracy and the anti-social logic of capitalism. No wonder he writes, and how erroneously: "But I certainly do not think we are destined and damned to the communist form of doom and am doubtful that the collapse of civilization has been ear-marked for your time and mine. Revolution is the alternative only to brute lack of brains in our present plight. I don't think we've reached that stage." What Seldes does not know about the sociology and economics of revolution in the modern world could fill three big volumes: in fact, they have been thus filled by Leon Trotsky. (These remarks of Mr. Seldes are quoted from his letter to Harry Hansen, *N. Y. World-Telegram,* Feb. 8, 1933).

tarian the older version had become. Hence the necessity and
tactical wisdom of labeling sincere socialism by its Marxian
title of Communism. The very concept Communism had to be
resurrected to differentiate sharply and sincerely between a
Socialism that had become insanely patriotic, nationalistic, joyously serving the imperialistic interests of Capitalism, supporting Governments that were brazenly bourgeois, intoxicating
the masses with anti-revolutionary propaganda, behaving quite
as though Marxism were as unreal to them as to the capitalists
and their liberal apologists; *and* a Leninism that was anti-capitalistic and anti-imperialistic to the core, thus creating the
dynamic post-war categories of reactionary versus revolutionary
socialism. If you look at it sentimentally, the breakdown of
socialism in the World War and its aftermath is the most tragic
event of the 20th Century.

For our present purposes it is important to note that the old
illusory distinctions between capitalism and liberalism on the
one hand, between liberalism and socialism on the other hand,
not forgetting the presumably deep difference between Capitalism and socialism, are all fit for the historic trash-basket. And
in this disillusioned insight lies the sufficient reason for lump-
ing these three groups into the one category of real or potential
fascists. Mussolini, Pilsudski, Noske, Scheidemann, MacDonald,
Chiang Kai-shek, Horthy, Hitler:—these "National Socialists"
constitute a wonderful gallery for the Leninist to study.

Communism is both the flaming concept and the desperately
sincere reality which connotes first of all the treason and failure
of that traditional socialism which got itself all messed up with
capitalist-imperialism (the liberals [5] having as their sacred
function the sprinkling of a perfumed rhetoric on the corrupt
contradictions of a predatory status quo) and then the reëner-
gizing of the masses of the world with a revolutionary faith in
their great proletarian destiny as the new creators of a classless
civilization.

The history of socialism since the War is a tide of black reaction against the revolutionary philosophy its mighty leaders
had mouthed for a generation as platitudes and pretences, to
the betrayal of the blind and credulous masses. Socialism every-

---

[5] "The tolerant and detached objectivity of liberalism is, in fact, compelled to
descend from its spurious judicial seat, and to take its place behind the machine
guns pointed against revolutionary thought." From Robert Briffault's powerful
analysis of the liberal mind.

where is the last defender of Capitalism *against* Communism.[6]

I think we can see now all the more clearly why War has been thought of and accepted as "natural" while Revolution has been shied away from as "unnatural." Something is natural when it has become a familiar part of the traditional scheme of use and wont. Tragically enough, war has been so regular a part of the capitalist-imperialist philosophy of Government that one of the most obstinate beliefs to root out of the mind is this drilled-in panicky conviction that war is inevitable *because* human nature is pugnacious, i.e. warlike. This evil logic, desperately plausible, gained a strange re-affirmation by the correlative conception of revolution as something unspeakable, most unnatural, representing the unseemly dregs of society. Why has revolution been given such a black eye?

First let us be clear on one point, to wit, that this glorification of war and damnation of revolution is the sheerest dishonesty. Our problem is to account for the high repute in which this dishonest theory has been held. Capitalism needs the State for its intra-territorial and extra-territorial purposes: tariffs and subsidies and special privileges for the home market, diplomacy and veiled threats and armed intervention for the sake of foreign markets. Capitalism cannot thrive without its foster mother, the State. Hence the intimate bond between Capitalism and nationalism. And since this bond has very little to do with love and a great deal to do with power-politics pursuing lucrative unearned income, we perceive the inherent finance-imperialism of this *entente cordiale* betwixt Capitalism and nationalism. They are both realistically one. Imperialism in the modern world simply means that each separate Capitalism as it builds, mainly by war, its recognized status as a full-blown nationalism, comes into conflict with all the other arrived nationalistic Capitalisms, venomously competing for the

[6] Max Nomad's *Rebels and Renegades* is a great book to consult on these radical renegades who used socialism for purposes of careerism, making a monkey of the masses in the cold-blooded climb to prestige, under capitalism.

Think of this candid confessional of Prof. Charles A. Beard, one of the founders of the Rand School of Social Science, a socialist institution: "If capitalism were cursed with all the evils ascribed to it by Communists (and it has plenty to its credit), still the American people, on a fair and free count, would vote one hundred to one for keeping it rather than enslave themselves to the kind of political and economic despotism regnant in the land of the former Tzars." Beard is not ashamed of this low estimate of the American people nor of his wildly false evaluation of Soviet Russia.

lion's share of the world's markets. This unholy trinity: Capitalism, nationalism, imperialism—has literally battened on the blood and agony of the masses of underlings in all lands. And it was this unholy trinity that perverted the minds of men into believing that revolution is the horror of horrors, not to be thought of, treasonably impermissible!

That capitalists should want to hold the workers down in a system of wage slavery is understandable enough; that imperialists should want to hold their colonials in a profitable subjection is logical, too; but that liberals and even socialists, though pretending to be outraged by war as sheer barbarism in a civilized world, shall in a patriotic crisis accept, participate in, and whoop it up for their respective capitalist-nationalisms, that's not so obviously understandable or logical. The situation is even more involved and incredible. That these self-same liberals and Socialists, in fierce actuality making an unforgettable mockery of their pacifist pretenses and socialist dedications, shall be among the most outspoken antagonists of social revolution is, at first blush, as baffling as it appears disingenuous.

If it can be even half reasonably argued that war is necessary, how can it be simultaneously argued that revolution is not necessary? War is initiated by the masters and fought by the slaves: Revolution is initiated by the slaves and fought against the masters. The rich approve of war and use every instrument at their disposal to *conscript* the poor for this alien purpose: the poor are driven by unbearable circumstance to inaugurate revolution for the dispossession of the rich. How can any mind sufficiently clear in its thinking to be utterly honest in its will, doubt the social and economic superiority of revolution to war—if what is at stake is the emancipation of the masses?

There is no longer any honest reason for imagining social revolution to be merely a study in mob [7] violence—the favorite conception of those publicists who find violence horrible only when it is perpetrated by the "lower" classes. Since the inspiring Russian revolutions we know very well that social revolution is not only revolutionary but sociological in its process,

[7] The eminent liberal Everett Dean Martin, one of America's most reactionary educators, has specialized since the war (which he joyously helped to sponsor) in trying to prove that the greatest danger in the modern world is "the mob" (i.e., the proletariat). He apparently does not know that the masses are driven to becoming mobs by their superiors!

goal, and cultural ideology. I know of no other effective anti-
dote for reactionary capitalism than revolutionary communism.
Reactionary Capitalism of course means in our day fascism.
The first critical difference between fascism and communism
—the only realistic choices before us—is precisely that the former is a fake revolution and the latter a sincere revolution. A
genuine revolution at this stage of capitalistic breakdown must
spring from a new class: the only significant new class is the
emerging proletariat (workers, farmers, jobless technologists,
disillusioned intellectuals) which has as its historic task the
rescuing of civilization from further destruction by capitalist
imperialism, a task that involves new social relations and new
economic motives, intra-nationally and inter-nationally. This is
revolution in the profound and life-enhancing sense.[8]

Look at the meager and uninspiring record of fascism. Its
audacious pretence that the State can transcend classes while
permitting classes to continue in economic operation and dif-
ferential status is as untenable in theory as it is vicious in
practice. For what actually happens is the merciless annihilation of the class status and revolutionary tradition of the proletariat, the forced subservience of the working class to a
capitalist class that now, under fascist auspices, shares its
exploitative power with the so-called "corporative" State. The
suppression of the proletariat, far from being diminished, is
actually doubled: two powerful masters now hold the whip
hand over the cringing slave.

Fascism is a forced equilibrium of elements so irreconcilable
that the merest relaxation of this compulsory coalescence would
release explosive energies intense enough to destroy the whole
system. Fascism is a very dangerous "solution" of the class conflict inherent in Capitalism. Not the least of its dangers is the
necessity of diverting the minds of the masses from the true
struggle at home toward fantastic nationalistic ambitions and
schemes of imperial grandeur that have not the remotest relation to the logic of reality. From a psychiatric point of view,
fascism clearly reveals itself as an insane solution of the modern
predicament inherent in the status quo. Since the emerging
proletariat—obviously the next social class to shape the historic process in response to the traditionally unsolved needs and

[8] Read *The Only Way Out* by Emile Burns, a splendid communist analysis of the
English situation by a well informed economist.

aspirations of the underlying population—is held in leash by this new police state,[9] the one significant source of creative energy, the energy that alone can build a future, is negated and arrested, the result being a backward-looking philosophy of values that seeks at all costs to reinstate a mythical past, to pit a renascent medievalism, all glamorous with rhetoric and false promise, against the threatening emergence of a new world.

Since fascism cannot accept the challenge of contemporary reality toward a true progression, it must perforce preoccupy itself with regression, in the psychoanalytic sense, and retrogression in the historic sense. The indoctrination of the minds of the people with pre-scientific superstitions, the vested interest of a medieval church, perverting the educational process to the reactionary purposes of a state that cannot dispense with theologic hocus-pocus, is of itself a remarkable illustration of that infantile regression in fascist thinking that marks it as immature and unreal. An age that by its very technological process is scientific in its innermost texture is hardly the period in history for resurrecting the myths congenial to the childhood of the race.[10]

Where reality is so real, as in our tormented epoch, the essence of wisdom is the facing of that reality. To camouflage it, to evade and distort it, to fly off on fantastic tangents, all this is social infantilism, though it be called by the hard-boiled name of fascism. Every observer, who has permitted himself even a small margin of critical-mindedness, has come away from his study of fascist ritual and pageantry, more obviously in the case of Hitler, only less obviously in the case of Mussolini, with the impression of its vast adolescent theatricalism and solemn buffoonery. In truth, fascism is the social hysteria of an economic system that is screaming to be saved while drowning. In all hysteria the element of pure theatricality is marvelously in

9 Count Sforza characterizes Fascism in Italy as "police despotism."

10 This is Benito Mussolini at his best: "Sometimes I play with the idea of a laboratory for making generations: that is, of creating the class of warriors, ever ready to die; the class of inventors, pursuing the secret of mystery; the class of judges, the class of great captains of industry, of great explorers, of great governors. And it is by means of such a methodical selection that the great classes are created which in turn will create the empire. To be sure this is a lofty dream; but I see it being realized little by little. . . . The goal is always—Empire!" (Quoted from Prof. Schneider's *Making the Fascist State*—p. 253).

evidence. Fascism is an insane solution of that modern predicament which is so palpably precipitating the complete breakdown of the capitalist-imperialist scheme of things.

The insanity of the solution is made manifest in the forced
coupling of such utterly irreconcilable principles as private
profit motive and mass welfare: this strange State that main-
tains the fiction of rising impartially above classes is thoroughly
capitalistic in one half of its brain and mock-socialistic in the
other half of its brain; the visible result being such a paralysis
of the people's energy that creative sterility, educational inhi-
bition, cultural emptiness prevail and stupefy the fascist mind.

"Fascism has no philosophy and wants none. Its inability to
formulate its ideas into a coherent system is not lamented as a
deficiency, but exalted as the most certain evidence of its creative freshness" . . . "Another chief work of fascist art is the
Duce himself—a genuinely creative 'invention' and a vital
synthesis of speech, bearing and deeds. The reader must not
take this metaphorically, for the whole point of the fascist doctrine is that genuine art must be expressed literally in the form
of practical action and not in so-called works of art; and the
whole essence of the fascist faith is this confidence in the aes-
thetic values of their practical achievements" . . . "And in
theory the *fascisti* can well afford to be unanimous; there will
be abundant opportunity for differences when it comes to ap-
plying it to particular works of art. But it is idle to anticipate
these differences, for as yet there are no particular works of art
to speak of" . . . "The external facts of fascist life really become quite insignificant once the true inwardness and spirit-
uality of the movement is grasped. Fascism's mind, then, is
contained in ideal fascist morals and its culture is the character
which every fascist thinks he possesses." [11]

Fascism is reactionary in economics, medieval in religion,
culturally sterile, scientifically tongue-tied, a newly "benevolent" feudalism attempting to save the masses from communism by leading them back to communionism. If you look at it
psychologically, the phenomenon that underlies fascism is
literally crack-brained. The origin of this split-consciousness
which is the fascist mind and vision derives from the post-war
breakdown, in Europe most graphically, of the capitalist order

[11] These quaintly sympathetic remarks are taken from Prof. Schneider's distinguished book *Making the Fascist State*.

and with it the painful liquidation of almost the entire middle class which, as a result of inflation and further all-around bankruptcy, has been hurled down into a quasi-proletariat. This crushed class, by economic catastrophe suddenly finding itself sinking to the level of the proletariat, but by traditional psychologic orientation remaining as of old an ally of the bourgeoisie, was caught in a terrible historic dilemma, namely, dispossessed and disinherited by its old landlord Capitalism, too proud and reluctant to accept orders from its new lord communism, what to do in such a crisis? Enter Fascism as saviour of this crushed class of bourgeois bankrupts.

The big business men and bankers are not in love with fascism, fearing its rivalry and in due time its positive hostility; but though they do not love fascism, they venomously hate communism: the choice is not a sweet one and capitalistic free will has apparently very little to do with the case. Hence we witness in several cracking countries this flirtation with fascism, a ludicrous honeymoon of an apparently ill-mated couple, the bridegroom far too old and wilily, the bride rather young and brainless, that threatens ever and anon to end in an ugly divorce or at least a scandalous separation. What obviously holds them in an unblest wedlock is not affection for one another but a common hate.

The bourgeoisie, big and little, major and minor, fears communism and communism alone, with a genuine biologic fear of a hostile force that will destroy it when the opportunity presents. Fascism is therefore welcomed by the dominant classes (still dominant in spite of everything) as the best solution for their unsolvable dilemmas. For deeper than all their immediate vexations and problems is the panicky need of staving off that fundamental transformation of civilization which will liquidate their costly and incompetent hegemony once for all, permitting the suffocated forces of life to flow vitally into new channels, creating through a new class a communist culture that will reënergize the broken wills of men and courageously re-make the slave status of humanity.

I was saying a while back that fascism is a fake revolution. The statement strikes me as wholly true. If we must use the concept revolution let us rather accurately describe fascism as a political coup d'etat, itself a prelude to the social counter-revolution. Fascism is not, by any possible stretch of terms, revolutionary; it is deliberately reactionary—that's its present pro-capitalistic and anti-communistic significance (and danger).

Surely the genuine Bolshevik revolution has taught us that a real social revolution *revolutionizes* every institution in civilization, transforms all economic and social and cultural relations, so that it is correct to speak of this change as bringing about something really new in the world's history. Everyone is sufficiently familiar by now with the vast amount of "catastrophic" change in Soviet Russia, and what is equally to the point, the unresting speed of these multitudinous changes: in the nature of the State, in the nature of the family, in woman's status, in the status of children, in the altered position of agriculture as well as of industry, not to overlook the profound transformations in sex, in morals, in marriage, in a whole catalogue of ancient behaviors and philosophies. This is Social Revolution in that inspiring and far-reaching sense which makes millions of awakened human beings in every perturbed portion of the globe look to Soviet Russia for great human experiments and solutions in this crucial 20th Century.

The contrast between Mussolini and Lenin yields a fair enough measure of the differences in their class status and social philosophy. The outstanding characteristic of Lenin's life was its marvelous sincerity. The most shining trait of Mussolini's career is its amazing insincerity. Is there any social philosophy more candid and courageous than Communism? Is there any political philosophy more opportunistic and disingenuous and chameleon than Fascism?

Surely there is the most intimate relationship between great sincerity and new creation, in art or in economics, and obversely, insincerity (which is a form of superficiality) is correlated with sterility. Scan the ten year record of Fascism! The incredible emptiness of the years is best attested by an official apologist's summary [12] which opens with these resounding sentences: "A great Fascist exhibition will open its doors in Rome

---

[12] *Ten Years of Fascism: Italy Remolded*, in *The New York Times Magazine*, Oct. 23, 1932, an article by Arnaldo Cortesi, dated Rome. The author, though slurring over the truth about Mussolini, including the mad murder of Matteotti, admits this much: "But of the changes that fascism has brought about in Italy the most significant will find no place in the exhibition, because it is not of a material but of a spiritual nature. Being that, it has more of the quality of permanence than other Mussolini achievements." For contrast effect, as well as for more knowledge and insight, read Count Carlo Sforza's *The Fascist Decade* in *Foreign Affairs*, Oct. 1932.

on Oct. 28 to celebrate the tenth anniversary of the march on Rome. In halls decorated in the flamboyant but not particularly beautiful style affected by the ultra-modern school of artists will be gathered a remarkable collection of mementos of the struggle which paved the way for the rise to power of the most dramatic dictatorship of modern times." Farther on, this cordial commentator apprises us of the following illustrious achievement of Fascism during its momentous reign of ten years: "The reclaiming of the Pontine Marshes, a work that defied the efforts of Emperors and Popes for centuries, is among the outstanding memorials of Fascist achievement. Another is the swift modernization of Italian roads during the last five years . . . Motoring in Italy used to be a trying experience. Now a network of smooth roads extends from the Alps to the tip of Italy."

It will be difficult henceforth for the sympathetic historian to deny that Fascism has been an astonishing success—for Mussolini, at all events. Pontine Marshes reclaimed: motoring improved—these are certainly great achievements. Our journalistic reporter, Arnaldo Cortesi, who is perhaps a greater unconscious humorist than even Curzio Malaparte [13] communicates this footnote on contemporary events: "To-day, when many countries are torn by revolution and unrest—the underlying cause of which is often economic—Italy has been completely free of manifestations of a similar nature."

Those who are against Communism and pretend or imagine that they are not for Fascism think they occupy a superior liberal position when they damn both as being dictatorships, the naïve assumption being that democracy under capitalism is generically unrelated to the dictatorial technique. But differences are all-important if our thinking is not to be merely academic and rhetorical. In Soviet Russia there is a socialized dictatorship, deeply imbedded in a proletarian class philosophy, while in Fascist Italy there is only too patently a personal despotism. Mussolini has more than once of late frankly confessed that he hopes to hold on until he dies, though he has his doubts whether there will be a successor. To make a personal despotism, which means in actuality a sort of glorified policeman, synonymous with a class dictatorship of the most fertile

---

[13] Whose recklessly brilliant book entitled *Coup D'Etat: The Technique of Revolution* contains a subtle chapter on Hitler which taken in conjunction with the one preceding it on Mussolini supplies some sidelights of an illuminating nature.

and creative resourcefulness that the world has known is to perpetrate a crime against lucidity—to put it mildly.

The mind of Italy has been put to sleep by Mussolini. The mind of Russia has been electrified into new thought and new life by Lenin. I do not deem it melodrama but accurate characterization to assert that the contrast is one quite literally between night and day, between death and life. Who does not know that Soviet Russia symbolizes the whole potential creative drive of modern life desperately confronting a new destiny on earth?

Mention any country, under capitalist or fascist domination, where so many *workers* coöperate enthusiastically toward the accomplishment of a goal consciously created by their associated minds and wills.[14] Here are authoritative words from Michael Farbman, one of the most distinguished students of economics, who has visited and re-visited Russia for the sake of special studies: "It was this enthusiasm, this zeal for working to full capacity, as illustrated by the so-called shock methods and socialist emulation, which is hailed as the cornerstone and guarantee of the ultimate success of reconstruction. During the last two years it has even led to a revision of the schedules of the Plan by the workers, called 'counter-plan.' That is to say, a mass meeting of workers in a factory would be held at which a planning committee would be appointed to discuss the official estimates with the directors of the factory in respect to output. The revised estimates thus obtained, if approved at the mass meeting, would then constitute the workers' counter-plan which almost invariably is in advance of what was demanded by the Plan. The new method of planning consists in adopting the counter-plan from the very start. That is to say, the mass of workers were now called upon to collaborate in the making as well as in the execution of the Plan . . . It is too early to decide whether a revision of government plans by factory

---

[14] Those who still hostilely imagine that there is something in England or America called democracy bulwarked by precious liberties will experience a salutary disillusion by reading Sidney Webb's article "Is Soviet Russia A Democracy?" (*Current History*, Feb. 1933) in which he shows so cogently how under the proletarian dictatorship the masses participate in, and significantly help to control, all the vital phases of economic and cultural life. "Thus, in literally hundreds of thousands of small public meetings, there goes on, from the Baltic to the Pacific, an almost ceaseless discussion of public affairs, to which there is in other countries no parallel." . . . "It is not easy to dispute the claim that the electoral system of Soviet Russia, however we may designate it, more accurately expresses the people's will than those of the United States, Great Britain or the German Reich."

workers has greater or less value than a democratic vote. I can only say that at present this collaboration is taken seriously by both the government and the workers, and that it is difficult to point out any other means of working out so onerous an operation . . . When in December the second Piatiletka is ratified by the Union Congress of Soviets, it will be claimed as the first national plan to be created by the collective will of the whole nation." [15]

If the personal despotism that fascism symbolizes and necessitates (the feudalism that still lies so deep in Capitalism in complete control once more) is to be called, though it be for invidious and malicious reasons, a dictatorship, it is still of the essence of intellectual honesty to differentiate concretely between a form of dictatorship that is repressive and life-constricting, and that dictatorship which has given abundant evidence of being liberative and life-enhancing. I doubt if within the past ten years any intelligent visitor to Russia has failed to comment upon the stir of energies, the bubbling new waves of life, the stimulating transformations in *every* field of thought and human activity.

H. N. Brailsford in his great book first made us aware more than ten years ago of the miracles of *will* which Bolshevism was releasing, destroying with such swift lightning effectiveness the traditional profit motive, turning the minds of men toward a qualitatively new order of civilization. And in the course of the inspiring years, thanks to Soviet Russia's fascinating every curious and forward looking thinker, we were being submitted here in America to a wonderful reëducation concerning the untapped potentialities resident in man, released by this revolutionary philosophy. The reports of competent and talented observers like Albert Rhys Williams on peasant life, revitalized and reborn; George S. Counts and John Dewey on education (than which the latter declared there was nothing more democratic and original and alive in the world); Maurice Hindus on the startling and deeply humanizing changes in marriage and morals; Sherwood Eddy and Jerome Davis on the great challenge held out by communism to the present inadequate order; Julian Huxley astonished and delighted with the enor-

15 This is the last of a series of four most excellent articles under the general title of *Russia Re-Visited,* in *The New Republic,* Nov. 30, 1932. The fourth article called *The Second Five Year Plan In The Making* is of the greatest interest and importance to students of Soviet Russia.

mous scientific achievement, not only practical and inventive
but in the fields of theory and research as well; Bertrand Rus-
sell's awakened sense of the new creative rôle in Soviet Russia
of youth, so dismally denied them in England and in America;
Elmer Rice's enthusiastic appreciation of the novelties and
originalities in the drama; the keen appreciation of a great new
era in music so happily commented upon by Albert Coates and
Olin Downes, for example; America's unforgettable new experience with the marvelous Russian films, the like of which
for sheer impersonal originality of theme and exquisiteness of
photography would be hard to match anywhere, except possibly
in Germany; Sidney Webb's calm and scholarly appraisal of
the remarkable economic and social achievements under Communist direction;—one could mention without difficulty a
hundred men and women, very few of whom would class themselves as Communists at all, all intensely agreeing that civilization has never known an "experiment" so fundamental and
ramifying, so significant scientifically and culturally and economically, not only for the Russians, but equally for the future
of humanity at large, as this incredible performance inaugurated by revolutionary socialism.[16]

We might profitably at this point ask and face the question
whether the principle of dictatorship is a vital part of any *fundamental* alteration of the status quo or whether, if enough
minds among the citizenry be sufficiently well disposed, it can
be dispensed with, as the socialists claim.

Has "our" own country perhaps been under a dictatorship,

[16] The intellectual collapse of Mr. Mencken, the ex-sage of Baltimore, is of course
one of the touching phenomena of our tragic era. His most manic excitement is
set off by Communism which his Fascist temperament can't abide. Isaac Don
Levine, who is conducting a private pogrom against Stalinism, is a fair-minded man
alongside of H. L. Mencken. Read our ex-sage's frenzied oration entitled "The
Russian Imposture" (*American Mercury*, Feb. 1933), which emits these red-hot
"Nietzschean" sparks: "The origin of these precious reformers sufficiently explains
their megalomania. With few exceptions they issue from the lowest orders of the
Russian population. The accidents of war and revolution gave them their start,
and they carry on by waging a venomous and relentless war against their betters.
An intelligent Russian must either grovel to them or starve. They prohibit every
rational exchange of ideas. They have driven almost all the more enlightened and
self-respecting people out of their unhappy country, and can carry on their witless
and bombastic schemes only with the aid of the foreigners they profess to despise.
. . . The sole winners in the macabre game are the politicians in the Kremlin,
strutting in the fading tinsel of the czars and thrilling over the hollow monuments
to their glory."

in ways not too visible at first inspection? If a man, in his capacity as historian, wants to speak mystically and dreamily of this land as James Truslow Adams, banker and author, finds it pleasant to do, lingering wistfully over the Epic of America, no one can stop him, since that false tune is so familiar as to sound genuine still. But a critical mind, possessing even a minimum of courage, knows different. Take these penetrating words written by Albert Jay Nock:[17] "Even if our elected officials all stand by us loyally, we cannot get what we vote for except on the sufferance of nine old men, irresponsible, inaccessible, appointed for life, and concerning whose appointment the people have nothing to say. The intelligent citizen knows this, knows that even with the President and Congress unanimously on his side, his actual sovereignty amounts to exactly nothing. The Supreme Court is the actual sovereign power, the final law-making authority—not law-interpreting, but law-making. How, then, can the citizen be interested?"

Is it not permissible to inquire whether in this free country we, the people, have not been living under a dictatorship of the judiciary? What becomes of all the oratorical babble about democracy? Of course I know the answer and feel it a patriotic duty to give it: simply insert the trenchant modifying adjective capitalistic before the magical noun democracy, and the mystery clarifies itself marvelously.

Capitalism lives and grows by a czaristic control over the economic process, making a camouflage compromise with "the people" by granting them—actually granting them—political freedom! Freedom to do what? To vote for candidates who in the first instance are crookedly chosen by politicians, themselves the tools of those vested interests that live and grow by the principle of czaristic control of the underlying economic process. Can you imagine a more amazing game? And that's what it is quite properly and picturesquely called: the game of politics. Of course, for the sake of that scientific accuracy which is the innermost heart of objectivity, we, the victims, might describe it as colossal chicanery. We, the underlying population, were obviously wage slaves [18] in industry but somehow,

---

[17] From his penetrating article entitled: *What The American Votes For* (in the *American Mercury*, February, 1933).

[18] If this phraseology seems exaggerated, look at these facts calmly presented by Dr. Harry Elmer Barnes in his enlightening column (Feb. 13, 1933): "I do not approve of the loose epithet of 'wage-slavery,' applied recklessly by Marxians to

by eucharistic transubstantiation, we became free-born American citizens on election day. Land of miracles.[19]

Even so tranquil and detached a publicist as Albert Jay Nock arrives, after reviewing the constitutionally undemocratic facts of our so-called republican form of government, at this revealing reflection: "There remains to us only the recourse to violence, which is no doubt our privilege, but is not to be considered, for we have no confidence in it. Probably our descendants will have to come to something of the kind, but it is nothing for us at the moment. We have learned something from our own revolutions and also from those in other lands; the outcome would be far too uncertain."

These sentiments are not as innocent as they sound. I think there is a great surprise in store for that large number of Americans who remember with great reverence and celebrate with patriotic ecstasy the *political* revolution that made these United States a happy hunting ground for Capitalism, while viewing with alarm and an almost biologic disgust the coming *social* revolution that will turn over the fertile lands and the ingenious factories to a triumphant proletariat, namely, the discovery of the large number of their fellow citizens who are convinced that it is the outcome of the present system which is "far too uncertain," and that no life-saving choice is left but to overthrow that system and establish a new one.

Are we or are we not living under a dictatorship of Capital-

---

our labor situation, but there is no denying the fact that our laboring classes in the United States today are in a far worse condition, materially speaking, than were the Negro slaves in 1861. Some 14,295,000 are unemployed and face possible starvation with no self-interested slave-holders to feed them. It is an understatement to say that there is more physical suffering among the unemployed in New York City today than among all the slaves in the entire South in 1861."

[19] Czar Nicholas Murray Butler, whose record in the war for violating ruthlessly the principle of academic freedom is one of the worst in America's history, favorite son for a long opportunistic life-time of that party of Junkers who go by the name of Republicans, recently delivered a most touching speech as President of "The Pilgrims" (in the Bankers Club, of course). He said: "Make no mistake about it. What is being challenged is liberty. Liberty is challenged in the name of compulsion. Compulsion may be that of the dictator or of the Communist State. But it is compulsion that is at open war with liberty and has challenged liberty to battle. . . . Look back and take courage, and remember that if we use liberty and prevent its abuse we have the answer to the compulsionist, be he dictator or be he Communist. . . ." The Pilgrims drank toasts to "the President of the United States and to his Majesty, the King of England." (From the *New York Times,* January 26, 1933.)

ism? [20] Is there or is there not a financial dictatorship? [21] Are there or are there not five old men in our Supreme Court that in a profound and almost incredible sense control the destinies of the "democracy"? Is the American Constitution—by its premeditated nature and origin, *pro-capitalistic*—on the side of the vested interests or on the side of the people! Is the Electoral College a democratic device or quite the reverse? How many decades is it since the electorate in these so-called United States have had a genuine choice between political parties: isn't the absence of genuine choice the true reason why personalities count immeasurably more in American life than ideas or issues or principles or sincere realities? Doesn't every school boy now know that the choice between the historic political parties for a half century has been the imbecile and indecent "choice" between Tweedledumb and Tweedledee? How can this Constitution—the legal basis of the dictatorship of the bourgeoisie—be radically revised, scrapped if necessary, by the people's will, *peacefully*? Quite out of the question!

The underlying assumption of the liberal-socialist position that there is a *rational* method of bringing about a social revolution assigns to reason an amount of dynamic influence in human affairs which it never possesses *unless* it is linked to power—in this case the power of the victimized workers; but if history teaches one lesson more clearly than another it is that the power of persuasion is powerless unless it is effectively backed by the power of coercion. A ruling class surrenders under coercion, not in response to rational persuasion! This is the dynamo-logic of power groups. Which is another way of saying that the principle of dictatorship, whether in the form of a reactionary personal despotism or in the form of a revolu-

[20] If you have any doubts as to how the political winds are blowing, watch this trial balloon sent up by our near-president Alfred E. Smith. "Now I say, and I've said all along, that in a depression we're in a state of war. This stagnation of business, or whatever you call it, is doing more damage at home to our own people than the great war of 1917 and 1918 ever did. The only thing to do is to lay aside the red tape and the regulatory statutes and do what a democracy must do when it fights.

"And what does a democracy do in a war? It becomes a tyrant, a despot, a real monarch. In the World War we took our Constitution, wrapped it up and laid it on the shelf and left it there until it was over." Quoted from the *New York Times* (Feb. 8, 1933) which runs a headline reading: SMITH URGES PUBLIC WORKS DICTATOR.

[21] On this point the reader cannot find more light than in the *New English Weekly*, brilliantly edited by A. R. Orage. A dictatorship of bankers! Nothing but.

tionary social control, is the principle of fundamental change.

It is worth recalling once more that those who favor the present system, even when they are its critics, at any rate to the extent of being opposed to Communism, in a final crisis preferring Fascism, have few worries or scruples concerning the dictatorial technique when it is exercised by the government they believe in, as for example in the Wilson administration during the Great War. The wills and minds of the people counted for just nothing at all. They were conscripted and bullied and manipulated—the whole process being called patriotism in war-time.

The rights and new liberties and expansive activities of the masses since the Bolsheviks inaugurated their scientific and social dictatorship constitute a remarkable study in freedom's true increase [22] compared with the known repressions under the Wilson dictatorship, accepted in a quite docile spirit by the free American people.

Talk about the cunning uses of reason when the mind is bent upon evading an unpalatable reality! We know very well what a brilliant chapter the psychology of rationalization is in psychoanalytic literature. The mind is far too ingenious in its employ of defense-mechanisms—against conscious realization of an aspect of reality it would rather be blind to or dodge as long as possible. I want to comment briefly on a few of these typical "defense mechanisms" which the capitalistic mind, instructed and inspired by the liberals and socialists (since they all wonderfully agree that no fate could befall mankind imaginably worse than the triumph of proletarian communism) is fond of these precarious days.

I have already discussed their doctrine of rationality as persuasive but ineffectual (disingenuous, when you come to think of it) since they know that power is not, by its very nature cannot be, reasonable. If the plight and urgent problems of the proletariat were as *real* to anyone of these groups of apologists for "rational" change as the more familiar problems of their own bourgeoisie, they would count it a small cost, speaking

---

[22] In Joseph Freeman's study *The Soviet Worker* there is a vast amount of detailed evidence on this point. He writes: "Appropriations for Social and Cultural activities in the financial plan (for 1931) are more than four times as large as the amount spent for defense. Educational and cultural expenditures constitute more than 18 per cent of the financial plan; and expenditures for defense amount to 4.1 per cent." (P. 312.)

historically, to lay the basis of a new social order by paying the price of dictatorship—since there is no other realistic choice in the Marx-Leninistic sense! [23]

Only a handful of lifelong pacifists have the smallest genuine right to oppose the technique of social revolution, with its necessary force and violence, in their opposition to the Marxian philosophy of change. Logically such persons occupy a position of complete alienation from the history of Western civilization, their viewpoint having more relevancy in an India inspired and led by Gandhi. But when one of these days the drastic pressure of economic and social forces, under the heel of imperialism, worsened by the oppression of the home-grown capitalist, drives the patient and long suffering Indians to revolutionary revolt under a leadership more realistic than Gandhi's, linking its destiny with world communism, how will it be with this aloof position of the wistful pacifists who cannot gulp down the fact that desperate problems require desperate remedies?

Listen to these eminently sane words of Lenin: "They are little more than imitators of the bourgeoisie, these gentlemen who delight in holding up to us the 'chaos' of revolution, the 'destruction' of industry, the unemployment, the lack of food. Can there be anything more hypocritical than such accusations from people who greeted and supported the imperialistic war and made common cause with Kerensky when he continued the war? Is not this imperialistic war the cause of all our misfortune? The revolution that was born of the war must necessarily go on through the terrible difficulties and sufferings that war created, through this heritage of destruction and reaction-

[23] No theme is more often rehearsed these anxiety-haunted days than the theme of America's uniqueness when it comes to revolutionary behavior and the creation of a basically new social order. It is worth while inquiring: Is America Different? Obviously, in a hundred historic and psychologic *particulars,* she is. But, how about the few central realities that determine the status of nations? Isn't it a little disquieting to realize that only as regards the creation of Communism do the rationalizing thinkers gravely assert gulfs between America and Europe? Why the oft repeated assumption that America is different as regards revolutionary (i.e. Communistic) technique and goal but is the same as Europe as regards capitalistic (i.e. counter-revolutionary) tactics? It is perfectly clear that capitalism found little difficulty in spreading all over the globe, and it is painfully evident that fascism is finding it only too easy to do the same thing. How does it happen that these very doubters who go on imagining America as essentially unique, are not at all surprised at the emergence of fascism in These States?

ary mass murder. To accuse us of 'destruction' of industries and 'terror' is hypocrisy or clumsy pedantry, shows an incapability of understanding the most elemental fundamentals of the raging, climactic force of the class struggle called revolution. . . . The bourgeoisie of international imperialism has succeeded in slaughtering ten million, in crippling twenty million in its war. Should our war, the war of the oppressed and the exploited, against oppressors and exploiters, cost a half or a whole million victims in all countries, the bourgeoisie would still maintain that the victims of the World War died a righteous death, that those of the class war were sacrificed for a criminal cause." [24]

Associated with these liberal defense-mechanisms that would have us believe the proletarian dictatorship barbarous and the capitalistic dictatorship civilized; that social revolution is unnatural, hideous, insane while the wars of plutocratic nationalism are necessary, normal, and beneficial; we find the argument that the concept class, particularly in this democratic land, has no authentic existence outside the somewhat deranged imagination of extreme radicals, since, so the smooth argument runs, we are all equal citizens in a great and free republic, loyal to "our" nation! That unforgettable man, named Al Smith by popular assent, out of the depths of his social knowledge of the historic process, writes these neighborly words: "We should stop talking about the Forgotten Man and about class distinctions. There is no other country in the world where individual initiative counts for so much, where opportunities to rise are so great, and where class prejudice is so unimportant. In no

[24] Excerpts from Lenin's *A Letter to American Workingmen*, Moscow, August 20, 1918. Quoted in Prof. Jerome Davis' informative volume entitled: *Contemporary Social Movements*, pp. 375, 377. Jerome Davis in his Introduction (p. XI) quotes this illuminating excerpt from Herbert Spencer's *The Study of Sociology*, appraising popular opinion about the French Revolution as contrasted with the Napoleonic Wars: "And when the mortality on both sides in battle, by wounds, and by disease, throughout the Napoleonic campaigns, is summed up, it exceeds at the lowest computation two millions. And all this slaughter, all this suffering, all this devastation, was gone through because one man had a restless desire to be despot over all men. What has been thought and felt in England about the two sets of events above contrasted, and about the actors in them? The bloodshed of the Revolution has been spoken of with words of horror; and for those who wrought it there has been unqualified hate. About the enormously greater bloodshed which these wars of the Consulate and the Empire entailed, little or no horror is expressed; while the feeling towards the modern Attila who was guilty of this bloodshed, is shown by decorating rooms with portraits and busts of him."

other country is there so little evidence of economic class
hatred, so little encouragement to the Communist, the Fascist,
or the Junker, and such responsible, far-sighted and loyal
leadership of labor. Just now all of our people are in trouble.
The old rich are the new poor. What is needed in the crisis of
to-day is the united, coöperative effort of all good citizens of
whatever class or creed to fight our way out of the bog of depression to the solid ground of good American enterprise and
prosperity." [25]

These bitter years have not yet burnt into the consciousness
of America the knowledge of the fundamental existence of
irreconcilable classes, though that realistic insight has been a
vital part of Europe's thought for well-nigh a century. Here
we have a truly remarkable country that belongs technologically
in the 21st Century, the world's advance guard in invention and
mechanical ingenuity, while it remains closeted in an 18th
Century ideology. No problem is more baffling than this gulf
between a revolutionary technology and a reactionary ideology.
And yet a man whom all the liberals admire for his intelligence
can seriously assert, in the year of catastrophic crisis 1932–33,
when a propertied class is doing everything in its power to
precipitate the wreckage of civilization rather than permit a
propertyless class to come into control of the essential means
of existence, can cheerily announce to the American people
that "We should stop talking about the Forgotten Man and
about class distinctions." Al Smith is quite right, but not in the
sense in which he intended: it is indeed high time for the
masses to stop talking, and to act!

There is just one more of these profitable rationalizations
and defense-mechanisms that I should like to comment upon,
namely, the traditional attitude toward religion as man's great
spiritual accomplishment, transcending the low materialisms
of existence, the mystic light within his dark brain, the still
small voice of God amid the clamor of merely human voices.
My intention is to concentrate my analysis on what I shall call
the psychiatric case against religion.[26] To make matters clear

25 This is one of his briefer editorials as new editor of *The New Outlook,* October,
1932. May I suggest to America's most illiterate political sage that he read John
Strachey's *The Coming Struggle for Power,* and then ponder its powerful analysis
in relation to his own country?
26 Read E. Boyd Barrett's *While Peter Sleeps* for more concrete analysis of the
neurotic nature of religious indoctrination in childhood. Dr. Barrett is the distin-

at the outset let me say that if religion be construed as the private poetry of transcendental imagining concerning man's fate in the Universe, I am not at all concerned to perturb that private mysticism. By religion, viewed historically, we can only mean vast organizations owning colossal real estate, imposing rituals beyond the reach of reason upon the masses of mankind presumably for their salvation, both here and hereafter, more particularly hereafter, the substitution of ghostly preoccupation for material amelioration of life on earth, the enthronement of irrationality and superstitious conjecture as higher principles of insight and guidance than experimental science and realistic sociology can afford men in their struggles toward a fuller life.

That religion is one of the most powerful of the vested interests even the devout are well aware. That religious organizations, pretending to be concerned about man's heavenly welfare have been preoccupied to the point of obsession with privileges and prerogatives of a most earthly quality, is pretty familiar information. What is not as generally known as it deserves to be is the psychoneurotic, and in sufficiently numerous instances, the psychotic effect of religious beliefs and admittedly irrational faiths upon the human nervous system. I have long maintained that if the communists in Soviet Russia had never done anything else of great moment than to undo the evil power of the church to make the minds of men (and women *and children*) irrational, they would deserve in the ensuing centuries of light and liberation the immortal thanks and affection of their mortal fellow men.

What is the best known technique for keeping men and women in a state of servility? Obviously by teaching them in childhood, through a ritual that frightens the wits out of them, to go on being anxiously dependent upon some "higher" power (or powers) that can catch them, punish and degrade, damn and torture, if their conduct is amiss in some prescribed particular. From a psychiatric point of view, religion is a compound neurosis: it specializes in teaching men and women to feel inferior, to enjoy this humiliated state of insignificance,

---

guished ex-Jesuit, who has not yet divorced himself from catholicism, but whose psychoanalytic training has made him aware of the diseased elements in religion. . . . Read also Freud's *The Future Of An Illusion*. What a book for the Pope to ponder.

to be spiritually proud of their helplessness; not only that, but to feel ashamed of their sexual impulses, to feel disgust, to think of themselves as lewd and lascivious, to go through a process of purification and ceremonial cleansing so that God can forgive them for being libidinous swine. The Adlerian and Freudian neuroses are the stock in trade of the church! Is it any wonder that human nature, under priestly guidance, is the distorted and crippled thing we know it to be: emotionally infantile, sexually neurotic, panicky and hysterical, servile and cowardly, loving irrationality, hating rationality, clinging to immaturity, fleeing from maturity,—a pathetically incompetent and self-defeating bundle of blunders and woes? Religion specializes in ignorance and irrationality.

What chance is there for the mind to develop its sanity and courage while under the weird domination of beliefs and rituals that make a ghastly mockery of both? Communism was wonderfully right in its understanding of the correlation between the technique of exploitation and the technique of religion; and how utterly wise, from the angle of reëducation and the new psychiatry these bolsheviks were to remove, by surgical operation (in the nature of the case far from painless), the tumor from the brain of man which churchianity throughout the exploitative ages had been, by an insidious festering process, responsible for infecting the mind of humanity with.

The culture of communism is humane enough to respect the mind of the child,[27] its right to honest knowledge and sincere scientific wisdom: no more spooks and sickly sentimental irrationalities! If the modern mind, and our civilized emotions, are to be saved by healing psychological and socio-

---

[27] Walter Duranty (New York Times, Feb. 5, 1933) communicates this fine bit of news: "The writer is prepared to state that there is no city of 4,000,000 inhabitants in the world in which the children are healthier and happier than in the Soviet capital. In point of fact, there is little appearance of adult privation in Moscow, though there are many care-worn faces. . . . But the chief reason is doubtless that Moscow has no slums like western cities—no dark, airless courts and human rabbit warrens. . . . One hardly sees an underclad or ragged child in the whole city, and the homeless waifs who were so shocking a sight during the New Economic Policy period, have disappeared. . . . This universal care and kindness to the littler ones—from adults to children and from the bigger children to the smallest—is a bright and warming thing in the harsh materialism of the Soviet scene. Medical records and vital statistics bear out the surface impression of juvenile Moscow's healthiness."

logical therapy from a disintegration that moves in the direction of insanity, the very first task of a new social order is to eliminate the church completely from among man's institutions. Only then will rationality and sanity and humor and sincerity have a chance to become effective in the lives of men. God, I happen to know, will be marvelously pleased with this genuine dawn, after the long night of theological misery.

Little jets of light bob up in the brain as one perceives with a new clarity certain significant relationships which were not always so obvious or clear. Take the famous shibboleth of the French Revolution: *liberté*: *égalité*: *fraternité*! Viewed in terms of their sheer abstract ardor these words are still capable of producing a drunken sense of exhilaration. Scanned more realistically, in historic perspective, the very order of the words is of the greatest tell-tale significance. Of course, a rising bourgeoisie was in love with liberty; the liberty to pursue its own bourgeois "ideals"; viz. unhindered pursuit of property and profit. Liberty of conscience and liberty of thought, though real enough within definite limits, were after all incidental to this fundamental freedom to be successful in business, to grow rich, to become a model bourgeois.

The ideal of equality could hardly come first under these competitive conditions let loose by new economic forces and a relatively new governing class. In theory, citizens of a great republic were of course all free to be equal to one another, if they could achieve it through prosperity and profit: if they couldn't, that was their bad luck. And as for the concept of fraternity, well, that would take care of itself in the long run if they all believed loyally enough in liberty as basic, in equality as desirable but secondary, and ultimately in fraternity as the wonderful consummation of these prior idealisms and pursuits. How transparent, in disillusioned retrospect, is this "revolutionary" philosophy of liberty!

It would not be difficult to show that the bourgeois revolution *had* to have this concept of liberty as its guiding star; and equally demonstrable is that growth of *inequality* which liberty in a capitalistic system inevitably engenders: and as for fraternity, if one means the Masons, Elks, Knights of Pythias, Kiwanis, Rotarians, of course, even though there is little fraternity one must gracefully admit that there is a plethora of fraternities. These very fraternities would hardly have any reason for existence at all if it were not for their exhibitionistic desire to make a fetish of conspicuous inequality—to neutralize the ego-diminishing *pretence* of democratic equality.

A proletarian revolution, immeasurably more deep and sincere by its very nature than a bourgeois revolution (clinging to the sacred dogma of private property but re-distributing unearned income) must revoke this liberty which is so precious to the classes pursuing profit and prestige.[28] There is no choice in the matter. Can one continue so blind as not to perceive the disastrous consequences to the exploited classes of this seductive "philosophy" of liberty? Hence, in a Bolshevik revolution, the concepts are reversed, to wit: fraternité: égalité: liberté.

Class consciousness is the newer and deeper type of fraternity. Comradeship in Communism represents the profound direction of a realistic equality, attained by means of the socialization of the State and the communization of cultural and human relations. And liberty, socially motivated, is the new by-product of these necessary preliminary processes: necessary first to the destruction of the capitalistic ethics of exploitation, and second to the desperate creation of a socialistic society.

Liberty is the most inspiring concept in a civilization that places more emphasis and importance upon the individualistic ego of the aggressive captain of industry than it does upon the welfare of the masses. How can such a point of view be anything but despicable in a *social* system that has come into existence in response to the needs of a *class conscious* (not ego-conscious) proletariat? [29]

Some final points remain for consideration. No matter what system supervenes in this or that part of the world, the individual in the old atomic sense will exist nevermore. The complexity of modern civilization will see to that. The continuing plight of nations reduces the stature of the atomic individual to a shadowy significance. The problem is no longer the individual but the nation and the class. The significant

[28] For a highfalutin defense of liberty that exists primarily in the dreamy minds of arm-chair philosophers, read Benedetto Croce's article in *Foreign Affairs*, October, 1932.

[29] It is amusing to watch Ortega's intellectual antics as he juggles with the new concept of the masses, with his left hand, while with his right he still performs some magical tricks with the bourgeois balls of liberty (vide: *The Revolt of the Masses*). He is simultaneously fascinated and frightened by this new *force* in modern history, occasionally admitting that there may be something great and creative in the new masses.

struggles of the next fifty, more likely one hundred years, will cluster about these two pivotal points: nation and class. We can see in the unfolding events right before our very eyes that Fascism is raising its menacing head and that the only effective antagonist is Communism.

Just twenty years ago millions of splendid human beings calling themselves Socialists imagined that they had rejected the patriotic point of view in behalf of the Marxian logic of class struggle and internationalism. The war brought a blinding revelation of the self-deluding nature of this seemingly sincere belief in class as more real than fatherland. The collapse of German Socialism taught us the binding power of bourgeois beliefs, the feeble potency of proletarian conviction, in time of national danger. In 1917 the Bolshevik revolution once more reminded the world that the class concept is genuine, is desperately real, more real than capitalistic patriotism. Hence the split and increasing divergence between the Socialism of the second international and the Communism of the third international.

But class logic was to receive another quite unexpected blow, once more lifting into prominence the problem of the rôle of the nation in contemporary life, and the difficulties of that concept's transcendence by the class philosophy of internationalism. What has transpired since the Treaty of Versailles, and more vehemently within the past half dozen years, is the most extravagant exacerbation of nationalistic consciousness. From a Communist point of view the danger lies in the close relation between this inflamed nationalism and the rise of Fascism.[30]

Nationalism, in its most hate-envenomed separatism, is feverishly on the increase and every scheme of "recovery" is more vigilantly nation-conscious than any theoretician could have believed to be possible, precisely in that impasse of the world's affairs that cries so loudly for inter-national and trans-national modes of appeasement and understanding. To begin with the more familiar facts: tariff walls more and more diffi-

---

[30] Comes the news from Berlin: "Adolf Hitler rode into power in Germany today on the rising tide of his militant Fascism. The desperate political experiments of the last two years were culminated when President von Hindenburg entrusted the Chancellorship to the fiery little Austrian from Munich, foe of Jews and Communists and leading exponent of a belligerent German nationalism." From *New York World-Telegram*, Monday, January 30th, 1933.

cult to scale; immigration barriers of a flagrantly hostile character, holding populations as in a trap, in coercive areas, against their will; the fast tempo of economic disintegration inducing a fierce sense of self-preservation, come what may in the sequel. And then these more subtle facts, tending like the others, only not so crudely, in the direction of an intensified nationalistic consciousness: autarchy, national planning, Fascism—wherever you look, civilization is trying insanely to preserve itself by going back to the principle of self-centered economies, tight-enclosed nations practicing a patriotic cockiness and belligerent provincialism that are more inflammable than the palpable materials of warfare.

And the main reason why I am lingering over this neo-nationalistic resurgence is because the one force in the modern world that genuinely, by its inherent social logic and demonstrated human purposes, opposes and transcends this patriotic revivalism,[31] namely Communism, is also caught in this worldwide reaffirmation of the nationalistic principle.

If the original Leninistic hope of imminent world revolution had had a chance, by historic good luck, to be translated into proletarian reality, we should have been witnessing these recent years two marvelous experiments: (1) the rise of Soviets in industrially advanced countries and (2) the inauguration of Socialist planning as the new technique for collectivization of agriculture and the communization of industry. The differing tempos of capitalistic and imperialistic development, accompanied by the differing tempos of revolutionary insurgence—Communism apparently having a better chance to triumph in "backward" Capitalisms, like China, Russia, possibly Spain, while in the most advanced countries, like Germany and England and France and the United States, Fascism, tragically enough, is making a powerful bid for sovereignty, the communists being forced to hold off their revolution until a more favorable moment arrives.

The Russian communists, seeing how matters stand, namely, that one country is now proceeding to lay the basis of that

---

[31] In his first public recital after his assumption of power, Hitler let loose these winged words: "The parties of class warfare may be sure that so long as the Almighty lets me live, my determination to destroy them will be unconquerable!" he exclaimed. "There is to be either the German nation or Marxism!" (From *New York Times*, Feb. 11, 1933.) What would Hitler do if he discovered that God had become a Jew—after the centuries of Christian bloodshed and brutalism?

genuine Socialism which is on the road to Communism, and that some other countries may not be ready to achieve their Bolshevik revolution for the next twenty-five or fifty years, have intelligently decided to quit an impossible situation—trying to "force" revolution upon lands that are obviously either not ready for it or are entangled in revolutionary dilemmas that still defy adequate solution at home, let alone by compulsion from the Kremlin!—and to concentrate their marvelous Communist intensity upon the building up of a proletarian economy and culture within their own vast territory.

This retreat, if you want to stamp it as such, from the preconceived theory of world revolution, is dictated by a double necessity: (1) the urgent problems of the internal Soviet situation: a state trying to solve in a decade the intricate problems of technology and productive efficiency which Capitalist nations have not been able adequately to solve in many decades; not to mention the heroic socialistic enterprise of collectivization, itself heralded as one of the great revolutions in history; (2) the desperate complexity of the problems in the world at large, both counter-revolutionary and revolutionary, which it is sheer madness to expect either the Soviet Government directly or the Comintern indirectly to solve.

What this bluntly comes down to is the realization that Communism in each separate country will be following a different tempo of emergence and development and must therefore fight out its major battles within its own familiar land. If it cannot do that, it is a confession of incompetence which Moscow cannot correct, even if it were desirable for it to do so. The argument that the Five-Year Plans now constitute Soviet Russia's revolutionary contribution to world Communism is a valid and impressive argument.[32]

[32] Louis Fischer (in *The Nation*, Dec. 28, 1932) writes: "The Bolsheviks are now concentrated on the task of national upbuilding. I do not wish to imply that they reject the thesis of world revolution. They do not. But they will not harm Russia by working for it." This sounds dangerously like a regression to nationalistic self-centeredness. But what is Russia's choice—in a world that is so slow in going communist? The question, as I see it, is this: Is the building of socialism in Soviet Russia, itself a revolutionary achievement of the first magnitude?

"The Izvestia concluded on a note, often repeated of late, that the Soviet does not want to interfere with anyone and does not want anyone to interfere with it. 'The government desires normal peace relations because it is building socialism, and peace is necessary to successful achievement of this aim,' it says." (This is quoted from an article on the renewal of diplomatic relations between Russia and China,

To conclude: we can see with the utmost clarity that the capitalist system saves itself by setting up a fantastic bogey-man against revolution, preferring the congenial slaughter of wars and alien imperialisms, since it is the lives of the masses that are sacrificed to prop up the "stakes of diplomacy." Against this recurrent nightmare of imperialistic wars, threatening the wreckage of civilization and the crucifixion of humanity, the philosophy of social revolution is a veritable dream of life's salvation, of man's emancipation from a doom utterly unendurable.

Any alternative, no matter how costly from a human point of view, is welcome to the apologists for the Status Quo rather than the profound and genuine solution symbolized in Soviets of Workers and Technicians! [33]

---

in the *New York Times*, Dec. 14, 1932). Construe this as sympathetically as we will, appreciating the tragic dilemma Stalinism is caught in—of finding it necessary to put a damper on revolution in other countries for the sake of guaranteeing the possibility of success to socialism in Russia—we dare not close our eyes to the momentous conceivable implications of this strategy. Listen to Louis Fischer on this problem: "Things have changed since the Comintern first met in 1919. At that time, no Bolshevik conceived of the continued existence of the Soviet Government in Russia if other revolutions did not come to its aid in foreign lands. Moscow was weak. Revolutions seemed to be imminent in Europe and Asia. The sanguine Bolsheviks therefore emphasized the importance of world revolt. The psychology which dominated the Comintern in those days closely resembled the psychology of the Soviet Government. Much water has flowed down the Moscow River since then. The Soviet Union is strong and can stand alone. A foreign Communist uprising, moreover, is quite unlikely at present. Many Russians feel, in fact, that it would be an embarrassment if it did come." Re-read this last sentence and you will have a vivid sense of what I have referred to as the tragic dilemma of Stalinism. Can anyone who profoundly cares about the world-wide spread of Communism doubt that what is most urgently needed everywhere today is an electrifying resurgence of revolutionary ardor and integrity, a renewal of Leninistic faith in the masses? And the painful problem is: What part is Soviet Russia, the leader and inspirer of revolution, to play in this Leninistic renascence?

[33] "Our primary remedy for present difficulties is not in the change of economic systems. It consists in an enlightened public opinion which will demand of our rulers that they seek peace, economic as well as political, and pursue it. . . . No, I am one who believes that we must rebuild on the basis that is still under us. We must, in Mr. Lippmann's phrase, continue to live in the house while we are rebuilding it. You may call that house, if you will, the capitalistic system. It has been in the building since the Dark Ages. It has, with all its ups and downs, brought to mankind increasing comfort and happiness. It is still a fairly tough structure and will not easily topple over. But it has developed some serious weaknesses which require more than patch work attention." This is the economic wisdom of the bankers as uttered with an appropriate serenity to university students

We in America need a revolutionary reëducation of our
pampered and confused and unstable minds. Our liberation
from liberalism is not yet complete. We mix up in a messy
linguistic hodge-podge concepts and realities that belong in
utterly different worlds of discourse.[34] It is too soon to expect
America, still betting, with the typical gambler's blindness to
realities, on that one of the old political parties which has not
yet had a sufficient opportunity to prove its ineptitude in time
of political and social earthquakes, to be ready to see in latter-
day socialism the rhetorically seductive twin of liberalism,
that pathetic cripple limping so awkwardly across the stage of
history.

We, the people, must *recover* from Capitalism, a disease that
has wasted and undermined our lives. Recovery through revolution! That's the road of sanity in our insane social order.[35]

---

by Mr. Thomas W. Lamont of J. P. Morgan & Company. (Address printed in
Scientific Monthly, Jan. 1933.)

[34] Among the incorrigibly amiable liberal-socialists who care not a continental about
"labels," the Nobel Prize for looseness in thinking must go to Heywood Broun.
"Such things must not be. If radical remedies are needed to prevent such episodes,
then radical remedies there will have to be. If liberalism can offer a remedy, let it
show its hand, but without further delay. In the same way it is obvious that protection must be extended to farmers who have already lost their homes or are
about to lose their homes through tax sales or mortgage foreclosures. Nobody can
afford to be bothered whether the way out is radical or revolutionary. It must be
done! Men and women have frozen to death in large cities. Some Governors still
contend that nobody starves, but that hardly applies to the slower disintegration
of malnutrition. . . . The point which the essentialists should stress is that the
necessary work of salvation must be done. Do the job first and then decide on the
label later." Excerpted from his column "It Seems To Me" (in *New York World-
Telegram*, Jan. 31, 1933).

[35] That eminent Professor Emeritus of History, Mr. Henry Ford, the auto-intoxi-
cated philosopher of Americanism, utters this staggeringly intelligent judgment on
the current depression: "This period that we are going through right now is the
recovery. The bad times were back in 1929 and before. That was the real panic—
that so-called prosperous period. Business, at bottom, never was so bad as it was in
what we called boom times. The managers were off the job. People weren't really
working or really thinking. Now they are. We are seeing now the passing of an old
era and the beginning of a new one better than anything the world has known
before." Farther on, he adds profoundly: "I don't think there's anything wrong
with the world. I think these are the best times we ever had. We are learning
something. We are thinking. What could be better than that? We're all here for
experience, and all experiences are good, even those we call bad at the time."
(Quoted from an interview in the *New York Times* for Feb. 1, 1933, attractively
entitled *Ford Sees Dawn Of A Golden Era*). For the leaden side of this golden era
the reader is invited not to forget to read Edmund Wilson's marvelously human

These bitter years. The "Great" War like a murderer who in his mania laughs hideously in crazy triumph as he sees his victim bleeding to death, cracked open the skull of humanity. The face of life is all scars and ugly wounds, terrible to behold. Life's become a grinning gargoyle from which a madman's eyes look out upon a madman's world. The bitter years. All the fields strewn with corpses. Living corpses of men that could not die. The trees in the spring fertilized by the agony of ten million living corpses of ten million sad boys who died so futilely. All the world in tears, senseless sad tears, remembering the insane war they never desired in their lone sanity. The dirty imperialist war and the dirty imperialist peace. Lunatic's nightmare.

Then the Russian Revolution! The skulls and corpses half forgotten, as in a dream at dawn but half remembered. Red dawn. The smell of the earth more fragrant as once, before the sepulchre of the war, man's faith was fragrant and sweet. Death's dominance fading out of life's new dawn, life flowing lustily through the minds of men, in red exultation, rejoicing amid the dimming graveyards, facing with triumphant thoughts, in song and folk ecstasy, the young red dawn. Life bursting the fetters of death, spilling magnificently over the fields and into the parched hearts of men: the rebirth of life, creation crying to be born again.

The drama of our epoch, enacted on a world stage, depicting humanity in agony, tossing between life and death as in a fatal fever, the womb of time in desperate travail, is the epic drama of an age that is dying and one that is coming to birth.

Life and creation belong henceforth to Communism. Decadence and death to Fascism.

Social revolution is the prelude to life in a dying world.

---

articles under the heading of *Hull-House in 1932*, particularly the third one which contains a heartbreaking picture of certain capitalistic realities that Henry Ford has neither the imagination nor the moral stamina to look at with honest eyes.

ROBERT BRIFFAULT

THE HUMAN MIND IN REVOLUTION

THE turmoil which disturbs the contemporary mind began to manifest itself at a time when bourgeois civilization stood on a pinnacle of unshaken power, prosperous and triumphant. In the closing decade of the last century those symptoms were already discernible which have to-day ripened into a crisis.

In all externals the scheme of bourgeois civilization seemed justified by the richest fruits. The world was marching to the tune of "progress." The cornucopia was flowing. Technology daily brought forth new marvels; and people speculated wistfully, in those *fin de siècle* days, upon the wonders which the new century surely held in store. Science, aglow with enthusiasm, was opening up undreamed of horizons and battling for new freedoms of thought. The mysteries of life, of man's upgrowth from animality and savagery, were being unveiled. Literature echoed with pæans and flashed Pisgah views. Poets sang of the onward march and of the coming brotherhood of man.

Yet into the hearts of men a secret uneasiness was creeping. A breath of doubt and cynicism was abroad. Instead of basking as theretofore in the mellow dignity of broad-based custom, the minds of men and women put forth strange exploratory tentacles in search of some unknown thrill of change. The complacent standards of established taste suffered the shocks of startling eccentricities. Exotic, semi-barbaric modes, *art nouveau,* revolts against the seemingly secure academic canons

478

surged into movements that pronounced the eternal ideals old-fashioned. A new literature and a new art took overt pleasure in the sport of *"épater le bourgeois."* Oscar Wilde was the wicked young god of the English decadents. Beaudelaire and Verlaine were in many quarters displacing Tennyson and Browning. Swinburne was chanting bacchanalian lyrics. The Russians were the rage. On the boudoir table of an evil-eyed Salome, Aubrey Beardsley placed the novels of Zola. In moral, Victorian England the word was going round that it was smart to be naughty, and amid a satirical cynicism tinged with disillusion, a new generation was seeking solace in outbursts of frivolous gaiety that prefigured the jazz age.

What had happened?

The great social structure which had blossomed into nineteenth-century civilization was the Dictatorship of the Bourgeoisie. A liberal priest had proclaimed the new sovereign ruler when, in the eighteenth-century revolution, the dictatorship of aristocrat and autocrat had been overthrown. "The Third Estate should be everything," Abbé Sièyes had declared. The power of that dictatorship was supreme. The material, social, economic foundations of the Dictatorship of the Bourgeoisie seemed as solid as rock. But the emotional, sentimental, intellectual premises that constituted its mental foundations were showing signs of sagging. Men and women, whether clearly conscious of the fact or no, believed no longer in the solidity of those foundations as their fathers and their grandfathers had believed.

No more sharply defined and rounded mental scheme ever served as the basis of a great social structure. The principles of "bourgeois ideology" were more categorical than any Marxian orthodoxy which is heard of to-day. The dictatorship of the bourgeois bore the inspiring name of democratic liberty. The language of liberal democracy was couched in the phrases of a lofty moral idealism. Its policies were ennobled by humanitarian sentiment, inspired by concern for the welfare of the lower orders and anxiety to carry the torch of bourgeois civilization to backward peoples and to shoulder the white man's burden. The moral sentiments of civilized democracy centered upon the sacred institutions which were the cradle of society; the rights of private property, the hearth, the home, the family. Reverence for the dignity of womanhood, the purity of childhood, the holiness of the marriage tie—those were the emotions which, together with the nobility of labor, the duties of industry and thrift, and respect for law and order, lent their glow to thought and purpose, inspired art and literature, heightened patriotism, and were the bulwarks of civilized society.

For over a hundred years those deep realities had furnished the unchallengeable mental foundations of the social order. In their contemplation the mind had been filled with an agreeable self-approving optimism which was of the nature of a duty. To divert attention from that moral excellence to such things as social injustice, suffering, poverty, was a mark of depravity, in much the same manner as concern with certain sexual values was admittedly a stigma of degeneracy. There were, of course, in the world, things which lay outside the rounded scheme of beseeming bourgeois optimism—things unpleasant, unseemly, base, ugly. But, as in art only the pleasant and pretty were admissible so in every outlook. To seek out things unseemly and unpleasant was the morbid propensity of base and ignoble minds. To be virtuous was to look upward, so as not to see the ground on which one trod.

Yet before the century of the Dictatorship of the Bourgeoisie had drawn to a close, the whole structure of that "ideology" was crumbling down in the minds of thoughtful Europeans. While yet no current consciousness of clearly formulated criticism had exposed the colossal falsity of that ostrich ideology, human feeling, surfeited with the orgy of moral righteousness and lofty idealism, had revolted against the sheer fulsomeness, meanness, and ugliness of the outward expression of that complacency, in life, in art, in sentiment. No feudal, aristocratic, despotic culture of the past had brought forth such intrinsically sordid mediocrity as bourgeois democratic liberty. Voicing the revolt of wounded human sensitiveness against its repellent offensiveness, the founder of the French realistic movement in literature had gone so far as to declare that "to hate the bourgeois is the beginning of all virtue." The blatant hypocrisy of those high moral sentiments, those sublime ideals was, in the European nineties, coming to be openly and generally derided and denounced. Against the fraudulent smugness of bourgeois optimism, the philosophic pessimism of Schopenhauer had acquired a vogue which expressed the protest of intelligence against the ostrich ideal of bourgeois virtue. The fabric of Victorianism, the foundations of bourgeois society were, to ordinary honest intelligence, becoming incredible. They were in fact collapsing. The same thing was happening on the American side of the Atlantic. While academic pundits, such as Dean Howells, were exhorting loyalty toward "those more smiling aspects of life, which are the more American," a generation of American writers was violently breaking away from the scheme of self-approval in indignant revolt, protest, and disgust, and were fiercely "muckraking" the ideals of bourgeois civilization.

The revolt of the human mind, that decadent authority of bourgeois ideology, took place with almost no reference to social or political issues. The *fin de siècle* rebels against bourgeois bad taste, blinkered fatuity, fulsome mediocrity, were for the most part uninterested in social theoretical issues. If their revolt included any criticism of the structure of bourgeois society, it took mostly the form of vague restatements of liberal principles, fanned into new Shelleyan flame, as in Swinburne's Republicanism, Walt Whitman's Democratism, William Morris's, Ruskin's, Edward Bellamy's idealistic socialism. Seldom did it venture beyond the restrained reformism of the "Fabian Essays" or of Henry George's "Progress and Poverty"—audacities as wicked in their day as any Bolshevism is to-day. But those incidental links with social theory were without importance, and bore no direct relation to the change that was taking place in the minds of men and women. It was against the mental structure, against bourgeois ideology, its smug, stuffy values, and the musty flavor they imparted to life, not against the social structure of society, not against the Dictatorship of the Bourgeoisie, that revolt, or rather, failure of belief, manifested itself.

That revulsion grew during the opening decade of the new century. A lonely thinker who had, mostly at his own expense, published books that had remained unread and unintelligible until explained to bewildered minds by George Brandes, became after his death the dominant articulate expression of the intellectual stirrings of the pre-war era. Nietzsche not only denied that bourgeois ideology which Flaubert had held up to execration, but smashed it with hammer-blows of penetrating thought, exulting in the transvaluation of its most consecrated values. Coinciding curiously with another obscure thinker, Marx, he recognized in those values, those "ideologies," the products and astute weapons of a social situation. Bourgeois

values, Christian values, owed their mediocrity, their meanness, to the conscious inferiority of the timid, servile parasite,
the emancipated slave. They were "slave morality," the shell
of fatuity wherein the poltroonery of the craven found shelter.
They were the exudation of the bourgeois soul, the incrusta-
tion of its greed, and crouching envy. Drawing from similar
premises to those of Marx, an exactly opposite conclusion,
Nietzsche proclaimed the proud aristocratic values which had
created the splendor of pagan cultures, the master morality of
the amoral individual, which were, at least, not mean, craven,
and mediocre.

The beseeming world of bourgeois ideology suffered a
further affront, felt to be perhaps more horrible, more revolting, than Anti-christian Nietzschean amoralism, at the hands
of a Viennese physician. Freud came forth with the horripilat-
ing declaration that sex—the thing which in the bourgeois
scheme of beseeming ostrich-like outlook had been suppressed
out of existence by the discretion of complete silence—was
actually the mainspring of life, the secret motive power of the
mind's activities. Truly a transvaluation more shameless than
any Nietzschean wickedness! What was a respectable bourgeois
world coming to?

Amid such shocks and such perplexities, on the shifting
foundations of a mental world in a state of flux, did the intelligence of bourgeois Europe face the cataclysm of the War.

The intellectual bewilderment was itself without systematic
foundations. Its restless uneasiness was unconnected with social
or political configurations. Entering the colossal conflagration
to the blare of the slogans of liberal ideology, the Allies represented that if those slogans had fallen somewhat short of their
promise, that was chiefly because they had not as yet had an
opportunity for complete fulfillment. Germany expressly threatened to impose upon European civilization its "Kultur," that is,
Prussian militarism and junkerdom, the blood and iron philosophy of a revived and glorified feudalism and autocracy
opposed to democratic liberty. The war was to "make the world
safe for democracy." It was to give the noble ideals of liberalism a free hand to initiate a new era. It was, among other
things, a war against militarism, a war to end war. And bewildered intelligence, unrationalized, unwitting of its own
social and economic foundations, was willing to lend an ear
once more to high idealism, and to conceive the hope that the

THE HUMAN MIND IN REVOLUTION

invalidities of bourgeois civilization would be rectified by so gigantic an ordeal.

The issue was the most opprobrious anti-climax of grotesque ignominy that has ever affronted human intelligence. No touch of irony was lacking to complete the fantastic sordidness of its cynical buffoonery. In order still further to emphasize the unspeakable effrontery, hypocrisy, and falsehood of the idealistic formulas, the American Presbyterian schoolmaster descended upon the scene chanting incredible moralistic psalms. The sophisticated old bourgeois politicians, Lloyd George and Clemenceau, not only kicked the solemn Presbyterian American about like a ridiculous clown, but, out of his own mouth, convicted him of being nothing but a hollow hypocrite, the worst kind of hypocrite, an unconscious one. The slogans and psalms and sacred formulas of liberal idealism were but wind. He himself meant not a word of them. No liberal windbag really meant a word of his prayer-mill formulas. The American Presbyterian babbled of permanent peace as the English Victorians had blethered of the brotherhood of man. But no babbler of high pacific purposes is willing to surrender a single imperialistic bayonet, any more than any capitalist economist is willing to surrender a cushion of his comforts or a coupon of his dividends for "social planning" or the brotherhood of man. It was all blether and wind. The bleating Presbyterian Saviour of Mankind was left foolishly perorating in mid-air; and with him all slogan-belching and prayer-mill grinding democratic liberalism, idealism, and humanitarianism. Not peace, but war; not idealism, but naked predatory greed; not humanitarianism, but unabashed business, and graft; not charity, but ruthless, murderous cruelty; not sweetness and light, but brazen lies and frauds—that was the fulfillment of liberal eloquence, of the opportunity to make the world safe for bourgeois democracy.

If in the doubting pre-war period the windy foundations of bourgeois society had been sagging, the War, and the issue of the War, dissolved them into the limbo of exploded incredibilities. It dealt the fatal blow, not to the material structure of the Dictatorship of the Bourgeoisie only, but to its mental foundations, to bourgeois ideology.

Among the thinkers who in the nineteenth century had unmasked the frauds of bourgeois ideology, and whose leaven had, for reasons presently to be noted, been excluded from the general cultural pabulum of the intellectuals, was a German philosopher, Karl Marx by name. He had, like Darwin, hit upon a key-thought, a master key, by means of which the relations of the basic facts of human society and of its mental foundations might be unlocked. Why, he had asked, as does every desolated thinker, those monstrous dishonesties of the human mind? Whence the passionate mendacity upon which every social system is built, and upon the defense of which every astuteness and perfidy of human power is desperately bestowed? And his answer was that the forms of men's ideas and opinions are not primarily determined by varying intellectual points of view or capacities of apprehension, but by social interests. Nor is it the social interests of the individual, who has little power to depart widely from the world of ideas which his social environment transmits to him, which mold his views and beliefs, so much as the interests of the social group, or class, to which he belongs, which determines the tenor of his concepts and sentiments. By those interests, and more particularly by the basic economic interests to which all others are in final analysis reduceable, are shaped the interpretations, the ideas, the systems of opinions and values, the ideologies of a social class.

The human mind is a social product. Naked, nescient, creedless, amoral, speechless and thoughtless, is the individual born into a world of speech that reverberates the formulas and fantasies and frauds that are of good repute. His mind is clothed with the cast-off garments of ages of sharp practice and deception. Whenever a human being, or a group of human beings, has wielded power over others, the purpose of their thought has been to confirm and protect that power, to make it appear "good." The natural function of thought, developed from the slime onward by stern experience of the disasters attending misapprehension of facts, the will to know, is supplanted in a social configuration where power over men is the economic foundation of life, by a more powerful motive. Thought ceases to perform its natural function as a cognitive instrument, and becomes power-thought, performing instead a social function as a weapon of class power.

The key-thought of Marx, explaining as it did for the first time the true nature of class ideologies, of passionate devotion to lies, was, by virtue of the very law which Marx had stated, providently prevented from impinging upon the ears and intelligence of those intellectuals who had ceased to credit the fatuous fictions of bourgeois ideology. For had they permitted such a thought to penetrate their minds, they would have found themselves placed in a terrifying predicament. They would have found themselves pitted not merely against ideas, tastes, theories of art, values, doctrines, but against the very structure of bourgeois civilization of which those ideas and doctrines were but the reflection, and against its power. Quite another predicament for a distracted thinker. It would have meant the conversion of thought into action. And the intellectuals were, after all, bourgeois, dependent economically, materially, in a culinary, sartorial, perambulatory, and in every easeful sense upon that very structure. They too, like the Presbyterian schoolmaster, Wilson, were willing to talk, and to do anything that might be accomplished by talking. But there are wide distinctions between academic controversies and controversies with the police, between signing a declaration of faith and signing a check. Intellectuals were willing to revolt in terms of impassioned eloquence and cutting satire against ideologies, but not against the social structure which the ideology supported. Hence the wholly unpalatable nature of Marx's key-thought—that the ideology and the structure were in fact one and the same thing.

Bourgeois intellectualism sought, on the contrary, every means and device whereby it might escape from the terrifying necessity of apprehending that key-thought. In the same manner as the sufferings inflicted by man's depredation of man had formerly, and is still by Vicars of God and Presbyterian preachers, set down to the divinely appointed order of the universe, or by academic perorators to the perversity of human nature tainted by original sin, so have many sought to convince themselves that it arises from the erroneous theories or defective information which misdirect the anxious efforts of humanitarian idealists at Versailles, or Wall Street, or Washington, Kentucky, or California to benefit the human race. Or they set down the ruin and misery resulting from those efforts to an innate propensity of the human mind to mendacity, blandly disregarding the trifling circumstance that the mind of social man and its mendacities are conditioned products of social, and not of biological causes.

Our favorite surrogate for the economic source of the un-

486 RECOVERY THROUGH REVOLUTION

easiness produced in their minds by the Dictatorship of the Bourgeoisie has by many been discovered in the Christian provisions for the suppression of the sexual functions. The preservation of those provisions has served the useful purpose of protecting the sacredness of the bourgeois family, the medium for the transmission of real and personal estate, and has likewise fed the high moral tone which, with the complement of pornography and prostitution, sustains the lofty idealism of bourgeois civilization. That intolerable mutilation has been supposed, by such as D. H. Lawrence, to be the main cause which has prostrated their mangled and crippled life-force. Sexual liberation is accordingly sought through the repudiation of superstitious tabus and bourgeois marriage, promiscuity, nudism, sex expression, and an intensified study of sexological literature which, by providing a thoroughly scientific and therefore perfectly frigid and impotent approach to sex, has had the pleasant effect of aggravating a thousandfold the neurosis it was intended to allay. The revolt against sexual tabus, rife in all quarters to-day, serves the useful purpose of a welcome alternative to revolt against economic tabus. Unfortunately the only effective way of abolishing the former is to abolish the latter, and it is quite impossible to reduce sex to sanity within a Christian civilization, or for women to cease being burdened by the marketable price of their pelvis under the dictatorship of bourgeois business.

Similarly of every surrogate evil which, in its desperate effort to avoid perceiving the source of it, crippled intelligence devotes itself to contemplating. Some devote their energies to the cause of pacifism, while carefully omitting to perceive that the monstrous evil of war is inseparable from the structure of bourgeois civilization, and can no more be rationalized away while that competitive structure for markets is retained than the depletion of the world's resources by capitalistic exploitation can be remedied by the efforts of the exploiters. So of all "causes" and reforms; not one can be effected without reforming away bourgeois civilization, of which those evils and those falsehoods are compounding elements. And the reformer or intellectual is thus condemned to batter his head in despairing futility against stone walls so long as he persists in regarding any of those elements as an independent evil or lie, and turns away his gaze in terror from the economic social structure which is the determinant of the evils and lies.

Karl Marx, who long ago previsioned the sole means of escape from those intellectual dilemmas, perceived that the alternative to the Dictatorship of the Bourgeoisie is the Dictatorship of the Proletariat.

Why the Proletariat? The proletariat is the antithesis to intellectual culture. The mob, through no fault of its own, of course, is gross, crass, crude, ignorant, bestial, and barbarous. How may the amendment of civilization be brought about by the barbarous mob? Thus: the proletariat is the only class which is not interested in deflecting the functions of its mind by power-thought. It is the only class which is not interested in being irrational, in guarding against perceiving the truth, in evading and circumventing social facts. It is, on the contrary, interested in giving the lie to ideologies whose sole function is to uphold the Dictatorship of the Bourgeoisie. The destruction of those mendacities constitutes the ideology which corresponds to the social and economic interests of the proletariat. And, once it is conscious of those interests, the mob, the gross proletariat, is not held back by any of the cautious qualifications which the intellectual bourgeois finds it so hard to set aside. The professed calm, dispassionate, "judicial," attitude, the detachment of judgment of the academic intellectual, is but one of the tactical devices whereby he may escape from facing squarely inacceptable facts. It is one more subterfuge for evasion.

The substitution of the Dictatorship of the Proletariat for the Dictatorship of the Bourgeoisie does not, therefore, represent the substitution of one falsified class ideology for another, for power exercised by the proletariat over the bourgeoisie does not mean the subjection of the bourgeoisie, but its abolition. It does not mean the exercise of the power of one class over another, and the protection and justification, by a falsified ideology of power thought, of the class wielding power, but the abolition of classes, class power, and therefore of falsified ideologies and power-thought. It means the abolition of the causes which have not only produced human social suffering, but have also brought into being intellectual irrationality and consequently the mental suffering arising from inner conflicts and contradictions.

Marx, like Nietzsche, was led, as a logical consequence of his key-thought, to set aside ethical values, to pass beyond bourgeois good and evil. Good means social good, all values being social values; and therefore the good of one class is necessarily the evil of another class. The usual judgment of the bourgeois intellectual produced by a moralistic civilization is that it is unjust. Marx, being logically compelled to discard ethical values and judgments, did not, and could not, any more than Nietzsche, denounce bourgeois civilization as "unjust." But the ethical term connotes nevertheless a social fact. Class civilization is made up of impracticable self-contradictions, among which is the class-conflict, whereby class civilization inevitably brings about its own disintegration, and results in the Dictatorship of the Proletariat, that is, a classless society. Class civilization is an unstable mechanism, a badly constructed putative society, which automatically causes its own destruction. It has destroyed itself over and over again. Theocratic power has been destroyed by military power; autocracy by landed aristocracy; landed aristocracy by the trading and industrial bourgeoisie; trade and industry themselves are being destroyed by speculative finance. The bourgeoisie must in like manner inevitably be supplanted by the dictatorship of another class suffering from "injustice."

The self-destructive and impracticable character of class civilization (its "injustice") is necessarily associated with the irrational character of its ideology, which consists of lies, in the same manner as its morality consists of injustice. The bourgeois intellectual may not be vitally interested in the social mechanism so long as he does not greatly benefit or greatly suffer from it. Marx was a bourgeois intellectual, Nietzsche was a bourgeois intellectual, Lenin was a bourgeois intellectual, I am a bourgeois intellectual. The bourgeois intellectual is able to attach greater importance to the values of ideas than the bourgeois solely absorbed in attention to business is able to do, and finds more satisfaction in the power of ideas than in economic power, which he is accordingly better able in some measure to renounce than the bourgeois who is incapable of ideas. The intellectual may thus revolt, as bourgeois intellectuals have done again and again, against the irrationalities and falsifications of bourgeois ideology without necessarily revolting against bourgeois economic dictatorship. The intellectual is, in other words, an idealist, that is to say, he has faith in the instrumental importance of ideas. Marx, who utterly repudiated idealism, (by the theory of economic determinism,) was an idealist. He had, it should be noted, the insight to distinguish

between personal idealism, which he practiced, and class idealism which he repudiated. The individual can be an idealist,
but not the class, for the behavior of a group or class is always
determined by the lowest common denominator of motives, that
is, by the most concrete, the economic motive.

The revolt against bourgeois ideology took place, as was
noted at the outset of the present article, before revolt against
bourgeois material domination, and independently of it. This
appears to be in contradiction with the Marxian formula of
economic determinism. In the eighteenth century intellectual
revolt against feudalism and absolutism also took place before
the outburst of social revolt. So again intellectual revolt in the
form of religious protestantism preceded direct action. But the
contradiction of those facts with Marx's key-thought of economic determinism is only apparent. By misrepresentation it
has been suggested that Marx, substituting economic or material determinism for idealistic determinism, repudiated and
ignored the latter. Of such stupidity Marx was not capable.
An idealist himself, he did not repudiate idealistic determinism, but affirmed its invariable association with economic determinism. The very means by which the Dictatorship of the
Bourgeoisie (as of all classes) is enforced is by the idealistic
determinism. Marxian communists are at present chiefly engaged in propaganda, that is to say, in idealistic determinism.
The obstacle which they are mostly concerned to overcome is
the effect of bourgeois ideology upon the proletariat, which
serves the purpose for which it is intended of preventing them
from being aware of their class interests, from being "class
conscious."

The entire strategy of Karl Marx and of Marxian communists depends upon idealistic determinism, or intellectual
preparation, without which the perception of class interests, or
"class consciousness," is not possible. That intellectual preparation, antecedent to social action, is nowise in contradiction
with Marx's key-thought of economic determinism, for class
dictatorship and class ideology are one. The ideology against
which the intellectuals of the late nineteenth century revolted
was itself a product of the economic dictatorship of the bourgeoisie. As Marx and Engels expressly stated, phrasing the relation in the then influential Hegelian jargon, "cause and effect
are one, and effect becomes cause." The intellectual who is
interested in rationality (or "truth") revolts against the lies of

class ideology without perceiving that those lies are but an aspect of economic dictatorship. But it is an economic situation against which he, unwittingly, is nevertheless revolting. In the same manner the petty bourgeoisie of the seventeenth century revolted against Popery, under the impression that they were interested in theology, whereas they were, in reality, interested in their social situation, in their "class-struggle." Puritanism was merely a disguise of the bourgeois class-struggle against aristocratic feudalism.

The abolition of the Dictatorship of the Bourgeoisie and the substitution of the Dictatorship of the Proletariat in the Union of Soviet Republics is naturally viewed as a social, economic, and political fact. The bourgeois judges it in Marxian terms. But to that political, social and economic fact there corresponds an ideological fact. The Dictatorship of the Proletariat has not only abolished the Dictatorship of the Bourgeoisie, but by so doing has also necessarily abolished bourgeois ideology. It has not only abolished social maladjustment, or "injustice," but has also abolished intellectual and mental maladjustment or the disabling of the human mind by the power-thought of bourgeois ideology.

The Dictatorship of the Proletariat is vitally important to the intellectual. That dictatorship is the only means by which his aims, rational validity of thought, can be attained. That aim cannot by any possible means be attained under the Dictatorship of the Bourgeoisie, which requires the falsification of thought. In the same manner as pacifism, the rationalization of the relation between the sexes, or any other rational social aim can only be attained in a classless society, so the liberation of the human mind from the traditional falsifications, that is, the vested interests of a class society. All the titanic imbecilities and dishonesties of thought which swarm under the Dictatorship of the Bourgeoisie, and drive the rational intellectual to despair, become impossible in a classless society without vested interests. The ideologies of morons, of well-to-do old ladies, of Babbitts, the pseudo-scientific forgeries of a Professor Keller, or a Professor Osborne, the idiocies of a Millikan, to cite but some fragments of the falsification of all thought under the Dictatorship of the Bourgeoisie, would be impossible and unthinkable under the Dictatorship of the Proletariat. They would be impossible, not because they would be censoriously repressed, but because they could not arise; they would be devoid of motivation. Such stupidities and mental contortions cannot occur in Russia.

The proletariat, concerned with its own class interests and not with the intellectual's interest in valid thought, is nevertheless fighting the battle of the intellectual, and is indeed the only force that can fight that battle to a finish.

That is why the intellectual, who is more interested in the mental than in the economic issue, is vitally interested in the overthrow of the Dictatorship of the Bourgeoisie. His economic interest, which he is willing to sacrifice under that dictatorship by the advocacy of "unpopular" thought, is secondary to his intellectual interest. But the latter requires the overthrow of the Dictatorship of the Bourgeoisie.

On the other hand, it is natural that during the period of increasing strain and war between the two ideological structures, the contrary effect will be produced upon a large number of intellectuals whose economic interests outweigh their intellectual interests. This we daily perceive. Bourgeois ideology sets up in their minds defenses whose purpose is to prevent them from effecting the identification expressed in the Marxian key-thought. Such a strategy of mental defense develops, as is well known, all the powers of ingenious astuteness of which the human mind is capable. Defense-mechanisms may take the form of criticism of Marxian thought, which is, of course, no more invulnerable than is Darwinian thought; such criticism, as in the case of Darwin, being totally irrelevant so far as the key-thought is concerned. But the intellectual critic detecting an error in some portion of Marx's thought, say, in his theory of value, will dismiss Marx's key-thought, with the same satisfaction as the theological critic, detecting an error in Darwin's theory of natural selection, will dismiss organic evolution in order to entrench himself in fundamentalism. Or the shallow intellectual performing verbal puns on the words "materialism" and "idealism," without any clear conception of their philosophical meaning, may declare his opposition to "materialism." Or he may protest the indispensability of "individualism," setting aside the fact that belief in intellectual validity is inconsistent with belief in the equal validity of opposite opinions. Or he may turn for comfort to the fetish of calm and judicial suspension of judgment. Innumerable in form may such defense-mechanisms be, and the more paltry they are the more will they be clung to with the stubborn persistence of a drowning soul.

From such defense-mechanisms in the mind of the bourgeois intellectual who is partially liberated from the toils of bourgeois ideology, to passionate reactionary opposition is but a step. The present time is a time of war. One of the consequences of the state of revolutionary war is the impossibility of middle terms. So long as war did not exist, people could wander unconcernedly in no-man's-land. They find such promenades increasingly unpleasant. In war there are two contending camps; there are no middle terms.

Parallel with the widespread advance of modern intellect toward a perception of actuality, liberated from bourgeois ideology, there is, of necessity, an enormous stiffening and hardening of that ideology. Whereas in the closing years of the last century, men of science, inspired by new key-thoughts, were battling against the mythologies of bourgeois ideology, and offered inspiration to intellectuals striving for freedom from those fictions, official, academic science is to-day almost to a man, conscripted in the desperate reactionary defense of the mythology. Academic science, which but thirty or forty years ago was the beacon of intellectual liberation, is to-day the bulwark of bourgeois ideology at bay. The physical scientists blab of theology; social science and anthropology are mere passionate pleas for the Dictatorship of the Bourgeoisie and its institutions; economic science is the pimp of business and finance; historical science is the sergeant of nationalism; biological science cleaves to outworn formulas and uses them to defend militarism and the elimination of the unfit, that is, of misfits in a bourgeois civilization; philosophical science blandly formulates the instrumentalism of industrial bourgeois civilization and does not blush to offer to "save the children of fortune from the uprisings of the poor." As with conscripted academic science, so with intellectualism in general, in press, in literature. Mere defense-mechanisms are being, and to a still greater extent, will be, cast aside, and bourgeois ideology will fight in the open, as unmasked Fascism, for unabashed reaction. Economic determinism is tightening its grip over every manifestation of the human mind.

Such a state of war has a very definite effect on logic. The ideal fallacy of liberalism or "democratic liberty," in other words "freedom of opinion" and (religious) toleration, was the abolition of rational validity. All opinions are equally free before "democratic liberty," alias religious toleration. Such freedom and equality demands and implies the repudiation of rational grounds for validity, for the opinion which is totally irrational is just as "free and equal," that is, valid and respectable, as the opinion which is rationally valid. The fiction of democratic liberty, or religious toleration, has thus enabled any inconsistent combination of the most disparate ingredients of lunatic thought to disport themselves unchecked in every no-man's-land of vague opinion. The state of war between bourgeois ideology and the rationalism resulting from its repudiation as a class weapon compels irresponsible opinions to evacuate an unhealthy no-man's-land. Bourgeois ideology is compelled to fight under its true colors; it is compelled to withdraw from positions of spuriously judicial detachment and to entrench itself in undisguised reactionary emplacements. In political parlance, all bourgeois ideology is driven more and more toward the right, and all opposition to it more and more to the left. A clear alignment of forces is thus being substituted for the chaotic disorder of "democratic liberty" and the illogical unrealities of bourgeois liberalism. The distress of many intellectuals arises from the increasingly unhealthy climate of no-man's-land. The Marxian key-thought is thus becoming more concretely and visibly illustrated. The pretense that diversities of opinion are the outcome of valid differences of logic, or individual mentality, is growing less and less plausible, and those diversities are compelled to show themselves more clearly for what they really are—ideologies determined by class-consciousness and the vested economic interests of the social structure. The tolerant and detached objectivity of liberalism is, in fact, compelled to descend from its spurious judicial seat, and to take its place behind the machine guns pointed against revolutionary thought.

In such a situation the place of idealistic determinism, that is, of argument, is becoming entirely changed. The basic fallacy of idealistic determinism lies in the fact that, notwithstanding the real power of ideas, they cannot alone, and independently of economic and social causes, determine events. Idealistic determinism is indispensable in the form of intellectual preparation operating in conjunction with economic determinism. But idealistic determinism, that is, reason and argument, is of no account against entrenched class-ideology. There are, we know, people with whom one cannot argue. To argue with a Christian, a businessman, a senator, an old lady of independent means, or an influential university pundit, is puerile. The absurdity of idealistic determinism is daily demonstrated by the impossibility of making an argumentative impression on entrenched bourgeois interests and ideologies. In the last resort, other means than idealistic determinism, other means than discussions, have to be substituted. The only instruments of persuasion relevant to the case are lethal weapons. Force is the only argument. Those who cannot be persuaded must perforce be liquidated. The social revolution, and incidentally the intellectual revolution, cannot be effected without a considerable liquidation of irrationalists. Idealistic determinism must of necessity pass into materialistic determinism; words into deeds; thought into action. Failure of gentle intellectuals to perceive that necessity is one of the most pathetic effects of their failure to apprehend the Marxian key-thought, the actual relation between ideology and class-power. Argument is of no account against economic determinism.

The interests of intellectuals are thus, by the force of the social process, reduced to terms of economic social determinism. Thought becomes, willy-nilly, transformed into action; idealism into materialism. The cultural history of all intellectual development is the history of that process. At a time when the uncontested power of bourgeois dictatorship was at its height, intellectualism disported itself in detached realms of thought, and quite sincerely imagined that those realms had no connection with social facts. Intellectuals were not concerned with social facts. They were concerned with the art of Boticelli, or of Marcel Proust, with folklore, with archæology, or linguistics, or numismatics, or what-not. They sought, and seek, refuge in Ivory Towers, hoping to escape. They were concerned with purely æsthetic and intellectual detached criticism of bourgeois taste, bourgeois superstition, bourgeois anthropological ignorance, bourgeois tabus. They were not concerned with social theories, and had scarcely heard of Marx. And now, lo and behold! it doth appear, to the dismay of terrified intellectuals, that while they had been innocently descanting on the theories of art, of science, of ethics, they had all along been sapping the sacred foundations of the bourgeois economic and social order, of the Dictatorship of the Bourgeoisie. For it was not the doctrine of bourgeois æsthetics, or this or that scientific, literary, or philosophical theory that was at fault. It was the structure of a society which rendered base artistic theories, false and mean literary and scientific theories necessary in order that the Dictatorship of the Bourgeoisie might be exalted and protected against intelligence. That social structure and dictatorship, not bad taste or false science, or imbecile philosophy, was the cause of the colossal defeat of reason. It was the cause of the intellectuals' suffering and mental martyrdom.

> It is the cause, it is the cause, my soul;
> Let me not name it to you, ye chaste stars!
> It is the cause.

No ideal theory, but the economic and social structure of bourgeois civilization is the cause.

That strange fellow of whom vague reports had been heard, the Jew, Marx, could have told them that almost one hundred years ago. Alas that it should have needed the stern voice of facts, a menacing Union of Soviet Republics, proclaiming far and wide the Dictatorship of the Proletariat, and the end of the Dictatorship of the Bourgeoisie, to bring to the notice of thoughtful people Marx's key-thought, that intellectual theories are but products of economic determinism.

The intellectual, whose perplexities, verging in these days upon agony, have been created by that situation, must learn a new test of thought, a new measure of its validity. Is his thought the outcome of his undeviated individual judgment? Hardly; for is he not, he and his thought, a social product? Is not his thought the "power thought" of bourgeois ideology, designed not to bestow upon his mind the apprehension of facts, but to safeguard the Dictatorship of the Bourgeoisie? No longer can the thinker evade that question. He supposed that he was free to disport himself in detached realms of pure intellect, disinterested, unconcerned with the turmoil and dust of sordid social issues. He must now face the fact that, not only can he not be unconcerned, but that before the validity and worth of his thought can be appraised, it is necessary that he should have *decided* the social question.

Is his thought the product of the Dictatorship of the Bourgeoisie, and of the mountain mass of falsifications, distortions, mental deformities which that dictatorship requires? Or is it the product of a human society that has declared itself classless, strifeless, nationless, priestless, and which therefore has no need for fraud, forgery, and fiction? That question is indispensable to the appraisal of all thought. Even more than the proletarian, the intellectual, he who values the things of the mind, the worth of thought and ideas, is interested—vitally interested—in the Dictatorship of the Proletariat.

*"*THE *capitalist system is dying and cannot be revived. That is the conclusion to which any honest investigator of the actual facts and possibilities of the present situation must be driven."*

JOHN STRACHEY

NOTES ON CONTRIBUTORS

CARLETON BEALS

Carleton Beals was born in Medicine Lodge, Kansas, November 13, 1893. A.B. University of California. M.A. Columbia University, 1917. Instructor, Private Staff, President Venustiano Carranza. Former Lecturer, National University of Mexico. Special correspondent: Mexico, Central America, Spain, Italy, Morocco, Turkey, Soviet Union, Germany. Special correspondent with army of General Sandino in Nicaragua. Lecturer, University of California, Summer, 1933. Guggenheim Fellow to Mexico, 1931-32. Fellow, National Geographic Society. Member anthropological and educational mission to the Mixe, Cuicatecan, Huatecan and Mazetecan Indian regions of Oaxaca, Mexico, 1930. Present in Mexico during Obregón, De la Huerta, Gomez-Serrano revolts; also horsebacked through Jalisce during the 1928 Catholic revolt in that state. Author of *Porfirio Díaz: Dictator of Mexico, Mexican Maze, Banana Gold,* etc.

H. N. BRAILSFORD

H. N. Brailsford; educated at Glasgow University, M.A. (Philosophical and Classical Honors). Editor, *The New Leader,* 1922-26. He is the author of *Rebel India, Olives of Endless Age, How the Soviet Works, Socialism for To-day, A League of Nations, The War of Steel and Gold,* and many other works.

ROBERT BRIFFAULT

Robert Briffault, M.D., was born in London, 1876. He was educated at Florence, in Germany, and later at Liverpool. After studying medicine in London, he went to New Zealand as a practicing surgeon, publishing a series of articles in *Transactions of the New Zealand Institute.* The war brought him again to Europe, where he served with a battalion at Gallipoli, also in Flanders and France. At Nieuport he was gassed and disabled for active duty. The Military Cross was twice awarded him for conspicuous bravery. He is the author of *Breakdown, Sin and Sex, Rational Evolution, The Mothers* (also abridged edition); *The Making of Humanity,* and *Psyche's Lamp.* He has contributed articles to various reviews and journals.

498

V. F. CALVERTON

V. F. Calverton was born in Baltimore in 1900 and graduated from the Johns Hopkins University. In 1923 he founded *The Modern Quarterly*, a journal of letters and social thought. He is the author of *For Revolution, The Liberation of American Literature, Three Strange Lovers, The Bankruptcy of Marriage, Sex Expression in Literature,* and *The Newer Spirit,* Co-editor of *Woman's Coming of Age, The New Generation,* and *Sex in Civilization.* He is also American editor of *La Paix Mondiale.* He is now literary editor of Ray Long and Richard R. Smith, Publishers. He has contributed to magazines in Europe and America and lectures on sociological, literary and historical topics.

G. D. H. COLE

Born 1889. University reader in economics, Oxford. Vice-President Workers' Educational Association. Vice-Chairman Society for Socialist Enquiry and Propaganda. Author of: *The Intelligent Man's Guide Through World Chaos; British Trade and Industry, Past and Future; Gold, Credit and Unemployment; The Next Ten Years in British Social and Economic Policy; Trade Unionism and Munitions; Guild Socialism Restated; Self-Government in Industry; The World of Labour,* etc.

LEWIS COREY

Lewis Corey was born in 1894, went to public schools until fourteen and then to work. Member of the editorial staff of the Encyclopaedia of the Social Sciences. Author of: *The House of Morgan.* Has contributed special articles to *The Annalist, The Advance, New Freeman, The Nation, The New Republic, The Modern Quarterly.* Wrote a special chapter on *The New Capitalism* in "American Labor Dynamics." Among his more important articles are: Technological Unemployment, Wall Street and Hard Times, Employees Stock Ownership, The Distribution of Income, The Distribution of Ownership, Wages and Income, Dividends are Insured —Why not Wages?

LOUIS FISCHER

Louis Fischer was born in Philadelphia, Pa. on February 29, 1896. Taught school in Philadelphia, began to write in 1922 from Germany. He first went to Russia in 1922, and since then has spent most of his time there. Author of *Machines and Men in Russia, Why Recognize Russia?, The Soviets in World Affairs* (two volumes), and *Oil Imperialism.* He has been *The Nation* correspondent since 1924, and has contributed to German, British, and American newspapers and magazines.

JOHN GUNTHER

John Gunther, newspaper correspondent, born in Chicago, Ill.
August 30, 1901. Educated at the University of Chicago, Ph.B. 1922.
Began work on the Chicago *Daily News* the same year and has
never left it. Is now Central European and Balkan correspondent
of the Chicago *Daily News,* resident in Vienna. At various times
has worked in London, Paris, Moscow, Rome, Geneva, Madrid, and
almost all the minor capitals, and has traveled fairly widely in the
Balkans and the Near East. Has recently interviewed Masaryk,
King Carol, Trotsky, and many others. Author of several novels,
among them, *The Red Pavilion* and *The Bright Nemesis.* Occasional contributor to *The Nation* and other magazines. Is rather
more interested fundamentally in literary work than politics, but
politics, especially the Balkan brand, take most of his time.

HAROLD J. LASKI

Harold J. Laski; Professor of Political Science in the University
of London since 1926; connected with London School of Economics
since 1920. Author of *The Crisis and the Constitution, Studies in
Law and Politics, An Introduction to Politics, The Dangers of
Obedience, Liberty in the Modern State, Communism,* and many
other works. He is a contributor to *The New Republic, Harvard
Law Review, The Nation, Manchester Guardian, etc.*

LUDWIG LORE

Ludwig Lore, born 1875 in Germany; graduate Berlin University; journalist on Socialist newspapers in Germany until 1903.
Joined staff of *New Yorker Volkszeitung* in 1905, became its editor-
in-chief in 1919. Contributor to American and European publications since 1931.

ROBERT MORSS LOVETT

Robert Morss Lovett was born 1870. Professor of English at the
University of Chicago. Dean of Junior Colleges 1907-20 Univer-
sity of Chicago. Author of: *The History of the Novel in England*
(with Prof. Helen Sard Hughes); *A History of English Literature*
(with William Vaughn Moody); *Richard Gresham* and *A Winged
Victory* (novels); *Cowards* (a play); *Edith Wharton* (criticism),
Compiler of an anthology on British Poetry and Prose. Editor of
The Dial, 1919. Editorial board of *The New Republic* since 1921.
One of the contributors to the Symposium entitled *Behold America!,* on *The Degradation of American Politics.*

MAX NOMAD

Max Nomad is a political emigrant from pre-war Europe who has been either a sympathetic observer of, or an active participant in, the left-wing revolutionary movements in most European countries before the War, and in the United States since the War. He is the author of *Rebels and Renegades* (1932), and a contributor to various magazines.

SACHIO OKA

Sachio Oka was born in Tokio in 1900 as a son of a socialistic artist and a college teacher. At the age of 13 he entered a Christian high school in Tokio, discovered the rôle of religion in the present society, and grew up as a rebel poet. In 1924 he entered the Imperial University of Tokio. There he joined the students' revolutionary movement and became a member of the Worker-Peasant Party. While in journalistic work, he was active in the movement against the censorship, a major issue of the Worker-Peasant Party. He was arrested several times for his articles and speeches. Has attended several institutions of learning in the United States. Is now a journalist and translator. His chief interest lies in a Marxian interpretation of literature.

MAXIMILIAN OLAY

Maximilian Olay was born in Oviedo, Spain, in 1893, where he was educated. Lived in Spain and Cuba, in addition to the U. S., and has been active in labor and libertarian movements from childhood. Has also contributed for many years to the Spanish labor and libertarian press, and occasionally to the English Press. Was co-editor of *Fiat Lux* of Havana, Cuba. Has contributed especially to *La Tierra, El Libertario of Madrid, Cultura Obrera, Cultura Proletaria, Voluntad, Aurora, The Road to Freedom, Freedom* (New York publication), *Solidaridad Obrera* (published in Chicago).

WALTER N. POLAKOV

Walter N. Polakov, expert Consulting Engineer to the Board of Estimates, City of New York, 1909-10. Superintendent of Power of the New York, New Haven, and Hartford railroad till 1915. Power Expert, U. S. Shipping Board, Emergency Fleet Corporation, 1918, and since that time in private consulting practice, here as well as in Europe. In 1929 was invited to Russia by the Supreme Economic Council. For the better part of two years he was management consultant to that body. Author of : *Mastering Power Production, Man and His Affairs, Power Plant Management*, etc. Contributor to *Harper's, Harvard Economic Review, The New Republic* and numerous engineering journals, Fellow, Institute of Management, member American Society Mechanical Engineers, Society of Industrial Engineers, American Management Association; member Taylor Society, Hon. member local 44 National Association Stationary Engineers. Inventor of remote control instrument boards and various devices in management technique.

ARNOLD ROLLER

Arnold Roller is the pen name of a journalist writing on Latin American affairs. He has traveled through all Caribbean and most South American countries to get acquainted with the background and the men behind the revolutionary and labor movements in these regions. Before coming to America, he was an electrical engineer and worked at his profession in Vienna, Berlin, Paris, London and Barcelona. In Europe he wrote a short history of the Spanish Revolutionary Labor Movement until 1909, anti-militarist and syndicalist propaganda pamphlets on Direct Action and the revolutionary General Strike, which latter has been translated into many languages including Chinese and Japanese. He edited propaganda newspapers in Switzerland, Bohemia, Berlin, Paris and contributed to magazines and newspapers in Spain, Holland and Belgium. He tramped on foot through Spain, Portugal, Morocco, Algeria, Tunis, Italy and Switzerland, and has so far been in thirty-five countries and eight jails. He was also a "native teacher" of various languages, a sheet metal worker in automobile factories, wireman, printer, translator, smuggler, hod carrier and even lecturer. In the United States he has contributed articles on Latin America to *The Nation, The Menorah Journal, New Freeman, New Masses,* and other publications.

GAETANO SALVEMINI

Gaetano Salvemini, Ph.D., Univ. of Florence, 1894. Secondary School Teacher in Palermo, Faenza, Lodi, Florence, from 1895 to 1901. Professor of Modern History at the Univ. of Messina from 1901 to 1909; at the Univ. of Pisa from 1910 to 1916; at the Univ. of Florence from 1916 to 1925. Editor of the weekly paper *L'Unità* from 1911 to 1921. Member of the Italian Parliament from November 1919 to April 1921. Arrested under charge of Lese Majeste in June 1925; amnestied on July 31st, 1925. Left Italy in August 1925, and sent in his resignation from his chair at the University of Florence on November 5th, 1925. On December 1, 1925, the Minister for Education, disregarding his resignation, dismissed him from his chair for being absent from his post. Has given courses of lectures on Mediaeval and Modern History at King's College, London;

Bedford College, London; The London School of Economics; Lady Margaret Hall, Oxford; All Soul's, Oxford; the Universities of Manchester and Edinburgh. He was visiting Professor at Harvard in 1930 and at Yale in 1932. His more important works deal with the history of the Italian Communes in the XIIIth Century, the French Revolution, the Italian Risorgimento, The Foreign Policy of Italy from 1871 to 1919, and educational problems. His recent books are devoted to Fascism: *The Fascism Dictatorship, Mussolini Diplomat,* and *Mussolini's Italy: Ten Years of Dictatorship,* in collaboration with Prof. George La Piana of Harvard University.

SAMUEL D. SCHMALHAUSEN

Samuel D. Schmalhausen, Ph.D. Columbia University, is the author of *Psychology For A New Age, A Mental Hygiene Inventory* (in collaboration with Prof. R. S. Woodworth) *Our Changing Human Nature, Why We Misbehave,* and *Humanizing Education.* He is the editor of *Our Neurotic Age* and *Behold America!,* and co-editor of *Woman's Coming of Age, The New Generation* and *Sex in Civilization.* He is a contributor to various journals, here and abroad, in the fields of psychology, psychoanalysis, and revolutionary social science.

EDWIN D. SCHOONMAKER

Edwin D. Schoonmaker was born in Scranton, Pa. in 1873, but spent his childhood and youth in Ohio and Kentucky, where he attended the public schools and later Kentucky Wesleyan College, Transylvania College and the University of Chicago. The first two years after his graduation he held the chair of Latin and Greek at Eureka College, Eureka, Ill., which he resigned to begin literary work. He is a writer of both verse and prose, and is the author of several verse dramas and also of two prose volumes, "The World Storm and Beyond," and "Our Genial Enemy, France."

HERMAN SIMPSON

Herman Simpson is a graduate of N. Y. U. Studied sociology, history and political economy, School of Political Science, Columbia. Taught history City College, N. Y. On editorial staff of New International Encyclopaedia. Editor of New York *Call, New Review.* Contributed to *Independent, Bookman, Freeman, New Freeman, New Republic,* and other publications.

CHI-CHEN WANG

Chi-Chen Wang was born in 1899 in a village in the province of Shantung, of a "plowing and reading" family. Entered Tsing-Hua College (American indemnity college) Peking in 1913 after studying under private tutors and government primary schools, and graduated in 1921, receiving the usual five-year scholarship to study in this country. Came to this country in 1922 and entered the University of Wisconsin as a junior, studying political science and journalism. After graduating from Wisconsin in 1924, he took courses in literature and philosophy for the next three years, intermittently, without taking a degree. Has been an assistant in the Far East Department of Metropolitan Museum since 1928 and a lecturer in Chinese language and literature, Columbia University, since 1929. Has done articles, reviews, etc. for various newspapers and magazines, including *The Dial, The Nation* and *The New Freeman.* Translator of *The Dream of the Red Chamber,* published in 1929, generally considered the greatest Chinese novel.